ALIEN WORLDS

ALIEN WORLDS

BLITZ EDITIONS

Published by Blitz Editions
an imprint of Bookmart Ltd
Registered Number 2372865
Trading as Bookmart Ltd, Desford Road, Enderby
Leicester LE9 5AD

Cover design: Peter Dolton
Text design: Jim Reader
Production Manager: Sue Gray
Editorial Manager: Roz Williams

Printed in the Slovak Republic
50980

ISBN 1 85605 135 8

Every effort has been made to contact the copyright holders for the pictures. In some cases they have been untraceable, for which we offer our apologies. Thanks to the Fortean Picture Library and the Hulton Deutsch Collection Ltd, who supplied most of them. Pictures have been provided as follows:

SECTION 1

The Aetherius Society (pp 60, 65), M. De Cet (pp 5, 31 middle, 77, 78 top), Hulton Deutsch Collection Ltd (pp 4, 10 top, 11 right, 12 top, 19 middle, 20, 23, 42 top right, 43, 45, 46, 56, 61 bottom, 63, 68, 73, 75, 79 top), McDonnell Douglas Photos (31 bottom), Orbis Publishing (31 top).

SECTION 2

M. De Cet (p 68), Estate of Frank Brookesmith (p 7), Tom Fox (p 67), HarperCollins (p 64 bottom), Hulton Deutsch Collection Ltd (pp 3–6, 8 top, 10 top, 11, 13, 16, 18, 20–6, 28–31, 32 top right and bottom, 33, 34 top, 35, 36, 39–41, 44, 45, 46 top, 47, 50, 51, 53–63, 64 top, 66, 70, 71, 73 left, 74, 77, 78, 79 bottom, 80 bottom), The Mansell Collection (p 73 right), Mary Evans Picture Library (pp 75 and 76).

SECTION 3

M. De Cet (pp 34, 52), Department of Defense, USA (p 78), Hulton Deutsch Collection Ltd (pp 4–7, 23, 24, 35, 50, 53 right, 54, 55 bottom, 56, 70–4), The Mansell Collection (p 80), Mary Evans Picture Library (pp 58, 59).

The remaining pictures, including those on the jacket, have been supplied by the Fortean Picture Library.

The Author

Reuben Stone has long been fascinated by the paranormal and the mysteries of the unexplained. He is the author of many books and articles on military history, popular science and technology, and various aspects of anomalous phenomena.

Contents

ALIEN WORLDS

There has to be something more than this.

THE POSSIBILITY of existence other than this meagre span we call life has always tormented the human mind. Legends and folktales, rituals and religions, are all attempts to come to terms with the awesome possibility that there are other forms of life – life after death, life in outer space, life running parallel to our humdrum everyday existence.

This book investigates those tantalizing visions. It examines the details of sometimes fantastic stories of spaceship sightings and abductions by aliens; it scrutinizes the evidence for and against existence beyond the grave; and it assesses the confusion surrounding poltergeists and other paranormal phenomena. It asks the questions we should ask, and demands sensible answers.

Our advanced science and technology should be able to provide us with comforting explanations and neat frameworks of rules about precisely what is, and is not, feasible. Unfortunately this is not always the case. Sometimes science provides us with convincing proof of hoaxes. Sometimes it offers a plausible interpretation of the facts. And sometimes science provides disturbing answers that raise even greater questions.

Alien Worlds assembles the evidence and allows us to make up our own minds. Whether the answers fill us with hope – or with fear – is for us alone to decide.

UFO INVESTIGATION

HOW LONG HAVE THEY BEEN HERE?

On a bright summer's day an ordinary man witnessed an extraordinary sight. Kenneth Arnold's cautious reports unwittingly launched the age of the flying saucer. His was only one in a long series of inexplicable sightings.

At about 7 pm on the evening of 2 April 1991, Dick Feichtinger was driving to work in Faribault, Minnesota, when he saw a curious, white, long and narrow rectangular object apparently hanging in the sky above the town. 'It seemed to be hanging up and down. Rather than horizontal it was vertical,' he told reporter Paul Adams of the Faribault *Daily News*. 'The fact that it wasn't horizontal is strange...the configuration and the way it was hanging, that was what drew my attention to it.'

Still more remarkable was the fact that the object was there again when Feichtinger returned home from work later in the evening. Now, instead of being simply white, it was red and green. Once home, Feichtinger, naturally somewhat excited and more than intrigued, urged his wife and children to come and look at what he had seen. His family rushed to join him. As the Feichtingers watched, the object hanging mysteriously in the sky changed colour from red and green to solid white. By this time, neighbours had come out to see what the fuss was about, and were equally astonished to see the weird rectangle in the sky – which, they later agreed, 'seemed to be intelligently guided'.

At this point something very strange happened: two aircraft came cruising incredibly low over the houses. Said neighbour Steve Kelly: 'I thought they were going to land on my house.' And they were flying extremely slowly – so slowly that Dick Feichtinger commented:

Above: *Kenneth Arnold, whose sighting of nine flying disks in the summer of 1947 ushered in the modern UFO era.*

Opposite: *A 'daylight disk', photographed in October 1974 by David Knutsen in Surrey, British Columbia. The picture is typical of many of UFOs – devoid of detail, yet apparently showing a flying craft of unknown origin.*

Left: *Kenneth Arnold collaborated with* Fate *magazine publisher Ray Palmer to tell the story of his sighting. Critics have alleged that Palmer sensationalized the book, but Arnold himself remained a sober and dedicated investigator.*

THEY HAD NO DOUBT THAT THE WEIRD RECTANGLE IN THE SKY WAS GUIDED BY AN UNKNOWN INTELLIGENCE.

'I couldn't figure out what was keeping them up there.' Undaunted, he waved at them as he stood under a street light, and one of the planes seemed to acknowledge the wave by briefly turning on a set of floodlights – possibly its landing lights.

Before long, more aircraft were on the scene. Some witnesses said they counted up to 11 planes, including helicopters and two large aircraft. When the local military were contacted, however, they had no knowledge of any aircraft in the area besides a pair of National Air Guard C-130 Hercules cargo planes – one of which, spokesman Lt Kevin Gutknecht admitted, had indeed turned on its landing lights, although why was not explained. However, the C-130 pilots did not report seeing any strange lights in the vicinity of the town. A puzzled Lt Gutknecht was reported as saying: 'I have no idea what it is. It doesn't sound like anything we have in the Minnesota military inventory.'

This case has all the ingredients of a certain kind of classic UFO sighting. There is the bizarre light in the sky, changing colour but seemingly under intelligent control, witnessed by a number of independent observers, none of whom apparently has any reason to lie, let alone organize a neighbourhood conspiracy. There are unexplained terrestrial aircraft associated with the sighting. The military deny all knowledge, as usual, although they give away a tantalizing and inexplicable detail: why did the Hercules pilot turn on his landing lights?

The role of the military in UFO lore is a subject on its own, but this case, like the hundreds of others reported each year, serves to illustrate that the UFO phenomenon is as strong as it ever was.

But how long have UFOs been seen in our skies?

SUPER INTELLIGENCE

The modern history of UFOs is traditionally considered to begin in 1947, when Idaho businessman Kenneth Arnold saw nine weird disks of light flashing through the air while he was flying over the Cascade Mountains in Washington State, USA. This extraordinary encounter is worth recounting in detail, for it is a key episode in any attempt to understand what UFOs are – and what they have been. For Arnold's experience was by no means the first recorded instance of unexplained aerial objects and ordinary humanity coming into contact with each other. The great difference between his and previous sightings was the interpretation that was very soon put on it – that the lights Arnold saw were extra-terrestrial craft.

Hardly anyone in the Western world was immune to this belief. Even US President Harry S Truman could say, at a press conference on 4 April 1950, 'I can assure you that flying saucers...are not constructed by any power on Earth.' Just a few years later, in June 1954, at another conference in Innsbruck, Austria, Dr Herman Orberth – often called the 'father' of the German V-2 rocket, precursor of all the spacecraft launched from Earth – stated his conviction unmistakably: 'These objects are conceived and directed by intelligent beings of a very high order. They probably do not originate in our Solar System, perhaps not even in our galaxy.'

Below: ***Harry S Truman, US President during the first sightings of 'flying saucers' after World War 2. Truman publicly stated his belief that UFOs were from outer space, and some ufologists believe that he instigated research into the phenomenon – research that remains super-secret even today.***

Whether or not UFOs are indeed material craft from outer space, messengers from alien civilizations, or the vehicles of galactic 'guardians' of humanity – or possibly even evidence of something far less benign that has a presence here on Earth – is a question that still vexes experts. The important point for the moment is that in the late 1940s, there was no other interpretation that made sense to most observers. Yet this was not Kenneth Arnold's own belief, and was certainly not the way that earlier witnesses saw the strange and bewildering lights and seemingly solid objects that from time to time have filled the skies throughout history and at the same time have filled the witnesses, too, with awe and wonder.

FLYING SAUCERS

Kenneth Arnold unwittingly launched the age of the flying saucer on the clear sunny afternoon of 24 June 1947. He was an experienced pilot, and that day was flying east across the Cascade Mountains from Chehalis to Yakima, Washington. Arnold had been enticed by the offer of a $5000 reward to spend an hour or so during his journey searching for a C-46 transport aircraft belonging to the US Marine Corps that had recently come down near Mount Rainier with 32 men on board. The Callair aircraft Arnold was flying was specially designed for working in the mountains. He took off from Chehalis airport at about 2 pm and made straight for the plateau of Mount Rainier.

Arnold was in the midst of his search at an altitude of about 9200 ft above the town of Mineral (about 25 miles south-west of the peak of Mount Rainier), and was making a 180° turn when 'a tremendously bright flash lit up the surfaces of my aircraft'. Understandably startled, Arnold thought at first that he was about to collide with another aircraft. He spent an anxious half-minute or so searching the sky for the source of the flash of light, but the only other plane in the vicinity was a Douglas DC-4 airliner, which he judged to be on the airlane from Seattle to San Francisco. Arnold then figured that he had seen the flash of the sun on the wings of a close-flying fighter; he thought he had been buzzed by a gung-ho young USAF lieutenant in a P-51, better known as the North American Aviation Mustang, the most powerful piston-engined fighter then in common service with the USAF.

Before he had time to start searching for a fast-moving Mustang, however, Arnold saw another flash – and this time saw where it came from. 'I observed,' he reported drily, 'far to my left and to the north, a formation of very bright objects coming from the vicinity of Mount Baker, flying very close to the mountain tops and travelling at tremendous speed.' Watching the craft near Mount Rainier, Arnold at first thought that he was watching a formation of nine jets at, he calculated, a distance of over 100 miles. 'What startled me most at this point was...that I could not find any tails on them.'

SCIENTISTS CONFIRMED THAT THE OBJECTS WERE CONTROLLED BY SUPER-INTELLIGENT BEINGS FROM ANOTHER GALAXY.

Above: ***A P-51 Mustang. When Kenneth Arnold first encountered mysterious flying disks in the air over the Cascade Mountains, his first thought was that he was being buzzed by one of these powerful fighters.***

The formation was flying almost directly across Arnold's own flightpath, which made it easy to make a rough calculation of the objects' speed, using the clock in his instrument panel, Mounts Rainier and Adams as markers, and reckoning the formation would pass about 23 miles in front of him. Arnold was amazed to discover that the nine craft were travelling at over 1700 mph – an astonishing speed for the time (it was only later that year that the sound barrier, about 750 mph, was first broken by a jet aircraft). What made this phenomenal speed all the more extraordinary was the way the craft were flying. Arnold said:

'They didn't fly like any aircraft I had

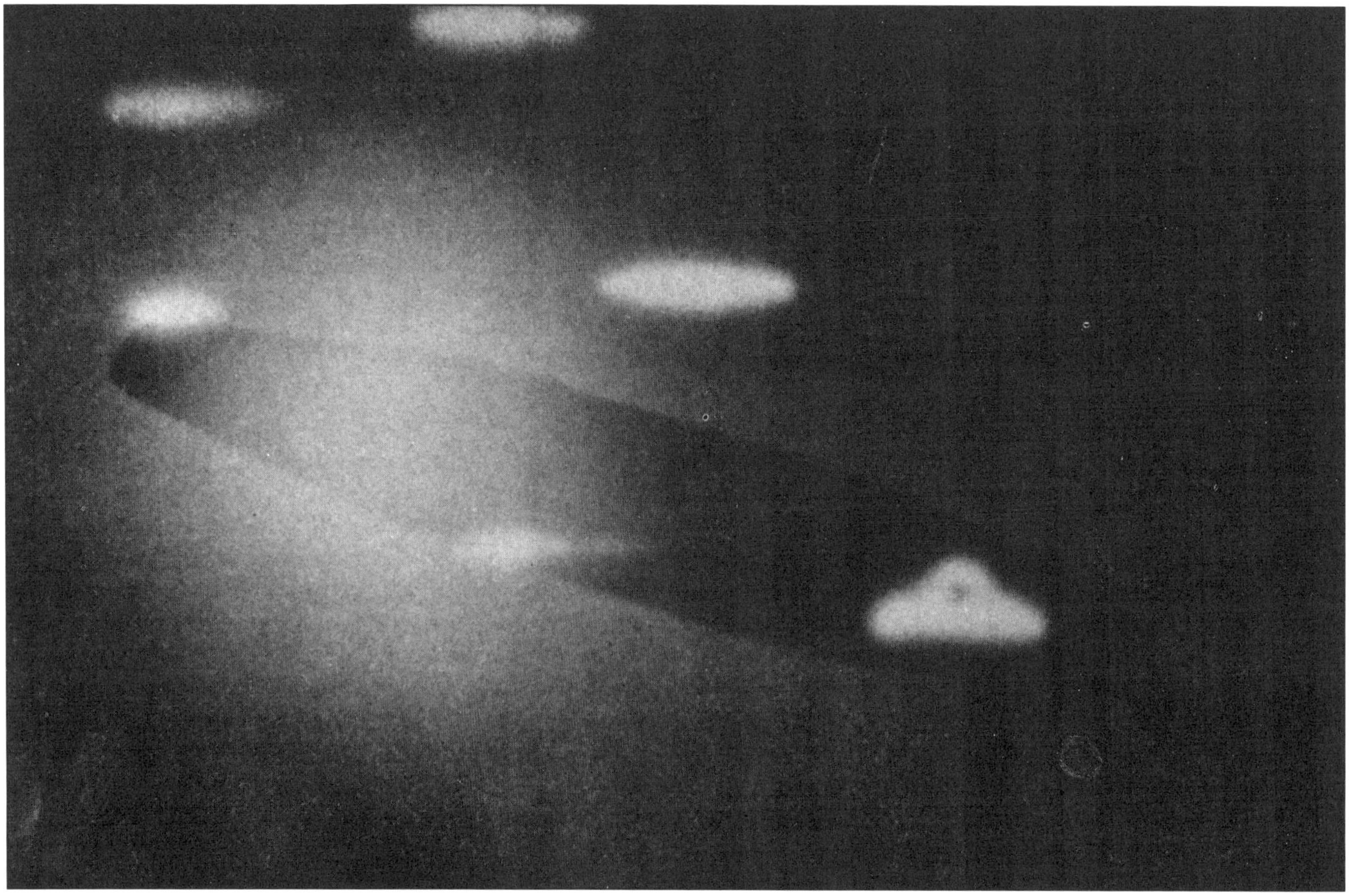

seen before...they flew in a definite formation, but erratically...their flight was like speed boats on rough water or similar to the tail of a Chinese kite that I once saw blowing in the wind...they fluttered and sailed, tipping their wings alternately and emitting those very bright blue-white flashes from their surfaces. At the time I did not get the impression that these flashes were emitted by them, but rather that it was the sun's reflection from the extremely highly polished surfaces of their wings.'

Above: ***George Adamski claimed to have photographed this 'mother ship' releasing smaller craft.***

Below: ***These UFOs have been dismissed by sceptics as a flight of geese.***

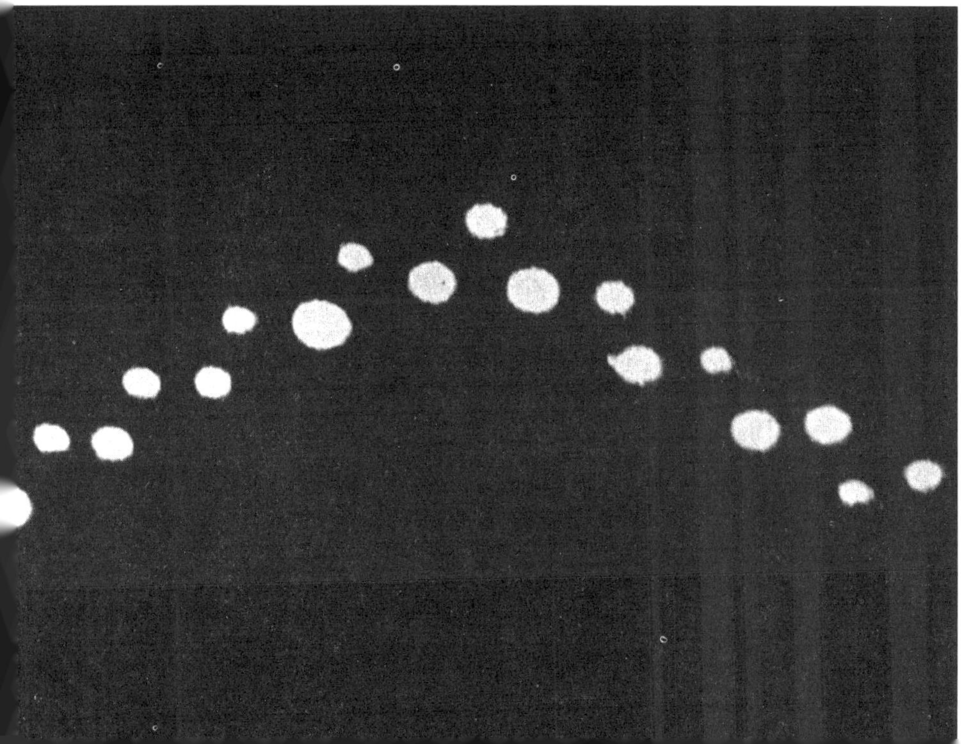

By the time the nine craft flew beyond the southernmost crest of Mount Adams, Arnold had decided to abandon his search for the missing C-46 and make for Yakima to report what he had seen. Landing there at about 4 pm, Arnold told his story to an airline manager and discussed it with other professional fliers, before taking off once more for Pendleton, Oregon. The news had travelled ahead of him: among the crowd of people to greet him there was Bill Becquette, from the local newspaper, the *East Oregonian*. It was during this time that Arnold described the craft he had seen as flying 'like a saucer would if you skipped it across the water'. This description was slightly garbled by Becquette, who thus originated the phrase 'flying saucers'. Then, with other pilots, Arnold cautiously recalculated his estimate of the UFOs' extraordinary speed. But even the most conservative reckoning still put their velocity at over 1350 mph. From talking to other airmen, Arnold was now convinced that he had seen a flight of guided missiles, 'robotly controlled'. He concluded that the government had chosen this way to announce the discovery of 'a new principle of flight'.

Then the story broke, put out on the Associated Press wire by Bill Becquette. For three days at Pendleton Arnold was besieged with enquiries. Finally, exhausted and unable to work, Arnold flew the 200 miles across the state line to his home in Boise, Indiana. It was shortly after arriving there that Arnold had a telephone call from Dave Johnson, aviation editor of the *Idaho Statesman*. That conversation changed everything for Arnold. As he put it:

'The doubt he displayed of the authenticity of my story told me, and I am sure he was in a position to know, that it was not a new military guided missile and that if what I had seen was true it did not belong to the good old USA. It was then that I really began to wonder.'

ALIEN CRAFT

Arnold might well have wondered, for in the three days that he was being harassed by newshounds he discovered that his was by no means the only, or even the first, sighting of such mysterious flying objects. ('I thought it wouldn't be long before there was one of these things in every garage,' he commented wryly, at the stage when he still believed that he had seen a flight of government-sponsored machines.)

In April 1947, a meteorologist tracking a weather balloon saw a saucer-shaped object fly by – a neat irony, as so many later UFO sightings have been explained away as, and sometimes have really been, misidentifications of weather balloons. On 5 May, a 'silvery object' was reported to have dropped out of the sky over Washington State and disintegrated before reaching the ground. On 12 June, shortly before Arnold's own experience, another chain of UFOs was seen over Weiser, Idaho, and on 14 June a pilot named Rankin also observed a flight of 10 saucer-like objects flying in triangular formation. At about the same time as Arnold saw 'his' flying disks, a prospector in the Cascades also witnessed a similar group of UFOs, whose presence made his compass needle go wild. Arnold's sighting in fact took place in the midst of a major UFO 'flap' – a flurry of sightings – in the late spring and summer of 1947. Between the beginning of June and 16 July that year, the US authorities received over 850 reports of UFOs from all over the USA. By September, the USAF had set up Project Sign to evaluate the reports and, among other things, consider the possibility that these were extra-terrestrial craft.

What made Arnold's report different was that it sparked an equally monumental flap in the media – whose underlying assumption throughout was that 'flying saucers' were indeed alien craft, and were probably not very friendly.

Curiously enough, Arnold himself did not share this view of the origins of UFOs. In 1962, in the magazine *Flying Saucers*, he published his own conclusion: '...the so-called unidentified flying objects that have been seen in our atmosphere are not space ships from another planet at all, but are groups and masses of living organisms that are as much a part of our atmosphere and space as the life we find in the depths of our oceans. The only major difference [is] that they have a natural ability to change their densities at will.'

Arnold, perhaps, was not a man of his age; but this was not the first time that UFOs had been identified with living things in the sky. On the other hand, the belief that they were nuts-and-bolts machines was not entirely new, either.

SHAKEN BY HIS EXPERIENCE, ARNOLD WAS CONVINCED THAT HE HAD SEEN A FLIGHT OF ROBOT-GUIDED MISSILES.

MACHINES OF DEATH

Probably the earliest report of a UFO on record is to be found in (of all places) a treatment of architecture and civic planning called the *Samarangana-Sartradhara*, an ancient Indian text that dates back at least to 500 BC. In this, one passage describes curious machines called *vimanas*, which can fly, and are controlled by pilots. There follows a number of lengthy descriptions of how the *vimanas*' various power systems work, but they are tantalizingly obscure. The same devices are also mentioned in the great Hindu epics in Sanskrit, the *Mahabharata* and *Ramayana*, where they are described as military machines with the range to 'carry death' anywhere in the world – an assertion that, like so many aspects of unexplained and paranormal phenomena, raises as many questions as it

GREAT HINDU EPICS DESCRIBED THE 'MACHINES OF DEATH' IN CHILLING DETAIL – WERE THE WRITERS FORETELLING A CATASTROPHIC NUCLEAR WAR?

Above: ***Shooting stars – seen here in a Victorian print – were taken to be portents in more superstitious times. Today, misinterpretations of such natural phenomena tend to have a technological flavour, and many reported 'UFOs' are in fact meteorites.***

Below: ***In medieval times and before, mysterious aerial phenomena were often believed to be dragons. But did people actually see dragons then, just as witnesses report seeing flying disks today? If so, have UFOs changed in appearance over the centuries to suit expectations?***

answers. One researcher has even gone so far as to say that 'we cannot but be struck [when reading these works] by the modernity of certain passages, where we seem to be reading an account of a nuclear war'.

Roman writers noted visitations by UFOs: Livy (59 BC–AD 17) described a sighting in 214 BC at Hadria in Italy that looked like an altar in the sky, while Pliny the Elder (AD 23–79) refers to 'gleaming beams in the sky' in his *De Rerum Naturae*, and describes how in 66 BC a 'spark' fell from a star to the Earth, became as large as the Moon, and then – shrinking in size – returned to the sky. And in his *Historia Naturalis*, Pliny makes an intriguing assertion:

'A light from the sky by night, the phenomenon usually called "night suns" was seen in the consulship of Gaius Caecilius and Gnaeus Papirius and often on other occasions causing apparent daylight in the night. In the consulship of Lucius Valerius and Gaius Marius a burning shield scattering sparks ran across the sky at sunset from east to west.'

The fascinating part of this passage is the words 'usually called'. Pliny seems to assume that 'night suns' were, if not commonplace, at least well-enough known to have a common name. And, although he was one of the first naturalists, Pliny was enough a man of his time to accept such wonders without comment.

The literature of medieval Europe abounds in UFO reports of various kinds. Among the earliest are to be found in the works of St Gregory, bishop of Tours in France in the 6th century. In his *Historia Francorum* ('History of the Franks'), the saint related how in AD 584 'there appeared in the sky brilliant rays of light which seemed to cross and collide with one another', while the following year 'in the month of September, certain people saw signs, that is to say rays or domes such as are customarily seen...to race across the sky'. Elsewhere he describes 'golden globes' that, on several occasions, flashed at speed across the skies of France. St Gregory also wrote seven volumes concerning miracles and – in keeping with his devout Christianity – seems to have been in little doubt that these were heavenly signs. The interpretation, in short, fitted the preconceptions of the chronicler.

In the same way, in AD 793, the *Anglo-Saxon Chronicle* reported: 'In this year terrible portents appeared in Northumbria, and miserably afflicted the inhabitants; these were exceptional flashes of lightning, and fiery dragons were seen flying through the air.' The *Chronicle* was written by secular scribes, and their report reflects the still thickly pagan atmosphere of 8th-

century England – for both people and place were far less orthodox in their Christianity than the monasteries of France had been two centuries previously. What today would have been called a UFO or even a 'flying saucer' was to them a dragon. It flew in the air, it lit up the sky, and it was fearsome and inherently inexplicable; it was a dragon because that was the nearest thing in human knowledge to match what people actually saw. This unconscious mental process also helps to explain why diehard sceptics, confronted with a UFO, will always believe they have seen the planet Venus, or a weather balloon – indeed anything other than an inexplicable and possibly alien craft.

Just as people see UFOs today, people saw dragons then. Kenneth Arnold was not the first to suggest that UFOs, in the most literal sense of being unidentified flying objects, were members of the animal kingdom. In England in 1113, a group of churchmen from Laon in France were going from town to town in Wessex (south-west England), bearing with them relics of the Virgin Mary, which they used to perform miracles of healing. At the coastal town of Christchurch, Hampshire, they were astonished to see a dragon come up out of the sea, 'breathing fire out of its nostrils'. There are plenty of reports of modern UFOs rising out of the sea, as well.

The 12th-century chronicler Ralph Niger recounts that on 9 March 1170, at St Osyth in Essex, south-east England, 'a wonderfully large dragon was seen, borne up from the Earth through the air. The air was kindled into fire by its motion and burnt a house, reducing it and its outbuildings to ashes.'

Dragons and UFOs show some interesting parallels. Whatever form UFOs take, they are always perceived as being on the very edge of human knowledge as it exists in any particular era, including some alluring extras that we can imagine but cannot (yet) achieve – such as faster-than-light travel today, or heavier-than-air flight in the Middle Ages.

Like UFOs today, dragons were familiar as *ideas*, but were also regarded as

Above: ***An astonishing aerial battle breaks out over the city of Nuremberg on 4 April 1561. A contemporary account speaks of a 'very frightful spectacle', in which luminous globes, crosses and tubes appeared to fight one another for about an hour in broad daylight. All then fell to earth, 'as if on fire'. The citizens saw this bizarre display as a divine warning to improve their sinful ways – but ufologists are divided over whether the event had its origins in a highly unusual freak of nature or some more alien source.***

Right: ***Edmund Halley was a pioneer of the scientific observation of astronomical events, and also seriously investigated reports of anomalous and enigmatic phenomena – in striking contrast to the attitude of much of today's scientific establishment.***

Below: ***A huge meteorite falls to Earth. Many apparent UFO reports from before the 20th century may refer to natural events like this, but just as many accounts describe extraordinary and inexplicable behaviour on the part of the heavenly lights.***

'impossible' in practical terms. To the medieval mind, dragons occupied a strange no-man's land between reality and imagination. Most people had not seen one – though they might know someone who had, or who knew someone else who had. But everyone was familiar with dragons and what they did (which was guard treasure, breathe fire, and fly), and everyone knew what a dragon looked like. Medieval people would have had no difficulty in identifying one if it landed in a bustling market place and snorted smoke and flame. But actual dragons remained elusive and magical, neither quite real nor quite imaginary, possible but improbable. Today, most of the same things could be said about UFOs, except that they are only magical in the sense that they are 'other-worldly' or paranormal.

AERIAL CONFLICT

As time went on, and the old Anglo-Saxon myths disappeared from memory in an England conquered by the Normans, the identification of UFOs with dragons faded too. The persistent appearance of inexplicable lights and objects in the sky did not fade with them, however. In his *Historia Anglorum* ('The History of the English'), another English chronicler, Matthew of Paris, tells how at sunset on 24 July 1239, 'a great star like a torch appeared. It rose in the south and climbed the sky giving out a great light...it left behind it smoke and sparks. It was shaped like a great head, the front part was sparkling and the back part gave out smoke and flashes.' And in his memoirs the French Duke of Bourgogne recalled that on 1 November 1461, an object appeared in the sky 'as long and wide as a half-moon; it hung stationary for about a quarter hour, clearly visible, then suddenly...spiralled, twisted and turned like a spring and rose into the heavens'.

Such accounts were not limited to Europe: records of strange lights over Japan go back at least to the 10th century, while in May 1606 the former capital of Japan, Kyoto, saw a succession of fireballs in the sky. One of them hovered near the Nijo castle in front of a host of witnesses, spinning like a red wheel.

And so the records continue: blue, black and blood-red balls, along with disks and blood-red crosses and two huge cylinders, battled together in the skies over Nuremberg, Germany, on 4 April 1561, and there was a similar aerial conflict a little more than five years later over Basel,

Switzerland, between black spheres: 'many became red and fiery, ending by being consumed and vanishing', wrote the 'student in sacred writings and the liberal arts', one Samuel Coccius, who reported the weird events of 7 August 1566 in the city's gazette.

A SKY OF FLAMES

In the centuries that followed, observers, including the astronomer Edmund Halley (1656–1742), continued to note a host of bizarre aerial phenomena. But now the tone of the reports starts to change yet again: as the so-called 'Age of Reason' dawned in the late 17th century and rigorously 'logical' scientific observation became the order of the day, so different explanations for sightings of what we would now call UFOs begin to creep in to the accounts. At Sheffield, England, on 9 December 1731, for instance, at about 5 pm, Thomas Short saw what he later described as 'a dark red cloud, below which was a luminous body which emitted intense beams of light...the light beams moved slowly for a while, then stopped. Suddenly it became so hot that I could take off my shirt even though I was out of doors [this in the dead of winter!]. This meteor was observed over Kilkenny, Ireland, where it seemed like a great ball of fire. It was reported that it shook the entire island and that the whole sky seemed to burst into flames.'

In the afternoon of the next day, local manuscript records show, this 'meteor' appeared over Romania: '...there appeared in the west a great sign in the sky, blood-red and very large. It stayed in place for two hours, then separated into two parts which then rejoined, and the object disappeared towards the west.' To the Romanian mind of the time, this was 'a sign'; to the cultured gentleman of Augustan England, it was a 'meteor', if a very strange one by our modern standards of judging meteors. The tendency to interpret such events according to the most easily available *existing* explanation – and one that at the time was the most acceptable socially – is even clearer in another account from 18th-century England.

On 18 August 1783, a small crowd of the gentry that included Dr James Lind (whose pioneering dietary work resulted in the eradication of scurvy from the Royal Navy), the renowned water-colour painter Thomas Sandby and the scientist Tiberius Cavallo, were on the terrace at the royal

In August 1783, a group of distinguished writers, artists and scientists that included medical pioneer Dr James Lind **(above)** ***witnessed the appearance of a weird luminous cloud, which seemed to be under intelligent control, over Windsor Castle*** **(left).**

residence of Windsor Castle enjoying the summer evening when, according to Cavallo's account published the next year by the Royal Society, at about 9.45 pm they 'suddenly saw appear an oblong cloud moving more or less parallel to the horizon. Under this cloud could be seen a luminous object which soon became spherical, brilliantly lit, which came to a halt…This strange sphere seemed at first to be pale blue in colour, but its luminosity increased and soon it set off again towards the east. Then the object changed direction and moved parallel to the horizon before disappearing to the south-east…the light it gave out was prodigious; it lit up everything on the ground. Before it vanished it changed its shape, became oblong, and at the same time as a sort of trail appeared, it seemed to separate into two small bodies. Scarcely two minutes later the sound of an explosion was heard.'

To the scientist Cavallo, the group had

The mysterious airships that plagued parts of the United States in 1896 and 1897 (**right:** *a contemporary illustration from the* **Chicago Times-Herald**) *were far in advance of American airship technology of the day and, according to all reports, far bigger than anything that did eventually fly – as can be seen from the scale of this early Spencer airship* (**above**), *taking off at Ranelagh in 1903.*

clearly witnessed a meteor: the proof was in the explosion, presumably made as the thing crashed to earth. The astonishing thing to modern eyes is the similarity between the cloud and the object beneath it seen in 1783, and the almost identical nature of the other so-called 'meteor' that visited England, Ireland and Romania some half a century before. But a person trained to look out for meteors will see them when something like one appears in the sky, however remotely like an actual meteor it may seem from our later perspective.

THE ALIENS HAVE LANDED

True to form, the next century saw another, no less consistent, interpretation of unexplained aerial phenomena. The Victorian era saw an astonishing leap forward in works of engineering, especially in transport – from the spread of railways around the globe to the introduction of iron steamships capable of crossing the Atlantic, and the production of the first cars. Land and sea had been conquered: but not the air. Airships seemed the most promising means of achieving sustained, controlled flight, but the major problem was power. It was not until light, compact internal combustion engines appeared in the late 1890s that airships became truly practicable. By then, they were being discussed everywhere – both as the next great advance in engineering, and as something more strange.

On 6 November 1896, the citizens of Sacramento, California, were amazed to see a light moving sedately through the night sky, apparently carried by a cigar-shaped craft. During the month further reports of this machine poured in from all over California. From March 1897, the American Great Lakes states and Texas were plagued by reports of lights in the sky, some like 'electric arc lights', others shaped like balls or wheels, that were attached to huge craft – which was at once dubbed an airship – shaped like a cigar, an egg, or a barrel, and apparently powered by propellers. On a number of occasions these machines landed, and the occupants, who appeared to be ordinary human beings, spoke to bemused witnesses on the ground.

Below: ***Ludvig Lindbäck points to where his brother Knut saw a mysterious rocket crash into Lake Kölmjärv, Sweden, on 19 July 1946. The Swedish government received some 1000 such reports in 1946, but the country's top aviation and rocketry experts were unable to provide an explanation – and none has been forthcoming since.***

Right: ***Karl-Gösta Bartoll trawls the bottom of Lake Kölmjärv in a fruitless attempt to find wreckage from the 'rocket' that crashed there in July 1946.***

The case for the alien origin of UFOs rests on numerous eyewitness reports – and many tantalizing photographs, whose credibility is usually in inverse proportion to their quality. James Lucci was taking a time exposure of the Moon over Beaver, Pennsylvania, on 8 August 1965, when, he claimed, this UFO **(opposite above)** ***came into view. Many ufologists have concluded not only that UFOs are alien, but that the US government has retrieved crashed saucers like this one*** **(artist's impression, opposite below)***, which allegedly was taken to Fort Riley, Kansas, in November 1964.***

IS OURS THE AGE WHEN THE WATCHERS IN OUTER SPACE WILL REVEAL THEIR TRUE PURPOSE TO US? ARE THEY OUR FRIENDS, OUR GUARDIANS – OR OUR MASTERS?

Then, at the beginning of May 1897, the reports dried up.

An airship as large as the objects that witnesses described would have had to be rigid, or it would have been uncontrollable. But it was not until 1900 that the development of rigid airships – 'dirigibles' – began, and that was in Germany. No airship then flying, either in the USA or elsewhere, was capable of the feats performed by these machines – if that is what they were. The first dirigible to fly in the USA was Thomas Baldwin's *California Arrow*, which took off from Oakland, near San Francisco, California, in 1904.

In August 1946, the Swedish authorities received nearly 1000 reports of mysterious rockets in their skies, some of which crashed spectacularly into the country's inland lakes. One theory was that the Soviets were testing captured German V-2 rockets – which, in the public eye at least, were the most advanced technology of the day. But Swedish aviation engineers, who by then had considerable knowledge of the V-2, failed to find any plausible explanation. Similar displays of rocket-like behaviour by mysterious aerial objects were reported early the following month by British Army units in Greece, especially around Thessaloniki. Midway through September they were seen in Portugal, and then in Belgium.

THE WATCHERS IN OUTER SPACE

UFOs have been seen in the form of dragons, meteors, airships, rockets...and as 'flying saucers'. To the sceptic, all these bizarre sightings are either natural phenomena, errors of perception or plain hallucination. Some, perhaps most, UFO sightings certainly are no more than that. There is certainly good evidence that many truly strange lights in the sky are the product of little-known and rarely seen natural forces, which seem to be released in areas of geological disturbance – along fault lines in the Earth's crust, for example. Such a theory may well explain a proportion, at least, of the long history of mysterious airborne lights over Japan, which is notoriously prone to earthquakes. But these explanations don't account for the UFO phenomenon as a whole.

The common belief since Kenneth Arnold's sighting in 1947 has been that UFOs are extra-terrestrial craft built by a civilization that is technologically far in advance of our own. There are very strong grounds for questioning this assumption, but it remains a possibility. Some of the people who claim to have spoken to aliens and extra-terrestrials also maintain that this civilization has been watching the Earth for a very long time. Presumably, there have been occasions when – for reasons we can only guess at – they have been unable to conceal their presence entirely. Or perhaps they have deliberately shown themselves, as part of a centuries-long programme of gently introducing themselves to us. In either case, when they have been obliged or have chosen to reveal themselves, they have come in clever disguises: just far enough within the bounds of human understanding, carefully matching the mood of the times, to be acceptable, if strange – and just far enough beyond normality to deter unwanted investigation or interference.

And we may just be living in the age when they have decided to reveal their true purposes to us.

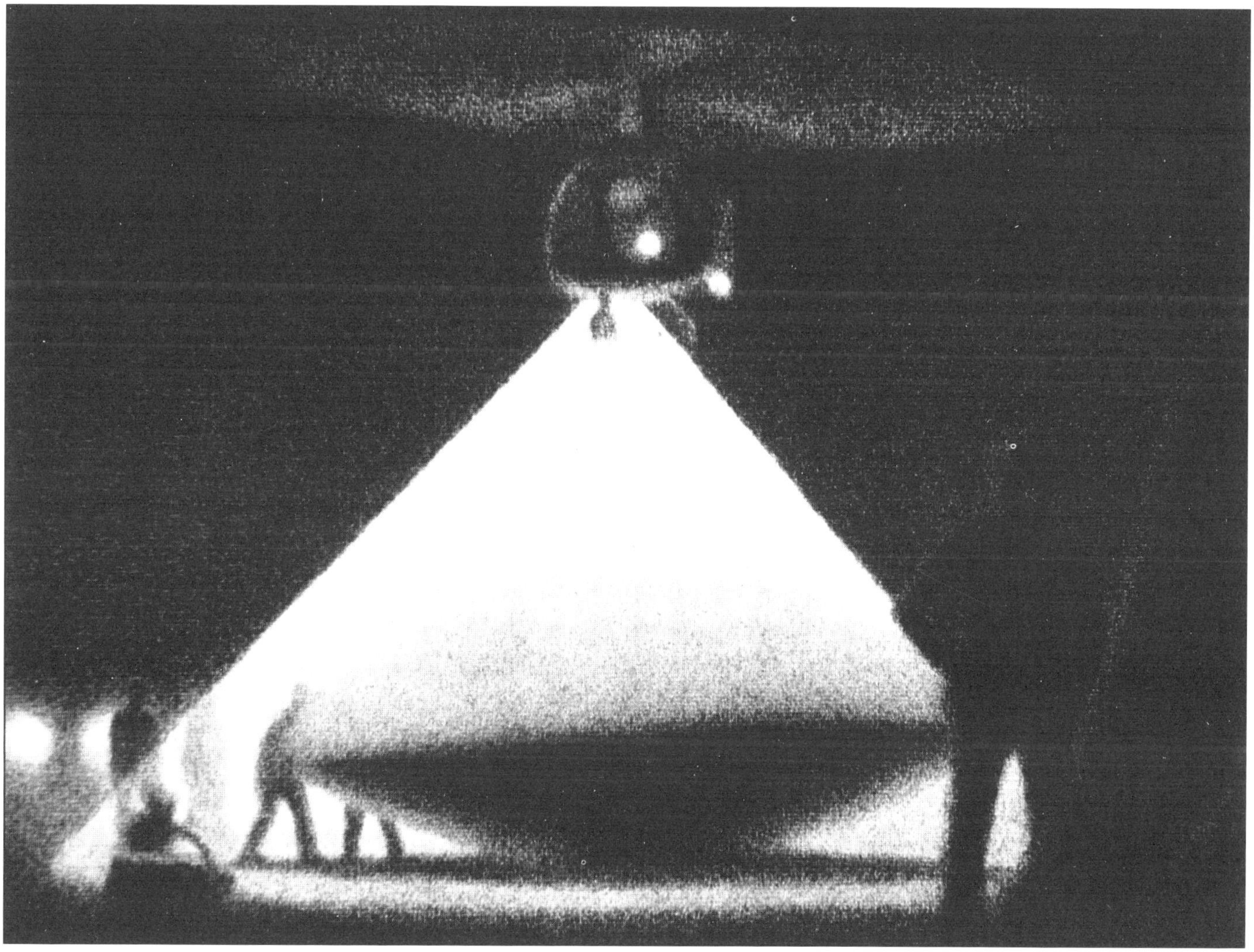

MESSENGERS FROM OUTER SPACE

George Adamski had spent years observing the skies on the lookout for UFOs. An impulse drew him into the desert where a figure beckoned him from the opening of a ravine...but with a sudden chill of fear he wondered whether his long vigil had been wise.

Is someone – or something – inhabiting the Solar System besides ourselves? Are they out there watching us, for some mysterious purpose of their own, or are they simply our elusive neighbours? Are they friendly or are they hostile?

The answers to these questions – the most perplexing and, many would say, the most crucial in the whole debate about UFOs – should have become apparent in the decades since UFOs first revealed themselves as inexplicable flying disks. For in that time numerous people have claimed to have had direct contact with the occupants of UFOs. One might expect a clear picture to emerge from these undoubtedly traumatic experiences of who the aliens are, where they are from, and what – if anything – they want. Yet cases of contactees, and more especially those of people who have been abducted by UFOs, present some of the most conflicting and perplexing evidence of all the vast array of data in the field of ufology.

There are, essentially, three kinds of witness who might help answer some of the fundamental questions.

First, there are those people who have come so close to UFOs that they have seen and described the occupants.

Second, there are those who have been approached by aliens in a friendly spirit and have come away with what amounts to 'a message for mankind' – not necessarily of enormous cosmic import, but at least containing some explanation of what the aliens are doing and why they are here.

Third, there is a small group of people who seem to have been forcibly abducted by aliens. These cases are the most difficult to assess and contain the most astounding claims: that the contactees were subjected to some kind of medical examination, for example, and in some cases were sexually used or abused.

EVADING CAPTURE

One of the most frustrating aspects of the UFO enigma is the inconsistency of the evidence. This is particularly apparent in the descriptions of alien beings given by those who claim to have seen them.

The first such contactee to come to public attention was George Adamski, a part-time caterer who described himself as a 'philosopher and teacher' and who lived in Palomar Gardens, on the southern slopes of Mount Palomar, California. Adamski's passion was astronomy; he had a 15 in and a 6in reflector telescope set up at home to watch the stars. He was also convinced that the other planets of our Solar System were inhabited. On 9 October 1946, while watching a meteor shower from his home, he saw what he later believed to be confirmation of his conviction. Along with others he saw 'a gigantic space craft' that was 'hovering high above the mountain ridge to the south of Mount Palomar, toward San Diego'. It was 'a large black object, resembling a gigantic dirigible'.

Above: *George Adamski's remarkable adventures with purported visitors from Venus were first chronicled in* **Flying Saucers Have Landed.** *Desmond Leslie's part of the book described many historical accounts of apparent UFO sightings.*

Opposite: *Adamski, who before his contact with alleged Venusians was a keen amateur astronomer, with one of his telescopes.*

Below: *Adamski, with Long John Nebel and the 'mother ship' and attendant saucers that he claimed to have photographed in March 1951.*

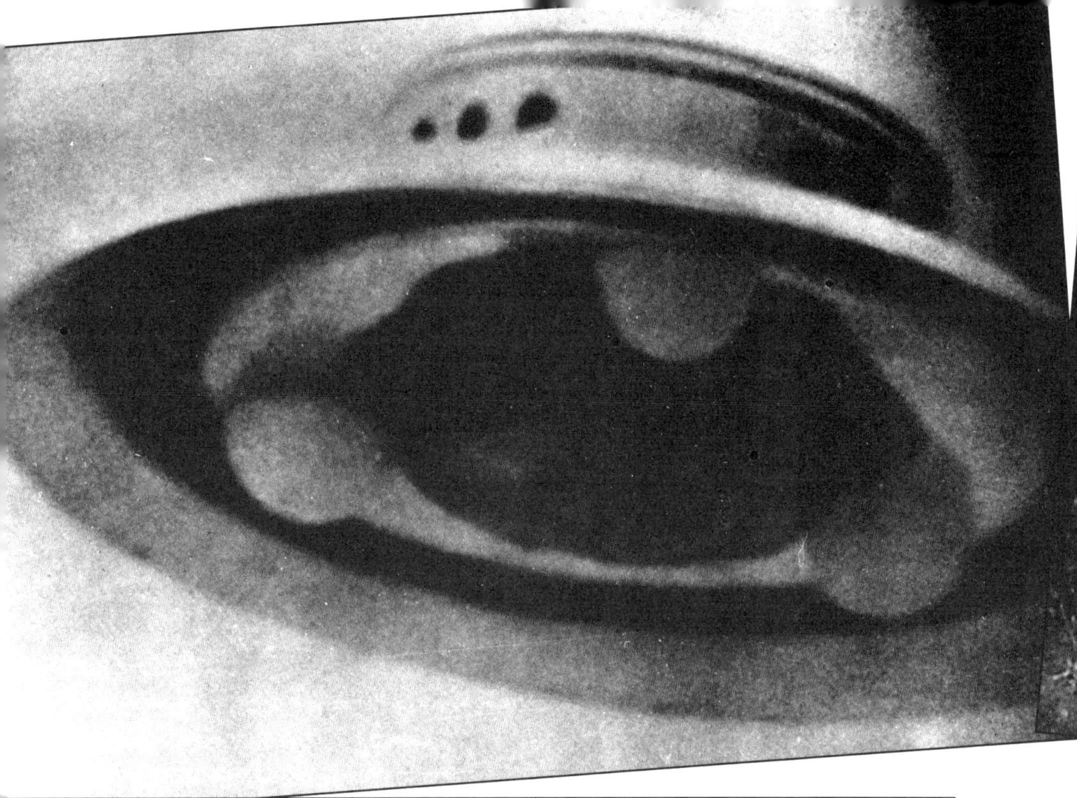

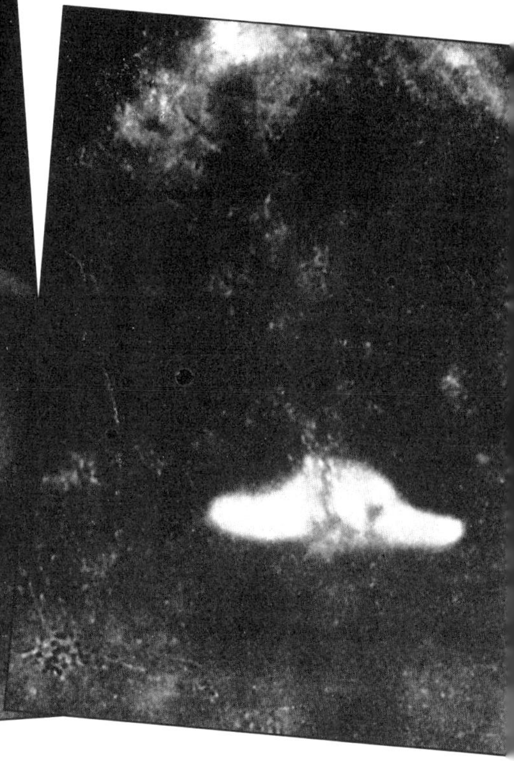

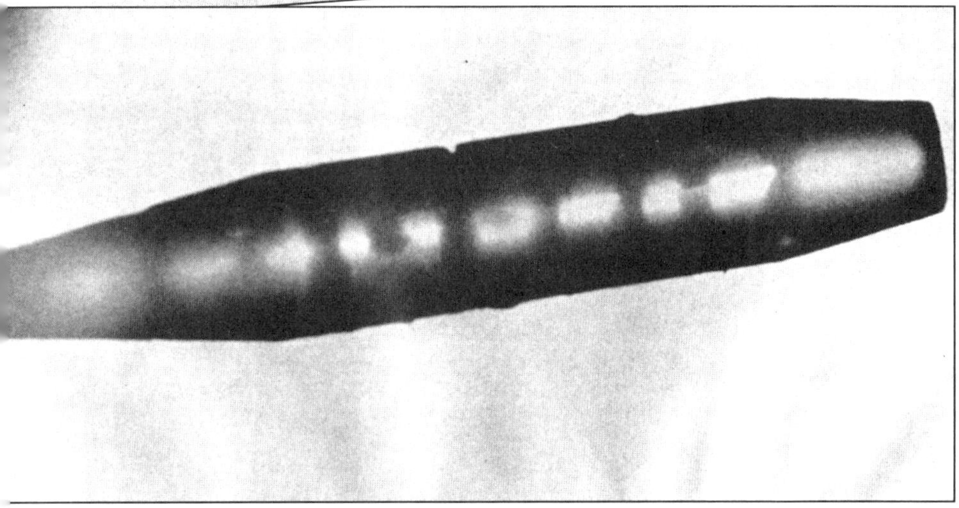

In his book *Flying Saucers Have Landed*, Adamski reports that he was first alerted to the possibility that this was 'a ship from another world' by a military officer, shortly after this sighting. From then on, Adamski spent hours every day on the lookout for another UFO. Between the winter of 1949–50 and the summer of 1952, he photographed a number of UFOs both with and without his 6 in telescope, some 18 of the photos being of high quality. Adamski began giving lectures on UFOs and extra-terrestrials to various interested groups, and as a result of these contacts began to hear rumours that flying saucers had been landing in 'various desert areas not a great drive from Mount Palomar'.

On 20 November 1952, Adamski, his secretary Mrs Lucy McKinnis, and the proprietor of Palomar Gardens, Mrs Alice K. Wells, met up with four such contacts – Mr and Mrs Al C. Bailey of Winslow, Arizona, and Dr and Mrs George H. Williamson of Prescott, Arizona – on the highway near Blythe, California, to go into the desert in the hope of seeing a UFO land. Adamski gives no reason for having chosen this day rather than another, but admits to following a hunch as to where they should start their vigil – about 11 miles down the highway from Desert Center toward Parker, Arizona. The group was richly rewarded.

Top left: ***This extraordinary craft, Adamski maintained, flew over his house in Palomar Gardens on 13 December 1952. Surprisingly, no other witnesses reported the event.***

Top right: ***This picture, according to Adamski, shows a UFO traversing the disk of the Moon on 6 June 1950.***

Above: ***This cigar-shaped UFO was photographed by Adamski on 1 May 1952. Unfortunately, there are no background or other contextual details by which the size or true nature of the image can be judged.***

After a stroll and a light lunch, the party sat scanning the sky. The only thing of note was the passage of a two-engine plane apparently on a routine flight. Then:

'Suddenly and simultaneously we all turned as one [*sic*] looking again toward the closest mountain ridge where just a few minutes before the first plane had crossed. Riding high, and without sound, there was a gigantic cigar-shaped silvery ship, without wings or appendages of any kind.'

The craft moved as if drifting in the direction of the group, then stopped, hovering. Adamski felt that the ship had come specifically for him, and on another hunch demanded to be taken down the road – the spot they were in, next to a well-travelled highway, was too conspicuous, he thought, and would discourage a landing.

With Lucy McKinnis at the wheel and Al Bailey accompanying, Adamski was driven off the highway onto a dirt road, while all the time the giant ship followed them silently. After half a mile or so they stopped. Here, Adamski set up his smaller

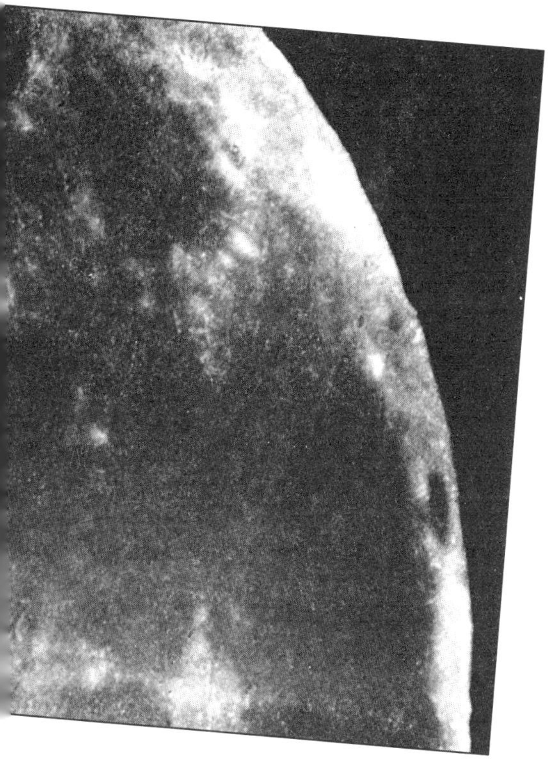

telescope and a camera and then, fearing the presence of his companions would deter the aliens, sent them back to their original parking spot, to watch from there. As they left, a number of aircraft – presumably fighters – roared into sight and tried to circle the huge craft above. In response, the ship 'turned its nose upward and shot out into space'. Wondering if the planes had chased it away for good, Adamski settled down to wait.

Before five minutes was up, he saw a flash in the sky and 'almost instantly a beautiful craft appeared to be drifting through a saddle between two of the mountain peaks'. It settled on a ridge, and Adamski took photographs. Then it lifted and flew back across the saddle, as two more aircraft came into sight, circled, and flew on. Apparently the saucer had evaded them. After some minutes Adamski realized that a man was beckoning him from the opening of a ravine about 450 yds away. Wondering who this was, Adamski made his way toward the figure. Only when he was within arm's length of the man did Adamski realize that he was looking at a visitor from another world.

A WARNING

'The beauty of his form surpassed anything I had ever seen,' he wrote later. That form was unmistakably human. The man was about 5 ft 6 in tall, weighed about 135 lb, and appeared – in Earthly terms – to be about 28 years old. He had shoulder-length, sandy-coloured wavy hair 'glistening more beautifully than any woman's I have ever seen'. His skin was the colour of a suntanned Caucasian's. His face was round, and he had an extremely high forehead, 'calm, grey-green eyes' that slanted slightly at the corners, high cheekbones, and a 'finely chiselled' nose. He seemed to be beardless. The alien was wearing a single-piece, finely woven chocolate-brown suit with no visible fasteners or pockets, but with a broad waistband and a close-fitting high collar. His shoes were ox-blood red and had blunt toes. Adamski thought the outfit was a uniform of some kind.

His attempts to speak to the creature failed, but by concentrating his efforts Adamski succeeded in communicating with a mixture of hand signals and telepathy.

A NUMBER OF SMALL FIGHTER PLANES TRIED VAINLY TO ENCIRCLE THE GARGANTUAN SPACECRAFT.

Below: ***The first photograph of Venus's full disk taken by a spacecraft from Earth – the NASA Pioneer Orbiter, in 1979. The planet's turbulent atmosphere – incapable of supporting humanoid life, despite Adamski's claims to have met a native – is clearly visible.***

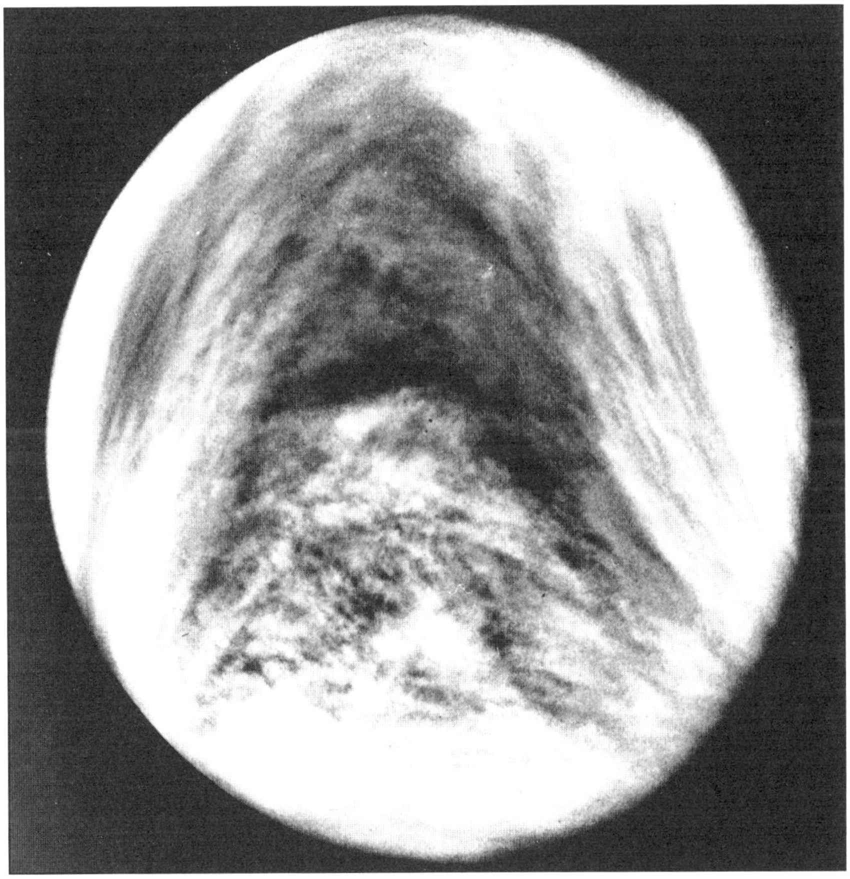

The first thing the alien told Adamski in this manner was that he was from the planet Venus. The Venusians were here, he said, because they were concerned about radiation from atomic explosions: too many of these explosions would destroy all of Earth.

THE WARNING WAS SIMPLE – THE EARTH WAS GOING TO BE DESTROYED.

***Below:** 'A giant leap for mankind' – one of the Apollo 11 crew on the Moon. As human knowledge of the Solar System became more accurate and detailed, so visiting UFO occupants stopped claiming to have come from neighbouring planets and made more and more extravagant claims. Some ufologists maintain that this is part of a game that aliens are playing with humanity – and some are certain that the game is a disguise for the fact that the aliens are not from outer space at all.*

And so it went on. The saucer which brought the Venusian – who did not divulge his name – to Earth had been launched from within the atmosphere by the giant 'mother ship' that Adamski had seen earlier. The craft was powered by 'magnetism'. Asked if he believed in God, the spaceman replied yes, but observed that Venusians lived according to the laws of the Creator and not the laws of materialism as Earthmen did. People from the other planets in the Solar System – all of which were inhabited – and from other systems too were visiting Earth. Some of their craft had crashed on Earth, shot down by 'men of this world'. Saucers landed only in remote places to avoid panicking people, but the time would come when they would land near centres of population. There were many aliens living in our midst already, and for this reason the Venusian refused to be photographed, lest his features become recognizable. All aliens were essentially human in form.

Adamski was then allowed to approach the saucer hovering nearby, but was not permitted inside it. After this, the Venusian climbed aboard his craft, and it glided silently away.

DESOLATE OF LIFE

It is interesting, to say the least, that as Earth's own space programme developed during the 1960s, and probes reported with monotonous regularity that our neighbouring planets were incapable of supporting life as we know it, so the occupants of UFOs have stopped claiming to come from our Solar System. They would certainly feel uncomfortable on Venus, which has an atmospheric pressure 94.5 times higher than our own – which alone would cause any Venusian lacking massive pressurized body armour to explode the moment he set foot on Earth – while temperatures are commonly around 900°F (five times hotter than the boiling point of water). Venusian rain consists largely of hydrochloric and sulphuric acid, and the 'air' is almost entirely carbon dioxide.

However, bearing in mind that one of the few consistent aspects of the UFO phenomenon is its habit of staying just within the borders of the human imagination, it makes some sense for an alien to suggest that he comes from a place that the apparently rather backward terrestrials can immediately recognize as habitable. And in 1952 many people did believe that Venus could support life. Even then, they were wrong – for as early as the 1920s scientists had deduced that Venus could either support 'only low forms of life...mostly belonging to the vegetable kingdom' or was a desert planet plagued by dust storms. By 1932 the Venusian atmosphere was known to be mainly carbon dioxide. This meant that even vegetation was absent.

By 1975, hardly anyone in the Western world was ill-informed about space: six years earlier, the first attempt to put men on the Moon had succeeded brilliantly, while a host of unmanned craft had been sent out to explore remote space, sending back extraordinary pictures of the Solar System along with a mass of information about its planetary environments. All were clearly desolate of any known forms of life.

AN INSANE SOCIETY

Just after 2 pm on 28 January 1975, a one-armed farmer named Eduard 'Billy' Meier was walking near his home at Hinwel, in the canton of Zürich in Switzerland, when he saw a silvery, disk-shaped craft swoop down with a strange throbbing sound out of the sky and land about 100 yds away from him. Intrigued, he began to run toward it, but some invisible force halted him after about 50 yds. A figure then emerged from the disk, which was about 25 ft in diameter, and approached him. When it and its vehicle departed an hour and 45 minutes later, Billy Meier knew he had met a cosmonaut from the Pleiades star cluster (of which seven are visible to the naked eye), 430 light years away from the Sun in the constellation of Taurus.

In all, between January 1975 and April 1978, Meier met five Pleiadians – Semjase, Ptaah, Quetzal, Plaja and Asket – in 105 encounters, photographed their five different types of flying disk on numerous occasions, and took 3000 pages of notes on their conversations and general wisdom. According to Meier, the Pleiadians look like terrestrial Scandinavians, although their lifespan stretches to the equivalent of 1000 of our years. They came from a planet named Erra 'in the system of Taygeta' in the Pleiades, and before that from a planet in the constellation of Lyra, from which they had emigrated millions of years previously. They had reached Earth thousands of years ago, as part of a continuous programme of space exploration, in ships capable of travelling faster than light through 'hyperspace'. Their general message for mankind was that we should concentrate on the arts of peace and cultivating the life of the spirit – otherwise, Earth was 'an insane society rushing headlong to our own destruction'. The Pleiadians communicated with Meier both through telepathy and by speaking his own dialect.

By astronomical standards, the Pleiades is young: a mere 150 million years old. Its 500-odd stars are virtually all 'B' type – ferociously hot, very large blue stars that burn themselves out very rapidly – most, in fact, have already consumed most of the hydrogen in their cores. In contrast, our Sun, a relatively cool, slow-burning 'G2' yellow dwarf, is some 4.49 billion years old, and it took a further 2.5 billion years or so before conditions on Earth were able to support even the most primitive forms of life. The chances that any planet in the Pleiades is habitable are about zero.

Above: ***Eduard 'Billy' Meier, the one-armed Swiss farmer who claimed to have had hundreds of contacts with cosmonauts from the Pleiades star cluster in the mid to late 1970s. The picture on the wall behind him, he claims, is of the Pleiadian Semjase.***

Assuming that extra-terrestrial entities of some kind did make contact with Meier, one can only conclude that they were lying about their present galactic address. The obvious question is: why? And if they lie about that, why should we take anything else they say seriously?

The claims made by the aliens in the Meier case are as incredible as those in another, almost equidistant in time between Adamski's encounter in California and the events in Switzerland, that occurred in New York State. On 24 April 1964, farmer Gary Wilcox of Newark Valley, Tioga County, noticed something shiny about 800 yds away, among some trees on a hill where he was working. He drove his tractor up the hill, dismounted, and approached a cigar-shaped object, that was hovering just off the ground.

Wilcox kicked it. It felt, he said, like metallic canvas. Then, out from under it, came two 4 ft tall but otherwise featureless creatures who, in the conversation that followed, claimed to be Martians. After an innocent conversation in which the two entities made two predictions that turned out not to be true (one foretold the death of astronaut John Glenn within the year), they departed in their noiseless, 20 ft long craft. This occurred at a time when no space

Above: ***Walter H. Andrus Jr, who has analysed thousands of 'alien visitor' reports and detected a number of recurrent patterns within them.***

Right: ***An artist's impression of an encounter with ufonauts that occurred near Cennina, Arezzo, Italy, on 1 November 1954. Note the craft – few real UFO encounters conform to the 'flying saucer with little green men' stereotype.***

scientist believed that any life form more complex than bacteria might be able to survive in Martian conditions.

THE MESSAGE WAS SIGNED 'F. SAUCER'.

VOLUPTUOUS FORMS

These contacts were elaborate and detailed for those who experienced them. They also contain elements of absurdity, illogic and falsehood on the part of the interstellar visitors, but one of the more surprising facets of ufology is the frequency with which these occur. The veteran ufologist and former editor of the internationally respected journal *Flying Saucer Review*, the late Charles Bowen, once offered his readers a few of the choice messages that ufonauts offer to witnesses.

For instance, in 1968 two beings with transparent legs handed an Argentinian farmer's son a written message that translated as 'You shall know the world' and was signed 'F. Saucer'. In 1964, a Venezuelan contactee, confronted by a pair of creatures who were hardly inconspicuous, in that they stood between 7 and 8 ft tall and sported long yellow hair and bulging eyes, asked – with commendable wit, in the circumstances – if any other 'human beings' like them were living on Earth. The reply was 'Yes. Two million, four hundred and seventeen thousand, eight hundred and five.'

Perhaps the most surreal of these utterances came in 1954, when a Frenchman came across a glowing, saucer-shaped UFO, in front of which was standing a diminutive entity who kept repeating, in a mechanical tone: *'La verité est refusée aux constipés'* ('Truth is denied to the constipated'), and *'Ce que vous appelez le cancer vient des dents'* ('What you call cancer comes from the teeth').

If these beings, who seem habitually to

lie about their origins and occasionally make obscurely hilarious observations to the humans they meet, are indeed aliens visiting Earth from other planets, one would expect some consistency at least in their appearance. In fact, they take many more forms than the voluptuous young man who greeted Adamski, or the shapely Nordic blondes of Meier's acquaintance. And they are by no means as friendly or concerned for our welfare as the beings that Adamski and Meier met.

A HEADLESS FIGURE

Walter Andrus, director of the Mutual UFO Network, studied thousands of contactee cases and concluded that there were four major categories of UFO occupants. These were: small humanoids; 'experimental animals'; human-like entities; and robots. ('Little green men', the staple mocking term of the media, however, are hardly ever seen in real UFO contacts.) But these broad categories blur a multitude of differences found from one witness's report to the next.

The term 'human-like entities' encompasses extremes as far apart as the two gigantic beings seen filling a sphere as tall as a two-storey house over the Canary Islands on 22 June 1976; the blue, scaly-skinned, 6 ft tall creature that confronted 19-year-old Maria Eliada Pretzel in Córdoba, Argentina, on 13 June 1968; the creature inside a UFO seen by William Bosak near Frederic, Wisconsin, in December 1974 that had a tan-coloured, furry body, a flat nose and mouth, protruding eyes and 'calf-like' ears; and the truly nightmarish creature that in November 1976 emerged from a UFO near Winchester, England, and stared into a car in which Joyce Bowles and Terry Pratt sat in terror: the thing was human in all visible details but for its eyes, which were entirely pink, with neither irises nor pupils, and luminescent.

The animal forms can be unexpectedly horrible. In 1960, during a UFO sighting at Yssandon, France, giant white maggots were seen crawling across a road. On 16 November 1963, two couples walking near Sandling Park in Saltwood, Kent, saw a bright golden oval UFO come down from the sky and then hover among some trees nearby. A figure emerged and approached them, but the foursome fled when it was close enough for them to make out its features: it was entirely black, had wings like a bat, and no head.

Perhaps the most common form taken by UFO occupants is the classic 'small humanoid' – figures on which Steven Spielberg based both 'ET' and the creatures seen emerging from the giant spaceship in *Close Encounters of the Third Kind* (for which Spielberg used the late Dr J. Allen Hynek, a global authority on UFOs who invented the title phrase, as a consultant). Even these pale, huge-headed, hairless, soft-eyed and innocent-looking entities, which so much resemble human foetuses, vary enormously in detail, according to the witnesses' reports.

They may stand from 1 to 5 ft in height. Their eyes may be like ours, or slitted, like a cat's. Sometimes they appear apparently naked; at other times in shiny black, yellow or blue garb, possibly with a cloak. Some have pointy ears, others none. Betty and Barney Hill, of New Hampshire, believed that in 1961 they had been taken aboard a craft belonging to such creatures (who were clothed in black) and given medical examinations; while in August 1990, five such beings, of various heights, apparently without clothes and with grey skin, and

THEY BELIEVED THE NIGHTMARISH CREATURE WAS HUMAN UNTIL THEY LOOKED INTO ITS EYES.

Below: ***Steven Spielberg, creator of 'ET' and director of the hit movie*** **Close Encounters of the Third Kind.** ***The film was the first to show a wide audience the alien forms most often reported by witnesses. But, while Spielberg's films show aliens as essentially friendly, many actual encounters have been with creatures that were both hostile and dangerous.***

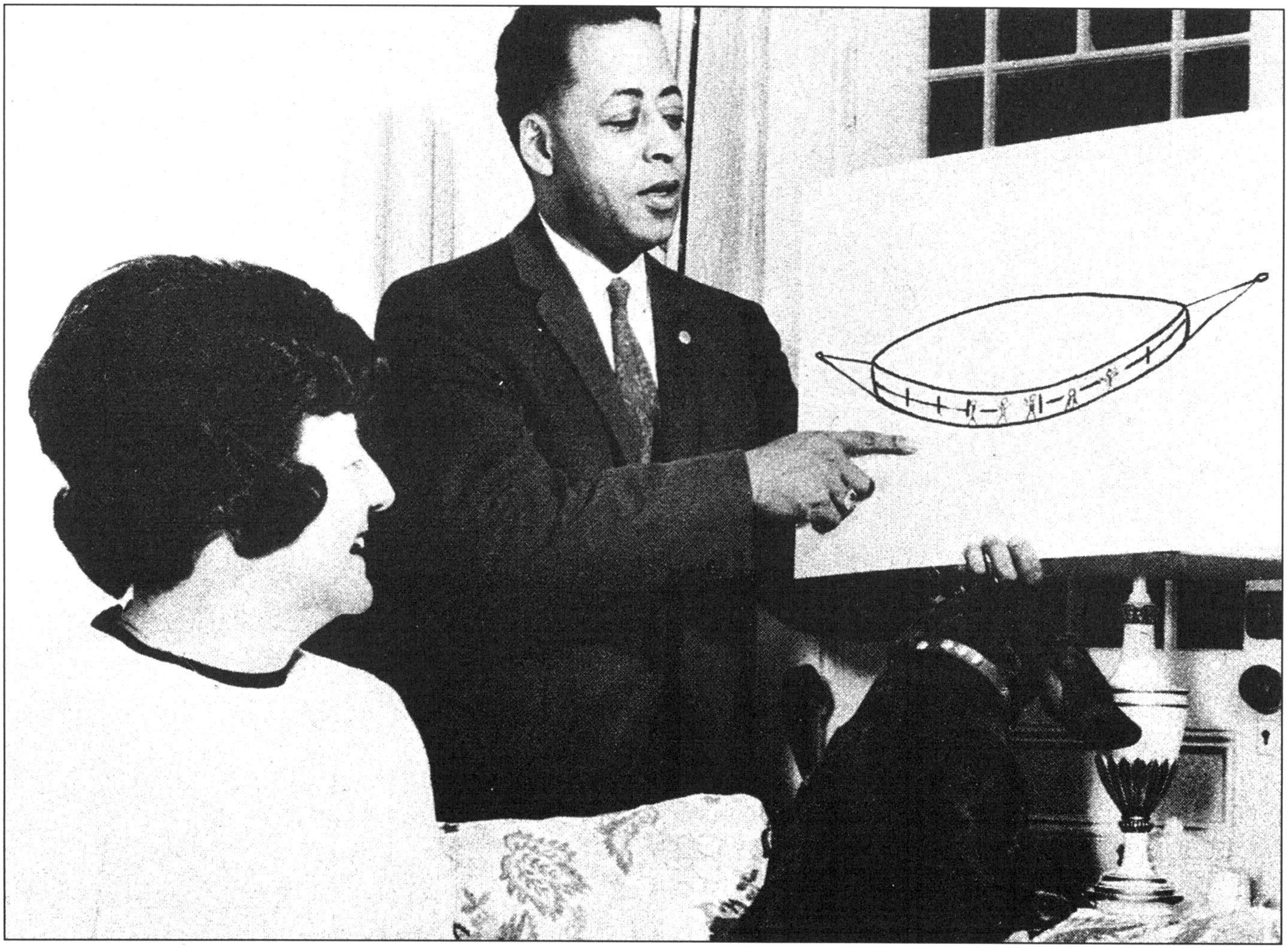

Above: ***Betty and Barney Hill, whose abduction aboard a UFO in 1961 has been the subject of innumerable analyses. None has entirely explained what the couple experienced, or why they were apparently chosen for an alien experiment.***

THE ALIENS ARE DELIBERATELY CONTROLLING THE MINDS OF THE WITNESSES TO PREVENT US LEARNING THEIR TRUE INTENTIONS.

with only three toes on each foot, were seen walking along a main highway in Puerto Rico by numerous witnesses, but made no attempt to molest anyone. These did have the virtue of slightly resembling the creatures seen at Rio Pièdras, Puerto Rico, on 3 March 1980, when teenagers Vivian and José Rodriguez surprised two pointy-eared creatures who were clothed, and had webbed feet.

On other occasions, such creatures have paralysed witnesses with lightbeams from their craft – or their eyes – or physically attacked people in daylight. In the hair-raising episode experienced by Lorenzo Flores and Jesús Gómez near Carora, Venezuela, on 10 December 1954, a band of humanoids tried to drag Gómez away until his companion retaliated with his shotgun (the pair were on a hunting trip).

Most bizarre of all the perceived occupants of UFOs have been the so-called robot figures, and possibly the weirdest of all was reported by Jerry Townsend, a radio station employee from Minnesota. On the evening of 23 October 1965 he was driving toward Long Prairie when his car's electrical systems went totally dead and the engine stopped. In front him on the road was a V-2-style 'spaceship', between 30 and 35 ft tall and resting on the tips of three fins, that might have featured in any 1950s sci-fi movie. Undaunted, Townsend got out of the car to investigate and saw, coming from beneath the rocket, three ludicrous objects walking towards him. They were no more than 6 in tall, reeling like drunken sailors on two fins, and shaped like beer cans. When they halted, a third, rear fin descended to keep them upright. In due course they tottered back to their antiquated 'rocket' and it took off – which part of the incident was also witnessed by two hunters who were some distance away.

MIND CONTROL

None of this catalogue of strangeness – which only scrapes the surface of the cases on file – suggests that the being that was

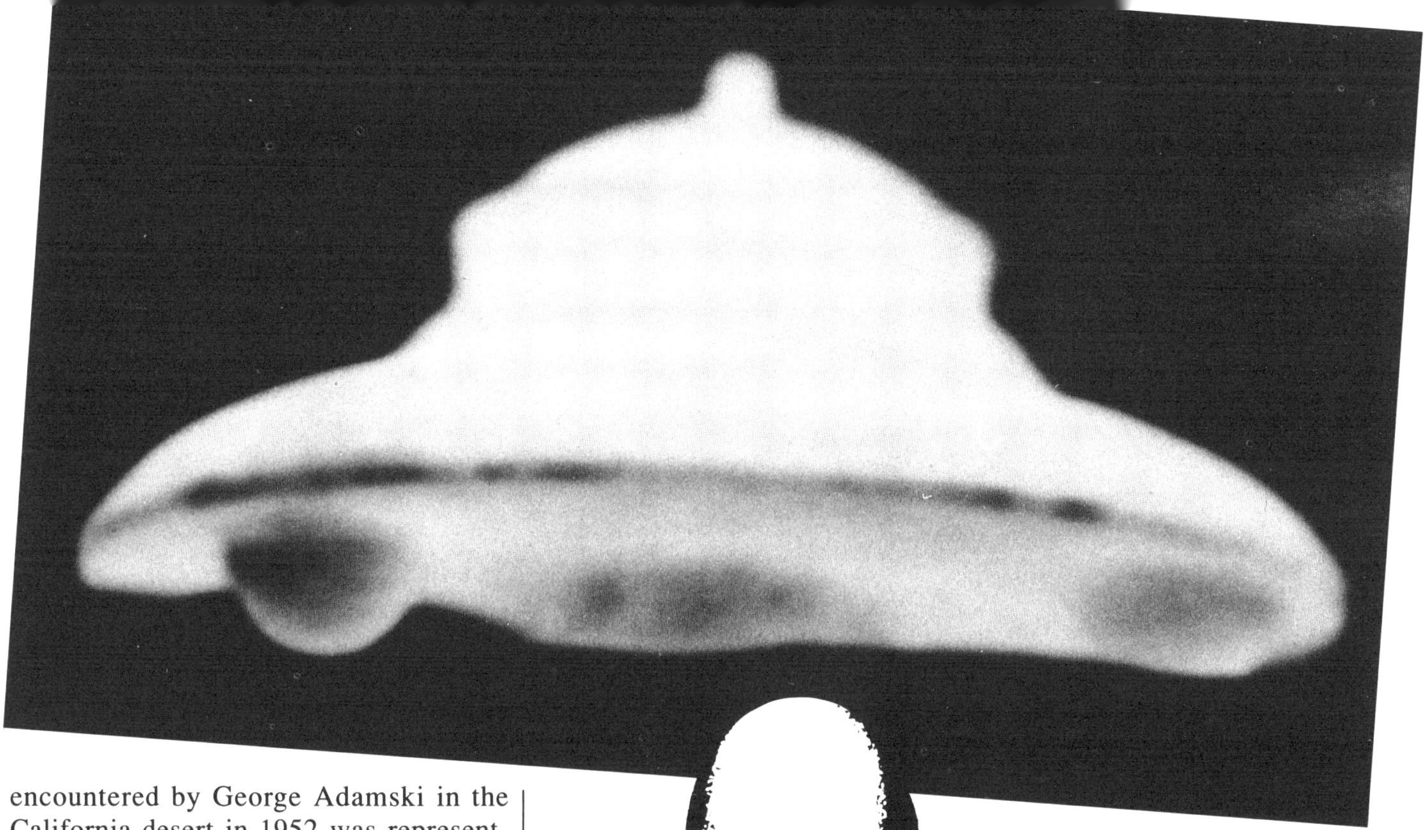

encountered by George Adamski in the California desert in 1952 was representative of its type. The brutal fact is that there is no 'type' at all when one is dealing with UFO entities, and no general conclusion to be drawn from the available evidence about their intentions and still less where they come from. So what are they?

Ufologist and specialist in radiation medicine Maxwell C. Cade once suggested that UFO occupants deliberately monitored, and reflected, what was in the mind of the witness: in some cases, homing in on their fears. Thus, the sceptics' dismissal of the contactee phenomenon that 'It's all hallucination' may be true, but with a significant and unexpected twist. According to Cade's hypothesis, the hallucinations are generated *from within the UFO*, not directly by the witness.

This would explain the huge variations in the degree of sympathy or hostility that contactees encounter among aliens, as well as the bewildering variety of shapes, sizes, colours and textures the entities display. And it would also explain the quality of alien behaviour so shrewdly noted by ufologist Peter Hough – that they 'act less like "aliens" than as if they are fledgling temporary beings hastily assembled and scripted to act out a brief scenario'.

If Cade's hypothesis is correct, it has a clear corollary: whatever they are and wherever they are from, the occupants of UFOs are doing everything in their power to prevent us seeing their true forms or learning their real intentions.

'Typical' flying saucers and alien figures, like these, in fact make up a minority of real UFO encounter reports. Both the craft and their mysterious occupants vary enormously in size, shape, and colour – and in the ufonauts' actions and statements, which range from the amiably banal to the savage and depraved.

ENCOUNTERS WITH THE UNKNOWN

There have now been so many close encounters with UFO phenomena that it is very hard to deny their existence. Terrible injuries have been inflicted on some of the witnesses – but were these encounters with rogue military hardware, or with alien craft on a mission?

Dr J. Allen Hynek (1910–86) was one of the most dedicated, and one of the best-informed, of ufologists the world has seen. A professional astronomer, long a professor, and in due course head of the astronomy department at North Western University in Evanston, Illinois (a suburb of Chicago), Hynek was also one of those fortunate beings who always happen to be in the right place at the right time. In the late 1940s, when still in his early thirties, Hynek was recognized as a rising star (so to speak) and appointed astronomical consultant to the USAF's Project Sign, the official – if not the only – government body established to gather and assess UFO reports. Sign collapsed in 1949, its belief in

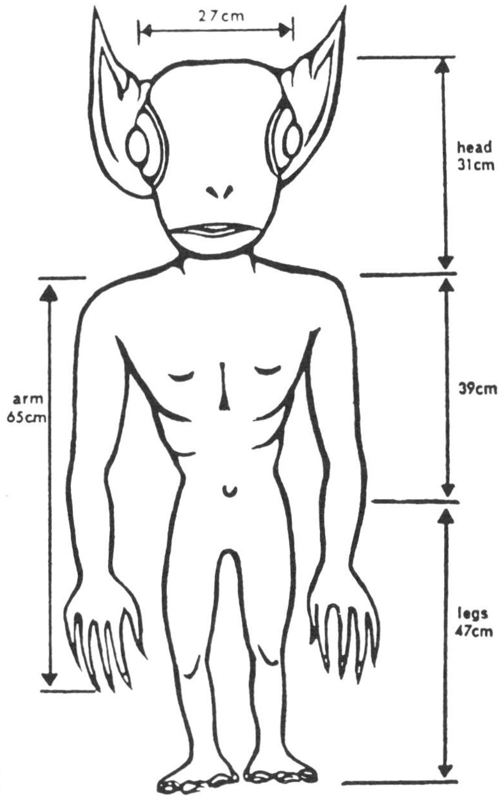

EVENTUALLY THE FAMOUS PROFESSOR WAS FORCED TO CONCEDE THAT SOME CLOSE ENCOUNTERS WITH ALIENS WERE POSSIBLY GENUINE.

Opposite: *This daylight disk was allegedly photographed from an aircraft at Barra da Tijuca, Brazil, on 7 May 1952. South America has always been a rich source of UFO reports, some of them of the most intriguing kind.*

Left: *A diagrammatic representation of one of the goblin-like entities that besieged the Sutton farm at Kelly, near Hopkinsville, Kentucky, in August 1955. The creatures were impervious to gunfire, and persisted in terrorizing the Sutton family through an entire night, although their purpose in doing so never became clear.*

Below left: *Dr J. Allen Hynek, the professor of astronomy whose tireless efforts did much to put UFO studies on a scientific basis. Hynek began analysing UFO reports at the behest of the US Air Force in the late 1940s, and did so at first as a sceptic. The nature of the evidence and the integrity of the overwhelming majority of witnesses soon convinced him that something real lay behind the UFO enigma.*

Above: ***Proof of alien contact and government cover-up – this picture, taken in Germany in the 1950s, shows a tiny alien corpse from a saucer that had crashed near Mexico City and had been sent to Europe for analysis. That, at least, was what many UFO buffs believed, until assiduous research showed that the picture was first seen in an April Fools' edition of a German student magazine in the early 1970s.***

the extra-terrestrial origins of UFOs disbelieved and savagely discredited by the USAF establishment, to be succeeded by Project Grudge and in due course by the longstanding Project Blue Book, which was eventually wound up in 1969.

Hynek survived these political shifts and upheavals, and remained a USAF consultant right through until the end of Project Blue Book, when the USAF officially proclaimed the end of its interest in UFOs. Always, from his earliest professional acquaintance with UFOs until his dying day, Hynek rejected the extra-terrestrial hypothesis – the belief that UFOs and their occupants come from some reach of space beyond this Earth – but in the course of 20 years spent investigating UFO reports on behalf of the USAF came to be convinced that something indubitably real lay behind the UFO phenomenon.

In 1984, in a brief survey of the subject, Hynek summed up his own belief concerning UFOs as follows:

'It is far from certain that UFOs represent a single phenomenon, despite the similarity in patterns of reports from all over the world...Perhaps I may presume to intrude my own opinion on these matters, based on more than 30 years of study. I believe that the UFO phenomenon is in some way directing us to consider an aspect of reality of which we have been hitherto largely unaware – an aspect, indeed, that may eventually be incorporated into our science and may prove to be of great value to the progress of mankind.'

During the International Symposium of the Center for UFO Studies (of which he was founder and director) in Chicago in 1981, Hynek confided to the author of this book that he believed that UFOs were directed by some kind of intelligence. 'That intelligence may be our own,' he added, but did not expand on his conclusion. Perhaps he felt he did not have to.

CLOSE ENCOUNTERS

So far in this survey of the UFO phenomenon, we have seen that while there is little doubt that the phenomenon itself is real, the hard evidence that it is a physical reality is singularly elusive. The proof, in the form of a solid and indisputable example of a grounded UFO or a captured alien, does not exist. Nevertheless, UFOs of considerable size, apparent complexity and the ability to affect the environment around them continue to be seen and reported. How should one start to sort this kind of evidence?

One of Hynek's most useful contributions to the often confused debate about UFOs was a scheme for analysing the evidence: a standard and non-controversial classification of UFO sightings that any interested party could use as a starting point from which to approach the subject. Hynek divided UFO reports into two basic categories, 'distant' sightings and 'close' encounters. 'Distant' meant that the perceived object was further than 500 ft from the observer; a 'close' encounter is one that takes place less than 500 ft away from the witness.

Under distant sightings he listed three sub-categories:

(1) Nocturnal lights – which qualify as UFOs when they make unusual manoeuvres, change speed or direction, show unorthodox configurations, colours or

intensity of lights, in such a way as to rule out the presence of conventional aircraft or natural phenomena.

(2) Daylight disks – unusual flying objects seen in daylight. Their shapes may be like cigars, spheres, triangles, boomerangs, eggs, and even pinpoints.

(3) Radar visuals – a comparatively rare event, when there is instrumental evidence of an unidentified object that correlates with the witness's 'subjective' report. Hynek rejected UFOs detected solely by radar because of the high proportion of 'clutter' that can appear on radar screens, especially those scanning near ground level. This distinction has perhaps become less important since many aircraft, civil and military, are now equipped with transponders that identify them individually on air traffic control and military radar screens. A consistent 'unknown' appearing in commercial or military airspace with no such electronic tag may well be a UFO.

Hynek also listed three 'kinds' of close encounter:

(1) Close encounters of the first kind: UFOs are witnessed at close quarters but do not affect the environment.

(2) Close encounters of the second kind: the UFO has physical effects on animate and/or inanimate objects around it –

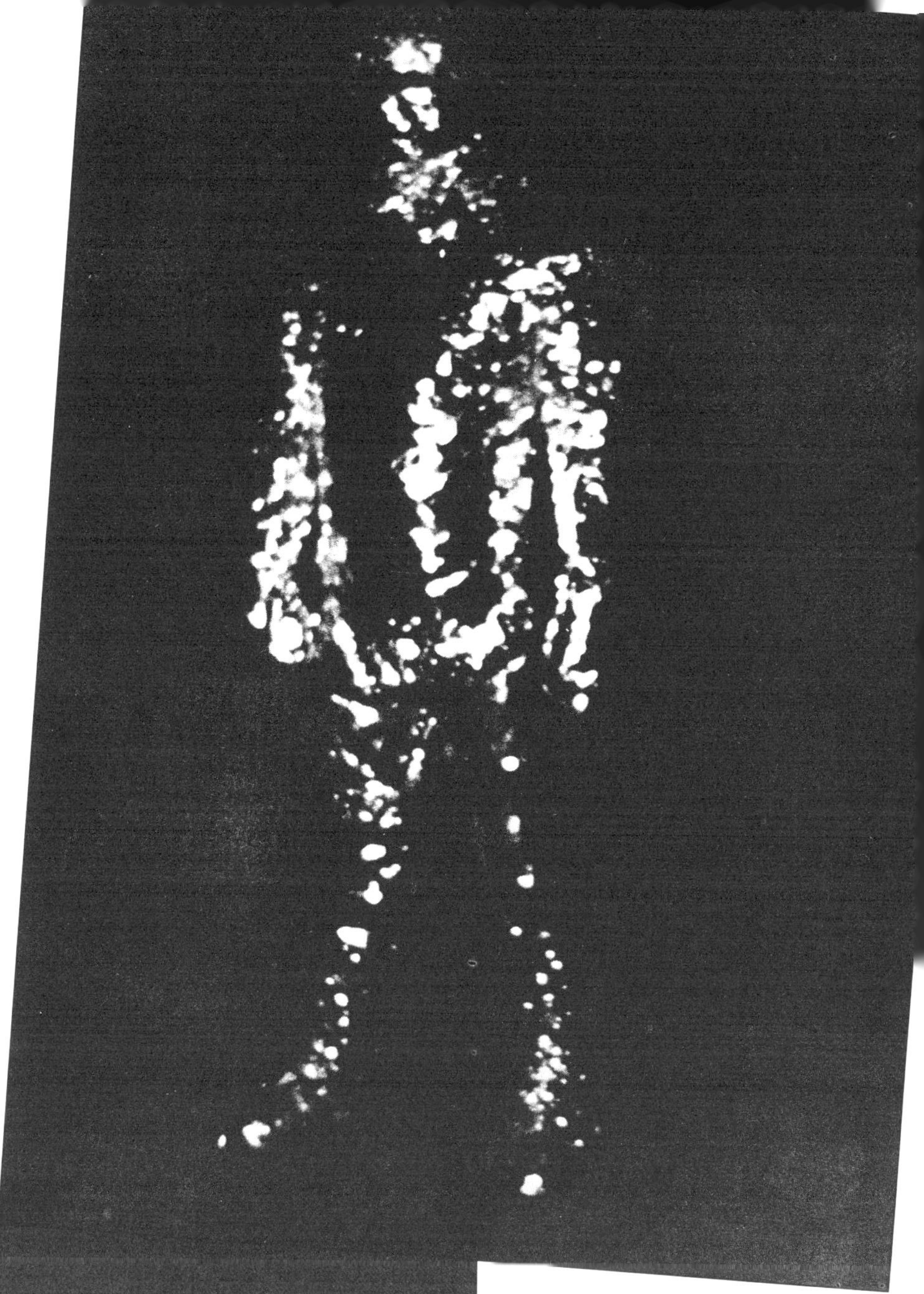

Above: ***The bizarre silver-suited creature that Jeff Greenshaw, police chief of Falkville, Alabama, encountered on 17 October 1973.***

Left: ***According to engineer Paul Paulin, who took this picture of a UFO over Paris at around 3.45 am on 29 December 1953, the craft remained stationary long enough for him to set up a 2-minute time exposure on his camera. During the exposure, the light leapt to a fresh position.***

animals are frightened, the ground is burned, electromagnetic systems such as radios or car lights and engines cease to function, and so on.

(3) Close encounters of the third kind: entities are seen in or near the UFO. Initially Hynek rejected reports that people had had intelligent communication with the occupants of UFOs, and reports of abductions, as never being made by 'sensible, rational and reputable persons' but did come to accept some experiences of this kind. Such cases are now often referred to as 'Close encounters of the fourth kind' in deference to the fact that his system of classification has now become standard among UFO analysts.

Hynek also referred to some UFO reports as having 'high strangeness', although he never made this term part of his system of ordering as such.

THE BLACK SQUADRON

The nocturnal light is the most commonly reported UFO and is the sighting most prone to misidentification, wishful thinking or even, in extreme cases, fantasy. The number of advertising planes, their sides ablaze with some promotional message, is legion in the USA, and so is the number that have been proved to be the source of the most authentic-sounding UFO reports.

***Close encounters of the third kind, as shown in artist's impressions – a meeting between a French farmer, two entities and their egg-shaped craft in a lavender field in the 1950s* (above), *and aliens seen apparently repairing their spherical craft in northern Italy* (below).**

Even the most orthodox aircraft, seen at night at an unexpected angle, especially if it is large and replete with tail illuminations, landing lamps and anti-collision beacons, can become a veritable festival of light – and look very strange indeed.

Daylight disks – unless the sighting is supported by high-quality photographs – can be equally ambiguous. The editor of the British partwork magazine *The Unexplained* once recounted how in the late 1970s he had been driving the sparsely travelled US Route 95 between Beatty and Las Vegas, Nevada, when around mid-afternoon he saw streaking across the sky an object that looked like no aircraft known to him (the son of an aviation engineer and inventor, he is familiar with a wide range of aircraft).

The craft performed no bizarre manoeuvres or aerobatics, but it was oval shaped, with a slight bulge at the rear end, apparently wingless and tailless, and 'the color of dried blood'. Its speed was 'no greater than might be expected from a large, fast strike aircraft – say an F-15 Eagle – at that apparent distance'. That would by most standards be very fast – the F-15 can top 1800 mph in level flight. But there was in any case no way of knowing whether the mystery object was very small and very near, or very large and very distant; the featureless desert terrain was no help in deciding how far away the craft was, or in giving some clue as to its real

size. But he was intrigued to find himself, some miles further on, passing the entrance to the USAF's Indian Springs base. Such installations seem to attract UFOs.

As it happened, the witness soon had a clue to what he may have seen: returning to Phoenix, Arizona, where he was the guest of a former USAF pilot, he learned that Indian Springs is indeed out of the usual run of USAF bases: it is the home of the USAF's 'black squadron' of covertly acquired Soviet aircraft, and over the years has been host to a number of experimental aircraft. The apparent size and, most particularly, the wingless shape and unusual colour of the object he had seen matched that of an aerofoil designed and built by NASA as part of its development programme for the space shuttle. The first shuttle was launched about a year after this sighting, so why a one-off experimental craft should still be flying, in such a location, so late in the life of NASA's programme is anyone's guess. But the point of this account was to illustrate the ambiguous nature of daylight disk sightings – even partly explained ones!

HIDDEN PURPOSES

Radar/visual cases, when they occur, offer much richer pickings to the ufologist, but they still offer no clear-cut clues as to the nature of what has caused the sighting, or what the purpose of the UFO may have been at the time.

At around 9 pm on 10 October 1990, residents around Skibo, Minnesota, began reporting unusual lights in the sky that were appearing to the south-east of nearby Hoyt Lakes. Two police officers who were sent to investigate saw, as did other witnesses, numerous objects 'of indeterminate shape, alternately hovering and darting about'. A little over an hour after the first reports were received, the Federal Aviation Authority's air traffic controllers at Duluth, the area's major airport, confirmed radar echoes from the Hoyt

Military fast-movers (**below:** *the McDonnell Douglas F-15 Eagle) and experimental craft from civilian programmes such as the NASA space shuttle* (**right**) *may easily be taken for UFOs by witnesses unfamiliar with the shapes of such machines. High speed and high manoeuvrability also give an 'alien' impression, as a staff member of the magazine* **The Unexplained** (**above**) *found in the Nevada desert in the late 1970s.*

JUST WHAT KIND OF BIZARRE REALITY ARE WE DEALING WITH?

Lakes area, and for more than an hour after that one of the ATCs at Duluth monitored the echoes. There were between three and five objects registering intermittently, in a roughly circular formation. The local National Air Guard radar also picked up the same returns.

Further confirmation came from the pilot of a commercial aircraft flying at 11,000 ft about 45 miles west of Hoyt Lakes, who reported seeing two steady, distinct, and unidentified lights at an estimated 1000 ft below him. They were a few miles apart and a deep, glowing red. Investigators noted that no other conventional aircraft were in the area, and 'no known weather factors accounted for the anomalous radar returns'.

Below: ***Patrolman Lonnie Zamora of the Socorro, New Mexico, city police, whose close encounter in 1964 has become a classic of ufology.***

HARD EVIDENCE

The most spectacular UFO cases are without doubt the 'close encounters', and it is in these, especially in encounters of the second kind, that we might best be able to judge whether Hynek was on to something in speculating that the UFO phenomenon is 'in some way directing us to an aspect of reality of which we have hitherto been largely unaware'. For here, the normal and the paranormal seem to meet at an interface – as they do to a lesser extent in radar/visual cases, but as they do not in the almost wholly paranormal and possibly entirely psychological experiences that constitute close encounters of the third kind.

This is not to say that something real does not happen in such encounters, but they are one crucial stage further removed from the everyday material world than those of the second kind. And this makes encounters of the third kind exceptionally difficult to analyse, for we are again, immediately, confronted with the old riddle about the *kind* of reality we are dealing with. In close encounters of the second kind we have at least a modicum of 'hard' evidence to add to the witnesses' accounts of their subjective experience. Hynek himself said close encounters of the second kind 'bear a special importance, for when it is reported that a UFO left tangible evidence of its presence...we find the real challenge to scientific enquiry'.

RED INSIGNIA

One of the classic such cases occurred at Socorro, New Mexico, in 1964 – the same town near which, in 1947, Grady L. Barnett reputedly found a crashed UFO. At about 5.45 pm on 24 April 1964 – a clear, sunny day with a strong wind blowing – patrolman Lonnie Zamora, on duty in the Socorro Two police cruiser, gave chase to a speeding Chevrolet. Whilst in pursuit, he heard a brief roar and saw a flame in the sky to his right. Zamora knew there was a shack containing dynamite in the vicinity, and his first thought was that it had blown up. He abandoned his chase and headed for the shack.

During this time the flame – blue and orange in colour, smokeless, long and narrow, and broadening toward the bottom

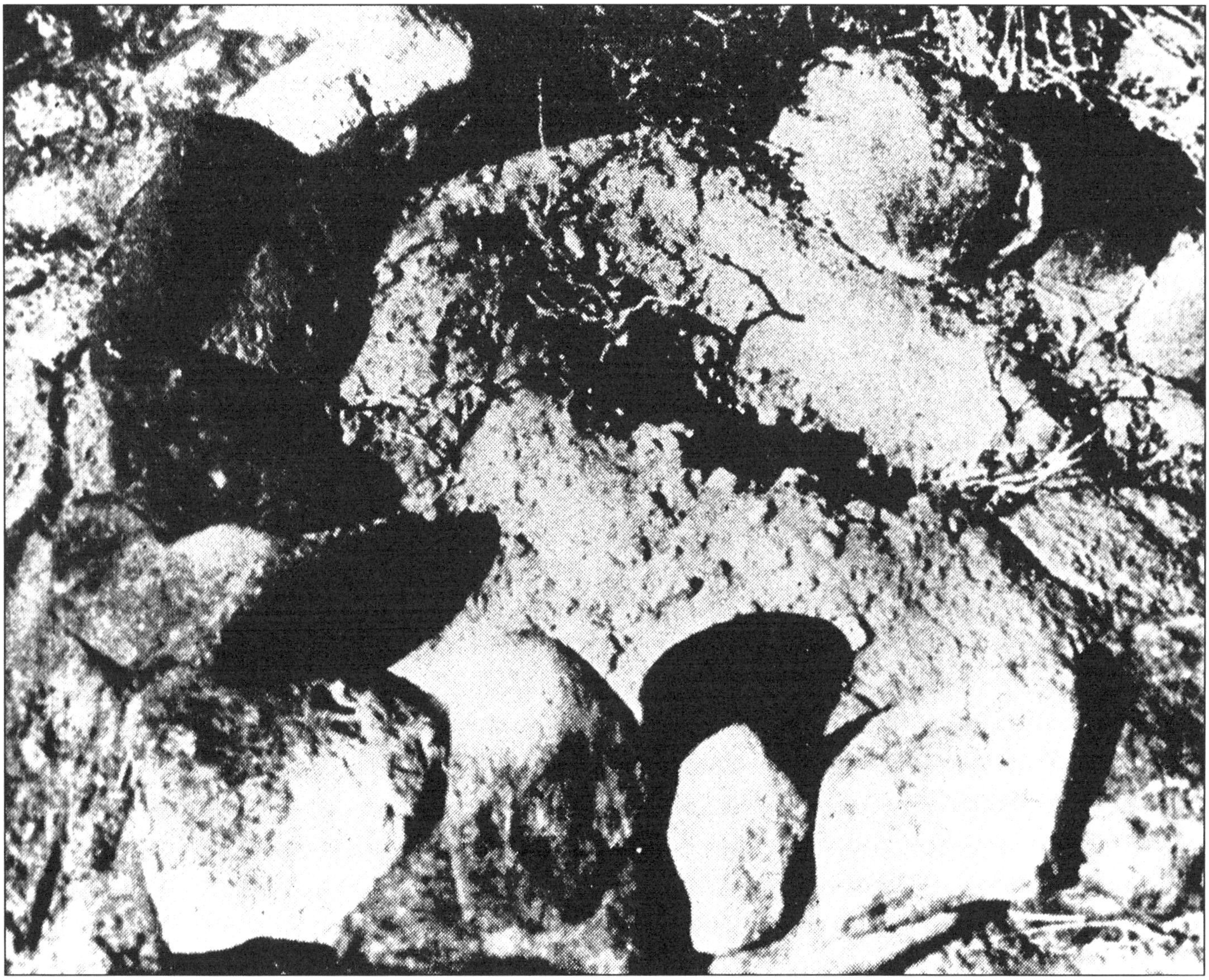

Above: *A 'footprint' left on the desert terrain by one of the stabilizer struts of the Socorro UFO. Stones were placed around the mark to protect it.*

– was descending toward the ground. The base of the flame was invisible behind a low hill to Zamora's left. Concentrating on his driving, he did not notice any object atop the flame and, besides, the sun was in his eyes.

While looking out for the shack, he noticed 'a shiny type object to [the] south' between 100 and 200 yds off the road and below him in a gully. 'It looked,' Zamora told FBI agent J. Arthur Byrnes Jr later the same day, 'like a car turned upside down...standing on [its] radiator or trunk.'

Next to the object were 'two people in white coveralls...One of these persons seemed to turn and look straight at my car and seemed startled – seemed to quickly jump somewhat.' They 'appeared normal in shape – but possibly they were small adults or large kids'. Zamora radioed Sgt Sam Chavez at the sheriff's office in Socorro that he was about to investigate a possible accident, then, as he got out of the car, his radio mike fell. While he turned back to replace it, he heard 'two or three loud thumps...a second or less apart'.

Zamora approached to within 75 or 100 ft of the object, which he now saw was oval and smooth, with no windows or doors, on girder-like legs. He also noted red insignia on its side, about 2 1/2 ft wide. Then the roar began again, low frequency at first, rising rapidly and getting 'very loud'. The object was emitting a flame and kicking up dust. There was no sign of the 'persons' he had seen before.

Zamora thought the object might explode, and ran. The roar stopped, and he looked back to see the UFO 'going away from me in a south-west direction... possibly 10 to 15 ft above the ground, and it cleared the dynamite shack by about 3 ft'. The UFO, now travelling very fast but no longer emitting either noise or

Above: ***Another of the traces left by the Socorro UFO. The depth of the impression suggested that the mystery craft weighed at least 4 tons.***

flame, rose up and sped away. It 'just cleared' a mountain in the distance and disappeared.

When Sgt Chavez arrived on the scene, he and Zamora went to investigate the spot where the UFO had landed, and where the brush was still burning. They were soon joined by FBI Agent Byrne, in Socorro on another case – and Deputy Sheriff James Lucky. They found four burn marks, and four V-shaped depressions, between 1 and 2 in deep and roughly 18 in long, in the ground in an asymmetrical diamond pattern around the burns. These corresponded to the 'legs' Zamora had seen on the mystery craft, and an independent engineer's analysis later declared that each would have been bearing a load of at least 1 ton to press so deeply into the dense earth of the district. Five other, smaller marks nearby were labelled 'footprints'. All these marks were photographed the following day.

Hynek arrived in Socorro on 28 April to investigate the sighting on behalf of the USAF's Project Blue Book. His first task was to establish the truth of Zamora's testimony, and that he could not fault. At his instigation, the USAF checked – to no avail – if any aerospace company had been privately developing such a craft. The USAF did not, however, follow up Hynek's request that they attempt to trace the car driver who told the manager of a gas station on US Highway 85 (since superseded by Interstate 25) that he had seen some kind of aircraft just south of town, obviously in trouble and landing – and a police car was approaching it.

Sceptics have had some difficulty in trying to dispose of the Socorro case, imputing motives for a hoax to the town's mayor and suggesting that otherwise Zamora saw a 'ball of plasma' and imagined the rest. The USAF initially thought that a lunar exploration module, then being developed, was somehow responsible, but no such vehicle resembles what Zamora saw; Blue Book finally classified the sighting as 'unidentified'. Hynek himself concluded that 'a real physical event' occurred in Socorro that day.

HYSTERICAL WITH FEAR

A less celebrated but no less intriguing case occurred in England three and a half years after the events at Socorro. Sometime between 1 and 2 am on 6 November 1967, Carl Farlow was driving his truck on the A338 trunk road between the villages of Sopley and Avon in Hampshire. He was approaching a junction when his lights died. The truck's diesel engine (which does not depend on an electrical ignition system) kept running and, assuming a simple short-circuit of some kind, Farlow pulled up to investigate.

Before he could climb down from the cab, he was astonished to see a bizarre egg-shaped object move from right to left across the road in front of him at about 25 ft from the ground. It was magenta coloured, with a white base, and was perhaps 80 ft long – big enough to overhang both sides of the road as it passed, exuded a smell 'like a drill boring through wood' and made a sound 'like a refrigerator'. As it crossed the road it accelerated gradually, then disappeared.

Farlow then realized that a Jaguar sedan, which had been coming in the opposite direction, was stranded on the other side of the UFO's path. Its driver, who was a veterinarian, approached Farlow, explained that his vehicle was out of action and his lady passenger hysterical, and suggested they call the police. The police arrived at the scene shortly afterwards. Their preliminary inspection of the site showed that the surface of the road seemed to have melted. The vet's passenger was taken to hospital to be treated for shock, while the two men were questioned first by police and later by a member of the Ministry of Defence.

Next day, Farlow returned to his truck. A bulldozer was at work levelling the road, the phone booth was being repainted, and other people seemed to be investigating the area with instruments. A week or so later, taking the same route in his truck, Farlow saw that some 70 yds of that particular stretch of road had been resurfaced.

BURNT BY RADIATION

Betty Cash, Vickie Landrum and her 7-year-old grandson Colby Landrum were driving home to Dayton, near Houston, Texas, on the evening of 29 December 1980, after a meal in nearby New Caney. Around 9 pm the trio, with Betty at the

Below: ***One of the most baffling, bizarre and frightening of modern UFO cases – the 'Cash-Landrum' encounter near Huffman, Texas, in 1980, which left the witnesses suffering all the symptoms of radiation poisoning and appeared to involve the US military.***

THE THREE VICTIMS SUFFERED TERRIBLE SIDE-EFFECTS AFTER THEIR EXPOSURE TO THE STRANGE ELECTROMAGNETIC RADIATION.

wheel, were on Highway FM1485, which runs through a forest of oak and pine. Then, Colby pointed to a bright light moving over the trees ahead of them. The light grew larger and larger – until it became 'like a diamond of fire', in Vickie Landrum's words – while every so often flames burst from beneath it. Suddenly, it was right in their way.

Betty braked hard. The three watched as the UFO hovered above the road about 60 yds away. From treetop level it sank to within 25 ft of the highway, gave out a blast of fire, and rose again. It did this several times, mesmerizing the car's occupants. They actually climbed out to see the object, which was lighting up the trees and the highway all around it, more clearly. It seemed to be made of dull aluminium, and the four points of its diamond shape were rounded. A row of blue dots ran across its centre. Now and then it emitted a beeping sound. A terrific heat was coming from the UFO, and Colby begged his grandmother to get back in the car. She and he both did, but Betty stayed outside until the object moved up and away. The car was now so hot that she could not touch the door with bare hands. Then a crowd of helicopters

Witnesses' drawings of UFO encounters, one from Lemon Grove, California in 1973 (right)*; the other from Dyfed, Wales, in 1977* (opposite)*. The Lemon Grove encounter was certainly with a material object of 'high strangeness' – one of the witnesses actually knocked on the side of the thing with his torch. But the Dyfed case turned out to be the product of a combination of mistaken identity (the 'UFO' was probably a council garbage truck) and a mild form of mass hysteria, which caused many schoolchildren to believe they had seen an alien craft.*

appeared. 'They seemed to rush in from all directions,' said Betty. 'It seemed like they were trying to encircle the thing.'

They drove on another five miles to where they could see the UFO in the distance, and the swarm of helicopters around it. One, a giant, twin-rotor CH-47 Chinook, roared right over them. They counted a total of 23 machines of various types apparently in pursuit of the clearly visible UFO.

But worse was to follow. Over the next few hours, the trio developed painful swellings and blisters on their skin and had severe headaches and stomach upsets. Vickie's hair began to fall out. Colby suffered a sunburn-like rash. Over the following week or so, Betty's eyes also became swollen to the point that she could not see, and she had to be hospitalized. In a few weeks all three had lost some hair and were developing eye problems. Their hair eventually grew again, although it was different from their original hair. Since their experience, none has entirely recovered their former good health. Doctors said that the symptoms shown by the three victims were consistent with exposure to intense electro-magnetic radiation in the ultra-violet, microwave and X-ray bands.

Investigators later established that other witnesses could confirm the UFO's flight path and appearance, and the presence of unusual numbers of CH-47 helicopters – which are quite distinctive – in the sky that night. Yet local civil airfields and military airbases deny that such a fleet used their facilities or showed on their radar. Vickie Landrum was convinced that a secret military device run haywire was responsible for her injuries, and she and Betty Cash sued the US government for $20 million in that belief. In 1986, the case was dismissed on the grounds that 'no such object was owned, operated or in the inventory' of the US Army, Navy, Air Force or NASA.

However, what the US government has *not* said may be significant, for it has not been obliged to admit whether or not it knows what the object was, irrespective of who owns it. So the origin and nature of the Texas UFO – like that of all other UFOs – remains an enigma. That is precious little comfort to those it affected, or to those trying to solve the mystery of UFOs as a whole. The Texas UFO case is perhaps the most baffling and frustrating of modern times, for what starts with solid evidence for a notoriously elusive phenomenon peters out in a maze of dead ends, official denials, and perhaps even deviousness.

Nonetheless, the three classic close encounters of the second kind discussed here show significant similarities. In the Avon and Texas cases there is a strong indication of military involvement, and it is possible, if by no means proven, that the military may have had some connection with the Socorro case – for by 1964, the White Sands Missile Range had acquired a further 883,910 acres of land that extended the range northwards, east of the town. There are certain physical similarities between the Texas UFO and the Socorro craft. And it is apparent that the authorities had no wish to admit to the existence of either the Avon or the Texas UFO – both of which involved multiple witnesses. And in all cases there were real physical effects, either on people or on the environment.

Are we dealing here with secret military hardware gone wrong, bursting disastrously into public gaze? Or were the UFOs alien craft that were busy trying to escape military scrutiny? Or – the wildest scenario of all, but one that some ufologists take seriously – was the military already well aware that the craft were alien, and simply trying to hide their knowledge, or even their collusion with the UFOs?

SOLID EVIDENCE PETERS OUT IN A MAZE OF DEAD ENDS, UNCONVINCING OFFICIAL DETAILS AND DEVIOUSNESS.

ARE THE MILITARY HIDING – OR EVEN COLLUDING WITH – THE UFOS?

UFOs: THE PHYSICAL EVIDENCE

Evidence of UFOs is dramatic and varied but too often the trail goes cold. Are the scientists being silenced? And, if so, is the controlling force a human mind or something far more powerful?

The three cases considered in the last chapter demonstrate that one part at least of the UFO phenomenon involves actual hardware – since we have to assume that only physical, mechanical objects have the capacity to melt road surfaces, crush compacted, dried-out desert earth, and maim witnesses.

It is also clear from that evidence that these cases do not really illuminate ufologist J. Allen Hynek's remark late in his life that 'the UFO phenomenon is in some way directing us to consider an aspect of reality of which we have been hitherto largely unaware – an aspect, indeed, that may eventually be incorporated into our science and may prove to be of great value to the progress of mankind'. Nor do they bear out his belief that close encounters of the second kind 'bear a special importance, for when it is reported that a UFO left tangible evidence of its presence…we find the real challenge to scientific enquiry'.

For here were three classic close encounters that seem to be all too real in worldly terms to indicate that some other order or aspect of reality is involved (although it may well be in other kinds of encounter, of course). Scientific enquiry bore very little fruit in the two American cases. If it was permitted in the English case, the scientists involved were clearly silenced by the Official Secrets Act. What they already knew, or what they discovered – if anything – is still under wraps.

The manner in which the scientific trail peters out in these cases is typical of the UFO phenomenon as a whole: the most promising clues to at least part of the phenomenon are leads only to dead ends. Even when investigators are presented with quite dramatic evidence, or material that can be put into a laboratory and analysed, the conclusions raise as many questions as they answer. Not the least baffling aspect of the physical traces that UFOs leave behind is that they are as varied as reports of the appearance of UFOs and their extraordinary occupants – as the following, necessarily brief, survey shows.

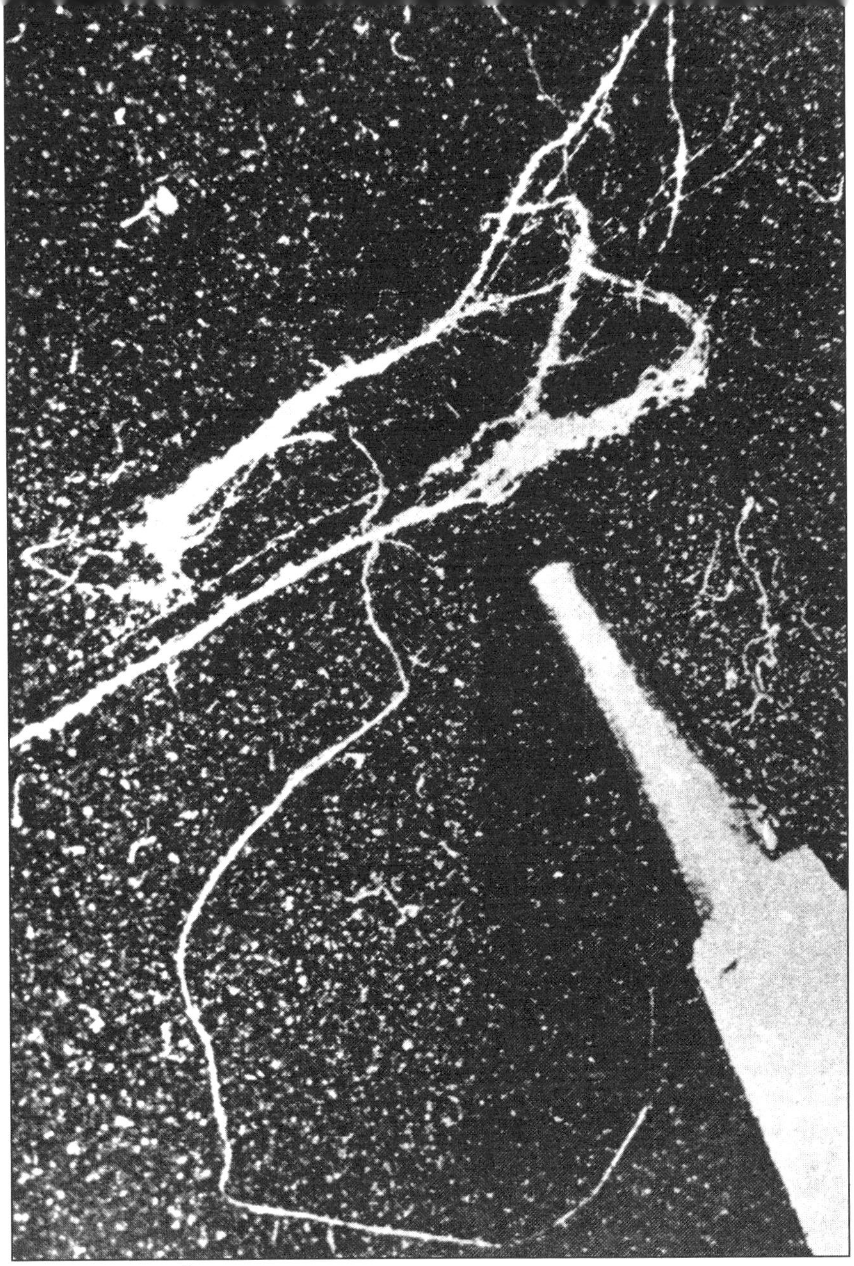

*Evidence of UFOs, or a so-far unexplained natural substance? So-called 'angel hair' (**opposite**, as found in Japan, and **above**) has drifted inexplicably from the sky during a significant number of UFO sightings. One of its more curious qualities is its tendency to evaporate, making scientific analysis impossible.*

WHAT THEY DISCOVERED IS STILL UNDER WRAPS – THE STARTLING REVELATIONS BLOCKED BY THE OFFICIAL SECRETS ACT.

ANGEL HAIR

French ufologist Aime Michel recounted this instance (of many on record) of the gossamer-like material called 'angel hair' that has occasionally fallen from the sky during a UFO sighting.

At about 12.50 pm on 17 October 1952, a M. Prigent, the headmaster of a school at

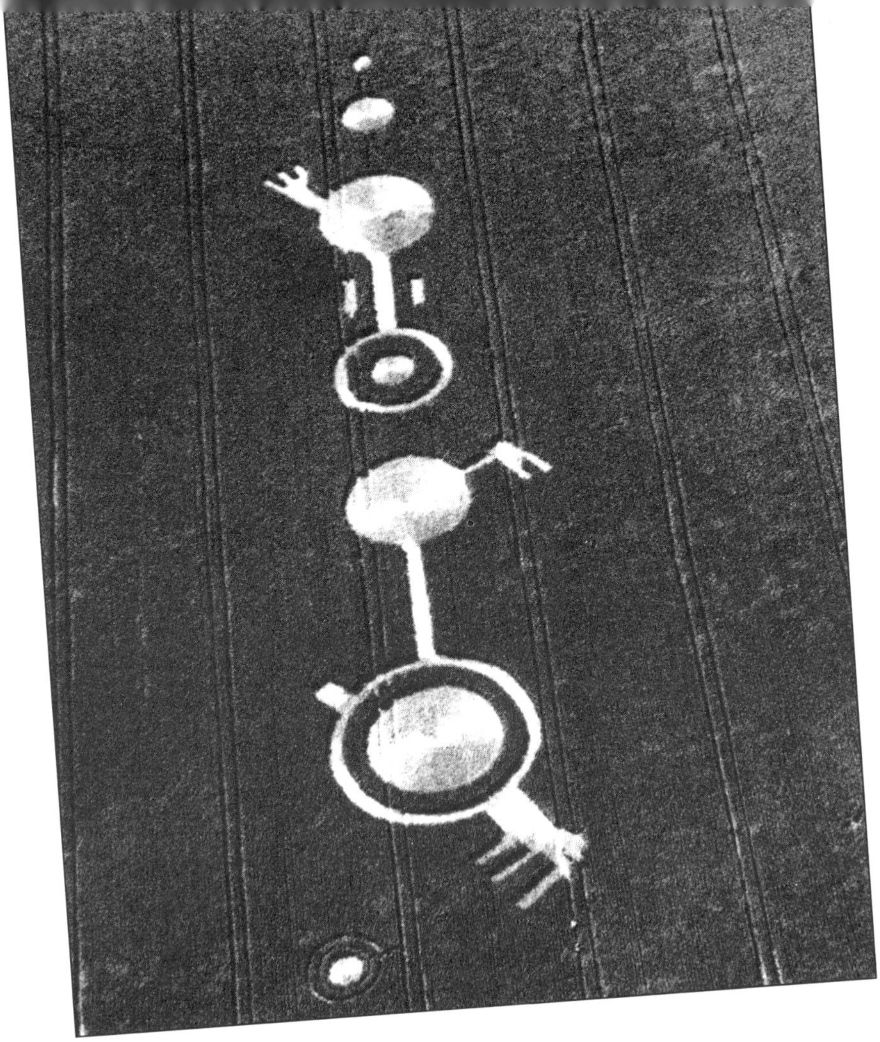

Crop circles **(above)** *were once taken to be UFO 'nests' or landing sites but, unlike the traces found at South Hill, Virginia* **(right and below)***, after a UFO sighting on 21 April 1967, the circles have been shown to be the work of hoaxers or caused by unusual atmospheric conditions.*

Oloron, France, was having lunch with his family when they saw a small fleet of UFOs and a 'mother ship' flying a zigzag course. The latter was a white cylinder, apparently tilted into the sky, at an estimated altitude of 8000 ft. Travelling in pairs ahead of it were some 30 spherical objects that, M. Prigent saw through binoculars, were red spheres with yellow planetary rings around them, like smaller editions of Saturn. From time to time all these objects seemed to give out puffs of smoke, but they also left long trails of some other substance, which drifted to the ground. A large number of witnesses testified that for hours afterwards the material kept falling; it was gelatinous at first, but eventually vaporized and disappeared.

Scientists could offer no clue as to its nature – and, of course, could not examine it.

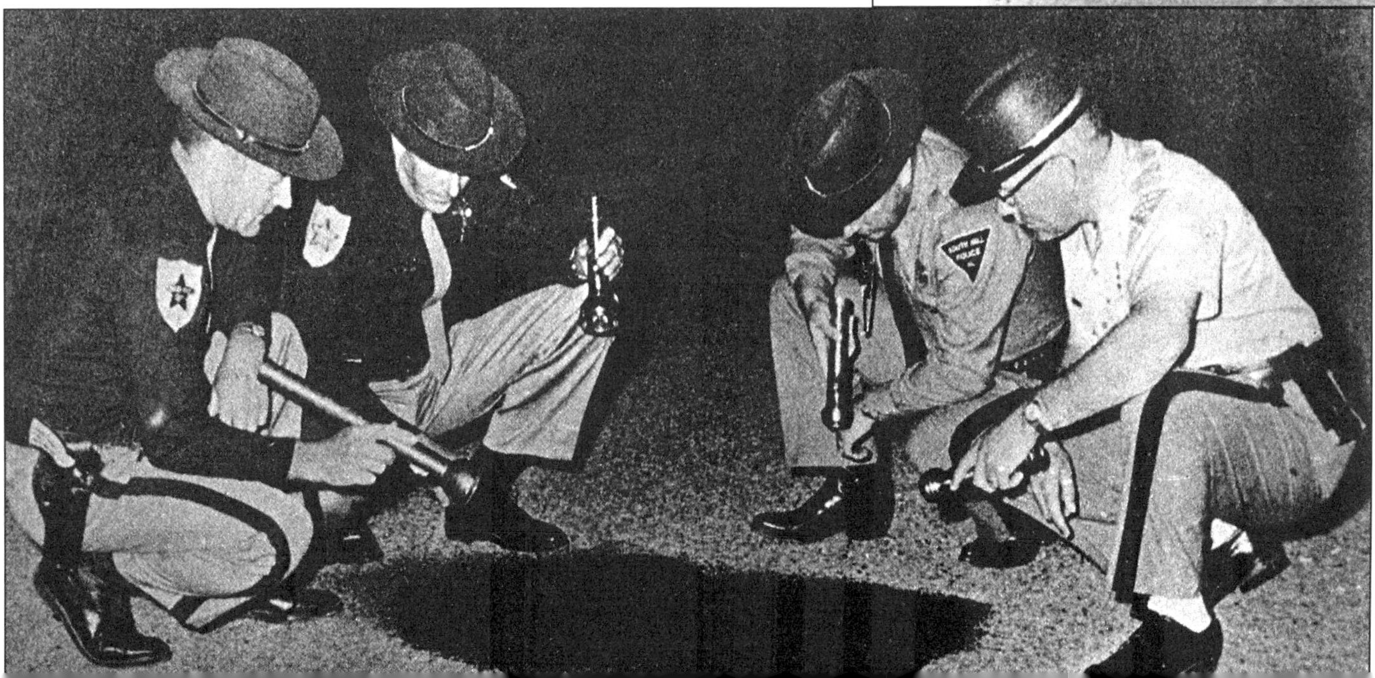

STEALTH TECHNOLOGY

One of the most dramatic reports of a radar/visual UFO sighting, with radical physical effects as well, hit the Russian press (including the district military newspaper *Za Rodinu*) in 1990, after a series of bizarre events at the long-range radar tracking station near the city of Samara (then called Kuybyshev) in Russia.

At 12.07 am on 13 September 1990, the radar watch saw a blip 'comparable to that of a strategic bomber' at a range of 60 miles appear on their screens. The station's automatic electronic IFF (Identify Friend or Foe) system then failed, preventing the watch from identifying whether the aircraft was hostile or not. Two and a half minutes after its first appearance, the large blip then scattered into a host of smaller returns. By the time these were within 25 miles or so of the station, the largest of them was showing as a triangular-shaped object, and heading straight for the radar post. As it approached, a team of soldiers was scrambled to investigate: the thing shot over their heads, less than 35 ft up, as they came into the open. Then it stopped, hovering about 100 yds beyond a barbed-wire barrier that lay less than 50 yds from a mobile, short-range radar array known as Post No 12. There was a flash, and No 12's paired aerials caught fire; the upper one collapsed to the ground. Later inspection revealed that all the steel parts had been melted.

***Many UFO photographs have been shown to be clever fakes, but some have passed the most rigorous computerized tests. Among the latter are those taken by Paul Trent at McMinnville, Oregon, on 11 May 1950* (above) *and from a Brazilian Navy research vessel off Trindade Island in the Atlantic on 16 January 1958* (right).**

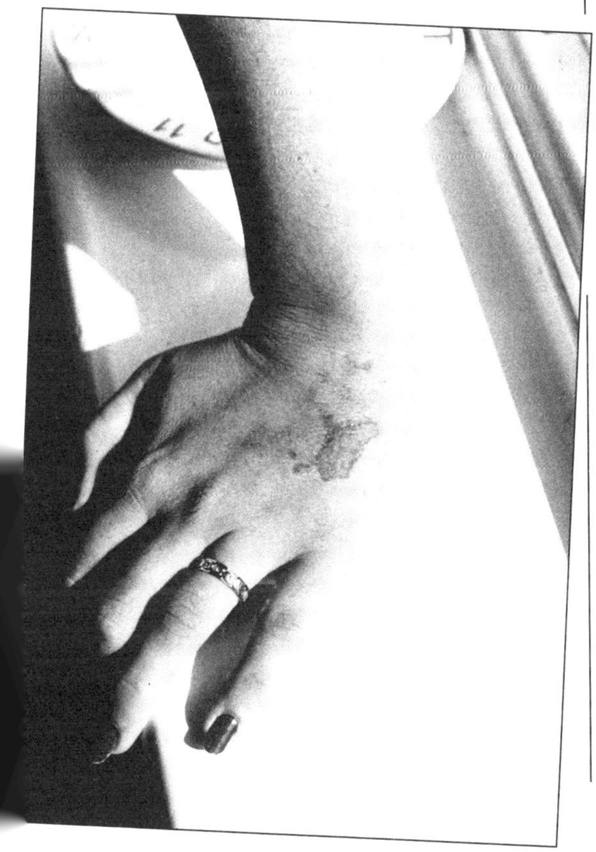

Left: ***UFOs may leave physical 'traces' on people as well as on the ground. Here, Denise Bishop displays the effects of her UFO encounter in Plymouth, Devon, on 10 September 1981.***

THE UFO BLOCKED THE ELECTROMAGNETIC DEFENCE SYSTEM AND DESTROYED THE RADAR. THE HELPLESS SOLDIERS COULD DO NOTHING BUT WATCH AND WAIT.

Witnesses – both officers and enlisted men – described the mystery triangle as black and 'smooth...not mirror-like – it was like a thick layer of soot'. Its sides were each about 45 ft long, and it was about 10 ft thick. There were no openings or portholes. The machine remained hovering for about 90 minutes after destroying the radar, while the post soldiers covered it – somewhat optimistically – with small arms. Then it took off.

After the press reports came official denials, and the announcement on 23 September 1990 that the story was a hoax perpetrated by a reporter on *Za Rodinu*. But it seems that a Soviet Defence

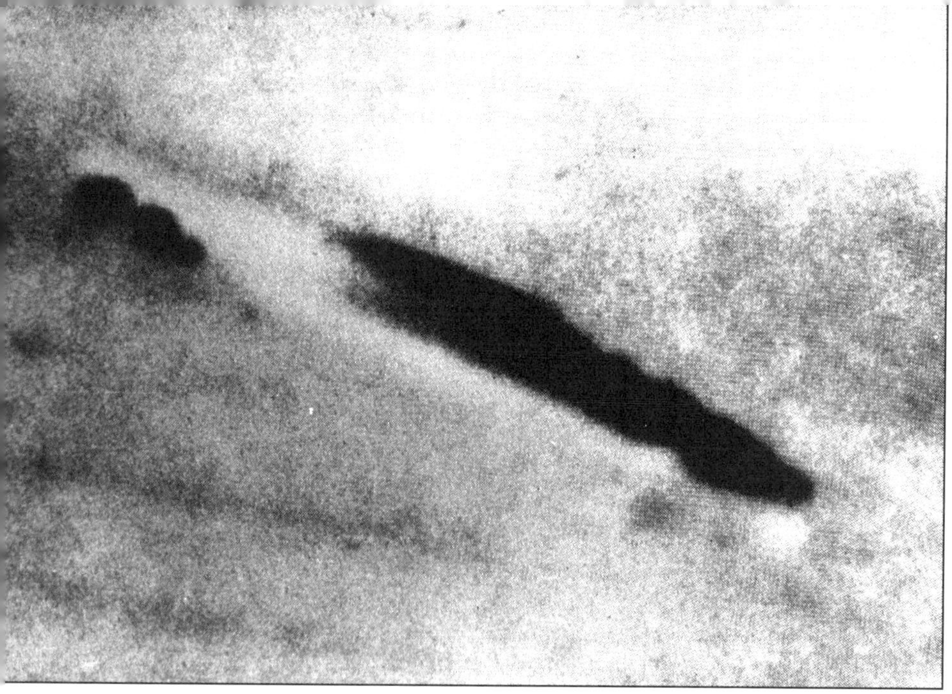

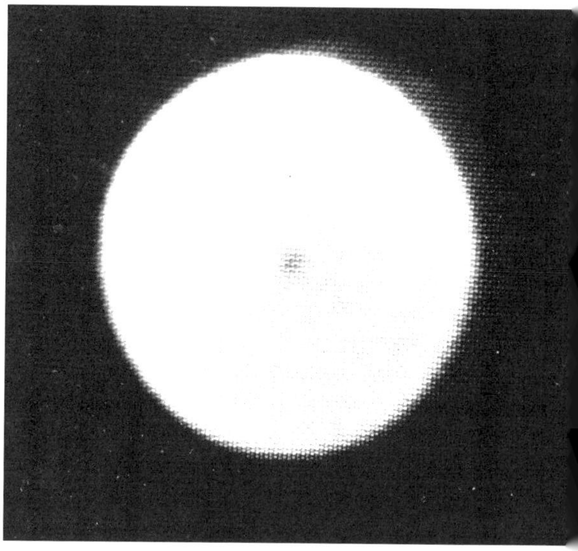

Right: ***A UFO apparently trails a Martin B-57 bomber as it flies near Edwards Air Force Base, California, in September 1957. No one in the B-57 or the accompanying aircraft detected the UFO (enlarged,*** **above*****) at the time; its image emerged only when the film was processed. Sceptics have suggested the image is the result of a flaw in the film.***

Above right: ***A UFO tracked and filmed for minutes on end by a New Zealand TV camera crew flying near the Clarence River in December 1978.***

Ministry commission investigated the site on 18 September, and removed the wrecked upper aerial of Post No 12 for study. Unnamed military sources claimed to have examined the site of the event and seen tapes of the initial series of radar returns.

The description of both these on-screen radar effects and the craft itself suggests all the characteristics of 'stealth' technology – another instance of a UFO suddenly adopting an ultra-modern but little-understood technological disguise. While the 'flash' and the destruction of the radar post could have been caused by a plain missile, it seems unlikely that an American stealth aircraft would have perpetrated such a provocation. And the USAF is the only military force known to have that kind of advanced aircraft in service.

SCORCHED EARTH

The notorious crop circles that plagued British farmers during the 1980s and early 1990s were very soon identified by some enthusiastic devotees of the paranormal as traces of UFO activity. However, the increasing elaborateness of the circles, the emergence of possible scientific explanations and finally the confessions of hoaxers have somewhat reduced the strength of the 'UFO hypothesis'. While hoaxers were certainly not responsible for all the circles, and even the scientists admit their explanation is far from complete, the evidence for UFOs in the usually accepted sense of the term being involved seems remote.

Among the commonest ground effects left by UFOs, however, is evidence of burning.

Over a period of two hours or so during the day of 8 October 1978, various members of the Sturgess family noticed 'something' in a field close to their house (the property is near Jenkins, Missouri) but thought little of it until it rose in the air. Six family members saw the object move away and meet another object; both then vanished, in broad daylight. Inspection of the site where the thing had been resting revealed a 4 ft circle of scorched grass, within which were three smaller circles burnt into the ground. Scientific analysis showed nothing unusual about the samples taken, however.

Samples of earth taken from a site at Medford, Minnesota, after a UFO was seen landing there on 2 November 1975 did, however, reveal some curious qualities. In radiation tests conducted by the Space Technology Laboratory at the University of Kansas, Lawrence, the samples showed ten times the thermo-luminescence of control samples from near the site, but appeared identical under the microscope. Dr Edward Zellner, the university's professor of geology, physics and astronomy, called these variations 'unusual' and 'an anomaly,' but added: 'Like so much of the other data [that] has been obtained on the UFO phenomenon, the results...are inconclusive.'

Below: ***Cameras can lie. This apparent formation of four UFOs was photographed by a US coastguard at the Salem, Massachusetts, Air Station in August 1952. Analysis has shown that the 'lights in the sky' are actually reflections of terrestrial lights on to the camera lens.***

Above: ***One of many UFOs photographed by contactee Daniel Fry in the 1960s. Few experts have taken these pictures at face value since computer analysis has shown that the 'flying saucers' are almost certainly models suspended close to the camera.***

On 30 September 1980, an extraordinary series of effects accompanied the UFO witnessed by 'Mr B', a farmhand and caretaker on a 600 acre property five miles from Rosedale, Victoria, in Australia. At about 1 am, Mr B woke to the sound of the farm's cattle going wild – accompanied by 'a strange screeching whistling'. He got up to investigate. There was no wind, and the moon was out; Mr B saw a domed object about 15 ft high and 25 ft broad with a white top, showing blue and orange lights. For a while it hovered over a concrete water tank about 450 yds from the house, then came to rest on the ground 15 or 20 yds further on.

Mr B clambered on a motorcycle and drove to within 50 ft of the object. There was no effect on his machine, but the whistling from the UFO suddenly rose to deafening heights, there was a huge bang, and the thing lifted off. At the same time, a blast of hot air nearly knocked Mr B over. The UFO dropped some debris and then flew away to the east, holding a height of no more than 100 ft.

FROM WITHIN THE RING OF BURNT GRASS THE FLOWERS HAD DISAPPEARED, BUT STRANGEST OF ALL, 10,000 GALLONS OF WATER HAD BEEN STOLEN.

Right: ***Masato Kohno points to a burn mark left by the UFO he saw land in Kofu City, Japan, on 23 February 1975. The witness also maintained that the concrete pile on the right was broken by the mystery craft.***

Mr B examined the site early next day. He found a ring of blackened grass, flattened in an anti-clockwise direction. Inside the ring was green grass, but flowers that had been growing there had disappeared. In a line to the east outside the ring was a trail of debris – stones, weeds and cow dung. For some days after the sighting Mr B suffered from headaches and nausea, and his watch refused to work normally. Strangest of all, the water tank over which the UFO had paused had been emptied of 10,000 gallons of water.

BIZARRE PHENOMENA

One of the commonest physical reactions to a UFO is the collapse of electrical systems, radios and similar equipment in cars driven by witnesses. This is sometimes, but not always, accompanied by witnesses suffering rashes and nausea after the sighting, a medically recognized reaction to certain kinds of electro-magnetic (EM) radiation. Two cases, more than six years apart and widely separated geographically, show a weird variation on this theme.

Ronald Sullivan was driving on a long, straight stretch of road nine miles east of Bealiba, Victoria, Australia, during the night of 4 April 1966 when his headlight beams suddenly and inexplicably bent part way along their length to the right – as if they had been pieces of pipe. Sullivan screeched to a stop, and was then treated to a brilliant display of coloured lights coming from a field by the road. After that, an object rose up from the field and vanished. Sutherland had his lights checked before reporting the incident to the police; they were in perfect order. When the police investigated the site they found a circular depression about 5 ft across and 5 in at its deepest in the field. Sullivan reported that he 'did not believe in UFOs'.

Six and a half years later, something similar occurred at Taize, in eastern France. At about 1 am on 11 August 1972, a group of about 30 people gathered at the Protestant monastery there, witnessed a 90 ft long UFO hovering against a hillside opposite the building. This then gave a bizarre light display that involved apparently solid beams of light extending slowly to the ground. Four of those present decided to take a closer look, and went across the fields toward it armed with torches. After about 600 yds they came across a dark mass about 20 ft high and shaped like a haystack. When they shone their torches at it, the beams turned upwards at right angles just a foot or so from the object.

Neither case has been satisfactorily explained, although it is perhaps worth noting that the EM effects here occurred on an unusual frequency – that of visible light – rather than on the longer radio wavelengths that more commonly are affected by UFOs. Even this is not much help, since so many of the data on UFOs are concerned precisely with bizarre phenomena involving light.

THE BLACK MASS DEFLECTED THE BEAMS OF THE TORCHES AND REFUSED TO REVEAL ITS DARK SECRETS.

Below: ***An early witness report form used by the British journal*** **Flying Saucer Review** ***in the 1950s.***

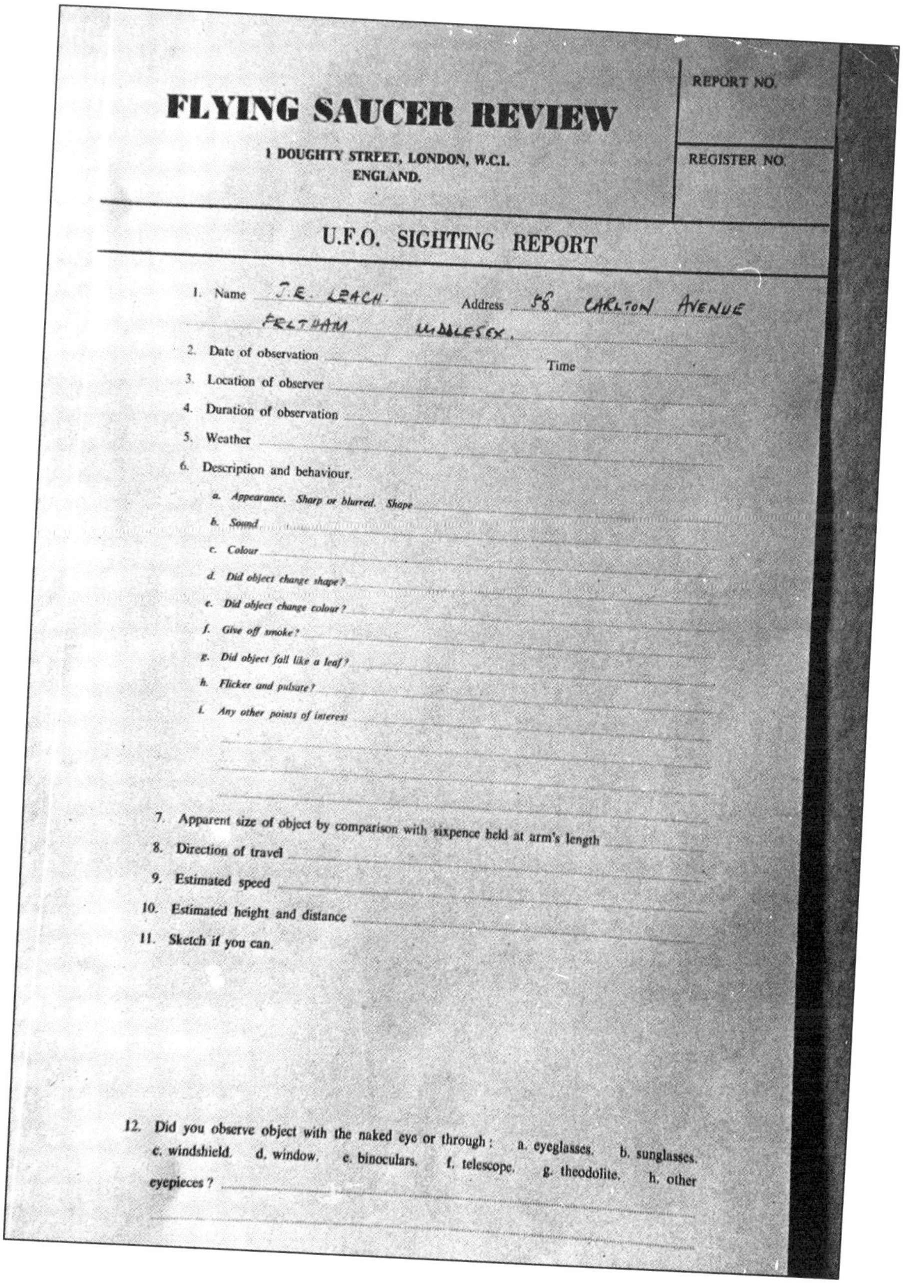

FLYING SAUCER REVIEW

1 DOUGHTY STREET, LONDON, W.C.1.
ENGLAND.

REPORT NO.

REGISTER NO.

U.F.O. SIGHTING REPORT

1. Name J.E. LEACH. Address 58 CARLTON AVENUE FELTHAM MIDDLESEX.
2. Date of observation Time
3. Location of observer
4. Duration of observation
5. Weather
6. Description and behaviour.
   a. Appearance. Sharp or blurred. Shape
   b. Sound
   c. Colour
   d. Did object change shape?
   e. Did object change colour?
   f. Give off smoke?
   g. Did object fall like a leaf?
   h. Flicker and pulsate?
   i. Any other points of interest
7. Apparent size of object by comparison with sixpence held at arm's length
8. Direction of travel
9. Estimated speed
10. Estimated height and distance
11. Sketch if you can.
12. Did you observe object with the naked eye or through: a. eyeglasses. b. sunglasses. c. windshield. d. window. e. binoculars. f. telescope. g. theodolite. h. other eyepieces?

ACCIDENTAL OR DELIBERATELY ENGINEERED? BY A CREATURE OF THE EARTH – OR FROM DEEP SPACE?

MARKS OF THE MIND

The disparate forms of the different entities seen around UFOs, the variety of shapes and sizes of the craft themselves (if craft they are), the rarity and ambiguity of the physical evidence: all these suggest that the UFO is not one thing, but several – and possibly many.

How does the UFO phenomenon divide up, given the evidence we have? What *kinds* of UFO are there?

The first essential distinction to make is that in many cases something undoubtedly physical has presented itself to witnesses. But what kind of physical thing is it? There are six possibilities worth serious consideration:

- UFOs are alien craft from planets in outer space.
- UFOs are alien craft from a shy and elusive culture that shares our Earth and perhaps our Solar System.
- UFOs are secret terrestrial craft, probably military in origin, which hide behind a screen of 'flying saucer myths'.
- UFOs are not 'nuts and bolts' craft of any kind, but some kind of biological phenomenon – although some (those without apparent occupants) may possibly be wild creatures, while those with occupants may have been domesticated.
- UFOs are natural phenomena that are related to ball lightning, plasma, and other little-understood manifestations of physics.
- UFOs are intrusions, accidental or deliberately engineered, from other physical dimensions or parallel universes.

As the reported behaviour of UFOs is so varied, it is quite possible that each of these hypotheses is true for a particular set of circumstances – although some of them are more probable than others. But there is no law to say that if UFOs are physical objects, they *have* to be all the same kind of object.

On the other hand they may not be objects at all. Not all UFOs leave physical

Below: ***Researchers in the 1950s used a chart of basic UFO types to help classify sightings. Note the variety of shapes and configurations – an aspect of UFOs that remains unchanged to this day.***

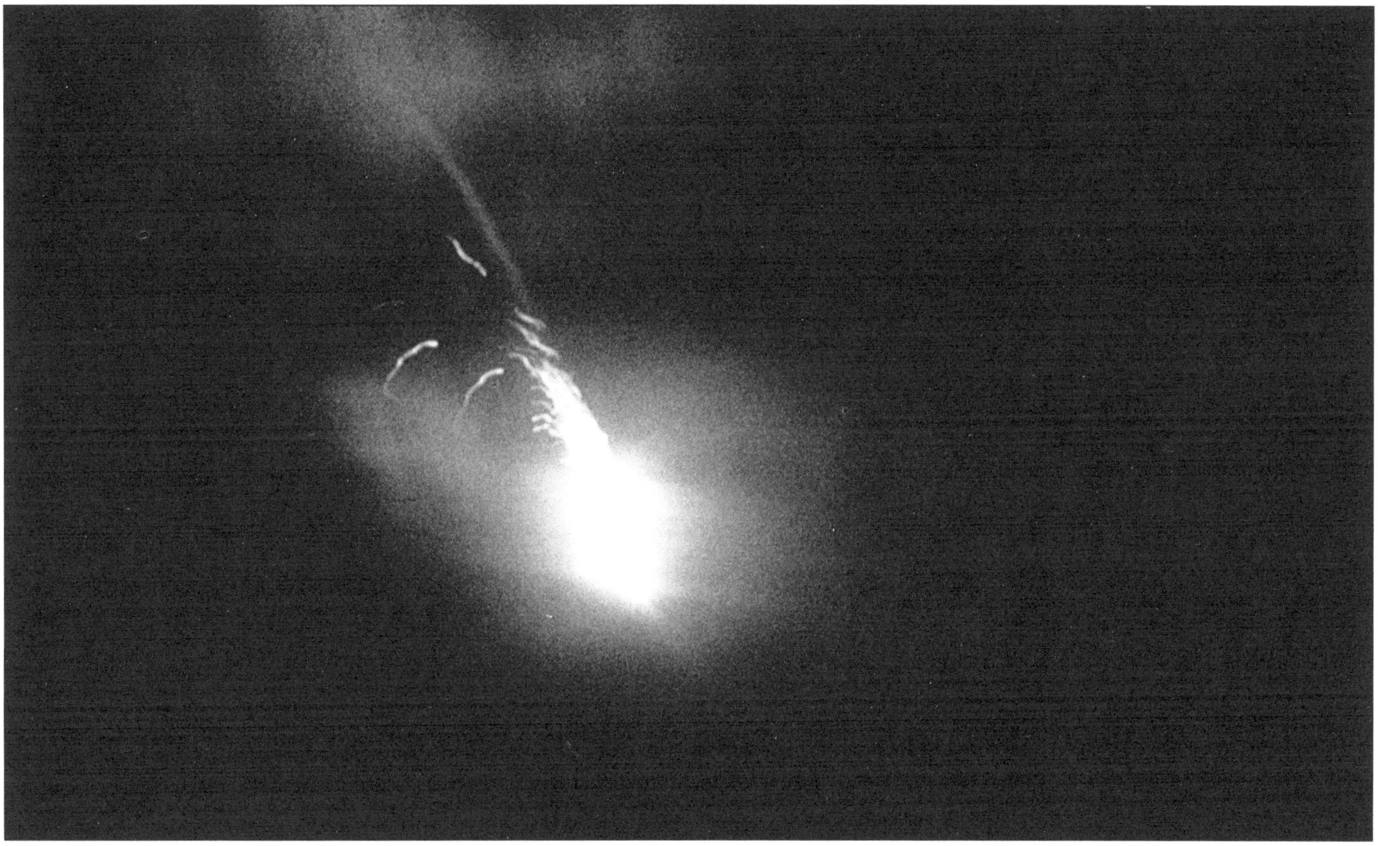

Above: *Ball lightning, photographed in Austria in summer 1978. Some researchers believe that all alleged UFOs are little-known or poorly understood natural phenomena such as this.*

traces, and many are seen by only a single witness, even over highly populated areas. So it is not inconceivable that the UFO phenomenon is an entirely psychological – even psychic – one. There are three major hypotheses that attempt to account for UFOs as immaterial phenomena:

- UFOs are hallucinations, triggered by some actual event but confined in reality to the mind of the witness.
- UFOs are indeed hallucinations, but the mental event has been induced by an alien intelligence, either from deep space or from nearer at hand. Both this and the previous suggestion would explain why UFOs present themselves in forms that are appropriate to the particular era in which the witness lives.
- UFOs are material objects – but they are brought into being only by the unconscious psychic working of the witness – or even by the working of the mass unconscious.

Once again it is not outside the bounds of possibility that all three explanations are true, one or another applying to differing circumstances and different sets of evidence.

However, there is another possibility. *All nine of the hypotheses offered here may be correct* – in other words, it may be the case that some UFOs are indeed hallucinations, while some are natural physical and biological phenomena, some are alien craft, others are military in origin, and so on. Just as there is no rule that dictates that all UFOs must be physical objects, so there is no law to say that UFO sightings must be *either* physical *or* psychic events. They may be one or the other; they may on occasion even be a mixture of both, the product of an interaction between physical and psychological states, planes of being, or even dimensions.

Judging from a number of remarks that he made in private, it is likely that it was some such insight that J. Allen Hynek had in mind when he suggested that UFOs should make us 'consider an aspect of reality of which we have been hitherto largely unaware'. The UFO phenomenon is almost unique in exhibiting almost every aspect of the paranormal there is; the physical traces that we have been considering in this chapter may, in fact, be the marks left by the mind – although whether it is the human mind at work here, or the mind of someone or something else, we cannot be certain.

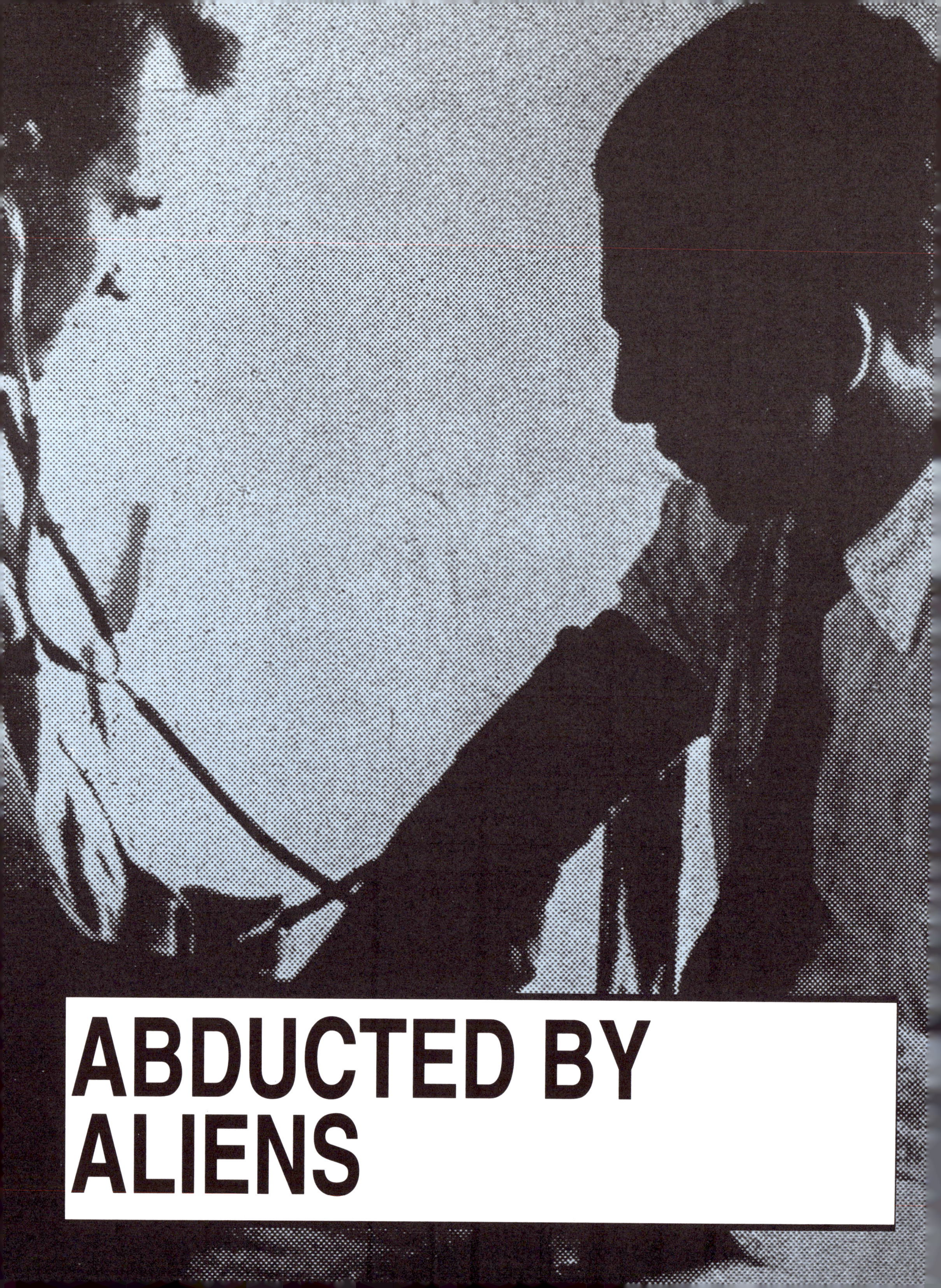

ABDUCTED BY ALIENS

Sensational stories of abduction and grotesque sexual experiments carried out by aliens may be easy to discount, but how do the 'experts' discredit the consistent testimony of a respected sober-suited lawyer?

At the age of 23, Antonio Villas Boas lived a hard but simple life with his parents, his brothers and sisters-in-law on a small farm near the town of São Francisco de Salles, in the Brazilian state of Minas Gerais. With his brothers, Villas Boas worked the farm: while the family had hired help in during the day, Antonio worked at night. On the night of 15–16 October 1957, he was out alone, ploughing the fields by the light of his tractor's headlamps.

He may not have been entirely surprised when, at about 1 am, he saw what he described as a 'large red star' descending out of the sky toward the end of the field he was working. At about 9.30 pm the previous evening, he had been out ploughing with his brother, and the pair had seen a dim red ball of light hovering about 300 ft above the northern end of the field they were working. He had then tried to get close to the light to see what was behind it, but it eluded him, darting from one end of the field to the other.

But this time Villas Boas was alone, and petrified, for as the red light came down to about 150 ft above him, he could see that it was an apparently egg-shaped object. Its brilliant glow drowned out the lights of his tractor as it landed – lowering three shafts as an undercarriage – no more than 50 ft from where he was sitting. The machine had a definite rim, in which were set purple lights. Three spurs were set at the front, lit up with red light. The upper, domed part of the machine was spinning anti-clockwise, and as it slowed to land, it changed colour from red to green.

Antonio tried to escape on his tractor, but the engine died after a few yards. He jumped from the seat and started to struggle across the ploughed field. Then someone grabbed him from behind. He knocked the creature flying, but was grabbed by three others – none higher than his shoulder, and he is only 5 ft 5 in tall – and dragged to the waiting craft. He was taken struggling up a flexible ladder into the machine, and found himself in a small, square, brightly lit room with metallic walls.

He realized that there were five small entities present: two kept a firm hold on him. They were wearing tight-fitting suits of thick, soft, unevenly striped grey material, and large, broad helmets reinforced with bands of metal. Pipes led down from the helmets to their clothes, two

Antonio Villas Boas **(opposite,** *undergoing medical tests in 1958) had one of the most extraordinary close encounters in the annals of ufology in October 1957. During his brief but astonishing visit on board an alien craft he attempted to steal a piece of equipment as evidence of his experience, but was thwarted. But he was able to recall a sign over one of the doors inside the vehicle* **(below)** *and reproduce it for investigators.*

Below: *A UFO approaches a witness and disgorges three aliens during a close encounter near Pirassununga, São Paulo, Brazil, in September 1976. When there is dialogue between aliens and witnesses, the encounter is classified as of the 'fourth kind'. Close encounters of the fifth kind are full-scale abductions.*

going under each armpit and one down their backs. Thick-soled 'shoes' seemed to be integral to their suits, as did thick, unwieldy gloves. All Villas Boas could see of the creatures' features through the helmets were their small, pale blue eyes.

He was then taken into another bright room, this time oval-shaped. Here, the aliens first attempted a conversation with their captive. Villas Boas later recalled that the sounds they made 'were so totally different from anything I had heard...They were slow barks and yelps, neither very clear nor very hoarse, some longer, some shorter, at times containing several different sounds all at once...But they were simply sounds, animal barks...I still shudder when I think of those sounds. I can't reproduce them – my voice just isn't made for that.'

Failing to communicate in words, the five diminutive aliens then proceeded to strip the protesting farmer of his clothes. One of the beings rubbed a wet sponge-like thing over his skin, and then he was led through still another door. This had an inscription over it in red 'letters', which he was able to reproduce later for investigators. (At first glance, this looks very like hastily scribbled Arabic, but it seems to relate to no known terrestrial alphabet.) In this chamber, sparsely furnished with a few chairs and a couch, the aliens produced 'a sort of chalice', which they used to take a blood sample. Then Villas Boas was left alone – only to find a weird odour filling the room, which soon had him rushing to a corner of the room to be sick. After that he began to calm down. But then came the most bizarre part of his experience aboard the alien ship.

SEXUAL ENCOUNTERS

He had been standing there naked for perhaps half an hour when the door to the

room opened – to reveal a woman whose body was 'more beautiful than any I have ever seen before'. This was something Antonio could hardly help noticing, for she was entirely nude.

The woman stood shoulder-high to him. Her hair was parted in the middle, and reached halfway down her neck before it curled inward. It was smooth, fair, almost white, except for her armpits and pubic hair, which was bright red. She had a pointed chin, straight nose, high cheekbones, and large blue eyes. Her arms were freckled. Her body, said Villas Boas, was 'slim, and her breasts stood up high and well separated. Her waistline was thin, her belly flat, her hips well developed, and her thighs were large.' What happened next was perhaps inevitable, and best told in Antonio Villas Boas's own words:

'The woman came toward me in silence, looking at me all the while as if she wanted something from me, and suddenly she hugged me and began to rub her head against my face from side to side. At the same time I also felt her body glued to mine and it also was moving.'

Villas Boas wondered if the liquid the aliens had spread on him had been some kind of stimulant, but he, at least, needed none:

'We ended up on the couch, where we lay together for the first time. It was a normal act and she reacted as any other woman would. Then we had some petting, followed by another act, but by now she had begun to deny herself to me, to end the matter.'

At that, Antonio too lost interest – and became angry, as it dawned on him that 'all they wanted [was] a good stallion to improve their stock…but [I] decided not to attach any importance to the fact, for

Above: ***UFO photographed by contactee Elizabeth Klarer in South Africa in the 1950s. Klarer was not abducted by ufonauts – she went willingly and, she claimed, lived with one on his home planet, where she gave birth to their child.***

THE ALIENS WERE AFTER A GOOD 'STALLION' TO IMPROVE THEIR STOCK – AND THE BEAUTIFUL BLONDE MADE IT EASY TO OBLIGE.

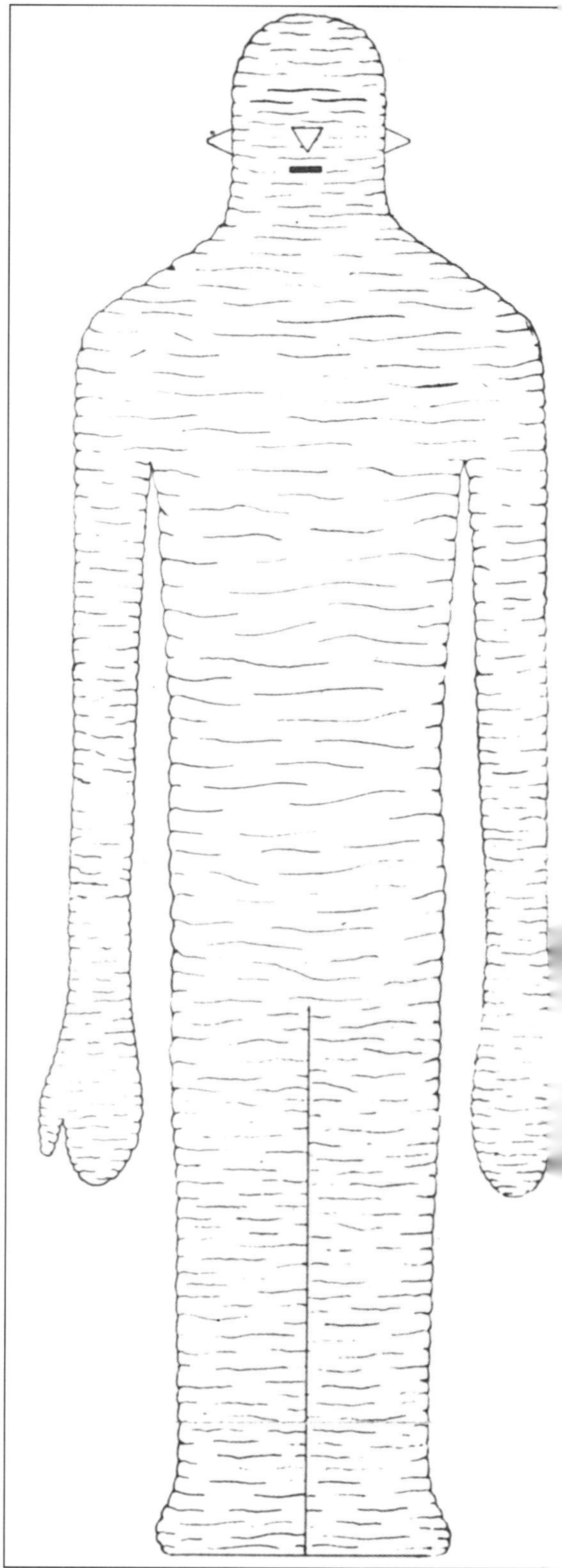

anyhow I had spent a few agreeable moments with the woman'. His impression that he was being used in a quite calculating fashion may have been reinforced by the fact that the woman never kissed him, although she did bite him gently on the chin.

Shortly after this (it seems not to have occurred to Villas Boas that his activities were possibly being monitored) the woman was called away. Before she left, she pointed to her stomach, and then at the sky, which he interpreted as meaning that sooner or later she, and the other aliens, would return to take him away. Brazilian investigators persuaded him, however, that she had simply meant that she would bear their child on her home planet. After this, Antonio Villas Boas was given back his clothes and taken on a guided tour of the alien craft, during which he tried, and failed, to purloin an instrument as a keepsake. Then he was carried back down the ladder to the ground, from where he saw the UFO take off, listing slightly to one side and then disappearing into the sky like a bullet. He had been aboard the craft for 4 hours, 15 minutes.

Charles Hickson* (above) *and his colleague Calvin Parker claimed that they were abducted by aliens in Pascagoula, Mississippi, in October 1973. The sketch* (right) *shows Hickson's own impression of one of the entities aboard the craft.

THE TERRIFIED ABDUCTEES WERE OFTEN STRIPPED AND SUBJECTED TO A PAINFUL MEDICAL EXAMINATION.

The Villas Boas case boggled the UFO investigators who heard about it so much that it was not until 12 years after these events that the witness's name was published. While the case became a classic in ufology, little was heard about Villas Boas himself. But in 1978 he surfaced again on a TV programme in Brazil – no longer a simple peasant farmer, but Dr Antonio Villas Boas, a sober lawyer with a practice in a small town near the nation's capital, Brasilia, happily married and with four children. The only item of his testimony that he changed was minor: the woman had taken a sperm sample from him during their second act of intercourse.

To the determined sceptic, the Villas Boas case has always been the fantasy of a simple Brazilian rustic. Yet the person who experienced what he did in October 1957, and the man who had gained academic distinction and a respected place in his community 21 years later were essentially one and the same. Intelligent, articulate, educated and determined, Dr Villas Boas was revealed as a person who cannot be dismissed any more as a mere 'peasant' – which is to say, ignorant, superstitious, and clod-hopping. And he did not change his mind, or contradict himself, when questioned 21 years later about his abduction.

Perhaps most important, his first account of that bizarre, frightening, yet exciting night was given straight from his conscious memory, and less than four months afterward. Unlike many who have claimed to recall – sometimes more than 20 years after the alleged events – being abducted by aliens and having sometimes grotesque sexual experiences while in their custody, Antonio Villas Boas did not need to be hypnotized to be able to give the most detailed account of what happened to him.

THE 'MISSING TIME'

The 'AVB' case, as it was known among ufologists, was long regarded as almost unique in the annals of abductions in that it involved a sexual encounter – although still more astounding claims were published in German in 1977, by South African Elizabeth Klarer. She maintained that between 1954 and 1963 she had numerous meetings with the two-man crew of a craft from the planet Meton, in the solar system of Proxima Centauri, the nearest star to the Sun, 4.3 light-years away. One of the aliens, the astrophysicist Akon, became the father of her child, and Klarer says she spent four months on Meton before her son was born, after which she was obliged to return to Earth while he remained on Meton with his father. Few ufologists took Klarer's claims seriously – as so often with contactees who allege they have visited known star systems, the laws of celestial mechanics spoil her story. Proxima Centauri is part of the triple-star system of Alpha Centauri, and as such is highly unlikely to have any planets. And even if it did, the star is a red dwarf – too small and too feeble to support life of any kind.

The typical pattern of abductee accounts did not, until the 1980s, involve any specifically sexual component at all. The classic scenario is reflected in the well-known accounts given by Betty and Barney Hill (abducted in New Hampshire in 1961), Betty Andreasson (in Massachusetts, 1967), Calvin Parker and Charlie Hickson (in Mississippi, 1973), David Stephens (in Maine, 1975), Whitley Strieber (in New York State, 1985) and others.

The events reported by these witnesses followed this basic pattern: first came a UFO sighting, sometimes involving electro-magnetic effects or other physical effects on the witnesses' vehicles. A key factor in the vast majority of such cases

Above: ***Betty Andreasson, who was abducted by aliens in Massachusetts in 1967 and given a bizarre 'pregnancy test' during her captivity.***

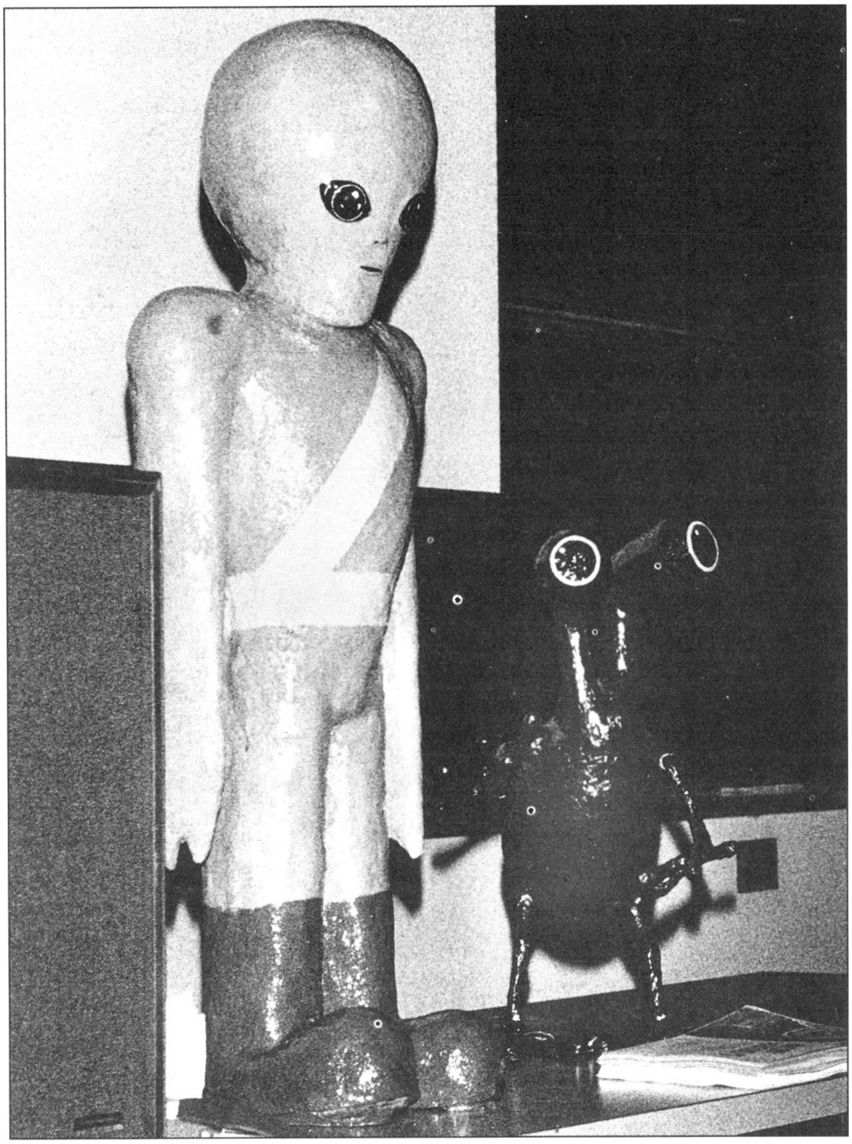

Above: *A model of 'Quazgaa', one of the alien entities that took part in the abduction and medical examination of Betty Andreasson.*

Right: *Artist Budd Hopkins, who believes that visiting aliens are performing a programme of genetic manipulation on the human race.*

emerges after the UFO has departed: the events of what seem like a few minutes' duration turn out to have taken an hour or more. The witnesses duly report their sighting to the police, local military authorities or the sheriff's office. Of their own accord, or encouraged by their family or members of a UFO investigation organization, witnesses then undergo hypnosis in an attempt to bring out the buried memory of what transpired in the crucial 'missing time' during their UFO encounter.

However, a handful of abductees do have clear memories of this part of their experience and need no such prompting or psychological dredging. But their descriptions of what happened to them in this segment of 'missing time' closely match the reports of hypnotized subjects even though the physical appearance of the aliens and the exterior of their ships often differ wildly from case to case.

Interiors of alien craft are, according to these witnesses, usually brightly lit, clinically clean, often shiny, with white or metallic appurtenances. The reason for this soon becomes clear, for the next stage in the abduction is a medical examination of some kind – usually a painful one.

Betty Hill and Betty Andreasson independently reported that they were examined with a machine from which needle-like wires protruded. Charles Hickson said his body was 'scanned' by a floating instrument resembling a large eye. Betty Hill and Betty Andreasson also said that needles were inserted into their navels for a 'pregnancy test'. Betty Hill had skin scrapings, samples of ear wax, hair and clippings from her fingernails taken from her. David Stephens had two blood samples taken, and was undressed and examined from head to toe with 'a box-like device'. Whitley Strieber maintained that 'an enormous and extremely ugly object', triangular in structure and with a tangle of wires at one end, was inserted into his rectum.

After this, the witnesses report, they are either allowed to dress and leave the ship – some are 'transferred' directly from the craft or 'floated' back to where the aliens first took them captive – or, occasionally,

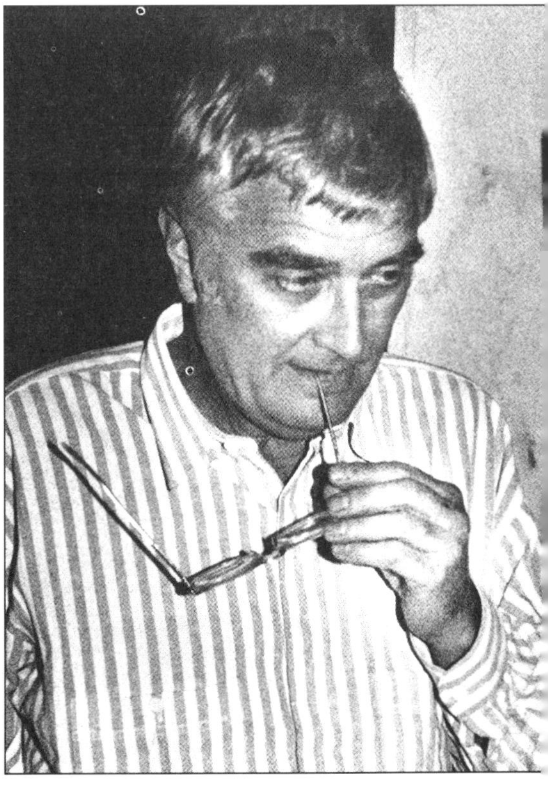

given a guided tour around the ship first. Once the victims have been returned to their starting point, the UFO leaves at high speed.

GENETIC SAMPLING

The reality, or otherwise, of UFO abductions became a major controversy among ufologists in the 1980s, and excited massive public attention as well. Budd Hopkins, a New York artist who as a result of his own UFO sighting became fascinated by abduction stories, used hypnotic techniques to uncover numerous witnesses' hidden memories of such experiences, and the bestselling book (later made into a film) *Communion* by novelist Whitley Strieber, in which he recounted his own gruesome and humiliating experiences as an abductee, was based on events recalled under hypnosis.

Undoubtedly, Hopkins's book received huge attention in the media because of the new element he had discovered in the cases he had investigated: and that was a constant sexual slant to the stories. Men reported having devices applied to them that relieved them of their sperm. Still greater number of women, notably one named Kathie Davis, told stories under hypnosis that suggested to Hopkins that aliens were conducting a deliberate and sustained programme of genetic sampling and possibly even manipulation among the human race, who were mostly unaware of what was being done to it.

According to Hopkins, hypnosis revealed that aliens first visited Kathie Davis when she was a child, and had implanted a device in her head so that they could keep track of her. (She and other members of her family had similar, mysterious scars on their legs, which Hopkins attributed to cell-sampling by the aliens, noting that other alleged abductees bore similar marks.) As a teenager, Kathie became pregnant, but the pregnancy ended suddenly and mysteriously. Hypnosis revealed that before her pregnancy, aliens had visited Kathie, performed an 'uncomfortable' and intimate procedure, and departed. Some months later they returned and removed her feotus. Years later, after she had married and had two children, the aliens returned again and briefly presented her with a little girl who 'looked like an elf or an...angel'. This was, apparently, her extra-terrestrially induced daughter. Kathie Davis was not the only woman who, according to Hopkins's research, had been impregnated by ufonauts.

Above: ***Novelist Whitley Strieber, who built a best-selling book,*** **Communion,** ***around his alleged abduction by ufonauts in 1985. Since then, he has hinted that the account is a fantasy.***

A FLAWED TOOL

Many serious ufologists – across the whole spectrum of the subject, from ardent 'believers' to those who border on scepticism – have had serious doubts about the validity of abduction accounts ever since George Adamski claimed to have met a Venusian in the California desert.

If, however – as is at least possible – the 'UFO experience' is a peculiar blend of material and psychic realities, there may be a kernel of truth in many abduction reports – though it may be truth of a very strange kind. But there is a vast difference between the account of a man like Dr Antonio Villas Boas and the stories that Budd Hopkins has

Psychologist Carl Gustav Jung* (above) *believed that a number of archetypal figures – from wise old men to monstrous semi-human creatures – lie buried in everyone's unconscious, emerging in the dreams of individuals and the myths and legends of whole societies. Jung considered UFOs to be a symbol of humanity's state of mind, projected on to the environment. Jung would no doubt have been fascinated had he lived long enough to learn that UFO occupants seem to follow the same patterns of appearance and behaviour as the archetypal figures that he identified in the collective unconscious.

put into mass circulation – and the key to that difference is the use of hypnosis.

Despite its many virtues in other contexts, hypnosis is notoriously unreliable as a tool for probing the memory, unless the hypnotist is scrupulously careful in the style and content of the questioning. One particular problem is that a false memory, unconsciously and even innocently suggested to the subject by the hypnotist through a leading question, will become part of ordinary conscious memory – and its impression, its apparent reality, will grow stronger the more the subject returns to it under hypnosis.

There is a powerful feeling among ufologists that Hopkins's conclusions from his hypnosis of apparent abductees are severely flawed. Critics say that he is too biased in his own beliefs to make a good examiner. Hopkins is not trained as either a hypnotist or a psychologist, and critics say he asks blatantly leading questions – letting the subject know the kind of answer that would please him most – and that he breaks all the other rules, too, that expert hypnotists observe.

Most damning of all to his case that for decades aliens have been performing genetic experiments on human subjects, a number of Hopkins's star witnesses have publicly repudiated the idea that they have been abducted. In 1987, the central character in his book *Intruders*, Kathie Davis, said bluntly at the US Mutual UFO Network's symposium in Washington DC: 'I can live with it because I don't believe it. I *really* don't. There's got to be something else' – in other words, another explanation.

Whitley Strieber, who in 1987 received $1 million in advance royalties for his best-selling book *Communion*, admitted in 1991 that there might be some quite different explanation for his experience besides an 'alien abduction'. Attentive readers of the book itself might have guessed as much, for in it Strieber recounts how he used to tell a number of dramatic stories about himself as truth but now candidly admits they were fantasies.

PUZZLING RESULTS

Still more serious is the discovery that under hypnosis, even people who have no knowledge or interest in UFOs will create essentially the same details of an abduction story as are reported by people who believe that they have actually been abducted.

This astonishing and potentially devastating piece of research was conducted in 1977 by Prof. Alvin Lawson, Dr W.C. McCall and ufologist John DeHerrerra at Anaheim Memorial Hospital, near Los Angeles. The experiment was inspired by the puzzling results of an investigation that DeHerrerra had conducted into a UFO sighting. In the hope of gaining further details of the event, the witness, Brian Scott, had agreed to be hypnotized and 'regressed' (that is, taken back in time) to the time of his encounter. In his hypnotic trance he had described being abducted by aliens. But in his normal waking state, Scott vehemently insisted that no such abduction had taken place.

Lawson and his colleagues recruited 16 volunteers who, in Lawson's words, 'knew little and cared less' about UFOs. They were given the bare bones of a typical abduction story: seeing a UFO land, being taken aboard and seeing the inside of the spacecraft, and being 'examined' by the aliens. The subjects of the experiment were simply asked, at each stage, what they saw or felt happening. And in detail after

Left: ***One of the frightening goblin-like creatures that besieged the Sutton farm at Kelly, Hopkinsville, Kentucky, in 1955, makes a determined attack on one of the family members. The creatures were archetypal fiends or demons such as are found in the folklore of every culture. Was the Suttons' experience proof that such beings really exist – or did something else call up these terrifying images from their subconscious minds, perhaps as a disguise for its own purposes?***

elaborate detail, the volunteers poured out images and experiences that were uncannily similar to those described by 'real' UFO abductees.

Lawson also noted that the alien figures described by both genuine claimants and his innocent creators of fictional abductions fitted with basic archetypes that the pioneering psychologist C.G. Jung suggested were part of everyone's unconscious imagery. It would be easy enough to conclude from this that people claiming to have been abducted by UFOs were simply calling on imagery that is buried deep in everyone's unconscious mind. But, interestingly, Lawson did no such thing. In answer to his own question, 'Do these similarities prove that close encounter cases are illusory?', Lawson cited four reasons why abduction reports might still be genuine.

First, he pointed out, many abductions and close encounter reports involve multiple witnesses; that they all would

WHEN THE RESPECTABLE MIDDLE-AGED WOMAN CAME ROUND SHE WAS TIED NAKED TO A METALLIC TABLE INSIDE THE SPACECRAFT. HER ORDEAL WAS ONLY JUST BEGINNING.

have *identical* hallucinations seems highly unlikely. Second, the physical scars that many abductees can show to be a result of their experiences 'suggest that *something* happened'. Third, close encounter witnesses recognize how unlikely the events are that unfold during their experience, yet are convinced of their reality. Fourth, psychologists can identify the 'trigger' that sets most hallucinations running in the human mind, but there is no consistent factor in abduction or encounter cases that lets investigators pinpoint an unmistakably imaginary experience.

Lawson's experiment has been cited time and again by sceptics who claim that it disposes of all abduction claims. But Lawson himself was not so convinced. 'I myself feel certain,' he wrote, 'that accounts given by witnesses reflect what their senses have reported – that is, they do actually perceive humanoids...and so on. But if [the entities they perceive are] already in the collective unconscious, they are already...in the mind of the witness before his close encounter.' The real mystery, Lawson suggested, was not what the witness saw but what stimulated those archetypal images to arise from the witness's unconscious in the first place. Neither he nor his experiment, he admitted, could answer that question.

A BRUTAL ORDEAL

Even if one rejects Budd Hopkins's belief that a secret alien programme of genetic sampling is under way in our midst, a genuine mystery remains – indeed more than just one mystery. One riddle is posed by that handful of abduction cases that have been reported by sober and upright citizens without recourse to hypnosis.

Antonio Villas Boas is not alone in this category. At about 11 pm on 16 October 1973, a 43-year-old woman (who, understandably, insisted on anonymity) was driving along a road near Langford Budville, Somerset, when the electrical system of her car failed. She climbed out to investigate, felt something touch her, and turned to see a 6 ft tall robot-like figure. She fainted on the spot. When she came round, a domed vehicle some 20 ft long and perhaps 40 ft high had appeared next to her. Again she fainted, and came round to

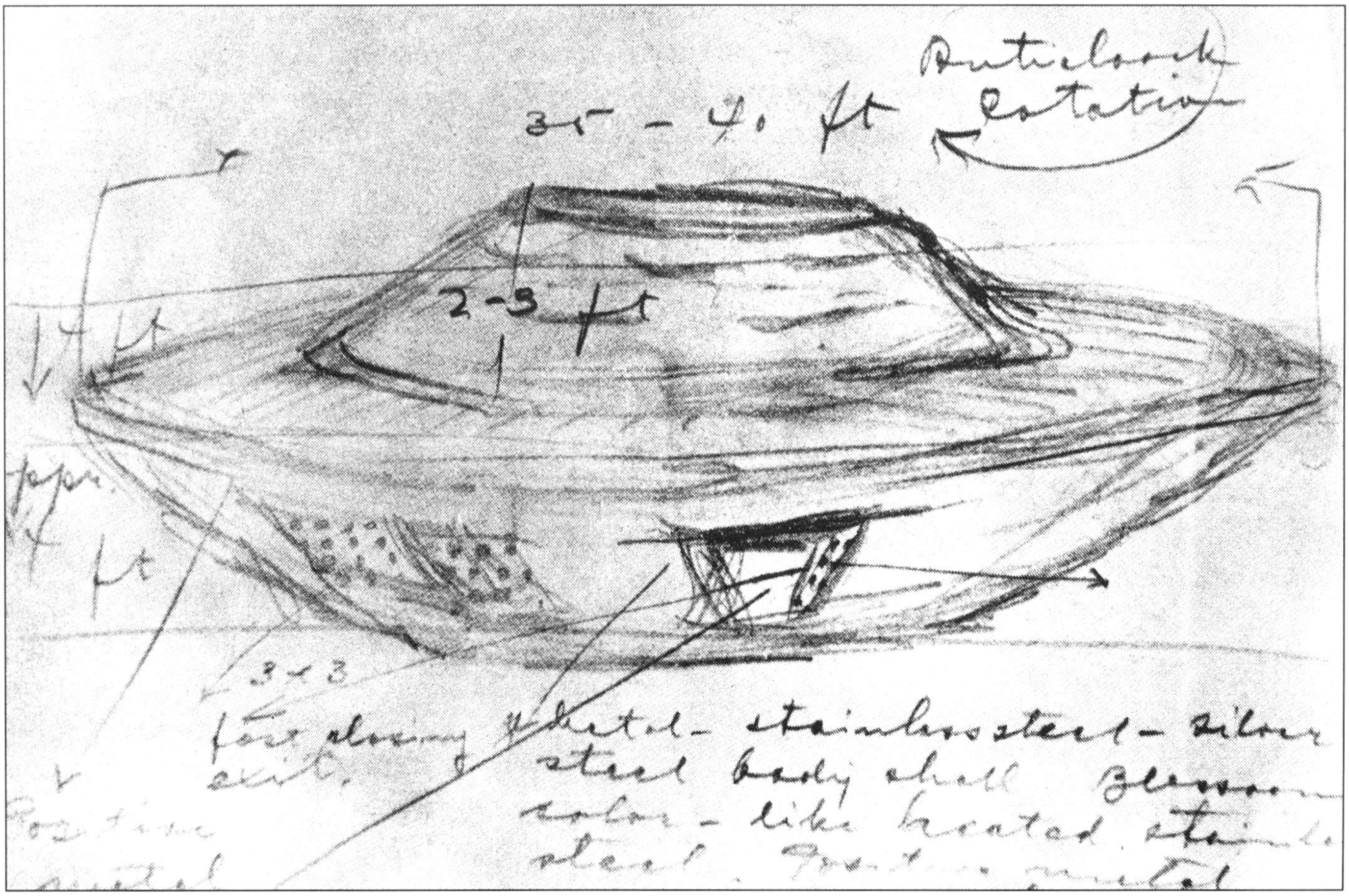

Below: ***Sketch by witness Steve Michalak of a huge metallic UFO, some 35–40 ft in diameter, which he approached and touched in a location near Falcon Lake, Manitoba, Canada, on 20 May 1967. Sightings like this suggest that some, if not all, UFOs are indeed material, 'nuts-and-bolts' craft, although their origins and purposes remain obscure.***

find herself tied naked to a metallic table in a room with glowing walls, inside the craft. When three humanoids – also about 6 ft tall – had finished examining her, two left the room. The third then raped her, and she fainted once more. She came to finally to find herself back in her car – which was now in perfect working order. By now it was 2 am.

But not all conscious abductions have a lurid sexual element. Brazilian military policeman Jose Antonio was on a fishing trip at a lake north of Belo Horizonte, Minas Gerais, one Sunday afternoon in May 1969, when he was paralysed by a burst of light and borne off to an upright, cylindrical craft by two 4 ft tall creatures in masks. Once inside, he was tied up and given a helmet to wear. The machine then took off and after an 'interminable' period, landed. Jose Antonio was next blindfolded and taken to a brilliantly lit room, in which he saw the bodies of four other humans, one of them a Negro, to be interrogated in front of about 15 of the tiny creatures. They removed samples of his fishing gear, and used drawings and sign language to suggest that he be 'their guide among men'. When he refused, he was blindfolded again and returned to Earth. Once on the ground he collapsed, and woke to find himself near Vitoria, in the state of Espirito Santo, 200 miles from where he had been fishing. He subsequently discovered that four and a half days had elapsed between his initial abduction and his return.

If abduction experiences were purely hallucinatory, a pattern would emerge within them, just as patterns are clear enough in states of neurosis and madness. The fact that Budd Hopkins perceives patterns in the abduction cases he has investigated is, in fact, almost as good as a danger sign. The genuine UFO case often signals itself by the way it only partly conforms to a pattern, and has only some aspects in common with previous cases of its kind.

Taken together, what the most genuine-sounding accounts of abduction by aliens most resemble, in fact, is not a pattern of deliberate and calculated intrusions by beings from elsewhere, but a series of bizarre accidents as they might appear to some innocent victims, only partly aware of the full circumstances in which they have been caught up. If there is anything to the notion that UFOs are not extra-terrestrial craft from within our own Universe, but exist in parallel with it, this image may prove highly fruitful in both comprehending, and coming to terms with, the entire perplexing enigma.

And not the least important of the answers to these mysteries lies hidden in the human mind, its nature, and its abilities.

THE GRUESOME AND HUMILIATING EXPERIENCES MIGHT BE A COVER-UP FOR A SUSTAINED PROGRAMME OF GENETIC SAMPLING OF THE HUMAN RACE.

Below: ***A mystery flying vehicle beams light into water in Pennsylvania in 1961.***

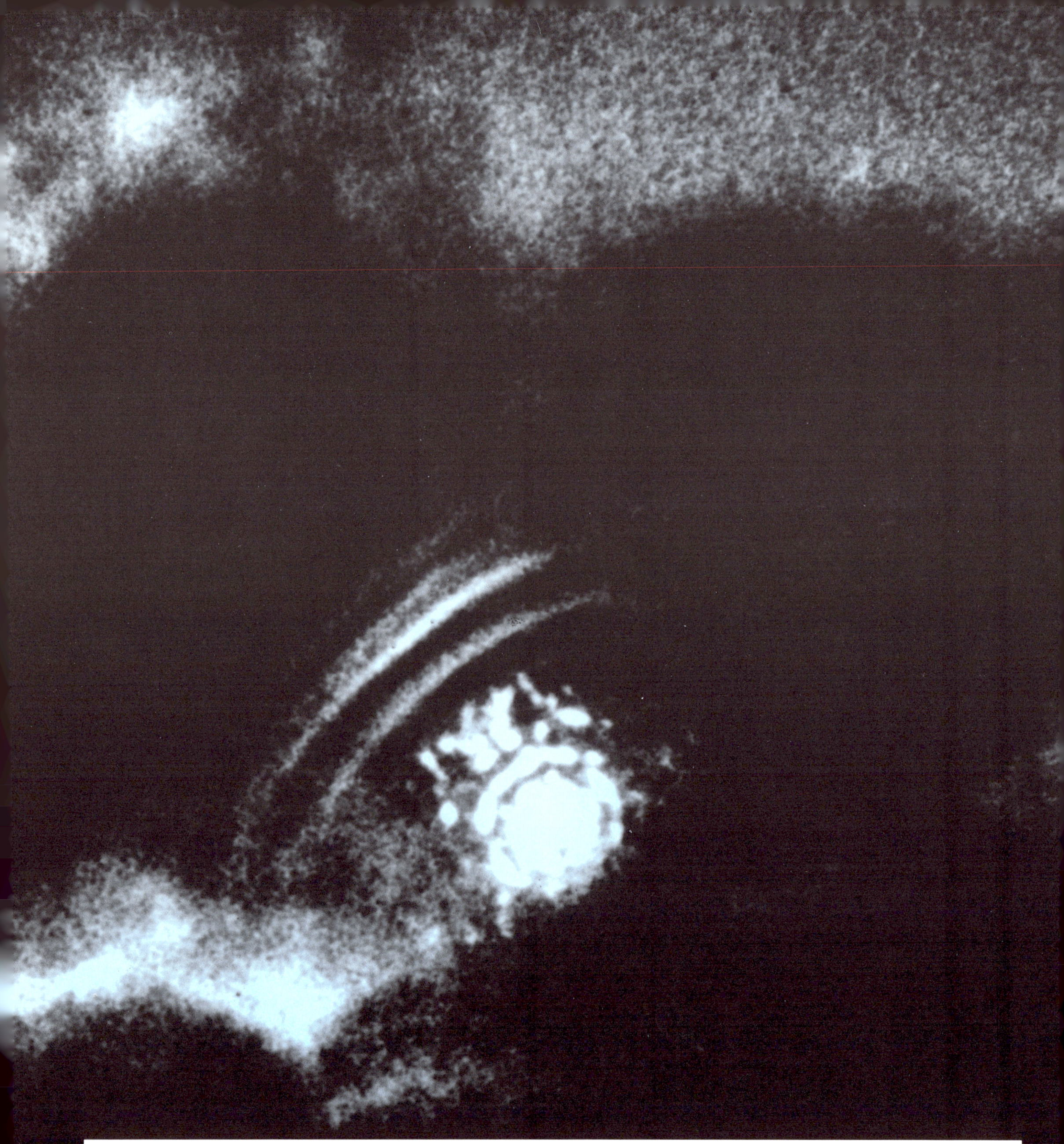

VISITS FROM THE GODS

For centuries individuals have accepted the possibility of alternative realities and other worlds. As humanity rushes headlong to its fate, many wonder about the nature of the beings that may control these realities.

Most people in the West have grown up with some knowledge of a reality that is quite different from that of the everyday world. Some believe in it without question; and while others would deny its existence altogether, the majority probably fall into a grey area of more or less nervous uncertainty. But everyone has an opinion about it, however vague. That other reality is, of course, the religious dimension, which encompasses the notion of God as all-seeing and all-powerful, includes the possibility of an evil power opposed to God, and involves images and traditions concerning the survival of the soul after death.

Whether or not each of us continues to exist in some conscious form when the body dies has little bearing on the problems thrown up by UFOs, but it is absolutely relevant that most people have no hardship in accepting the possibility that another order of reality beside our own may exist – and some people are absolutely convinced of it. (Convinced and committed atheists, on the other hand, are surprisingly hard to find.) This other reality is, besides, by definition beyond our comprehension. Moses hid his face in the presence of God, whose 'explanation' of Himself as I AM THAT I AM can be understood only intuitively, not rationally.

Many people feel similarly awed when confronted by the utterances of the secret priests of our own epoch, scientists and mathematicians. Physicists blithely tell us that certain sub-atomic particles may be seen travelling backwards in time, and that time itself may be stretched, shrunk, or bent. Indeed built into Einstein's theories of relativity is the concept of not a single universe – the one that visibly fills the night sky – but an infinite multiplicity of universes.

Such concepts are extraordinary, but they are grounded in extremely rigorous mathematical proofs. The immemorial claims of religions the world over that there is at least another plane of existence beyond the reach of our immediate senses has thus, in this century, been paralleled by the discoveries of science – although these are no more than parallel ideas: not even the most religious scientist would maintain that he or she has found the source of the Creator.

There are people, however, who would say that the mysteries of religion, of good versus evil, the ultimate fate of humankind,

Above: ***The age-old battle between the forces of good and evil. In this illustration from a 13th-century manuscript, Satan attempts to seize a magician with whom he has made a pact, while a lay brother defends the wizard. Some ufologists believe that UFOs are part of this eternal struggle between the powers of light and the powers of darkness.***

Opposite: ***A UFO photographed over Cheshire, England, by a bank employee in 1987.***

Left: ***Albert Einstein, whose theories of relativity show mathematically that other universes may exist in parallel to the one we inhabit.***

THE SENSE OF HUMOUR DISPLAYED BY SOME UFONAUTS IS OF THE VERY CRUELLEST KIND.

and the mysteries of UFO phenomena, are closely related. To an impartial observer, it may seem that such ideas result from a confusion between the scientific concept of other distinct but equal planes of being, and the religious apprehension of an absolute reality that underpins, justifies and verifies our life on Earth. It would also appear that if genuine UFO entities are really communicating messages of cosmic import, the ufonauts have a singularly cruel sense of humour. These suspicions may seem more reasonable after a survey of what various religious cults have made of the UFO phenomenon.

TELEPATHIC MESSAGES

The longest-lived UFO organization to recognize the religious significance of flying saucers is undoubtedly the Aetherius Society. The society was founded by Western Master of Yoga Sir George King in 1955 following an alleged instruction proclaiming 'Prepare yourself! You are to become the voice of Interplanetary Parliament!'

Sir George King then set up the Aetherius Society in response to growing interest in his messages from a being from Venus called Aetherius. The information that he allegedly received telepathically was, according to the Aetherius Society, relayed over millions of miles of etheric space for the benefit of mankind.

The Aetherius Society believes there is a strong link between man's nuclear activity and the presence of flying saucers. It is claimed that the occupants of these UFOs are concerned that a nuclear disaster on Earth could affect the Solar System too. Therefore, the Aetherius Society considers that part of the role of these aliens is to act as 'guardians' who impart information to mankind which would help avert such a catastrophe.

One of the major missions of the Aetherius Society is to charge 'prayer batteries' designed by Sir George King. In collaboration with various 'space agencies' the prayer energy, often amounting to 2500 'prayer hours', is frequently discharged to areas of the world which are, according to the Aetherius Society, in desperate need of spiritual energy. Pilgrimages are often made to charge these batteries from the tops of holy mountains in various parts of the world, where the adherents form a circle and recite mantras. The society says that often as a result of these efforts, extraterrestrials then add their own energy.

PROPHECIES OF DOOM

Few UFO religious cults have lasted as long as the Aetherius Society. More than one has come to an abrupt end through making grandiose prophecies about future events

Right: *At 2 pm on 4 February 1990, schoolboy Dima Girenko took this photograph of a UFO in the Achtyrka District of the Ukraine. The Moscow Aviation Institute declared that it was no hoax.*

that then fail to come to pass. One such was Human Individual Metamorphosis (HIM), founded in the mid-1970s by a couple known variously as The Two, Him and Her, Bo and Peep and, to previous acquaintances (who included their former fellow inmates within the Texas penitentiary system, and others at the mental hospital where they met, he as patient and she as nurse), as Marshall Herff Applewhite and Bonnie Lu Nettles. Seized by a sense of destiny, the pair turned up unannounced in small communities around the southern and western states to divulge their message, which Applewhite had received through mediumistic contact with a 19th-century monk.

This was in essence that 'the level above human' was a physical place, and could be reached by UFO. This would happen only when Bo and Peep – who said they were themselves aliens, millions of years old, in human form – had first been assassinated, and left dead in the street for three and a half days: they would then return to life and at this point the UFO would arrive and bear them away. Others could join The Two on the trip to salvation, on condition that they renounced all private possessions and family ties. Astonishingly enough, The Two soon gathered about 1000 disciples.

Unfortunately, at an inaugural meeting of HIM in Waldport, Oregon, on 14 September 1975 Bo and Peep had promised that their deaths, resurrection and translation by UFO would occur within six months. When no assassin obliged with the necessary act, they hastily revised their

The 'aliens' knew they would be assassinated and left for dead in the street.

Below: *Unholy alliance – a 17th-century representation of witches, imps and Satan. Some ufologists would now add UFOs and aliens to the forms that evil may take.*

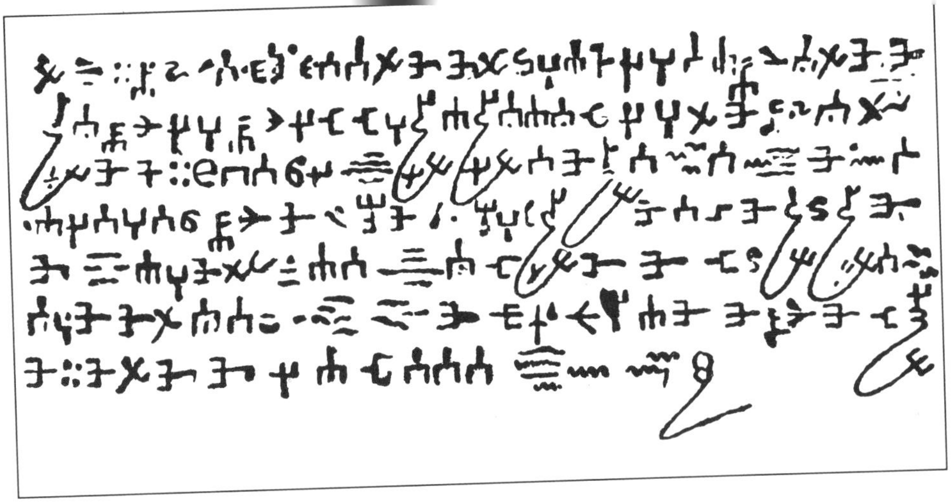

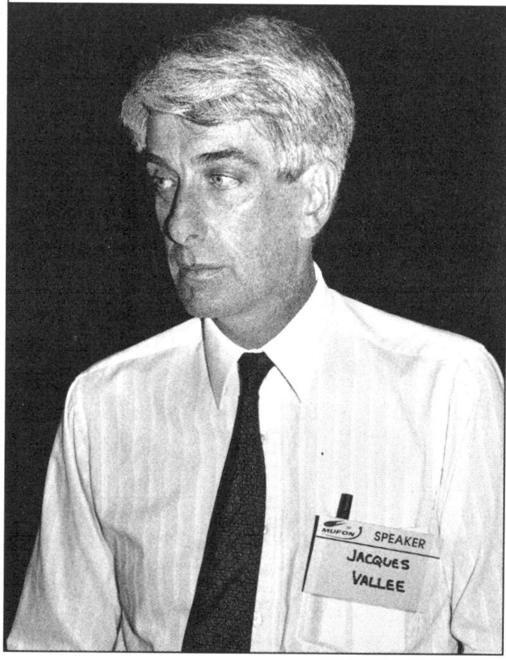

Above: ***John Ashton's intriguing volume* The Devil In Britain And America*, published in 1896, contains this curious script, which purports to be 'the only known specimen of the Devil's handwriting'.***

Above: ***The Devil gains a small victory – and succeeds in stealing the church at Over, Cheshire, as told in a local legend.***

Below right: ***French Dr Jacques Vallée, who maintains that the UFO phenomenon is a 'control system' that 'acts on humans and uses humans' – although he does not suggest that the controlling power is either divine or demonic.***

timetable and announced they would remain on Earth for at least a further ten years. The number of devotees soon declined drastically and, 15 years later, Bo and Peep were still on Earth, living a nomadic existence with their few remaining followers in Wyoming and Texas.

A similar fate befell the cult that grew up around the British Columbian channeller Robin McPherson (a.k.a. Estelle), whose extra-terrestrial contact Ox-Ho predicted that prodigious natural disasters would begin on Earth on 22 November 1969. The 'Chosen' – i.e. members of the cult, Light Affiliates – would be removed beforehand by the Space Brothers and returned when the Earth had recovered. No major disaster of any kind began on Earth that day.

It remains to be seen whether the prediction of Ruth E. Norman, channeller for an entity called URIEL (Universal Radiant Infinite Eternal Light) will come true. According to URIEL, spacecraft from the 33 members of the Interplanetary Confederation will land in the year 2001, to usher in a 1000-year epoch of peace, contentment and cultural achievement.

TIME IS RUNNING OUT FAST...WAVES OF SENSELESS IRRATIONAL VIOLENCE WILL DROWN THE EARTH.

SUBVERSIVE INVASIONS

The cosmologies of the various UFO cults are wildly different – far more incompatible with each other than any established Earthly religion. The California-based One World Family, for instance, declare that they will one day take over the government of the USA and the administration of the United Nations – but not before all professing Christians have been 'eliminated'. In contrast, the Aetherians have no political ambitions, and maintain that the Christian prophet is recognized as an intergalactic 'Master' who lives on, or near, Venus – which happens also to be the alleged abode of Ashtar, the One World Family's extra-terrestrial contact. Allen-Michael Noonan, the leader of the sect, claims to be the sole authentic mouthpiece for Ashtar – but Tuella, of the Utah-based cult, Ashtar Space Command, regularly channels messages of a gentler nature from an 'interplanetary space commander' of the same name.

All these cults differ fundamentally, however, with the small band of commentators who see UFOs not as harbingers of peace and plenty, but as unambiguously evil. Chief among these is probably linguist and former diplomat Gordon Creighton, editor of the international UFO journal *Flying Saucer Review*. Creighton's own theory is that *djinns*, supernatural creatures who work on behalf of the forces of evil and can take on human form, are UFOs in appropriate cultural disguise. Curiously, Creighton has an apocalyptic view of the present era that is not far removed from the beliefs of some 'space brother'-types of UFO cult who are expecting the End Times to begin at any moment:

'Time is running out fast. All the indications are that before the close of this century, cataclysmic and apocalyptic events will rend the planet. As the waves of senseless, irrational violence rise higher and higher on the Earth...who can doubt that certain of the "UFO entities" have a hand in the wrecking, and in the stirring of the nauseating brew?'

How he knows these things, Creighton does not reveal. But there is a long fundamentalist Christian tradition of identifying UFOs with the work of the Devil. As early as 1954 Gordon Cove offered the novel insight that 'Satan is the cleverest military genius ever known.' Exactly which battles in history he has planned and won, Cove did not say, but was certain that the aliens aboard UFOs were possessed by the Devil, even when appearing to be most benign.

Commentator Dan Lloyd likewise sees the UFO cults who look forward to mass contact with our intergalactic guardians as deluded: their 'distorted religious longings' are directed toward entities who merely appear benign in order to win our trust and thereby subvert humanity. He follows ufologist Jacques Vallée's suggestion in his book *Messengers of Deception* that the UFO phenomenon is 'a control system which acts on humans and uses humans.'

Vallée points to recurrent patterns in UFO cases that echo patterns of behaviour by evil spirits, goblins and other creatures from folklore, and suggests that something – perhaps human, and perhaps not – is making such patterns. Lloyd first argues that UFOs are not from another physical dimension, but are 'deliberately distorted etheric effects, and it should surprise no one to learn that such effects can influence physical matter and create, in turn, physical effects' and then identifies the maker of the patterns noted by Vallée: 'Behind whatever human group may be active in this area, there hovers the invisible presence of...the cosmic being who has been known since ancient Persian times as Ahriman. In the Bible he is known as Satan.'

EXTRA-TERRESTRIAL SALVATION

From this brief survey of the various points of contact between UFOs and religious beliefs, a number of things emerge. We previously suggested that such beliefs rest on a confusion between the *scientific* concept of other planes of being, distinct from but equal to our own, and the *religious* apprehension of a quite different kind of 'other dimension', the absolute reality that informs all existence.

Above: ***Scale model of a UFO constructed by the Aetherius Society. Note the resemblance to the UFO that George Adamski claimed to have seen in California in the early 1950s.***

This confusion is nowhere more evident than in the message of The Two, who seemed to think that Heaven, or something like it, could be reached in a spaceship. Such a literal, physical religious cosmology has not been contemplated by any major religion since the Middle Ages.

In conventional religious terms, there is no conflict between the levels of reality inhabited by God and those of parallel universes or additional dimensions. The Creator of one universe is still the Creator of all the others; and the God that created humanity also created ufonauts. But what, in effect, many of the cultists have done is to create a kind of substitute set of gods – the aliens, 'space brothers' and the rest,

Above: ***A UFO, caught on film by Guy B. Marquand, skims the hills near Riverside, California.***

of the major world religions would regard this belief as heresy, the UFO cults actually have little in common besides a common faith in some kind of extra-terrestrial salvation. If *all* these cults have any claim to truth, the immediate regions of space around Earth must be unusually crowded with our intergalactic brethren.

If these cults *are* in touch with genuine UFO entities, there are only a few logical conclusions to draw. One is that the ufonauts themselves are confused, with no greater claim to the truth than anyone on Earth. Or they themselves are at the mercy of rival systems of thought, and for all we know may be deeply hostile to one another's beliefs. Or they may simply be hopeless at prophecy, which also puts them on much the same level as anyone on Earth. Or, worst of all, they are cosmic cats, playing with the dying mouse of humanity.

This leads us to one further possible explanation. We have seen in previous chapters how both UFOs and their occupants, in all kinds of context, indulge in apparently meaningless, often contradictory, and most often simply incomprehensible behaviour: disguise, trickery, deceit, cruelty that, if the reports are to be believed, does not balk at rape or murder. One does not have to believe that UFOs are evil to wonder if the 'messages to mankind' and the cults they inspire are not simply another facet of this taunting game. If, that is, it is a game.

who will come down like cosmic cavalry to save humanity from itself.

Leaving aside the question of how many

THE UFOs ARE COSMIC CATS PLAYING A TAUNTING GAME WITH THE DYING MOUSE OF HUMANITY.

Right: ***A black UFO photographed as, allegedly, it hovered for almost half an hour over Shiogama City, north of Tokyo, Japan, on 27 September 1986. If the picture is genuine, the shape of the craft is not unlike the all-black F-117A 'Stealth' strike aircraft – but that cannot hover.***

FATAL ATTRACTION

Most attempts to explain the UFO phenomenon assume that there is some coherent purpose behind their presence here – and even a game, even the one a cat plays with a mouse, has a purpose. The struggle of most serious ufologists has been to discover that purpose; the UFO cultists believe they have the answer. But such an assumption may be the most naïve error that ufology has ever made, the fatal result of supposing in the first place that aliens are in any way at all like us.

In his book *Perspectives: a Radical Examination of the Alien Abduction Phenomenon*, ufologist John Spencer presents his 'Moth Proposal', which is possibly the most successful attempt yet made to reconcile all the contradictions within the reams of evidence for UFOs.

Spencer notes first that if certain sense-receptor cells in the brains of both humans and other mammals are not stimulated very early in an animal's life, they do not develop. This means that if, say, a child's long-sightedness goes undetected for very long, the brain is incapable of interpreting objects at close range properly, even when the image reaching the retina and hence the brain has been corrected with glasses. The brain simply has not developed a mechanism for dealing with this kind of input.

Spencer suggests that UFOs have had the same effect on people today (and one might add, throughout recorded history). We do not see UFOs correctly – hence the plethora of shapes and sizes reported – because we have not been conditioned to see whatever it is they really are. And he quotes the Russian UFO researcher Vladimir Rubstov, saying that an image is created in the mind 'as a result of the interaction between the sensory data and "anticipating patterns" that are kept deep in human memory. Seeing a completely new object means building promptly a new pattern to assimilate the non-standard sensory information. Such a pattern is usually constructed by association.' Rubstov remarks that this is no guarantee that the mental image will conform with 'the real structure of the observed phenomenon, and [this] may lead to various illusions'.

Spencer then describes the view of the world enjoyed by a family of moths living near a major motorway. What, he asks, would the moths understand of human society from their observations of vehicles, the occasional person walking from a car to the emergency telephone, or even relieving himself behind a bush? Would moths assume that 'the "visitations" of our vehicles are for a specific purpose relating to moths? From their interaction with telegraph poles, could they ever understand the telephone? Would they assume that the lighting, switched on when they are most active, is a device for luring and killing them? From their perspective, could they ever understand the true meaning of the lights, could they comprehend that when we constructed them, we never even thought of moths?'

Our mistake, Spencer suggests, in trying to understand UFOs, is the assumption that we are the object of the aliens' interest, rather than, like the moth dashing itself against a street light, 'caught up in something that may not even concern us'.

Any attempt to answer the crucial questions that John Spencer has raised must address once again the vexed question of where UFOs may come from.

Above: ***Contactee Paul Villa claimed to have snapped this UFO near Volcano Mountain, outside Albuquerque, New Mexico, in April 1965. All the many UFO pictures taken by Villa have been shown to be fakes.***

HUMANITY WILL BE DESTROYED IN SOMETHING THAT MAY NOT EVEN CONCERN IT.

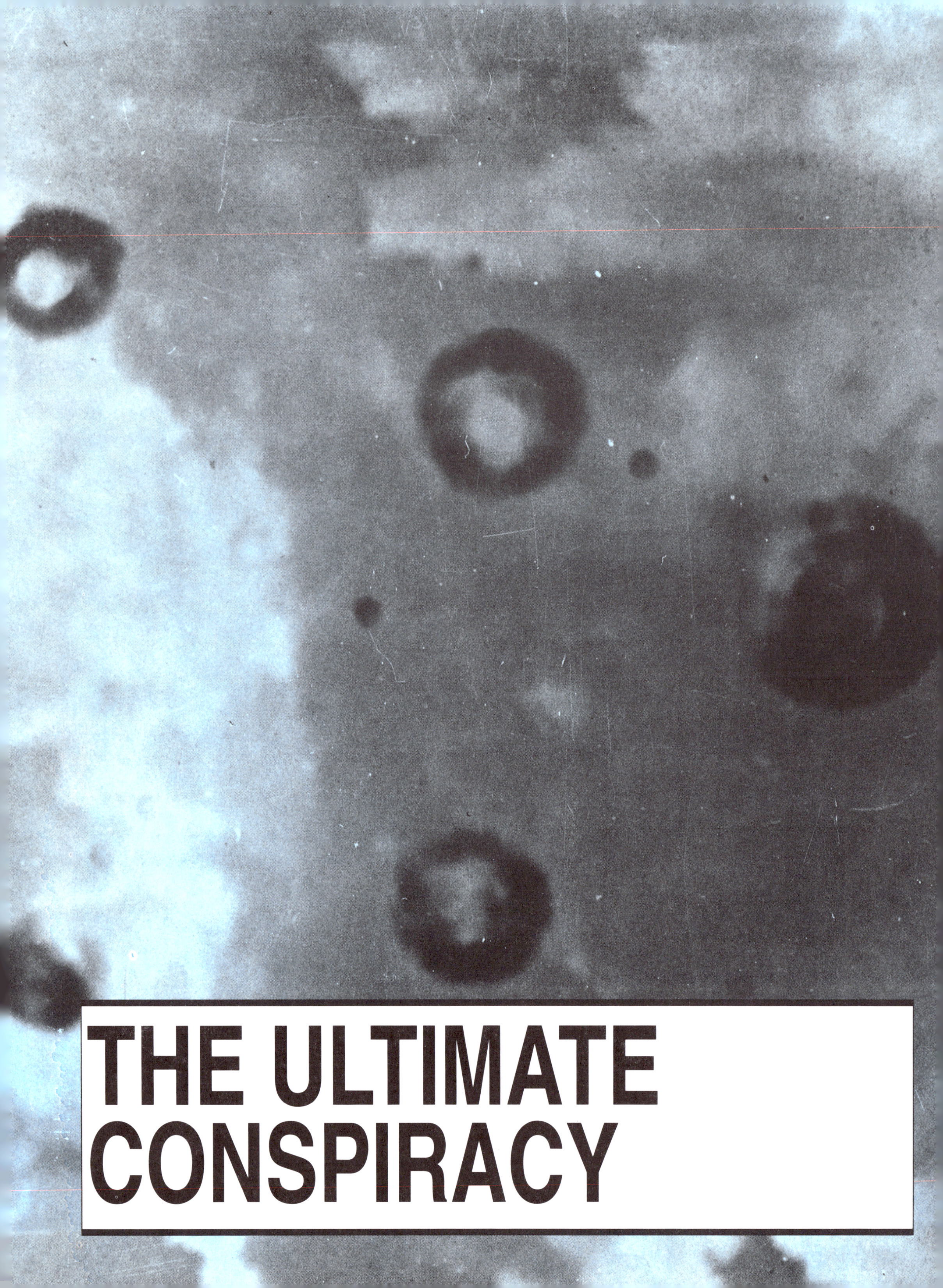

THE ULTIMATE CONSPIRACY

The 'thorough' scientific study, funded by the USAF, was designed to end the speculation about UFOs for once and for all. When its cover was blown, the public demanded to know exactly what the Pentagon was hiding.

If UFOs do not come from other inhabited planets in our galaxy, or from even further afield, how can we account for the widespread belief that they do?

When Kenneth Arnold opened the modern UFO era in 1947 with his sighting over the Cascade Mountains, it was perhaps inevitable, in the atmosphere of post-war America, that people would jump to the conclusion that he had seen craft from another world. The possibility that space might be explored, possibly even settled, had been glimpsed in the development of rocket technology in the USA before World War 2. During the war that technology advanced spectacularly in Germany, but these projects were always ambiguous, for while space was the 'last frontier' for humanity to conquer, there was also a more cynical use to which the technology could be put. And that was to provide vehicles with which to deliver weapons of mass destruction. For this was also the dawn of the nuclear age, with its 'balance of terror' and strategy of mutually assured destruction, or 'MAD'.

In 1947, Americans were deeply concerned that the USSR would soon develop nuclear weapons of its own – which would, in theory, make an invasion of the USA feasible. Kenneth Arnold's sighting of 'flying saucers' came at a time when the Western world, and the USA in particular, was obsessed with a fear of Communist invasion. Besides the military threat, there were fifth columnists, agitators, sympathizers and spies – 'the enemy within' – to beware of.

Worse, the Reds were prepared to invade

Opposite: ***Published in the*** **Irish Teen-Age Times** ***in March 1950, this obviously faked still was hailed as the first-ever photograph of a flying saucer. It was accompanied by the sensational revelation that flying saucers were space stations loaded with nuclear bombs, capable of being positioned anywhere above the Earth. The story did not divulge who controlled the craft. This was not the first time that UFOs were to be identified as secret weapons.***

Below: ***A UFO leaves a trail of vapour or smoke as it streaks across the sky at Madre de Dios, Peru, in 1952. Was this a secret terrestrial weapon being tested, or an alien craft in yet another unexpected guise?***

your mind. Since the 1930s it had been suspected that the Communist authorities used far-reaching psychological techniques to remould the opinions of dissidents. Veterans of the Korean war 'confirmed' this nightmare, with accounts of the most soul-destroying and violent attempts to 'brainwash' Western prisoners of war.

In 1947, then, the intriguing notion of life in space combined with political anxieties about invasions of all kinds, to produce a 'logical' conclusion about Arnold's sighting: if these silvery disks were not from an Earthly power, they had to be invaders from outer space. The reaction to Arnold's sighting was simply a very early sign of the conditions that produced the long nuclear winter of the Cold War. The fretful temper of the times was reflected in films of the era, which portrayed aliens in flying saucers as ready to colonize the world and, given the slightest opportunity, to enslave humanity in the process.

The extra-terrestrial hypothesis (ETH) has remained popular ever since partly because the media have tended to ignore alternative interpretations of UFO events – and partly because similar kinds of fears and uncertainties to those common in 1947 have remained with us ever since.

Above: ***Falling on stony ground – Connie Menger, wife of contactee Howard Menger, talks to arch-sceptic Dr Edward U. Condon, whose study of UFO phenomena effectively ended official US Air Force interest in the subject.***

THE TRUTH BEHIND THE 'INVADERS FROM OUTER SPACE' WAS EVEN MORE SINISTER.

But there may be a more sinister reason why the ETH has remained the paramount interpretation of UFOs.

DEBUNKING EXERCISE

Many serious UFO researchers hoped that when the University of Colorado began a thorough scientific study of the UFO phenomenon in 1966, government and military sources would have little choice but to open all their files on the subject to the research team and, perhaps, to public gaze as well. In charge of the project was a distinguished physicist, Dr Edward Condon, and the funding – all $572,146 of it – came courtesy of the USAF, which had finally agreed to the study under pressure from Congress. Condon's committee started work on 6 October 1966. Its brief was to sift the USAF's mountain of UFO sighting reports – an archive that contained nearly 20 years' worth of material – and draw whatever conclusions it could.

As far as both public and ufologists were concerned, the mystery that had baffled everyone for almost two decades would be given the kind of attention it deserved. That hope must surely have been swept away for all time in the autumn of

Right: ***Robert J. Low, who set up Condon's study at the University of Colorado so that it would show 'there is no reality' to UFO sightings.***

1968, when Dr David Saunders, a scientist at Colorado, blew the cover on what was supposed to be the most elaborate and exhaustive study of UFOs ever undertaken.

Out of disgust at the way the work was actually being done, Saunders published a memo that the committee's co-ordinator, Robert Low, had written in August 1966 while negotiating the contract for the work at Colorado. From it, one can only infer that the university was looking for ways to meet a presumably unofficial – even secret – Air Force brief to make the study a debunking exercise instead of a cool appraisal of the evidence.

Low wrote: 'Our study would be conducted almost exclusively by non-believers who...could and probably would add an impressive body of evidence that there is no reality to the observations. The trick would be, I think, to describe the project so that, to the public, it would appear a totally objective study but, to the scientific community, would present a group of non-believers trying their best to be objective but having an almost zero expectation of finding a saucer.'

Saunders further charged Low and Condon with ignoring the most difficult evidence in favour of weak cases that would bolster the impression that the UFO enigma was a chimera.

The Condon Report, as *The Scientific Study of UFOs* is usually known, was published on 9 January 1969. It was a 1485-page dossier, and in deference to busy journalists Condon's summary of the report was printed first – and the summary was all that the media initially reported. The key finding was: 'Careful consideration of the record...leads us to conclude that further extensive study of UFOs probably cannot be justified in the expectation that science will be advanced thereby.'

'KOOKS'

For those who bothered to read the rest of the report, Condon's summary was bizarre, for it bore no relation to what his committee had actually written. Of the 87 UFO sightings that it had documented and investigated, about 25 per cent were admitted to be inexplicable. In a further 8 per cent, the debunkers had become desperate indeed as they strove to find 'natural' explanations for the otherwise inconceivable.

One analysis concludes implausibly: 'This unusual sighting should therefore be assigned to the category of some almost certainly natural phenomenon which is so rare that it apparently has never been reported before or since.' Any real scientist would have sought at once for other, similar

Above: ***Serious UFO studies have always been hampered by hoaxes and fake photographs. This shot was taken in July 1952 by Gianpetro Monguzzi. Ostensibly of an entity standing beside a landed UFO in the Bernina Mountains of Italy, it was later admitted to be a hoax made by using tabletop models and photomontage.***

UFOLOGISTS WERE FURIOUS AT THE GOVERNMENT'S ATTEMPTS TO HOODWINK THEM.

Above: ***Traces allegedly left by a UFO when it landed at Morrill Farm, Piermont, New Hampshire, during the winter of 1974.***

Right: ***The USAF Project Blue Book's last commanding officer, Major H. Quintanilla, with his staff. This tiny team was expected to investigate and evaluate thousands of UFO reports every year.***

reports – but there is evidence that Condon did not allow his committee to address themselves seriously to the whole 25,000 or so reports held by the USAF's UFO-watching unit, Project Blue Book. Ufologists have held ever since that the Condon Report is one of the grossest examples of government trying to hoodwink the people on a matter of major importance.

Was Condon, in fact, covering up deliberately? Was he a willing dupe of the USAF and the US government, 'just following orders'? Or was he chosen for his role by those who knew his scepticism, and knew that his conclusions would serve their own mysterious purposes? Edward Condon was certainly a lifelong debunker of UFOs, who delighted in regaling people with tales of the crankier devotees of UFO lore and who regarded even serious ufologists simply as 'kooks'.

But the US government itself has always taken UFOs seriously. The USAF set up its first UFO unit, Project Sign, on 22 January 1948. Its task was to try to assess whether the recent, persistent and growing evidence of mysterious and hitherto unknown aerial craft in the skies signalled a technological breakthrough by a potential enemy (in short, the USSR).

A COVER-UP

There was every reason to believe such a hypothesis. It is now known – and was surely known to the security agencies of the time – that among the papers found at the secret V-2 rocket proving grounds at Peenemunde in Germany were plans for a saucer-shaped flying machine. During the same period Avro Canada were developing for the US Navy the VZ-9AV, a saucer-shaped craft intended to fly at 300 knots at

30,000 ft. No one knew that this revolutionary design's best performance was in fact to be a rather sedate 30 knots at a maximum altitude of 3 ft. The point was that saucer-like flying vehicles were believed to be viable and potentially very powerful.

By early 1949 those working on Project Sign had enough data to conclude that while UFOs might pose no security threat, their technical capacities were so extraordinary that they could only be extra-terrestrial. The Air Force's reaction was surprisingly violent, and swift: Chief of Staff General Hoyt Vandenberg ordered all copies of the report to be burned, and then the USAF shut the project down. A new team, disconcertingly code-named Project Grudge, was set up on 11 February 1949 to make a fresh assessment. Grudge proposed a campaign of debunking.

In the light of the reaction to Sign's report and Grudge's advice, it seems strange that three years later, in March 1952, the USAF set up Project Blue Book to collect sighting reports and investigate them. But Blue Book's budget and staff were totally inadequate to the size of its task. Many commentators have wondered if this inadequacy was deliberate, and if the project's real purpose was simply to act as a front to reassure an anxious public that the origins of UFOs lay either in misidentifications of natural phenomena or aircraft, or in occasional hoaxes.

Blue Book's astronomy consultant, Dr J. Allen Hynek, wrote years later:

'Blue Book was a cover-up to the extent that the assigned problem was glossed over for one reason or another…[in the 18 years of the project's existence] I do not recall even one serious discussion of methodology, of improving the process of data gathering or of techniques of comprehensive interrogation…The charge was frequently made that the publicly visible air force "investigation" of UFOs was merely a front for a real investigation being carried on somewhere "higher up"…for instance, one time when I inquired into the specifics of a certain case, I was told by the Pentagon's chief scientist that he had been

Top left: ***Roscoe H. Hillenkoetter, pictured in the rank of captain USN. It has been claimed that later, as an admiral and first head of the CIA, he was involved in an 'above top secret' panel charged with handling contacts with alien civilizations.***

Above: ***A German V-2 rocket launching pad. Trials of these rockets after World War 2 in the USA almost certainly gave rise to erroneous UFO reports. This gave the military the opportunity to use 'UFOs' as a cover for many other secret activities, and sometimes for its own blunders.***

Right: ***This UFO was photographed at Lake Tiorati, New York on 18 December 1966.***

advised by those at a much higher level to tell me "not to pursue the matter further".'

What did the Pentagon have to hide?

DRUGS

William H. Spaulding, of the Arizona-based organization Ground Saucer Watch (GSW), has developed the 'Federal Hypothesis', the result of a careful analysis of hundreds of top secret UFO-related documents declassified under the Freedom of Information Act. The Federal Hypothesis offers a new solution to the puzzle of what governments are not telling us about UFOs.

BEHIND THE SMOKESCREEN, TECHNOLOGY, DRUGS AND PSYCHOLOGICAL MANIPULATION COULD BE ILLICITLY TESTED ON INNOCENT VICTIMS.

Spaulding noted that areas of apparently high UFO activity in the USA were also near proving grounds for secret weapons and aircraft. (The same, as it happens, is also true in the UK.) He also realized that waves of American UFO sightings frequently followed moments of crisis for the US government, and cited the 'flap' in New Mexico and West Texas that followed the Soviets' successful launch of Sputnik II (only 30 days after Sputnik I) in November 1957 as an especially shocking example. At the time, the US space programme was suffering repeated, ignominious and nationally televised failures of its own satellite rocket launchers.

Spaulding suspected that many other aspects of the UFO phenomenon might be attributable to interference run by the CIA, and perhaps by a rogue cell within the organization. Close encounters and abductions may be the result of illicitly administering mind-expanding drugs to the unwary (the CIA did do this, under controlled conditions, in the 1960s). If that is so, the agency gathers much useful information. Not only are the victims' reactions monitored, but so too are media and general public reaction to accounts of events that are real in the mind of the witness but incredible to almost anyone else.

MEN IN BLACK

This may be the explanation for some abductee cases. It may also explain one of the weirder and more frightening 'side-effects' of some UFO sightings, the visits that some witnesses receive from the 'men in black' or MIB.

A typical instance occurred in Canada in 1981. At around 9.30 pm on the evening of 2 October, 16-year-old Grant Breiland saw a UFO from his home in Victoria, British Columbia, in Canada. It resembled an inverted dome, bright white in colour, with a red light that moved around the dome in a regular pattern. Above, below and on each side of the object were further white lights.

These details he saw by looking through binoculars and through the powerful zoom lens of his Ricoh SLR camera. Breiland used his CB radio to discover if anyone was on nearby Mount Tolmie, three miles distant, who could also see the object. A young man of 19, identified by the case investigators only as 'N.B.', 'came back' on the CB and confirmed that he too could see the object. After moving around the sky for about half an hour, the UFO vanished, like a light being turned out.

The next day, the two young men met for the first time to discuss their sighting. Breiland had never seen a UFO before and had read only one book on the subject when he was aged about 12. He could not remember its title.

The next Monday, at about 3.30 pm, Breiland was in a local supermarket when he saw two sun-tanned men watching him. They were dressed in extremely dark blue suits, shirts and shoes. Neither had eyelashes, and their eyes reflected no light. They approached him, and one asked, in a monotonous, mechanical voice: 'What is your name?' Breiland refused to tell him. The other then asked him where he lived. When Breiland again refused to help, they turned and walked away stiffly in complete unison. Breiland followed them as far as the edge of a muddy building plot, which they began to cross. Distracted momentarily, he looked away; when he turned back, they had vanished. He followed their path across the plot, but was so alarmed when he realized that they had left no footprints that he fled the scene.

MIB typically resemble G-men from a 1940s or 1950s Hollywood B-movie, and they may actually produce some form of ID and claim to be from a government department or, occasionally, a UFO research group. And they almost always know of witnesses' experiences even before they have reported them to anyone, and threaten that the witnesses or a member of their family will suffer if they reveal anything

Below: ***A UFO over Bulawayo? Photographer Barney Wayne was uncertain about what the curious object could be. The most likely candidate is a lenticular cloud – if, indeed, the object is in the sky and not solely on the film.***

Right: ***Sketch by Connecticut ufologist Albert Bender of a 'man in black' (MIB) who visited him in September 1953. The MIB so terrified Bender that he abandoned UFO research and did not tell the story of his encounter for several years. Despite the sometimes horrific threats that MIB utter, they have never been known to follow them up when a witness breaks silence. For this and other reasons, some researchers believe MIB are apparitions, while others suggest they may be real enough, but part of a long-term clandestine experiment in the psychology of fear.***

about it. Another weird aspect of the MIB is their transport. The cars they drive are usually Cadillacs or some other luxury model – which looks brand-new but has been out of production for years.

One of the strangest MIB encounters occurred to Dr Herbert Hopkins, who investigated the abduction of David Stephens in Maine in 1975, and his son. In September 1976, not only was Dr Hopkins visited by a MIB, who apart from being dressed 'like an undertaker' was deadly pale, totally bald – lacking even eyebrows or eyelashes – but was apparently wearing lipstick; but, a few days later, his son John received a visit from a man and a woman who, if not a stereotype MIB pair, were certainly quite peculiar.

They visited John Hopkins and his wife Maureen at home, and asked them a number of personal questions. While this was going on, the man kept 'pawing and fondling' the woman in a startling, intimate manner, and from time to time asked John if he was doing it correctly! When John left the room, the man asked Maureen 'how she was made', and if she had any photographs of herself naked. They left without even saying goodbye.

In this case, the MIB involved made no threats, but the threats they do make are never fulfilled: it is as if they are actually testing the effectiveness of empty menaces.

SECRET OPERATIONS

The creation of a series of such unlikely events – enough to fuel the mystery and the media, and keep ufologists busy – would serve two purposes. Bear in mind that the 'cover-up' has largely succeeded in diverting the scientific community from the UFO phenomenon already, by exercises like the Condon Report and persistent official denials (now, perhaps, seen to be true, in an unexpected way!) of the 'reality' of UFOs. First, the events that witnesses describe are so outlandish that most ordinary people tend to dismiss them as incredible, while the media make fun of them – and consequently no scientific body will investigate closely. And so, behind this smokescreen, secret technology, unusual aircraft designs and psychological manipulations can freely be tested.

For example, since the late 1980s there have been many reports from Puerto Rico that feature aircraft, notably the US Navy's F-14 Tomcats, chasing UFOs. Here are summaries of three of those reports.

At around 8.30 pm on 4 July 1989, F-14s from Roosevelt Roads Naval Air Station at Ceiba were seen by witnesses from the nearby town of Luquillo, in pursuit of 'a very big and brilliant blue-white star' that performed bizarre manoeuvres near Mount El Yunque before heading south-east across the Sierra de Luquillo, with the jets still trailing it.

In the evening of 22 June 1990, three witnesses saw four F-14s chasing 'a round ball of yellow light with a very bright red light in its center' that was flying in a south-westerly direction over the Rio Guyate near Route 52, in the eastern part of the island. The F-14s were followed in turn by an AWACS radar surveillance aircraft.

At 5.30 pm on 19 December 1990, residents of Caguas, also in eastern Puerto Rico, saw unmarked military helicopters apparently in pursuit of a similar yellow and red light 'as big as a 747 [jumbo jet]' and 'flying totally noiselessly', which disappeared among the mountains.

The US Navy's Atlantic Fleet Weapons Training Facility (AFWTF) has its headquarters hard by Roosevelt Roads NAS, and controls two huge ocean firing ranges – Alfa, some 120,000 square miles in area, to the north and east of the island,

and Bravo, 74,000 square miles in extent, to the south-east. Among the hardware tested by AFWTF are cruise missiles and electronic warfare devices. The US Navy is also funding development of advanced fighters using unconventional airfoils – swept-forward wings, for instance. Any of these could either be deliberately disguised as a UFO to cover tests that the local population might otherwise find objectionable (such as flying a cruise missile over populated areas) or could easily be mistaken for a 'flying saucer' – especially when flying at dusk, and especially if of unconventional shape.

Two instances cited by Spaulding will further illustrate how the UFO phenomenon is used as a cover for secret operations.

In October and November 1975, the North American Air Defense Command (NORAD) received a series of UFO reports from USAF bases and missile sites in northern Montana, northern North Dakota, northern Minnesota, Maine and Michigan. Common factors were that few of the sightings showed on radar; stationary lights; and lights that flashed on and off in various colours.

In one instance on 8 November, two F-106 fighters armed with missiles were scrambled from Great Falls, Montana, to

In 1990 a number of UFO sightings in Puerto Rico involved US Navy F-14 Tomcats **(top)** *and USAF AWACS* **(above)**, *apparently in hot pursuit of seemingly alien craft. However, Puerto Rico is home to the headquarters of two vast US Navy ocean firing ranges, where cruise missiles* **(left)** *and other still more exotic hardware are routinely tested. It would serve the military's public relations only too well if the public were to ascribe highly secret craft or test firings that went awry to 'UFOs'.*

investigate seven objects flying at between 10,000 and 13,000 ft that the 24th NORAD Region had picked up on radar, and that could be seen as lights from the ground. The fighter pilots were instructed to fly no lower than 12,000 ft and at moderate speed (the F-106 is capable of Mach 2, or about 1500 mph). When the jets approached, the lights went out. The fighters returned to base without having made contact with the 'unknowns'.

Spaulding concluded that this was not a classic case of 'saucers spying on military bases'. The 'entire November flap,' he wrote, 'represents a contrived military exercise, possibly involving both US and Canadian Special Forces, to covertly test detection capability and response...The UFOs were stealth (low detectability) helicopters...The whole "crisis"...reeks of a military mission [in which] a few individuals [know] the facts and the operators within the military system are kept in the dark.'

Stealth technology – seen in the USAF's B-2 bomber, F117A fighter (sometimes, before its public unveiling, erroneously identified as the F-19) and the experimental A12-ATA attack aircraft – has been under development since 1966. In 1975 a USAF mobile radar unit picked up an aircraft leaving Edwards AFB, California, at over 460 mph. In one sweep of the radar, the 'blip' had vanished – a feat possible, in theory, only if the target had accelerated to over 2000 mph.

In other words, this was another case of a UFO spying on a military installation, and was reported as such. And in fact, in a sense, it was exactly that – a plane testing the effectiveness of stealth technology against a military unit that had deliberately been given no warning of its presence. The aircraft switched on its electronic counter-measures systems in that sweep of the radar, and became electronically 'invisible'. How many civilian air traffic controllers reporting UFOs on their radar screens have been the unwitting victims of such tests?

Above: ***The USAF's B-2 'Stealth' bomber, which is virtually invisible to radar, thanks to a combination of shape, materials and a powerful armoury of electronic counter-measures carried on board. The aircraft and the effects of its technology were so unorthodox that both were more than once linked to UFOs during their development phase.***

IN THE UPROAR NO ONE NOTICED THAT THE AFFAIR CLEARLY INDICATED THE ORIGIN OF THE CRASHED SAUCERS.

CONSPIRACY

The difficulty with the Federal Hypothesis is that, like all the other UFO conspiracy theories, it cannot be conclusively proven. But it does fit many of the known facts better than most other conspiracy theories, and certainly better than the extra-terrestrial hypothesis. Nowhere is this better illustrated than in the case of the 'documentary proof' and 'highly placed intelligence sources' cited by those who

Right: ***TV producer Jaime Shandera, who in 1984 received a package of allegedly top-secret documents that, if genuine, had world-shaking implications.***

have been promoting the 'Majestic 12' legend since the early 1980s.

Los Angeles TV producer Jaime Shandera received a package in his mail on 11 December 1984 that, if it was genuine, was of world-shaking importance. Inside were photocopies of two documents, one dated 24 September 1947, the other 18 November 1952. The first was signed by US President Harry S Truman. The second was addressed to President Dwight D. Eisenhower by Admiral Roscoe H. Hillenkoetter. Both were marked TOP SECRET.

The first was perhaps the more momentous of the two. It purported to be a classified executive order from Truman to Secretary of Defense James Forrestal, and it authorized him, after due consultation with nuclear scientist Dr Vannevar Bush, to establish a board of suitably qualified persons to be answerable directly and only to the president, and to be known as 'Majestic 12' (or 'Majic-12' or simply 'MJ-12'). Their job was to investigate the case of the flying saucer that had crashed near Roswell, N.M., in July 1947.

Here, it seemed, was proof that the crash, long a subject of rumour and speculation among ufologists of all persuasions, had really happened. The second document backed the first. It was a top secret briefing for the newly elected president on the members and progress of the MJ-12 group. It consisted of 12 eminent scientists, engineers, military men and intelligence experts – some of whom, such as Hillenkoetter, combined more than one of these roles – and even included Harvard astronomer Dr Donald Menzel, who in his public utterances was a ferocious opponent of any suggestion that UFOs were remotely 'real'.

Menzel's presence seemed at first sight like a classic case of the sheep in wolf's clothing. To scholars of UFO conspiracy theories, Hillenkoetter's involvement was still more fascinating. The Admiral had not been purely a Navy man. He was also the first Director of the CIA (also established in September 1947; Hillenkoetter had also headed its predecessor, the Central Intelligence Group, since 1 May that year). He retired from the Navy in June 1957 and soon afterwards joined the Board of Governors of the National Investigations Committee on Aerial Phenomena, one of the first and most influential civilian UFO organizations. Conspiracy theorists have always maintained that Hillenkoetter – once a spy, always a spy – was a fifth columnist of the first water. Here, it seemed, was conclusive proof.

In view of the somewhat cataclysmic nature of the MJ-12 documents it seems strange that it was more than three years (on 29 May 1987) before Shandera, along with his associates, the writers W.L. Moore and Charles Berlitz, and crashed-saucer

Above: ***Dwight D. Eisenhower in 1944. There is circumstantial evidence that when US President he inspected evidence of alien contact held at Wright-Patterson AFB.***

Below: ***Dr Donald H. Menzel, renowned for his debunking of UFO reports.***

Right: ***Stanton Friedman, the nuclear physicist who has amassed much evidence that shows, to his satisfaction at least, that the US government has a secret collection of crashed UFOs and dead aliens.***

expert Stanton T. Friedman, made them public. Thc quartet claimed to have contacted a 'highly placed military intelligence operative' who could authenticate the story.

However, the 'highly placed' intelligence source turned out to be a lowly USAF sergeant once found guilty of falsifying official documents, and the papers themselves soon took a battering. Meticulous research by ufologist Philip J. Klass revealed that the machine used to type the Truman 'executive order' of 1947 was a Smith-Corona model that had not been manufactured until 1963. Hillenkoetter had dated his memorandum to Eisenhower in an odd hybrid of civilian and military styles and signed himself 'Roscoe H. Hillenkoetter'. Neither of these forms appear before or since in any of his voluminous surviving correspondence.

Finally, Klass's close inspection of the signature on the Truman document showed beyond reasonable doubt that it was a photocopy of the signature on a letter from Truman to Vannevar Bush, written on 1 October 1947. And as the Hillenkoetter memo of 1952 refers specifically to the Truman 'special classified executive order' of 1947, it follows that both are fakes.

There is indeed a UFO conspiracy, but exactly who is conspiring against whom is far from obvious. And what no one seems to have noticed in the uproar over the MJ-12 affair is the clear indication that the 'crashed saucer' stories are not only hoaxes, but would appear to have their origins inside US intelligence. Some part of the US intelligence network is still interested in fuelling one of the most outlandish aspects of the UFO enigma. The Majestic 12 affair may not prove the Federal Hypothesis, but it certainly helps to make it more credible than any other conspiracy theory concerning UFOs.

Below: ***Philip Klass, relentless UFO sceptic and tireless researcher, stands beside a display board showing material from the Gulf Breeze case, one of the most controversial modern claims for a sustained series of encounters with a UFO.***

LIFE AFTER DEATH

GHOSTS AND APPARITIONS

A troubled lady, haunting the place she was bound to in life; a dead father, unable to rest easy until his will is carried out; a piratical sailor whose love of adventure defeats even death – the many shades of ghosts present intriguing, if inconsistent, evidence for survival beyond the grave.

In 1968, Frances Little and her husband were delighted with the adobe house they had bought in the desert setting of California's Kern County, but after a few weeks, Mr Little became disturbed at seeming to see his wife in two places at once. He'd leave her in one room, or outside, only to see her immediately afterwards, wandering around at the other end of the house. Finally, it dawned on him that the 'other woman' must be a ghost. But whose ghost? And why was she haunting the house?

Then, alone at home one night, Frances Little herself saw a 'tall thin woman in a long dark old-fashioned dress' come out of a back room and go into her bedroom. From there, she went into the family room and Mrs Little was able to see her features quite clearly.

Not long after this, Mrs Little was sorting through some junk that had been left in the garage by the previous owners. To her amazement, she came across a photograph of a woman who looked exactly like the ghost she had seen. Careful enquiries revealed that this was Alice Margaret Kolitisch who, with her husband, had had the adobe house built in the 1920s. She was, Frances Little felt, still concerned about the house she had loved when alive.

This is a ghost story in a classic mould: the troubled shade of the dead haunts a place it had been bound to emotionally in life. But not all ghost stories are like this,

Opposite: ***The spectre of the Brown Lady of Raynham Hall, Norfolk, photographed in 1936 as she floats down the stairs of the house. The Brown Lady conforms to the most common notion of a ghost – the shade of a dead person who haunts a place where he or she enjoyed or suffered a crucial emotional experience. But by no means all ghosts fit this pattern.***

The Battle of Gettysburg* (below) *was a turning point in the American Civil War. During the war's worst days, US President Abraham Lincoln sought help from a medium.

Abraham Lincoln rides in triumph through Richmond, Virginia, on 4 April 1865 **(above)**. *Just one week later he was shot dead by the actor John Wilkes Booth* **(above right)** – *an event that Lincoln had apparently foreseen in a dream. Lincoln's interest in psychic matters and his mordantly ironic sense of humour may account for his haunting the White House* **(below right)**, *seen here as it was shortly before Lincoln took up residence as 16th president of the United States.*

and because hauntings are so varied in kind, they make intriguing, if inconsistent, evidence for some kind of life after death.

Legend says that US President Abraham Lincoln had a strong belief in ghosts: he apparently consulted a medium during the worst days of the Civil War and, according to W.H. Crook, one of his bodyguards, Lincoln had a number of psychic experiences. At the beginning of April 1865, he told Crook that he had had a dream in which he had been in the hall of the White House, and had seen a coffin draped in black there. When he asked who it was for, he was told: 'The president.'

On 11 April, Lincoln told Crook that he had dreamed of his own assassination; and on the morning of 14 April he had a vision of a ship carrying him to some unknown place. That night, against the advice of Crook and other members of his staff, Lincoln went to Ford's Theater in Washington. There, he was shot dead by John Wilkes Booth. Within months of Lincoln's death, rumours began to circulate that his ghost was haunting the White House.

Lincoln's spectre took a long time to take

visible form. Theodore Roosevelt, president from 1901 to 1909, maintained that he 'felt the presence' of Lincoln at 1600 Pennsylvania Avenue. The first person actually to see his ghost was Grace Coolidge, wife of Calvin Coolidge, the 30th president, who was in office between 1923 and 1929. Mrs Coolidge saw the ghost standing at the window of the Oval Office, staring out onto Pennsylvania Avenue in the attitude of a man deep in thought. Staff members and presidential aides have reported the same thing – and the apparition always appears at the same window.

The next president, Herbert Hoover (at the White House from 1928 to 1932), heard no more than 'odd sounds' but said that 'many of them were fantastic'.

Between 1932, when Franklin Delano Roosevelt became president, and 1945, when he died, Lincoln's ghost was allegedly seen many times. On one occasion Queen Wilhelmina of the Netherlands, who had long had an interest in spiritualism, had gone to bed in the Lincoln Room – formerly used by Lincoln himself as a dressing room – when she heard a gentle tap on the door. She opened it, and there stood the dead president, gravely doffing his famous stovepipe hat; then the apparition vanished. When the queen told Roosevelt of her encounter the next morning, he confessed that he knew the room was haunted; Winston Churchill had also seen the ghost of Lincoln while sleeping there, and Mrs Roosevelt had detected Lincoln's presence on several occasions.

Harry S Truman, who succeeded to the presidency on Roosevelt's death and lived in the White House from 1945 to 1952, often joked to his guests about Lincoln's ghost. He once admitted that though he had never seen it, he was certain that he had heard it, in the form of footsteps which approached his bedroom door, followed by a knocking.

There had certainly been no rational explanation for these sounds, he said, and they always occurred in the early hours of the morning. A White House stenographer who served both Roosevelt and Truman allegedly saw Lincoln frequently. The first time was in the Lincoln Room; the spectre was sitting on the bed pulling on his boots. The girl was badly scared, although with repeated appearances she seems to have got used to seeing the ghost. Both John and Robert Kennedy saw the spirit of Lincoln, according to friends of the Kennedy family.

Above: ***Franklin D. Roosevelt, 32nd president of the United States. During his tenure at the White House, two distinguished visitors saw the ghost of Lincoln there – Winston Churchill and Queen Wilhelmina of the Netherlands.***

Left: ***Grace Goodhue Coolidge, wife of President Calvin Coolidge, who saw Lincoln's ghost in the presidential office on several occasions between 1923 and 1929.***

Right: ***Winston Churchill gives his famous 'V for victory' sign. That such a prestigious individual freely admitted to seeing ghosts – Churchill also had a number of remarkably accurate premonitions – argues for the reality of the shade of Lincoln.***

Above: ***Robert* (left) *and John Kennedy. Both brothers saw the Lincoln spectre at the White House during John's presidency, although neither was noted for his interest in psychic or spiritual matters.***

The White House ghost is intriguing for several reasons. First, it hardly seems likely that several presidents, their wives, a queen, and a statesman like Winston Churchill would lie about seeing the wraith of Lincoln: 'seeing ghosts' might call their fitness for high office into question. The credentials of the witnesses, then, are beyond question.

But is this ghost really the spirit of Abraham Lincoln, bound to the scene where he worked and thought so hard and so deeply? Or is the apparition brought into being by something else? Could it be the result of a collective feeling that the White House really ought to be haunted by Lincoln, the greatest of all the men who lived there, and who died so tragically – so that those who have seen him, presidents included, somehow projected the 'spirit' to suit their own unconscious wishes? Or might the apparition be some kind of recording of Lincoln, impressed upon the place somehow and played over and over again? Or is the Lincoln ghost not one ghost, but several – sometimes one thing, sometimes another, depending on the circumstances and the person who perceives it?

Such questions take us to the heart of the mystery surrounding ghosts of all kinds.

HOARSE WHISPERS

What is a ghost? That the belief that a ghost is present and active can be created by circumstances is beyond doubt. Given some specious evidence, a credulous collection of witnesses, and a background of fear, a ghost will make itself heard, seen or felt. This is very clear from the story told by New Zealander Frank Brookesmith, who until his death in 1991 was one of the last few survivors from the age of square-rigged sailing ships.

In his book *I Remember the Tall Ships*, Brookesmith recalled a haunting that briefly afflicted the tanker *Orowaiti* on a voyage across the Pacific from Wellington, New Zealand, to San Francisco, in the early 1920s. What happened was this. After one of the sailors on board the ship had committed suicide, the rest of the crew, understandably distressed at the incident, swore that the dead man was haunting the bow end of the ship. The ghost was invisible, but its constant, eerie whisper could clearly be heard. Determined to find out what was really going on, Brookesmith went forward at about 4 o'clock one morning to investigate.

'The ship was rolling quite moderately and I paced the deck from right forward to the after rail on the weather side. I heard nothing. I walked along the lee side and paused by the windlass.

'I froze, and the hairs on the back of my neck stood on end...It felt as if *all* my hair was standing on end. Someone was talking in a hoarse whisper!…I ran down the ladder to the foredeck and I walked into the space under the focsle head. It was all as dark as the inside of a cow but I knew what was there…I stood quite still and listened. There was no sound save the usual creaks and cracks of a ship in a seaway…

'I went back…to the after rail and I could hear a faint whispering. I could not distinguish the words but there was no mistaking the sound…My skin crept. I knew that I could easily imagine words but I simply had to find the source of the sounds. I moved about and found that, the nearer I was to the gypsy [a small winch], the clearer was the sound. It was an indistinct asthmatic whisper.

'I put my hand on the [anchor] chain where it went down the pipe into [its] locker and I *felt* it! As the ship rolled the rusty links moved against each other to make this harsh sound.

'Rub two pieces of rough iron together and you will hear what we heard,' Brookesmith wrote many years later. 'Add to it unhappiness and superstitious fears and you will have a haunting.' He silenced the 'ghost' by lashing the chain down with rope. 'I've found the ghost and I've bound him hands and feet,' he reported with a certain grim satisfaction.

Frank Brookesmith was, on that occasion at least, driven to get to the root of the shipboard 'haunting' partly by curiosity and partly by a determination not to be prey – or to be in thrall – to what he called 'superstitious fears'. But he also told his family of another and quite different experience of the supernatural that he had as a young man, before he went to sea, in the last years of World War 1.

He was then working as a clerk in a bank in Christchurch, New Zealand; one of the few perks of the job was a free flat above the bank premises. The perk in turn had its price – which was that he had to be on the alert for any attempt to raid the bank. To help terminally dissuade any villains intent on relieving the bank of its customers' cash – or perhaps simply as a psychological support – he was issued with a hefty British Army officer's .455 Webley revolver and several boxes of ammunition. He used most of the ammunition practising with the pistol in the deserted hills outside the town, but he slept with the weapon loaded at his bedside every night.

One night he awoke suddenly, inexplicably disturbed. Peering warily at first down the length of his bed through half-closed eyes – half-expecting, half-fearing to find an intruder in his room – he found himself staring round-eyed at the figure of a young woman, dressed in white, kneeling as if in prayer beside his bed – and leaning her weightless arms on the covers over his knees.

This apparition, he swore, bore no relation to any image from any dream he had been having immediately prior to waking up. In fact he had been in a dreamless period of sleep when he was so strangely disturbed. What he saw, he admitted, frightened him. But his reaction to this extraordinary sight was weirdly rational: he wondered if it were not some outlandish decoy – the gangsters' moll pretending to be a ghost! – set up by some

Above: ***Frank Brookesmith as a seaman in the early 1920s. He experienced two hauntings in these years – one of a spectral young lady, another that seemed to be of a shipmate who had committed suicide. One had an entirely natural explanation, while the other appeared to be a genuine ghost.***

'IT FELT AS IF ALL MY HAIR WAS STANDING ON END. SOMEONE WAS TALKING IN A HOARSE WHISPER!'

Right: ***Christchurch, New Zealand, in the 1920s.***

particularly cunning set of burglars. With unusual presence of mind, he reached for his gun. As he swung it into aim, the image of the girl kneeling by his bedside faded away.

Brookesmith found himself rather foolishly waving a heavy revolver at his own bare feet. Making the best of a bad job, he salved his wounded pride by creeping around his flat and then the ground floor – the working area of the bank – looking for any sign of a break-in. He found nothing out of order, but neither could he explain the apparition that had woken him up.

Here we have a witness to two very different kinds of haunting, and a witness, to boot, with a certain rather startlingly logical reaction to both. Unfortunately, we don't know (because he did not say) whether Brookesmith made any attempt to discover if anyone else had ever seen the female phantom that rested so lightly on his bed, or if he made any effort later to find out whose phantom she may have been.

However, the real importance of these two stories, side by side and from the same source, is that someone can on one occasion believe he is really seeing a ghost and accept it as such, and on another occasion, confronted by another apparent haunting, take a thoroughly sceptical view and investigate and effectively exorcize it. To that person – and this is the point – the existence of false ghosts does not preclude the existence of real ones. And no one can say that Brookesmith's extraordinarily cool reaction was essentially different from one case to the other. On each occasion he responded according to a certain logic (despite his fright). The witness, if not the phenomenon, was consistent throughout.

DEATH-OMEN

Does any of this get us any nearer the answer to the question: what is a ghost?

In a way, no, this last story does not, because there is no evidence to suggest that the phantom lady seen by the conscientious bank guard and bluff, no-nonsense sailor Frank Brookesmith was not, in any case, a figment of his own momentarily disoriented imagination. But it does tell us that the most sceptical and practical of people can believe that they have genuinely seen a ghost. In short, the key to ghost stories may be the *witness*, not the ghost. And these two stories together also tell us that the most common presumption about ghosts is that they are the spirits – or at least the inexplicably immaterial records – of people once alive and now dead.

Before sorting out the vexed question of the role of the witness in ghost reports, it's as well to establish how varied the phenomenon of hauntings itself can be.

Ghosts of people may or may not be images of the spirit world, but they are not always apparitions of dead people, or even of animals.

Christina Hole comments in *Haunted England*: 'There is scarcely an old road in England along which the Spectral Coach has not trundled at some time or another. It

Left: ***The head of a phantom small boy mysteriously appeared in this photograph of a 1950s car, taken in March 1974 by David Broadbent of Bradley, Yorkshire.***

THE SPECTRAL COACH WITH ITS BLACK HORSES AND HEADLESS DRIVER IS A DEATH-OMEN FOR THOSE UNLUCKY ENOUGH TO ENCOUNTER IT.

may be either a genuine coach or a hearse; but whatever form it takes, it bears certain distinguishing marks [that] prove it to be something from another world. It is always black, and so are the driver and his horses. Often both are headless. It appears suddenly on the roadway and moves very fast and usually without noise. Only in a few cases do we hear of the rumble of wheels on the road or the clattering of horses' hoofs to give warning of its approach. Like most apparitions of its kind, it...often serves as a death-omen for those unlucky enough to encounter it.'

Why vehicles should take on spectral form, no one knows (let alone how), but phantom conveyances appear time and

Below: ***The spectral coach and coachman, of whom it has been said that 'scarcely an old road in England' lacks an example. But how does a coach acquire a 'spiritual' form, if ghosts are the shades of the dead?***

Above: ***Golden Gate Bridge, San Francisco Bay, under construction in 1936. Six years later Jack Cornelius and another seaman saw a ghostly sailing ship nearby.***

again in accounts of ghosts and hauntings. Furthermore, this is a tradition that refuses to die (so to speak). Modern accounts of ghost vehicles are rife with phantom trains, buses, ships, cars, and even aircraft.

SPECTRAL SHIP

In the winter of 1942, the destroyer USS *Kennison* was returning from an anti-submarine patrol along the California coast, coming up to the Golden Gate at the mouth of San Francisco Bay, when a heavy fog came out of nowhere. The *Kennison*'s engine-room bells rang for dead slow, and the ship began to nose carefully through the water, its foghorn sounding.

Then the fantail lookout, torpedoman Jack Cornelius, yelled into the ship's tannoy for everyone to look aft. Cornelius and another seaman, who was on the aft gundeck, both reported that a huge, derelict, two-masted sailing ship had passed within a few feet of the destroyer's stern. They had had the hulk in full view for about a half a minute before the fog closed in around it. The radar operators, however, had not seen a thing before, during, or after the sighting of the seemingly immaterial ship.

There is one ghost ship that has been seen dozens of times over the years by sailors. In a letter to *Occult Review* in 1921, F.G. Montagu Powell recounted an incident that had occurred many years previously, when he was serving with the Royal Navy:

'Somewhere in July 1859, when I was on HMS *Euryalus*, we were off the Cape of Good Hope when a curious thing happened. It was about six bells (11 am) in the forenoon, and I was midshipman of the watch, when a dull and heavy mist fell upon

us. We were under steam and sail and very light airs from the south were hardly filling our sails, the sun breaking out through the mist like a fiery copper ball every now and then, when we sighted a sailing ship right ahead of us, lying in fact right across our track and so close that before we could hail her or alter our course we were on top of her and in fact cut clean through her.

'Her sails seemed to me flat, lifeless and discoloured, no "bellying to the breeze" about them. Her crew, clad in sou'westers and tarpaulins and the traditional breeches, moved lifelessly about the decks, coiling up ropes or leaning over the hammock netting, and paying not the slightest attention to us, not nearly so much as we paid to them.

'I remember the curious vague look she had as, apparently undamaged by this tremendous impact (though of course there was no impact, it was just like cutting through a shadow or a cloud) she vanished slowly astern, the mist overwhelming and enfolding her like a shroud. I remember hearing one bluejacket saying to another, "Yon's the Flying Dutchman, I expect."'

The Flying Dutchman, Hendrik Vanderdecken, blasphemed against God and was condemned to sail the seas until the Last Judgement. That is a legend. But here we have dates, names, a specific location – and an account of a genuine personal experience. Was this spectral ship the Flying Dutchman? Or did the legend spring up to explain all such ghostly encounters at sea?

RECORDINGS OF THE PAST

In their way, steam trains are no less romantic than full-rigged ships – although no less problematic when it comes to explaining how ghost trains could be in any sense 'spiritual'. But there is no lack of them in the annals of ghost lore.

John Quirk, of Pittsfield, Massachusetts, reported that he and several customers at the Bridge Lunch café saw a phantom train hauled by a steam engine one afternoon in February 1958. The train consisted of a baggage car and five or six coaches, which the witnesses described in great detail. A month later, a similar train passed the same location at top speed, barrelling towards Boston, at 6.30 one morning.

Railroad officials insisted that no steam engine had run on that line for years. On yet another occasion when the phantom train was reported, the railroad stated categorically that no train of any material kind had been on that section of track at that time.

As trucks have largely replaced trains for hauling freight – and as the trucker and his big rig have become romanticized as modern exemplars of the great American tradition of rugged individualism – so ghost trucks have appeared on the highways.

In *Fate* magazine for February 1986, truck driver Harriette Spanabel of Brooksville, Florida, recalled an experience that unnervingly echoes Steven Spielberg's eerie movie *Duel*:

'I drive a tractor trailer and haul produce from Florida up the East Coast and west as far as Texas. For the past year and a half, always on my return run, a phantom truck follows me at least part of the time. At first I thought it was my imagination. One minute nothing would be behind me but the next minute a tractor trailer would be there.

'This truck has followed me on both Interstate highways and narrow two-lane roads. It is always behind me at night, moving over every once in a while so that its left headlight hits my left mirror directly. It disappears just as quickly as it appears.

'I now know for sure that I am not imagining the truck because I have a witness who also watched my mystery

Above: *US steam locomotive on a special excursion in the 19th century. Many such trains appear in ghostly form – as, increasingly, do trucks.*

Opposite below: *Two phantom faces, photographed from on board the oil tanker SS* **Watertown** *in December 1924. The ghost faces apparently had the features of two sailors who had died in an accident on the voyage down the Pacific coast of the USA and had been buried at sea. The faces appeared for days afterwards, though only for brief periods each day.*

THE PHANTOM TRUCK VANISHES JUST AS QUICKLY AS IT APPEARS.

Major disasters such as this train crash **(opposite)** *sometimes generate the phenomenon known as a 'near-death apparition'. Victims of the tragedy appear at the point of death to their nearest and dearest – although the witnesses may be hundreds of miles from the fatal event.*

vehicle. I recently took my friend Kelly Rose with me to Miami to make a delivery. I picked up the load in Philadelphia on March 8, 1985. It was a load of dry freight with two drops. It was when we were coming back from Miami that the truck first joined us at approximately 11:30 the evening of the 12th. I drove out of Lakeland, Fla, on US 98 going north. I planned to turn onto [State Route] 471 which runs through the middle of the Green Swamp. The phantom truck first appeared behind us on US 98 about two miles before I made my turn onto [State Route] 471. It followed us from there until we had almost reached [State Route] 50 where I turn to go west into the town where I live.

'On a narrow two-lane road which runs through a state forest, about 50 miles from my house, the truck again appeared behind us. Kelly immediately asked where it had come from. Of course I couldn't tell her but it followed us for 30 miles before it disappeared this time.

'Kelly, who had been watching the truck intently in her mirror, was astounded. I stopped my truck on 471 and we got out and looked for the other truck. It was completely gone. On this road there are no side roads where a truck could pull on or off. There are no shoulders where a truck could pull off without either tipping over or ending up tangled in a mass of big trees. And let me add there was no other traffic on 471 going in either direction.'

There is no difficulty in believing that these various witnesses are telling the truth – especially as in each case there was more than one witness to the strange events they describe. But these phantoms of the inanimate can hardly be spirits of something dead – since they weren't alive in the first place. So we may be forced to conclude that many ghosts are some kind of recording of the past. But then the problem still remains as to why a particular train, ship or even mighty, snarling 18-wheel semi-trailer should record itself on a particular place: why them, and not any of the hundreds of others that have passed that way?

GHOULISH APPEARANCE

Probably the most frequently told of all kinds of ghost story are those concerning apparitions of people at the moment of their death. Here at least the ghost is inextricably linked with the notion of a life after death – or, at least, with some kind of spiritual existence that is able to project itself across time and space from the dying person to someone near or dear to them. Two instances of this kind of haunting – if that is the word – show how different they can be.

One morning in the spring of 1973, 58-year-old Mrs Martha Beckwhite was doing one of the things she likes best – working in her garden – in Blandford, Dorset. Without warning she felt, without knowing how she could identify it, the presence of one of her youngest daughter's friends, Luke Fore. Then, she distinctly heard his voice say 'Goodbye, Martha'. Again without knowing why, she knew that he had died. When the telephone rang in the evening of that day and she heard her daughter's voice on the line, she said: 'Don't worry, darling; I know why you've called. Luke's just died, hasn't he?'

Indeed he had, of cancer of the liver. Two things about this case are intriguing, however. First was that she had met Luke Fore only once or twice (he was the husband of one of her daughter's closest friends at the time). Second was that she had no idea that Luke was ill. For various reasons Luke's cancer had been kept a secret from everyone but his immediate family: no one outside that small circle knew that he even had a cold, let alone was terminally ill.

There are two ways of stating the mystery here. Whatever the ultimate answer, there may be some clue in the fact that Martha Beckwhite and Luke Fore got along famously together on the few occasions that they met, although they were perhaps 20 years apart in age. Why did he appear to her, though, whom he had met but a few times? Or perhaps the problem should be put another way: why and how did she alone of all the people who knew Luke (and many knew him more intimately) 'tune in' to the fact of his death? Whatever the answer, there is no doubt that Martha Beckwhite received and understood, by some paranormal means, a message from someone who was dying, and whom she had no reason to suppose was even remotely at risk of death.

A much more typical case of a near-death apparition was recounted in the

October 1957 edition of *Fate* magazine.

Mary Travers was sitting up late waiting for her husband George, who was an insurance salesman, to come home. Shortly after the clock struck 11, she heard a cab coming down the street. It stopped in front of the house, and Mrs Travers heard a voice, presumably the driver's, call out 'Good night!' Then she recognized the familiar sound of her husband's steps on the porch. She hurried to the front door to welcome him home.

He came in silently, with his hat pulled down over his eyes, and then he stood with his back to his wife while she shut the door. She thought he was behaving oddly, and asked did he feel all right? He turned to face her – and in place of George's face she saw a hideous white death-mask. She screamed, and continued to scream, so that the neighbours rushed in to see what was wrong. By then, the apparition had vanished. Minutes later the phone rang: the caller regretfully announced that George Travers had been killed in a train crash.

It is difficult to account for such an apparition except as a spirit of the dead. It seems unlikely that by sheer coincidence Mrs Travers imagined his ghoulish appearance on the very night he died. It makes more sense to assume that the spectre was indeed her husband's spirit, or at least a projection from his mind, sent to warn Mrs Travers – albeit silently and shockingly – of what had happened to him.

AS SHE HURRIED TO WELCOME HER HUSBAND HOME SHE SAW THAT WHERE HIS FACE SHOULD HAVE BEEN THERE WAS A HIDEOUS WHITE DEATH-MASK.

Below: ***No natural explanation has been found for the ghostly image in this picture. But in 1991, 2-year-old Greg Maxwell*** **(seated)** ***began to point upwards and say, 'Old Nanna's here', although no one was visible to anyone but the child. Is this the shade of his dead grandmother?***

THE DEAD MAN'S WILL

The classic example of a haunting that seems to prove the continued existence of an individual in some form after death is the famous case of the 'lost' will of the North Carolina farmer James L. Chaffin. This is one of the best-documented cases in all psychic research. As several writers have remarked, even the lawyers involved seem to have been honest.

James L. Chaffin, a farmer of Davie County, North Carolina, had four sons: John, James, Marshall and Abner. On 16 November 1905 he made a will, attested by two witnesses, leaving everything he owned to his third son, Marshall. Why he singled out Marshall, no one knows. But, a little over 13 years later, the old man had a change of heart. He made a new will. It read:

'After reading the 27th chapter of Genesis I, James L. Chaffin, do make my last will and testament and here it is. I want, after giving my body a decent burial, my little property to be equally divided between my four children...and if she is living, you must take care of your mammy. Witness my seal and hand. James L. Chaffin. This January 16, 1919.'

This second will lacked the signatures of any witnesses, but would be legally valid under the laws of North Carolina if it could be established that the whole of the document was in the testator's own handwriting. Chaffin, unknown to anyone at the time, put the will between two pages of the family Bible on which were printed the 27th chapter of Genesis. The paper was folded over to make a kind of pocket. Chaffin never mentioned the second will to anyone, but he did scribble on a roll of paper, which he stitched into an inside pocket of his overcoat, a note that said: 'Read the 27th chapter of Genesis in my daddie's old Bible.'

On 7 September 1921, James L. Chaffin died unexpectedly after a fall. Marshall, the third son, obtained probate without fuss; there was no reason for anyone to challenge the will, and there was no enmity or rivalry among Chaffin's children.

But in June 1925 the second son, James P. Chaffin, began having vivid dreams that his father was standing silently beside his bed. A week or so later the apparition, dressed in the old black overcoat his son knew so well, spoke: 'You will find my will in my overcoat pocket.' James was convinced this was significant, and hurried to his mother's house.

His father's coat, however, had been given to her eldest son, John, who lived some 20 miles away. James went to John's home, and explained the situation. The two brothers examined the coat together. They found that the inside pocket had been stitched closed; when they cut it open, they found inside the rolled-up strip of paper in their father's handwriting. 'Read the 27th chapter of Genesis in my daddie's old Bible' was not a will, as James's dream had indicated, but the two brothers felt they must follow the message up.

John felt he could not look at the family Bible without independent witnesses, and took a neighbour, the neighbour's daughter, and his own wife and daughter with him. After a long search in his mother's house the old Bible was discovered in a top drawer in an upstairs room and, as it was

being taken out, it fell into three pieces. The neighbour picked up the front section containing Genesis, and it opened automatically at the place indicated in the cryptic message. There lay the second will.

This will was tendered for probate in 1925. Marshall Chaffin had died a year after his father, but his widow contested the application on behalf of her young son.

The court assembled in December 1925 to decide the issue: the public areas were crowded at the prospect of seeing a classic family squabble burst into open view. The scandal-hungry locals were to be disappointed. On the advice of her lawyer, Marshall's widow withdrew her opposition when she saw the will itself, unmistakably in the old man's handwriting.

There are really only two stark alternatives in explaining this case. Either the Chaffin brothers were lying, and set up the whole elaborate hoax in order to lay their hands on their share of their father's estate, or the story is true from start to finish. But the business of the Chaffin will is one of the best-documented and best-attested cases in ghost lore; and as such it stands as reasonable proof that in some cases, at least, ghosts do represent the consciousness of the dead – and that the physically dead do survive in some form of afterlife.

LOVE OF ADVENTURE

Some famous hauntings, however, leave one wondering to what extent some ghosts are purely subjective entities, existing solely in the mind of the witness.

Captain Joshua Slocum, the great American sailor, had a remarkable experience in July 1895, while on his historic solo voyage around the world in his sloop *Spray*. In the Atlantic, between the Azores and Gibraltar, he ran into squally weather. At the same time he began to suffer an attack of severe stomach cramps. These so distracted him that he went below – without taking in sail as he should have done. He threw himself on the floor of the boat's cabin, in great pain. In his account of the voyage he described what happened next:

'How long I lay there I could not tell, for I became delirious. When I came to, as I thought, from my swoon, I realized that the sloop was plunging into a heavy sea, and looking out of the companionway, to my amazement I saw a tall man at the helm. His rigid hand, grasping the spokes of the wheel, held them as in a vice. One may imagine my astonishment. His rig was that of a foreign sailor, and the large red cap he wore was cockbilled over his left ear, and all was set off with shaggy black whiskers.

Above: ***The image of a ghost that appeared in a picture taken inside Newby church, Yorkshire, by the vicar, the Rev. K.F. Lord, in the early 1960s. The ghost was not visible to the priest when he took the photograph.***

'I GAZED UPON HIS THREATENING ASPECT AND WONDERED IF HE HAD COME TO CUT MY THROAT.'

Right: ***Christopher Columbus, whose first expedition to the Americas in 1492 consisted of three ships, among them the* Pinta, *a caravel. Over 300 years later, Captain Joshua Slocum believed he was visited by the ghost of the pilot of the* Pinta *while sailing in the Atlantic. The spectral sailor guided the ship safely through a ferocious storm while Slocum lay in a delirium.***

He would have been taken for a pirate in any part of the world. While I gazed upon his threatening aspect I forgot the storm, and wondered if he had come to cut my throat. This he seemed to divine.

'"Senor," said he, doffing his cap, "I have come to do you no harm." And a smile, the faintest in the world, but still a smile, played on his face, which seemed not unkind when he spoke. "I am one of Columbus' crew, the pilot of the *Pinta*, come to aid you. Lie quiet, senor captain, and I will guide your ship tonight. You have a *calentura* [a reference to the stomach cramps] but you will be all right tomorrow...You did wrong to mix cheese with plums..."

'I thought what a very devil he was to carry sail. Again, as if he read my mind, he exclaimed, "Yonder is the *Pinta* ahead, we must overtake her. Give her sail, give her sail!"'

Next day Slocum found that the *Spray* was still on the same heading as he had left her when he staggered below in his 'swoon'.

'Columbus himself could not have held her more exactly on her course,' he wrote. 'I felt grateful to the old pilot, but I marvelled some that he had not taken in the jib. I was getting much better now, but was very weak...I fell asleep. Then who should visit me but my old friend of the night before, this time, of course, in a dream. "You did well last night to take my advice," said he, "and if you would, I should like to be with you often on the voyage, for the love of adventure alone." He again doffed his cap, and disappeared as mysteriously as he came. I awoke with the feeling that I had been in the presence of a friend and a seaman of vast experience.'

Perhaps so. And perhaps, in his delirious state, Slocum imagined, or hallucinated, the whole thing. But if he did, another small miracle seems to have occurred: the *Spray* kept her course, with no one at the wheel, through a long bout of foul weather and a hostile sea.

'MERE' COINCIDENCE?

The best evidence that some ghosts present proof of a life after death comes from pacts made between friends or relatives in which each party promises that whichever dies first will 'come back' to the other to show that they still survive.

The best-known of these cases is that of Henry, Lord Brougham (1778–1868), the famous and fiery British reformer. Brougham made just such a pact with his old college friend Geoffrey Garner, one that eventually unravelled in a manner so hilarious that it has to be true. Some years after making this agreement, Brougham

Right: ***Henry, Lord Brougham, who made a pact with a college friend that whichever of the pair died first would appear as a ghost to the other. Brougham's friend kept his word, and showed a mischievous sense of humour in doing so.***

went travelling in Sweden with a group of friends.

'Arriving at a decent inn, we decided to stop for the night,' he recalled. 'I was glad to take advantage of a hot bath before I turned in, and here a most remarkable thing happened to me – so remarkable that I must tell the story from the beginning.

'After I left the [Edinburgh] High School, I went with Garner, my most intimate friend, to attend the classes in the University...We frequently discussed and speculated upon many grave subjects – among others, on the immortality of the soul, and on a future state. This question, and the possibility, I will not say of ghosts walking, but of the dead appearing to the living, were subjects of much speculation: and we actually committed the folly of drawing up an agreement, written in our blood, to the effect that whichever of us died the first should appear to the other, and thus solve any doubts we had entertained of the "life after death".

'After we had finished our classes at the college, Garner went to India, having got an appointment there in the Civil Service. He seldom wrote to me, and after a lapse of a few years I had almost forgotten him; moreover, his family having little connection with Edinburgh, I seldom saw or heard anything, and I had nearly forgotten his existence.

'I had taken a warm bath, and while lying in it and enjoying the comfort of the heat, after the late freezing I had undergone, I turned my head round, looking toward the chair on which I had deposited my clothes, as I was about to get out of the bath. On the chair sat Garner, looking calmly at me.

'How I got out of the bath I know not, but on recovering my senses I found myself sprawling on the floor. The apparition, or whatever it was, that had taken the likeness of Garner, had disappeared.'

On his return to Edinburgh after this farcical episode, Brougham learned that Garner had died in India on 19 December, the precise date of the apparition. Many years after the event, Brougham tended to be sceptical about it:

'Singular coincidence! yet when one reflects on the vast numbers of dreams which night after night pass through our brains, the number of coincidences between the vision and the event are perhaps fewer and less remarkable than a fair calculation of chances would warrant us to expect. I believe every such seeming miracle is, like every ghost story, capable of explanation.'

Others, too, have suggested these cases are the result of 'mere' coincidence. But in their monumental collection *Phantasms of the Living*, published in 1886, the Society for Psychical Research described nine examples of an apparition following on a pact of this kind. It is surely stretching scepticism to breaking point to suggest that *all* these apparitions are purely 'coincidental' with the death of the parties concerned, especially when such a pact is involved. And even if they are, the sceptics still cannot satisfactorily explain *what* those phantasms are or where they come from.

Nevertheless, it is clear from the apparitions and spectres we have discussed in this chapter that ghost stories, however well documented and however fascinating they may be, do not make the best or most consistent evidence for life after death. That evidence comes in subtler and, often, even stranger forms.

Above: ***Borley Rectory, dubbed 'the most haunted house in England', showing the gates at which a ghostly nun was allegedly seen. The dubious nature of the investigations of the phenomena at Borley has led many to wonder since if the house was haunted at all – but the legend lingers on.***

ANOTHER TIME, ANOTHER LIFE

The ancient Celts were terrible in battle as they had no fear of death – they would even lend money on the understanding that if it were not repaid in this life, it would be in the next. What made them so sure that this was not the only life?

The idea that the soul may journey through time, using successive human bodies as vehicles for the journey and the lives of those personalities it adopts as food for its spiritual journey to perfection, is foreign to Western thought. Judaism, Christianity and Islam differ widely in their notions of the kind of afterlife that awaits us, and of heaven and hell, but their broad message is the same.

'It is appointed for men to die once,' says St Paul in his epistle to the Hebrews, 'and after that comes judgement.' If we live in an upright, tolerant and kindly fashion, we shall be rewarded in the life to come – and if we do not, we shall be punished. The fundamental belief is that this is the only life each of us has, and that this life is the only chance we have to prove ourselves morally and spiritually.

So deep is this idea ingrained in Western thought that even in the increasingly irreligious 20th century it has actually proved possible to make money by gently mocking any idea of reincarnation at all. The New York journalist Don Marquis made a small fortune from regaling an eager public with the adventures of his characters Archie, the cockroach who had formerly been a *vers libre* poet but continued to write his versified diary by jumping up and down on the keys of a typewriter, and Mehitabel, the alley cat who 'once accused herself of being Cleopatra'.

However, belief in reincarnation is widespread, ancient and powerful, and the religions of some of the world's greatest civilizations have held that reincarnation may be combined with transmigration – the entry of the soul into the body of an animal. Such beliefs were common in the West before the rise of Christianity. One reason why the ancient Celts were so devastating as warriors was that they had absolutely no fear of death – so convinced were they of the reality of reincarnation and the continuity of their consciousness. They would even lend money on the understanding that if it could not be repaid in this life, it surely would in a future one.

The torments of Hell* (above, as envisaged in a 12th-century illustration) *are one possible outcome of a single earthly lifetime granted the human soul, according to the great Western religions. Others, such as Buddhism, however, believe that the soul may journey towards its fate through many earthly lives. Whenever the Dalai Lama* (opposite) *dies, Tibetan Buddhists make a special search for the child in whom they believe the soul of their leader has been reincarnated.

Above: ***A wealthy household in ancient Athens. The Greeks, for all their famous rationalism and philosophy, believed both in a pantheon of gods notorious for uproarious behaviour, and in personal reincarnation.***

PYTHAGORAS CLAIMED TO REMEMBER HIS PREVIOUS LIVES AS A FISHERMAN, PEASANT, SHOPKEEPER'S WIFE – AND PROSTITUTE.

DEATH AND BIRTH

In ancient Greece, belief in reincarnation was not incompatible with belief in the orthodox pantheon of gods. The Orphic sect, which flourished about 100 years before the golden age of Athens, had a view of earthly life that for gloom and self-punishment matched that of the most zealous medieval Christian flagellator. The Orphics called human existence a 'sorrowful weary wheel', and the only way to escape it was to live with the utmost self-denial and asceticism. Even then, only after many physical deaths and rebirths in both animal and human form would the soul be free.

The belief in reincarnation as such in ancient Greece was not confined to such killjoy cults, however. The mathematical genius Pythagoras, who lived around 500 BC, claimed to know that in former lives he had been variously a fisherman, a peasant, a shopkeeper's wife and a (female) prostitute. Pythagoras, it is true, also held fast to many quite eccentric beliefs, including some concerning the certain fearsome consequences of eating beans.

But Plato, one of the most profoundly original minds of the ancient world, was convinced of the truth of reincarnation. He held that the soul chose its new life at the moment of death, and might enter one of nine levels of being. Plato believed that this was not an endless cycle, and the soul was neither eternal nor did it necessarily progress, or even learn, spiritually from one life to another. Progress could be made if a soul chose its next life wisely, but Plato held that in creating a new physical body for its next life, the soul expended energy. Once its energy was finally consumed, the soul itself died out.

The Roman notion of reincarnation was somewhat different; the 1st-century AD political thinker Sallust, for example, maintained that children born with handicaps were bearing punishments for evils they had committed in former lives.

The other great ancient culture that firmly believed in reincarnation was Egypt. At first, the Egyptian religions held that only 'great souls', destined to lead mankind, were born again, but this belief gradually relaxed and expanded to include everyone from the highest to the lowest social classes. By the time the *Book of the Dead* came to be compiled, matters had become distinctly formalized. The book contains incantations that would free the

Left: ***The Sphinx, with the Great Pyramid in the background. These monuments were part of the ancient Egyptians' massive and elaborate system of belief and ritual concerning the afterlife. The Egyptians believed in transmigration as well as reincarnation – the soul might return to earthly life as a plant or an animal or in human form.***

Below: ***The prophet Muhammad besieges a castle in the course of spreading his new religious vision. Islam replaced many local animistic religions in the Middle East, and gradually suppressed older beliefs in reincarnation.***

soul from its earthly prison in the tomb and prepare it for reincarnation. And it might come back as a plant – a lotus, say, or a sycamore – or as an animal; after 3000 years of such transmigrations it would be ready to be reborn as a human being once again.

RETURN OF THE GODS

Christianity gradually expunged such ideas as it spread west from the Middle East, and seven centuries later Islam suppressed them as it began to spread south and east. But in places where these religions have arrived only within the last few centuries, native faiths continue to hold fast in their belief in reincarnation.

Throughout the Pacific, for instance, reincarnation is a bulwark of most native religions. The religions of many American Indian tribes endorse reincarnation, too. It has even been suggested that one reason why the 16th-century Spanish *conquistadores* found it so easy to conquer huge tracts of South and Central America, despite the existence of highly developed civilizations there, was the prevailing local belief in reincarnation. The Spanish leaders were seen as reborn, returning gods: in Mexico as Quetzalcoatl, and in Peru as Virochas. The Spanish lost no time in taking advantage of this 'heathen' error, and laid the country waste.

In Alaska, where gold and oil rushes have had more effect on local culture than any missionaries, the indigenous Tlingit people have retained to this day a powerful reverence for reincarnation, which they

THE AZTECS BELIEVED THEIR GODS HAD BEEN REBORN – AND THIS BELIEF LED TO THEIR DOWNFALL.

regard as a direct and immediate continuity from one life to another. Tlingit women pay careful heed to their dreams when they are pregnant, for it is then, in dreams, that a previously incarnated but now disembodied soul announces its intention to them to be reborn in the body of the new baby. At birth, diviners take great care to ascertain whose soul has been reborn, and then the baby is given the tribal name of the person it had been before. The child then takes credit for the good deeds done by its predecessors – but also has a powerful moral example that it must live up to.

THE WHEEL OF REBIRTH

In India, attachment to the idea of reincarnation has never wavered since the Hindu religion took hold and, some 3000 years ago, its sacred writings began to reflect a belief in rebirth and reincarnation. In the *Bhagavad-Gita* ('The Song of Krishna'), the warrior, hero and god Krishna explains that he is the eighth incarnation of the god Vishnu, saying to Arjuna: 'Both I and thou have passed through many births. Mine are known to me, but thou knowest not of thine.' Hindus call reincarnation *samsara*, 'the wheel of rebirth'.

For Hindus, the number of reincarnations one may go through is infinite (and may include transmigration to lower forms of life, or even into rocks and stones), for the purpose of them is to give the soul the opportunity to rid itself of the imperfections that inevitably afflict it from its creation. Between each incarnation the soul enjoys a period of rest, in which it ponders on its progress towards *moksha*, the Absolute, which is also perfection and liberation – from which, paradoxically, the soul first emerged.

To rid oneself of these congenital flaws requires turning one's back on the world and realizing one's best, true nature. At the same time *karma*, the law of cause and effect, is at work: in essence this means that good is rewarded and evil is punished, and what is good or evil for the soul is judged on deeds and effects, not (as in Western religions) on intentions. Thus the *Upanishads* say quite clearly, 'Those whose conduct has been evil will have an evil birth as a dog, a pig, or an untouchable outcast.'

Earthly life is regarded as a burden, and at the same time as an illusion, called *maya*. The opportunities that this ostensibly unworldly outlook, combined with the rigid Hindu caste system, have offered for the exploitation of the poor by the rich have been plentiful, and usually avidly grasped.

Below: ***A Hindu raja celebrates the festival of Krishna with his wives. In orthodox Hindu belief, social class – caste – was related to the degree of virtue the soul had shown in a previous incarnation.***

THE SEARCH FOR THE DALAI LAMA

This observable corruption of a high ideal may have contributed to the inspiration of Siddartha Gautama, born a Brahman, the highest Hindu caste, around 566 BC. He was the heir to the crown of the Sakya clan on the Ganges in India, and is now known universally as Buddha.

The legend says that as soon as he was born Buddha vowed to end birth, old age, suffering, and death – in short, to break the endless grip of earthly life upon the soul. By the age of 29 he had realized that all were inescapable, and eventually propounded his Four Truths: that existence is suffering, and suffering is inevitable; that suffering is caused by desire; that eliminating desire will rid one of suffering; and that the right conduct – the Eightfold Path – will rid one of desire.

Central to these principles was the belief that the soul was not (as Hinduism taught) an individual and personal thing, which

Left: ***The present Dalai Lama, born in 1935. About three years later, he was recognized as the reincarnation of his predecessor.***

Below: ***A 12th-century gilt lacquer Chinese figure of Buddha. Born around 566 BC in India as Siddartha Gautama, Buddha radically questioned the Hindu attitude to reincarnation with which he had grown up, and so became the founder of a new religion.***

drove the cycle of reincarnation. Rather, reincarnation was fuelled by the ego, which was constantly changing from life to life, and was an illusion besides. Rid oneself of ego, therefore, and one would attain *nirvana* – which does not mean heaven or the absolute, but simply extinction. Buddhism thus rejects any connection between social caste and the condition of the soul, although successive rebirths are inevitable if one is to work off the burden of *karma* from previous existences. But this is a matter of purifying the life force, not redeeming the individual.

One of the most fascinating ways in which the Buddhist belief in rebirth has

Above: ***Constantine, emperor of Rome early in the 4th century* AD*. According to testimony given under hypnosis by Welsh housewife Jane Evans, she had once lived as the wife of Constantine's tutor during his residence in Britain.***

THE SIGNS WERE PLAIN TO THOSE WHO COULD READ THEM: THE CORPSE, THE STAR-SHAPED FUNGUS, AND THE DRAGON FLOWER.

practical effect is in the search for a successor to the Dalai Lama, leader of Tibet's Buddhists, when he dies.

The Dalai Lama is regarded as the incarnation of Chenrezi, the Buddhist god of grace, and he has taken earthly form 14 times since 1391. Each time the Dalai Lama (the term means 'greatest teacher') dies, the lamas of Tibet have the task of finding his reincarnated form – a male child born after the death – who will then be brought up to take on the leadership of the Tibetan Buddhist community. When the 13th Dalai Lama died in 1933, it took the monks six years to find his successor.

The search involves sifting a variety of normal and paranormal clues: the lamas scrutinize astrological signs, visions, dreams, and other omens to establish where they should start their quest. After the 13th Dalai Lama's death, the corpse itself offered one clue. It turned its head toward the north-east. Then, in the mausoleum where he was laid, a star-shaped fungus grew on the north-east wall. In the main courtyard of the monastery housing the tomb, a dragon flower unexpectedly grew by the north-east wall.

The lamas decided that it was in this direction that they should begin their search. To help them came a vision in a dream granted to one of the monastery's monks. He saw a place sacred to Buddhists – the lake at Chos Khorgyal, in China, and also a house with carved gables and eaves painted blue. Near here, the lamas concluded, they would find the child they were seeking.

In 1937 a group of lamas and monks set off for China to find the house. Two years later, at the village of Takster, they found it. One of the high lamas in the party disguised himself as a servant and went into the house. He found inside a two-year-old boy, Tenzin Gyatso, who instantly demanded the rosary that, beneath his disguise, the lama was wearing around his neck. This was not the lama's – but it had belonged to the Dalai Lama. Tenzin Gyatso then identified – or recognized – other rosaries, a drum and a walking-stick that had also belonged to the former Dalai Lama.

Encouraged by these initial signs, the lamas went on to look for physical confirmation that the boy was the current embodiment of Chenrezi. The various bodily characteristics, moles and birth-marks found on every Dalai Lama were indeed in place, and the lamas set about making arrangements for the boy and his family to travel to Tibet. Among these was paying a $300,000 ransom to the provincial governor for allowing Tenzin Gyatso to leave China, but eventually the infant Dalai Lama was installed in the Potala Palace above Lhasa to begin his long and arduous training to become the spiritual and temporal leader of the Tibetan nation.

The alleged reincarnation of the Tibetan Dalai Lama is not, in itself, proof of the reality of repeated rebirth. Without casting doubt on the sincerity of those involved, one could if one wanted pick holes in a number of aspects even in this one case. And the key to the matter, here, is profound religious belief; driven by that, a sceptic would assert, the law of averages says that sooner or later the lamas are bound to find a suitable child to proclaim as their reincarnated leader.

On the other hand, there are many cases from the West, where there is no established traditional belief in reincarnation or rebirth, of people who to their own surprise have discovered that they have apparently lived more than one life on Earth.

THE SECRET MEMORY

The evidence for these claims has been gathered exclusively from hypnotic regression – that is, from subjects who have been hypnotized and then led back into the past to recall what they can of any former lives. Unfortunately, the most plausible of these – notably the alleged reincarnation of the Irish woman Bridey Murphy (1798–1864, according to the account given under hypnosis) as Wisconsin housewife Virginia Tighe (born in 1923), and the various lives recounted by Welsh housewife Jane Evans – have fallen apart in the light of detailed research.

Of these, the claims of Jane Evans were the most transparent. Once researcher Melvin Harris had burrowed into them, they looked more like a highly aerated Swiss cheese than evidence for reincarnation.

Jane Evans produced an astonishing wealth of detail about (for instance) life as the wife of the tutor to the young Constantine (later to be Emperor of Rome) in 4th-century Britain, or as a young Jewess caught up in the massacre of the Jews in York in 1190. This latter account in fact contained a wealth of thoroughly *inaccurate* information both about York and about the Jews of the 12th century, and most of it seems to have come from a play broadcast on BBC radio.

Jane Evans's life as 'Livonia' in 4th-century Roman Britain was taken almost word for word from a novel called *The Living Wood* by Louis de Wohl. It seems that Jane Evans had, quite honestly, forgotten that she had ever read any of the books on which her 'former lives' were based, but retrieved her memories of them from her subconscious while in a hypnotic trance. This phenomenon, known as cryptomnesia (from the Greek for 'secret memory') is familiar to hypnotherapists, and has indeed proved useful in digging out facts – often traumatic – about their subjects' early lives that they have often deliberately forgotten.

Another detailed recall of an actual historical event was provided by a subject known only as 'Jan' when she was put into trance by hypnotist Joe Keeton. Jan became 18-year-old Joan Waterhouse who, she said, was tried for witchcraft at Chelmsford Assizes, Essex, in 1556. All the details were proven to be historically correct – including the existence of Joan Waterhouse and her presence in the dock. The only original source for Jan's – or Joan's – account that survived in the 20th century was a contemporary pamphlet, and the only surviving copy was in the library of the Archbishop of Canterbury's London residence, Lambeth Palace. Jan swore that she had never been there and had never seen the document.

THE WOMAN BECAME AN 18-YEAR-OLD GIRL WHO HAD BEEN TRIED FOR WITCHCRAFT OVER 400 YEARS AGO.

Above: ***Lambeth Palace, London residence of the archbishops of Canterbury. Here was the only known copy of an account of a 16th-century witch trial held in Cheltenham, Essex. Its details were reproduced with uncanny – but crucially flawed – accuracy by a subject of hypnotic regression who claimed to be the reincarnation of one of the accused.***

But there was one bizarre anomaly. As Joan, Jan insisted that she had been tried in the reign of Queen Elizabeth I. Unfortunately, the English monarch in 1556 was Queen Mary I; Elizabeth did not accede to the throne until 1558. Given the ferment in religious life at the time, the supreme importance of the monarch in deciding and directing what religious practices were acceptable, and the sensitivity to such matters of people at the local level and their readiness to act in their own obsessive interests, this seems an extraordinary confusion.

And, indeed, there was an extraordinary

confusion – in the mind of Joe Keeton and his subject 'Jan' – about what constitutes proper research. For the Lambeth Palace pamphlet had been reprinted during the 19th century, its solid black-letter type substituted by a fair attempt to reproduce a more legible typeface and design of Shakespeare's time. But there was one crucial error. The 19th-century printer had set the date of the Chelmsford witchcraft trial as 1556 – the date insisted upon by Jan and Joan. But the original plainly reads *1566* – by which time Queen Elizabeth had been on the throne for eight somewhat tempestuous years.

The only logical conclusion is that Jan had not, as she and Joe Keeton thought, once existed as Joan Waterhouse, accused of witchcraft, but had read, absorbed and – to be charitable – forgotten the reprint of the 16th-century trials at Chelmsford. But Keeton did not do this fundamental piece of research: a sceptic had to do it, and so debunk the case.

Perhaps the final word on hypnosis and progressive reincarnation should go to a travel courier who, in the late 1980s, was accompanying a group of middle-aged American ladies on the Nile steamer from Port Said to Luxor. In the middle of a conversation about the politics of the Middle East, she said to this author: 'You think you got problems? I've got *nine Cleopatras* on this tour with me. You try keeping *them* from fighting.'

THE CAUTIOUS PROFESSOR BELIEVED THE CASES WERE 'SUGGESTIVE OF REINCARNATION'.

Right: ***An engraving from Zucchero's portrait of Queen Elizabeth I of England. The date of her accession to the throne, 1558, was the key to revealing the alleged reincarnation of the Cheltenham witch Joan Waterhouse.***

A MATTER OF FAITH

Is there, then, any real evidence for reincarnation?

Actually, and sadly for those of us who would like to have another crack at life in the hope that we might not make the same terrible mistakes again, the answer is most likely a resounding 'No'.

Some of the most apparently convincing evidence for reincarnation has come from the researches of Dr Ian Stevenson, professor of psychology at the University of Virginia. Dr Stevenson has travelled the world, conducted innumerable in-depth interviews, and assiduously researched and reported a huge collection of cases that are, in his cautious words, 'suggestive of reincarnation'.

The British historian Ian Wilson has noted a number of problematic inconsistencies in Stevenson's evidence, and has also pointed out two particular but telling consistencies.

First, Stevenson has had to rely, on his extensive travels, on interpreters who generally already shared a belief in reincarnation with those he was interviewing. In some cultures people will tend to tell foreign visitors what they *think* the stranger wants to hear rather than the precise truth as they know it.

Second, Wilson has completed a careful analysis of the social backgrounds of the children claiming to have been reincarnated and compared them with the families of the people they allegedly once were. In an astonishing preponderance of cases, the family that the 'reincarnated' child has claimed to belong to has been of higher social status – from anything to an artisan (as opposed to a peasant) to a millionaire (as opposed to – a peasant). In a society in which belief in reincarnation is basic, and that is also circumscribed by a class system that is deeply underwritten by religious orthodoxy, any evidence that offers escape from certain wretched individual circumstances will surely be grasped at the earliest opportunity. Wilson does not say so directly, but it is not difficult to suspect from his evidence that the families involved in the claims Dr Stevenson has investigated have perhaps coached the children in question.

The truth or otherwise of reincarnation, then, has to remain, for the time being at least, a matter of faith. This does not mean that reincarnation does not occur – perhaps only for some people and not for others – but it does mean that there is no conclusive evidence for it at the moment.

It is still an attractive idea. And it remains a bulwark of many ancient and respected cultures around the world.

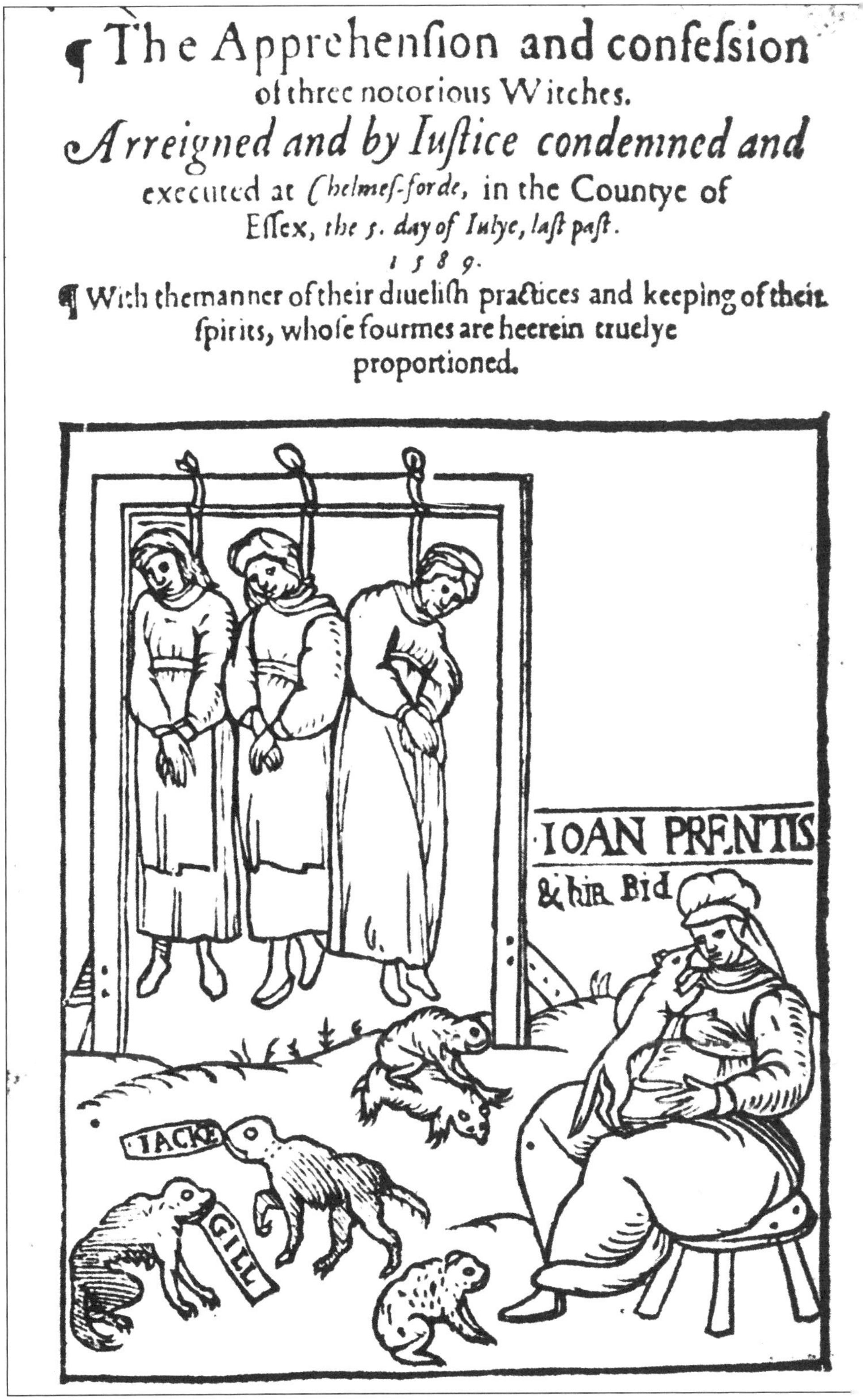

Above: *Account of the execution of three witches at Chelmsford, Essex, in 1589. Under hypnosis, Joan Waterhouse appeared to recall being tried there for witchcraft some years earlier – but there was a significant anomaly regarding the date.*

THE MOVING HAND

The lady was ashamed of what had happened in the second-class compartment of the express train, and had intended to tell no one about her unpleasant experience. The famous journalist uncovered her guilty secret in a most unexpected manner...

Opposite: ***Journalist William T. Stead, who had the ability to communicate telepathically with one of his female acquaintances by means of automatic writing.***

Author Alex Haley **(left)** ***discovered when helping Malcolm X*** **(below)** ***to write his autobiography that the Black Muslim leader habitually committed his unconscious thoughts to paper. His conscious, spoken thoughts at the same time might concern something quite different – or even contradict what he was writing.***

The great 19th-century British journalist William T. Stead, the founder of the *Review of Reviews*, was also a spiritualist. Appropriately enough for a professional writer, he was also an adept at automatic writing – which he used as a vehicle for telepathic communication with a certain lady friend. As proof of its efficacy, he recounted the following incident:

'[My friend] was to lunch with me on the Wednesday if she had returned to town. On the Monday afternoon I wished to know about this, so taking up my pen I asked the lady mentally if she had returned home. My hand wrote as follows:

'"I am sorry to say that I have had the most unpleasant experience, which I am almost ashamed to tell you. I left Haslemere at 2.27 pm in a second-class compartment in which there were two women and a man. At Godalming the women got out and I was left alone with the man.

'"He came over and sat by me. I was alarmed and pushed him away. He would not move, however, and tried to kiss me. I was furious and there was a struggle, during which I seized his umbrella and struck him with it repeatedly, but it broke, and I was afraid I would get the worst of it, when the train stopped some distance from Guildford. The man took fright, left me before the train reached the station, jumped out and took to his heels. I was extremely agitated, but I kept the umbrella."'

Stead immediately wrote to his friend to commiserate, and explained how he had come by the information. He also asked her to call on him, and bring the broken umbrella with her. She wrote back, slightly disturbed that she had, apparently unconsciously, communicated the details of this event to him: she had intended not to mention it to anyone. She added that there was one incorrect detail in the account his automatic writing had produced – the umbrella had been her own, not her assailant's.

THE HAND THAT BETRAYS

This is an unusual case of communication by automatic writing, if not indeed a unique one, in that the person generating the message was alive at the time. Communication by automatic writing is usually thought of as the preserve of the dead.

In itself, automatic writing is not paranormal. Alex Haley, who assisted with the autobiography of the Black Muslim and political activist, Malcolm X, noted very early in their collaboration that 'while Malcolm X was talking, he often simultaneously scribbled with his red-ink ballpoint pen on any handy paper...I began leaving two white paper napkins by him every time I served him more coffee [which he drank in enormous quantities], and the ruse worked...'

Haley admitted that the projected autobiography 'got off to a very poor start', but by reading Malcolm X's scribblings (which, Haley said, 'documented how he could be talking about one thing and thinking of something else'), he was able to latch on to Malcolm X's real interests at the time, and steer their discussions so that the Black Muslim leader finally abandoned his reserve. Through these scraps of automatic writing, too, Haley was able to tell Malcolm X's true reactions to current events in his life – which were often quite different from what he would be saying publicly and to Haley. When he was officially silenced by the leader of the Black Muslims, for instance, he wrote: 'I was going downhill until he picked me up, but the more I think of it, we picked each other up.' Before he was assassinated, Malcolm X had set up his own rival mosque and militant black political organization.

The example of Malcolm X demonstrates clearly what Dr Brian Inglis has remarked – that automatic writing is 'the outcome of a different level of consciousness' rather than anything intrinsically paranormal. But that level of consciousness has often proven to be one that is sensitive to paranormal information: whether it is received from other people through extra-sensory perception or whether it 'tunes in' to entities on a quite different level of being – for instance, those who have died.

DEAD CERTAINTIES

In *The Paranormal*, Dr Inglis cites two fascinating examples of automatic writing that seem to have come from dead people and that produced information that no one living could have known by any normal means.

Sir Edward Marshall Hall (1858–1927), reckoned the premier English barrister of his day, was staying with his sister; among the guests was her friend Miss K. Wingfield, who was an adept in automatic

Below: ***Sir Edward Marshall Hall, who received news of his brother's death through automatic writing, three weeks before official notification of his loss reached him.***

writing. When she agreed to give a demonstration of her gift, Hall took a letter that he had had from South Africa the previous day, sealed it in a fresh envelope, handed it to Miss Wingfield and asked her where it came from.

The immediate response was: 'The writer of that letter is dead.' After further questions the automatic writing answered the original question: the letter had come from South Africa. What Sir Edward had not told anyone present (not even his sister) was that it had in fact come from his brother, and had been posted three weeks previously. Three weeks after his visit to his sister's house, Sir Edward received another letter from South Africa – telling him that his brother was dead. He had died in his bed the day before the session with Miss Wingfield.

The English healer Matthew Manning found that, when he was a teenager, automatic writing helped divert whatever psychic energy was wreaking havoc in his parents' home through poltergeist attacks. On one occasion the Manning family decided to get in touch with the spirit of Manning's great-grandfather, Hayward Collins, who had been a racehorse owner. They asked if he could give them the winners at a race meeting scheduled for the following day. None of the family had read what horses were running then, and deliberately did not do so until the end of the next day's racing. They found that great-grandfather Collins – or his shade – had correctly 'named six horses, which turned out to be runners: two came in first, one second, and two third, which would have netted a good each-way profit, had money been put on them'.

Collins, later, also gave this message through automatic writing: 'Put your money on Red Rum which will come in first, and on Crisp which will come in second. The third will be a tight spot so leave well alone.' Red Rum won the race. Crisp was second. The third place, a photo-finish, was won by a short nose.

THE GLASTONBURY QUEST

One of the most dramatic indications that automatic writing may genuinely come from entities in the world hereafter resulted in the uncovering of Glastonbury Abbey. In the process, the career of the archeologist concerned was ruined.

From 1191 onward Glastonbury Abbey flourished, as pilgrims flocked to the site of King Arthur's tomb, which was – so the monks said – discovered that year. The Abbey had a long history: it had been founded early in the 5th century by St Patrick before his mission to Ireland, which began in AD 432. In 1539, however, the powers behind the English Reformation cast their eyes on Glastonbury. King Henry VIII's commissioners executed the abbot, Richard Whyting, confiscated the Abbey's lands and wealth, and wrecked the building. Over the next four centuries its stones sank from sight under the encroaching loam and a tangle of weeds.

In 1907 the Abbey ruins were bought by the Church of England. By then the neglected, overgrown site had become an enigma. The Church appointed 43-year-old archeologist and architect Frederick Bligh Bond to excavate it. Bond was recognized as one of the leading English experts on Gothic architecture and a past master at restoring medieval buildings. Unknown to his new employers, he was also a devotee of psychic studies.

Bond's brief included the task of locating two chapels whose whereabouts

Above: ***Red Rum, named as a sure-fire winner in a race described through automatic writing by the shade of an English healer's long-dead great-grandfather.***

'THE WRITER OF THAT LETTER IS DEAD.'

The presence of the alleged grave of King Arthur at Glastonbury Abbey, Somerset **(above)**, *and the legend that Joseph of Arimathea had brought there the Holy Grail, the drinking vessel* **(right)** *used at the Last Supper of Jesus of Nazareth with his disciples* **(below right)** *made the Abbey a prime site for archeological investigation.*

were by that time a complete mystery. They were the Loretto and the Edgar chapels, built by Richard Bere, the last abbot but one at Glastonbury. Bere had also revived and promoted the legend that Joseph of Arimathea, the uncle of Jesus of Nazareth, had visited Glastonbury twice – first with Jesus when he was a child, and later, after the crucifixion, bearing the Holy Grail – the vessel from which the disciples had drunk at the Last Supper.

Bond was faced with a big problem: he

had insufficient funds for a full-scale dig, and breathing down his neck was a rival architect, officially appointed to preserve the ruins Bond found but in reality deeply interested in finding them, and taking credit for the fact, before him. Bond decided to undertake what he politely called a 'psychological experiment' to aid him in a job whose success otherwise depended on guesswork. The experiment was, in fact, a direct appeal to the spirit world through automatic writing.

DISTINCTIVE HANDWRITING

In the afternoon of 7 November 1907, Bond and his friend John Alleyne Bartlett sat down at a plain wooden table in Bond's Bristol office. They were about to make their first attempt to communicate with the dead.

Bartlett had had considerable experience with automatic writing. He held a pencil lightly over a sheet of blank paper, while Bond rested his fingers lightly on Bartlett's other hand. After a false start, the pencil traced an outline that Bond recognized as the plan of Glastonbury Abbey. Then, curiously, it added a rectangle at the eastern end, beyond the high altar. Asked for more detail, the pencil – or whatever entity was behind it – confirmed that this building was the Edgar chapel. It had been built, the writing continued, by Abbot Bere; Abbot Whyting had made additions to it. The pencil also traced another chapel to the north of the main Abbey building.

Asked who was writing, the entity replied: 'Johnannes Bryant, monk and lapidator' (i.e. monk and stonemason). Four days later, they learned that he had died in 1533, and had been curator of the chapel during the reign of Henry VII, and that the monks were 'very eager' to communicate. Further sessions of automatic writing with Bartlett over the following months produced a mass of information about the original Abbey buildings. It all came ostensibly from a number of long-dead monks, each of whom had his own distinctive handwriting, faithfully reproduced by Bartlett's pencil.

When Bond finally started work at Glastonbury in May 1909, he was faced with a dilemma: either he could follow the information he had acquired through psychic means, or he could take the view that he and Bartlett had invented it all, and depend on his own luck and guesswork. But in a sense Bond had no choice: the leads provided by the 'dead monks' were as good as any intelligent guess he could make, and they might be just what they appeared to be. He staked his reputation on the monks, and started digging according to their advice.

THE COMPANY OF AVALON

Bond's workmen duly dug trenches at the east end of the visible ruins and discovered

TENSE WITH ANTICIPATION, THEY MADE THEIR FIRST ATTEMPT TO COMMUNICATE WITH THE LONG-DEAD MONKS OF GLASTONBURY ABBEY.

Below: ***Monks at Mass, in a 15th-century illustration.***

By the mid-19th century, Glastonbury Abbey **(above)** *was fast disappearing beneath weeds and loam.*

OUTSIDE THE WALLS OF THE ABBEY CHURCH A GIANT WAS BURIED; BETWEEN HIS LEGS LAY A HUMAN SKULL.

a huge wall, more than 30 ft long, whose existence no one had suspected. Further digging revealed the whole of what could only have been the remains of the lost Edgar Chapel, precisely where the monks – who were now calling themselves 'the Company of Avalon' and 'the watchers from the other side' – had said it was.

Bond found time and again that the monks' automatic writing was absolutely reliable. For example, they told him that the chapel roof had been painted in gold and crimson, and Bond's workers dug up arch mouldings with the red and gold paint still intact on them. The monks said the chapel windows were stained azure, and Bond found fragments of blue stained glass among the ruins – to his own surprise, since most glass of the period was stained white or gold. Still more unusual was the monks' claim that at the east end of the chapel was a door leading to the street. Most churches simply don't have doors behind the altar, but the Edgar Chapel, it turned out, did indeed. The monks even told Bond the precise dimensions of the chapel, although he was sceptical when he first read them, for they seemed enormous. But they were correct.

The 'Company of Avalon' produced a mass of other information that explained finds at the Abbey; but Bond could not reveal what he was sure were the facts without revealing his sources. One of the more mysterious finds, as far as conventionally available knowledge went, was the skeleton of a 7 ft tall man found buried – without a coffin – just outside the walls of the Abbey church on the south side of the nave. Stranger still, between the giant's legs was another human skull.

According to the Company of Avalon, the skeleton had belonged to a monk named Radulphus. He had come to England in 1087, after the Norman invasion led by William the Conqueror. William had installed a Norman abbot, named Thurstan, at Glastonbury. Radulphus had been Thurstan's treasurer. Before the giant monk died at the extreme old age of 103, he had asked to be buried as

Right: *The ruins of the Abbey today, neatly exposed – thanks, largely, to messages given to the archeologist Frederick Bligh Bond through automatic writing.*

near as possible to the church he loved. But what about the extra skull?

A curious tale attached to this, the shades of the monks informed Bond. Abbot Thurstan and his Norman monks were notoriously cruel to the Saxon monks who had had charge of Glastonbury before their arrival, and at one point incited, or engineered, the slaughter of a number of the Saxons by Norman soldiers. A local earl, Eawulf of Edgarley, had led a reprisal attack against the Normans. In the battle he came up against Radulphus – whom he managed to wound severely with his axe – and then Radulphus slew him. He was buried in the Abbey grounds. When, decades later, the brothers were digging Radulphus's grave, they came upon Eawulf's bones. By chance he been buried at the same spot that was chosen for Radulphus. The former enemies had been joined in death, their bones mingling in the same plain grave.

Bond spent months poring over old manuscripts to uncover some surviving documentary evidence of what the 'watchers' had told him through automatic writing. There was no known record of Eawulf; no scholar of the period had heard of him. But at the end of this odyssey through the crumbling chronicles of Saxon and Norman England, Bond had established that there had indeed been an earldom of Edgarley in Somerset in the ninth century at least; the obvious inference – at least it was Bond's – was that this was an ancestor of the Eawulf whose story had been told him by the dead monks of Glastonbury.

A DOOMED MAN

For more than 10 years Bond kept secret the source of his seemingly – and, in fact – uncanny ability to unearth the most surprising new facts about the Glastonbury site. His discretion was not the result of any lack of faith in what he and Bartlett had been told – the times his scepticism had been confounded were too many for that. The problem was the Church of England, which had always been hostile to spiritualism. Bond, already surrounded by jealous colleagues and suffering from a reputation for a dictatorial, even cranky, style of managing the Glastonbury project, would be bound to suffer if he described his experiments with automatic writing – no matter how fruitful they had proved.

In the end, the strain of remaining silent grew too great, and he decided, fatefully, to go public with the truth. In 1918 he published *The Gate of Remembrance*, which detailed the whole saga of his communications with the 'watchers' through automatic writing since 1908. As soon as it went on sale, Bond was a doomed man as far as his professional life was concerned.

The budget for the Glastonbury dig was slashed. Bond was saddled with an unsympathetic co-director, whose job was, plainly enough, to keep him in line. A monstrous Church bureaucracy suddenly took a singularly obstructive interest in his work at Glastonbury. Toward the end of his direct association with the Abbey he was demoted to cataloguing his finds for a miserly stipend of £10 a month. In 1922 he received a letter that, in the scrupulously

Above: ***The restored Galilee – the porch outside the main, west door – at Glastonbury today.***

THE GLASTONBURY EVIDENCE FOR LIFE AFTER DEATH IS PROBABLY AS GOOD AS ANY WE WILL EVER HAVE – UNTIL WE DIE.

polite but utterly chilling language of officialdom, summarily fired him from even that lowly position. His career, all too literally, was now in ruins. Even the most scholarly of his books were banned from sale within the Abbey precincts. Bond spent much of the rest of his life in the USA, pursuing psychical research rather than archeology. He died alone, impoverished and embittered, in 1945.

Do Bond's and Barrett's ventures into automatic writing constitute reasonable proof of survival of death? That is certainly what they seem to offer, but one of the many ironies in the way the Establishment treated Bond lies in the sobering fact that he himself came to believe that they did not. Bond himself maintained that he and Barrett had gained access not to the words of the dead but to a storehouse of buried – perhaps racial – memory. This was something akin to psychologist Carl J. Jung's notion of the 'collective unconscious', but one specific to England and the English and their peculiar myths and traditions. The gateway of remembrance was his own intuition, released to run free through the discipline and concentration of preparing for his experiments in automatic writing. The power of intuition, he wrote, 'from the depths of the subconscious mind...has evoked these images'.

Such an argument is appealing, but its attraction may be somewhat specious. Because 'intuition' is familiar to us all, and because so many of Jung's ideas have acquired a kind of veneer of truth because they have been successful in treating people in psychotherapy, many people feel more comfortable with this form of words as they seem to describe the inexplicable rather than proof of survival of death. In a rigidly secular age, it may even be that most people do not *wish* to survive after the death of their physical bodies: perhaps their worst fears will come true. Perhaps, even, they fear that they could not cope with their deepest yearnings coming true, either. But to argue that 'intuition' is a better explanation than straightforward communication with the dead, for what Bond and Barrett discovered, is merely to substitute one unknown for another.

Sometimes things really are as simple as they seem. The evidence from the 'Glastonbury scripts' for life after death is probably as good as any we will ever have. That is, until we die.

Below: ***Henry VIII of England, with his second wife, Anne Boleyn, whom he had executed in 1536. In 1921, an Anglican canon began a long and strange correspondence with Anne Boleyn through automatic writing.***

RULING PASSION

Frederick Bligh Bond, curiously enough, was instrumental in a case of apparent communication with the dead that, in contrast, throws up almost every question possible about the nature of psychic communications with the hereafter – ones that do not, however, seem relevant in his own involvement with the former tenants of Glastonbury Abbey.

In 1963, three years after the author's death at the age of 92, an intriguing book titled *A Tudor Story* by an Anglican clergyman, a canon of Peterborough Cathedral named William Packenham-Walsh, was published. It was in essence the record of one man's obsession with a woman who had died 332 years before he was born: in short, Packenham-Walsh's passion for Anne Boleyn, the second wife of King Henry VIII of England, born in 1507 and executed, after Henry had successfully pressed rather dubious charges of high treason, which included claims of adultery with her own brother, who was executed with her, on 15 May 1536.

Packenham-Walsh's interest in Anne Boleyn had first been aroused when, as a missionary in China, he read a biography of the dead queen in 1917. By the time he returned to England, the cause of Anne Boleyn – 'a queen who has been much misunderstood' – had become a ruling passion in his life. In August 1921 he instigated the first of many sittings with mediums that supposedly put him indirectly in touch with the dead queen – and with her husband, who was as temperamental in death, it seems, as he ever was in real life.

This first session, with a medium called Mrs Clegg, did not involve automatic writing, but it did produce a wealth of information, unknown to the canon until his own researches confirmed it, about Anne Boleyn. For the disinterested observer it also raised the most fundamental questions about the nature of Mrs Clegg's mediumship. This is not to imply that she was in any way a fraud or a charlatan, but to question whether she herself understood the real nature of her gift (a problem we shall meet again in discussing other mediums and their alleged communications with the dead). There are two reasons for waving this flag of warning.

In the first place, during the sitting, Packenham-Walsh was unable to restrain himself from telling Mrs Clegg the reason for his visit: she soon learned who her visiting 'spirit' was supposed to be, so breaking a cardinal rule of objective psychical research. In the second place (at a later sitting), the purported Anne Boleyn made a curious prediction. The canon, she said, would be 'offered a parish with the snowdrops' and would 'go to it with the daffodils'. Not long after this Packenham-Walsh was offered the living of Sulgrave, Northamptonshire. When he first visited the parish it was covered with snowdrops. When he took up residence there, daffodils were everywhere. The vicarage gardener, according to Packenham-Walsh, said he had never seen anything like it in 40 years' service in his craft.

Even assuming that Packenham-Walsh's account is accurate and uncoloured by his deep desire to prove his particular point, and presuming a great deal of other things as well, there is no particular reason to infer from all this that Mrs Clegg actually was in contact with the shade of Anne Boleyn. She knew of Packenham-Walsh's interest and it seems much more likely that she was picking up information about the dead queen from Packenham-Walsh's own mind, and was dramatizing it as the word of the dead, than that she was in direct contact with Anne Boleyn herself. This is if anything borne out by the prediction that came true. Mrs Clegg was probably clairvoyant in a wide degree, but her understanding of her gifts had to be translated in terms of her spiritualist beliefs in survival after death. So, she was bound to present – just as Packenham-Walsh, for his own reasons, was bound to accept – her precognition of the canon's future through the secondary medium of Anne Boleyn's allegedly discarnate soul.

Above: ***A modern Italian medium, Anita, at work. Although normally right-handed, she uses her left hand to receive messages.***

SIMPLE DECEPTION

Frederick Bligh Bond became involved in Packenham-Walsh's psychical researches into Anne Boleyn because another medium, a Miss Eleanor Kelly, had received messages through automatic writing mentioning both himself and Bond. In due course, Bond introduced

WAS THE MEDIUM GUILTY OF DECEPTION?

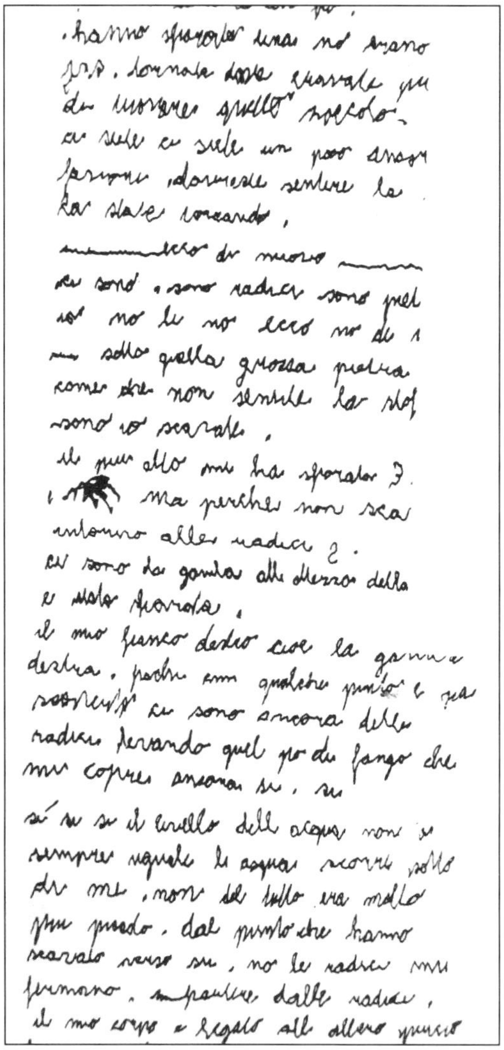

Right and below: *Samples of writing apparently from the spirit world. That at right is automatic writing from the Italian medium Anita. That below appears to be written in blood, and materialized during a seance with a trance medium in Naples. The writer claims to be Prince Raimondo de Sangro de Sansevero, a 17th-century alchemist and freemason.*

Packenham-Walsh to Miss Kelly, and they began sittings together.

Here, the case takes – temporarily – a more plausible turn. Before meeting Packenham-Walsh, Miss Kelly had received messages through automatic writing concerning Anne Boleyn and Henry VIII, indicating their emotional states in the afterlife. Whether she knew of Packenham-Walsh's interest in Henry's second queen – in other words, whether she was guilty of drawing Packenham-Walsh to her through simple deception – Packenham-Walsh himself does not, of course, say. But the world of psychics is a small one, now as then. News, which cynics would call news of opportunities, travels fast.

On the other hand, if Miss Kelly's interest was genuine and disinterestedly concerned, and if these communications were equally genuine, it remains as likely that clairvoyance was responsible for the initial messages as for the later ones received in sittings with the canon. For nothing in the later messages revealed anything that Packenham-Walsh himself may not have concluded from his by then encyclopedic reading on the subject of the Tudor king and his tragically misused and betrayed second wife.

The basic matter of these sittings boiled down to the apparent fact that Henry was still locked in his ego – 'stuck', as modern psychobabble has it – and was busy either justifying his earthly actions or roundly abusing his 20th-century interlocutors. Anne Boleyn, not surprisingly, approved the canon's record of these proceedings as 'one of the ladders...by which many may climb to true knowledge'. By June 1924 – this time with two other and different mediums – King Henry was wanting it known that he had repented of his misdeeds. Few things can have been more musical to the ears of William Packenham-Walsh, but even by his own account few desires can have been less secret than his to rescue Anne Boleyn's reputation or to know that Henry had admitted how dreadfully he had used her.

Automatic writing, as such, then, is as ambiguous as any other means of communication in establishing the reality of life after death. But the experience of Frederick Bligh Bond remains to tantalize us with its implication that sometimes, somehow, we really can get in touch with those who have died – but who live on elsewhere.

GIFTS FROM THE OTHER SIDE

Previous page: *Guardian angels, as depicted by the Victorian artist Frederick Goodall. Spiritualists regard their 'spirit controls' as a species of guardian angel, who mediate their contacts with those 'on the other side'.*

The investigator had checked for any sign of trickery and was convinced that the spiritualist was concealing nothing. Then, as he watched in astonishment, a fresh carnation materialized and began to fall from the medium's lips...

The late Anita Gregory was a distinguished scholar, a stalwart of the Society for Psychical Research in Britain, and by no means gullible when it came to paranormal matters – she spent considerable energy on showing how weak she believed the evidence was that anything truly strange had happened in the famous Enfield poltergeist case, for example. But at a seance held by medium Paul McElhoney in London in the early 1980s, Mrs Gregory was astonished and baffled when a small, metal model of Cologne cathedral landed in the palm of her hand 'from nowhere'.

McElhoney's spirit control, which called itself Ceros, explained through McElhoney that the model was a gift to Mrs Gregory from her dead father. At the time, this made little sense to her. Only later did she discover that her father and mother had spent their honeymoon in a hotel that looked out onto Cologne cathedral.

Paul McElhoney was a relatively rare phenomenon himself for the late 20th century: a spiritualist medium who produced physical phenomena. His peculiar talent was to produce objects, as Mrs Gregory so plainly put it, apparently 'from nowhere' – otherwise known as apports. His specialty was to bring forth flowers, often from his mouth; however he managed this feat, there was no doubt among the witnesses that they were all fresh. Unlike many other mediums, McElhoney would do this as often in good light as in the more traditional – and for sceptics, more suspicious – circumstances of a darkened seance room.

In November 1981, Michael Cleary reported in *Psychic News* how – though a believing spiritualist – he had carefully searched both Paul McElhoney's person and his seance room for any sign of trickery before 'Ceros' had come through and entranced the medium.

Cleary noted: 'When Ceros brought the first flowers, the lights were on. I looked into Paul's mouth. There was nothing there. Then a flower began to fall from his mouth. Carnations are very significant in my family. I had previously asked my mother in the spirit world to bring that kind of flower. When Ceros apported a carnation for me he said it was a present from a woman in the spirit world.'

SPIRIT GUIDES

It is a paradox of spiritualism that apports of material objects are regarded as proof of an immaterial life after death – immaterial, at least, as we understand the term. Mediums who produce such objects, and who create a wide variety of other physical effects during seances, are called, plainly and unsurprisingly enough, 'physical' mediums.

Below: *One of the most basic effects witnessed at seances in the 19th century and even today – the levitation of a table.*

Victorian seances were essentially middle-class affairs, and provided an acceptable forum for men and women to meet and, to some extent, shed their inhibitions. Mediums might be from any social class; some used their talents as a convenient means to rise in society. Floating furniture (left) *and musical instruments, which sometimes played spontaneously* (below), *were the least those attending expected to witness.*

The hey-day of the physical medium was the 19th century; spiritualism actually had its beginnings in the late 1840s in the most basic of physical-cum-spiritual phenomena – paranormal rappings that gave every sign of being intelligently controlled by someone, or something, that had survived death. Over the next two decades, mediums developed the ability to create an extraordinary repertoire of physical effects with the aid of spirits. (Mediums themselves would say, of course, that the spirits did this, and that they were indeed no more than the media through which these phenomena were produced.)

An outside observer would say that individual physical mediums tended to specialize in particular effects. A sceptic would say that that is because it is easier and better to perfect one kind of conjuring trick than to take on a number and suffer indifferent results. Mediums would reject both those ways of describing what happens, preferring to account for the difference between one and another medium's phenomena as the result of the predilections of their spirit guide, and as a matter outside their own personal control.

No medium claims to get directly in contact with a spirit on the 'other side'. It has become a convention, almost, among mediums, to have a 'guide' or 'control' – itself the spirit of a dead person but one seemingly more advanced than others – with whom they initially make contact, and who in turn mediates between the medium

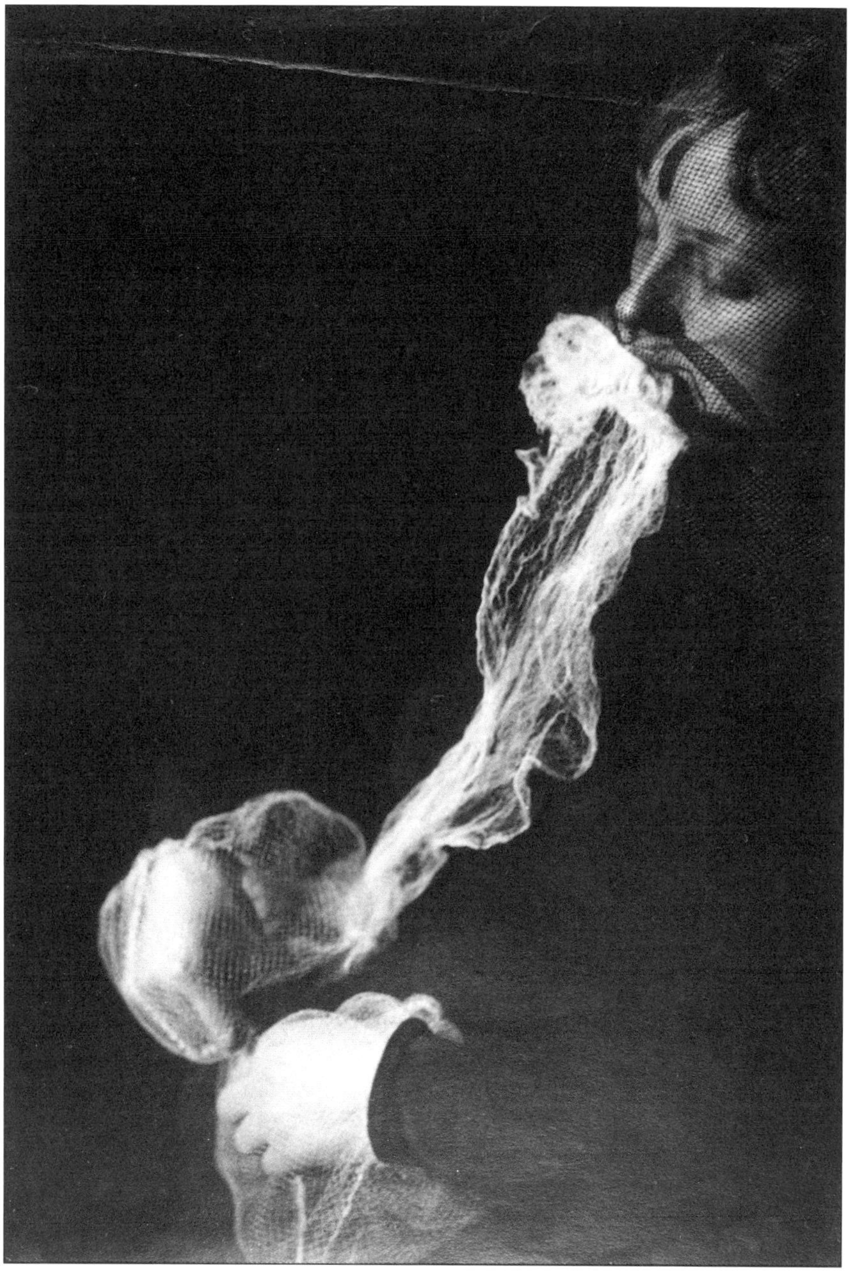

Above: *Ectoplasm pours from a medium's mouth. According to one unimpeachable source, its characteristic smell was of body odour.*

Right: *Ectoplasm produced by medium Stanislava P. during an experiment in the 1920s conducted by Baron von Schrenck-Notzing. The baron stitched the medium into a 'fraud-proof' coat to prevent any sleight of hand.*

and the rest of the world of spirit. No one seems to have addressed the question of why this should be so (perhaps everyone has such a 'guardian angel' from the afterlife, but only mediums have the good fortune to be able to communicate with theirs). But mediums find that that is the way things are, and seem to have no difficulty in accepting it. Nor do they seem to balk at the remarkable number of American Indian medicine men or Zulus who seem to figure among spirit guides. That is the way things are. And if one wants to argue about the truth or falsehood of mediums, these are details; there are better and larger grounds for dealing with the truth of their claims.

'THE STUFF OF THE UNIVERSE'

Some mediums hear the voices of the dead; some communicate through automatic writing; some receive in the mind's eye photographic visions of pertinent material; and some produce physical phenomena which, they or the spirits believe, offer a concrete proof that spiritual life continues after physical death. The very fact that such phenomena are outside the bounds of normal physical possibility is deemed to be proof that only the spirits could have produced them.

Physical mediums have demonstrated an enormous range of such phenomena to prove their point. Among the effects that staid and reliable witnesses have reported are paranormal and apparently intelligently produced raps, as mentioned before; table tilting; disembodied voices speaking through 'trumpets' (essentially no more than paper or cardboard megaphones), or directly through the mediums themselves (a phenomenon closely related to modern 'channelling'); levitations of any number of objects from pieces of paper through pieces of furniture to the persons of those present at seances, witnesses as well as the mediums themselves; elongation of the medium's body; materializing detached and

disembodied limbs; playing musical instruments that were well outside the reach of either medium or witnesses; and, most frequently of all in the 19th century, the production of that mysterious substance ectoplasm, which has been claimed to be the formative 'stuff of the Universe', the prototype of matter before it coalesces into recognizable physical form, from its original, allegedly spiritual state.

There have been reports too about individual mediums who have shown still more extraordinary capacities when under the influence of the spirits: they have been immune to the effects of fire, for example, or have produced materializations of their own spirit controls so real that those who saw them could not tell them apart from living flesh.

Here, we review a selection of the more interesting physical mediums from the great days of the seance room. If their manifestations were genuine then, according to them, so is the existence of an afterlife of some kind.

IMPERFECT HARMONY

Among mediums who produced apports, one of the most remarkable during the 19th century was undoubtedly Madame Elizabeth d'Esperance, actually a lady of English origin, whose more astonishing effects were produced through the spirit of a 15-year-old Arab girl named Yolande, who actually materialized as an entire physical form during Madame d'Esperance's seances.

At a seance held on 28 June 1890, this medium and the materialized Yolande produced a flower – not just any flower, or some sparkling cut hothouse bloom, but the seedling of a golden lily that in front of the astonished sitters grew before their eyes to a height of 7 ft, and in the process seven of the eleven flowers on the plant came into bloom and exuded a powerful scent. If this had been some species of vaudeville act, a professional conjuror would have made sure that the plant was either whisked away from prying eyes and sceptical inspection or equally 'magically' made to vanish. In this case, the spirit form of Yolande was disconcerted when she announced sadly that the giant lily could not remain in the material world, and then found that it refused to de-materialize.

Finally she told the sitters to keep the recalcitrant plant in a darkened room until they next met – a week later, on 5 July. The instructions were obeyed, and at the next seance the oversize lily was put squarely in

IS THE FACT THAT SUCH PHENOMENA ARE OUTSIDE THE BOUNDS OF NORMAL PHYSICAL POSSIBILITY PROOF THAT THE SPIRITS PRODUCED THEM?

THE TINY SEEDLING GREW INTO A GIGANTIC GOLDEN LILY IN FRONT OF THE INCREDULOUS WITNESSES.

Below: ***An alleged 'spirit' materializes behind Polish medium Franek Kluski at a seance held in Warsaw on Christmas Day 1919. Crude effects like these may have impressed the gullible, but brought the most scrupulous mediums into disrepute along with the charlatans.***

Above: ***Confucius, the 6th-century Chinese sage whose spirit corrected errors made in transcribing his own writings during a seance in New York in the late 1920s.***

the centre of the seance room at 9.23 pm. Within seven minutes it had disappeared, but not before two of the flowers had been kept as mementoes of its brief existence and photographs had been taken of the massive plant in company with the medium.

Another reasonable proof, in the eyes of spiritualists, that the dead were able to communicate paranormally with the living was their apparent ability to play musical instruments without the assistance of any visible musician. Such phenomena were recorded from the earliest days of spiritualism. In the early 1850s, for instance, the Ohio farmer Jonathan Koons was, by his own account, instructed by the spirits to build a specially dedicated log cabin alongside his farmhouse in which to demonstrate his powers as the 'greatest medium on Earth', in company with his eight children.

HIS CHILDREN WERE ATTACKED, HIS FIELDS AND BARNS WERE SET ALIGHT, AND THE FAMILY WERE FORCED TO FLEE THE DISTRICT.

The cabin was not the humble abode from which American country boys traditionally set out to crown their achievements with a spell in the White House. It was constructed like a miniature theatre, and had room for an audience of 30 people. Musical instruments were placed around the tiny auditorium. In this setting Koons and his children would take their places on a small stage. The lights would be put out, and Koons himself would take up his fiddle and play hymn tunes. Gradually, the spirits would take up the other instruments dotted about the room and join in – not, according to reports, always in perfect harmony. At the same time, a tambourine would be seen circling above the heads of the audience, trumpets floated into the air, and ghostly voices were heard speaking.

Koons did not make money from his bizarre presentations, and indeed actually encountered outright and aggressive hostility to his demonstrations from his neighbours. His motives seem to have been genuine and, in the light of the persecution he and his family received – the children were set upon, his fields and barns were attacked by arsonists, until in the end the Koonses left the district to become missionaries for spiritualism – it seems unreasonable to assume that the phenomena were not genuine too.

SPEAKING WITH MANY TONGUES

It's almost a commonplace today to see mediums 'channelling' the voices of the dead – reproducing the accents and idioms of the individuals coming through from the 'other side'. The seance rooms of 19th-century and early 20th-century Europe and America witnessed a similar phenomenon – but with a distinct and remarkable difference. For the 'direct voice' mediums who have emerged from time to time in the history of spiritualism have neither used their own voice-boxes to convey the words of the communicating spirits, nor have they been limited to being the channel for a single voice at a time. The voices, sometimes several at once, have come straight out of thin air to deliver their messages to the living.

New York medium George Valiantine demonstrated just such powers in 1924 in England. In seances held virtually every day over a period of five weeks, Valiantine was the medium for over 100 different voices. Numbers of them spoke simultaneously – and not only in English. The Welsh novelist Caradoc Evans held fluent, idiomatic conversations with his dead father in his native language (not an easy tongue to learn, with its difficult inflexions and unique system of 'mutations', and hardly one a New Yorker could mug up at short notice), while other spirits spoke with equal facility in German, Spanish and Russian.

The clinching demonstration of Valiantine's mediumship came in the late 1920s in New York. At a number of seances some voices that were frankly meaningless to the sitters had come through. On the off-chance that he might be able to identify the language, the orientalist scholar Dr Neville Whymant, though sceptical of claims for the paranormal, agreed to attend a seance. He pricked up his ears and became strangely interested, however, when he heard a voice speak the name K'ung-fu-T'Zu – Confucius – in an impeccable Chinese intonation and accent.

Whymant responded by quoting a passage from the works of the ancient sage. This was more than a matter of finding out whether the shade of the long-dead philosopher would recognize his own work. Whymant was reasonably sure that the passage, though it made good sense, had been altered as it had been copied by generations of scribes.

He had got no further than the first line when 'the words were taken out of my mouth, and the whole passage was recited in Chinese, exactly as it is recorded in the standard works of reference. After a pause of about 15 seconds the passage was... repeated, this time with certain alterations [that] gave it new meaning. "Thus read," said the voice, "does not its meaning become plain?"'

Whymant could hardly fail to be impressed. He reckoned there were perhaps half a dozen scholars in the West besides himself who knew enough Chinese – *and* were sufficiently familiar with the writings of Confucius – to have picked up his quotation with such ease, let alone subtly shifted the reading to give it a different sense. None of these learned men was in the USA at the time of the seance – and there was no question that any of them would have lent themselves to cheap trickery in the seance room.

Above: ***Italian medium Eusapia Palladino. She preferred tight controls over her seances, claiming that otherwise, if sceptics were present, she would be encouraged to cheat.***

A CURIOUS CHEAT

One of the more consistent exponents of physical mediumship in the 19th and early part of the 20th century was Eusapia Palladino. Born to peasant parents near Bari, Italy, in January 1854, Palladino made a name for herself as the focus of the most extraordinary physical manifestations during seances held in Naples. In 1891 the first of a series of tests and controlled observations, held all over Europe, were made of her powers by Cesare Lombroso, professor of psychiatry at the University of Turin.

Lombroso had had nothing but contempt for mediums, but came away from his encounters with Palladino remarking that he was ashamed to have disbelieved reports of what happened in spiritualist seances, adding, 'I am still opposed to the theory. But the facts exist, and I boast of being a slave to facts.'

THE ACADEMIC SCHOLAR COULD HARDLY FAIL TO BE IMPRESSED.

The facts were indeed astonishing. Unlike the vast majority of mediums at the

Right: ***Criminologist Cesare Lombroso, whose scepticism toward spiritual phenomena was shattered by Palladino's performances.***

THE MEDIUM CLAIMED THAT IN THE PRESENCE OF SCEPTICS SHE MIGHT EVEN REACT TO THEIR CONSCIOUS OR UNCONSCIOUS SUGGESTIONS – AND CHEAT.

time, Palladino did not insist on working under cover of darkness, and did not hide herself away in a 'cabinet' (a small chamber, rather like an enclosed pew, with a curtain across the front) as so many mediums did – often in order to hide the mechanics of their hoaxes. Palladino always allowed those present to tie her hands and feet if they wished, or take other precautions against her cheating. Another Italian scientist, Dr Ercole Chiaia, reported what he saw at her seances:

'Either bound to a seat, or firmly held by the hands...she attracts to her the articles of furniture which surround her, lifts them up, holds them suspended in the air...and makes them come down again, with undulatory movements, as if they were obeying her will. She increases their height or lessens it according to her pleasure. She raps or taps upon the walls, the ceiling, and the floor, with fine rhythm and cadence...

'This woman rises in the air, no matter what bands tie her down. She seems to lie upon the empty air, as on a couch, contrary to all the laws of gravity; she plays on musical instruments – organs, bells, tambourines – as if they had been touched by her hands or moved by the breath of invisible gnomes...'

The French astronomer Camille Flammarion reported that in one of her seances Palladino became irritable for some reason. As a result:

'The sofa came forward when she looked at it, then recoiled before her breath; all the instruments were thrown pell-mell upon the table; the tambourine rose almost to the height of the ceiling; the cushions took part in the sport, overturning everything on the table; [one of those present] was thrown from his chair. This item – a heavy dining-room chair of black walnut, with a stuffed seat – rose into the air, came up on the table with a great clatter, then pushed off.'

One of Palladino's most bizarre talents was to extrude, or somehow materialize, human limbs around her. On occasion she would produce entire human forms. In March 1902, one of the many scientists who investigated Palladino, Professor E. Morselli, had tied her carefully and thoroughly to a camp bed before a seance in which no less than six materialized forms appeared and disappeared. As each one vanished, Morselli checked the medium: she was still tied firmly to the bed.

One reason why Palladino was happy to be constrained in this somewhat undignified way was that she was, she freely

Below: ***Palladino levitates a musical instrument during a seance with psychical researcher Baron von Schrenck-Notzing in the 1890s.***

admitted, incapable of controlling her actions when in trance. She claimed that in the presence of sceptics she would even react to their unconscious or conscious suggestions – and cheat. She was in fact caught cheating on at least two occasions: once during a visit to Cambridge, England, in 1895, and again in New York in 1910. This last occurrence ended her international career as a medium. But it is a curious kind of hoaxer who admits to her own propensity for fraud, and is caught only when a researcher deliberately lets go his guard to see what will happen – as was the case during the Cambridge series of tests administered by the Australian lawyer Richard Hodgson.

ENORMOUS REPERTOIRE

The greatest of the Victorian physical mediums was without doubt Daniel Dunglas Home, who impressed a huge range of witnesses from all walks of life from emperors to elevator attendants, who never took money for his seances, and who was never caught in any deception or hoax.

Home believed himself to be the illegitimate son of a member of the Douglas-Home family – better known as the Earls of Home – and he pronounced his name as they do, to rhyme with 'spume'. He was born in Scotland in 1833, but was brought up by an aunt in Connecticut, in the USA. In 1855 he was told by doctors that his consumptive lung condition would worsen if he remained in America, and in the spring of that year he left for England.

Home had very little money, but he did have a wealth of psychic talent. He began giving seances when he was 17, after a classic spasm of poltergeist raps and bangings in his aunt's home had left him with powers of clairvoyance and healing. Within a very few years Home was to develop an enormous repertoire of bizarre and astonishing physical effects in the seance room.

In August 1852, Home levitated for the first time, at a sitting in the house of a Connecticut silk manufacturer, Ward Cheney. The editor of the *Hartford Times*, Frank L. Burr, described what happened:

'Suddenly, without any expectation on the part of the company, Home was taken up into the air. I had hold of his hand at the time and I felt his feet – they were lifted a foot from the floor...Again and again he was taken from the floor, and the third time he was carried to the ceiling of the apartment, with which his hands and feet came into gentle contact.'

Then, Home began to materialize disembodied hands. Burr told how one – 'very thin, very pale, and remarkably attenuated' – first took up a pencil and wrote. 'The hand afterwards came and shook hands with each one present. I felt it minutely,' he wrote. 'It was tolerably well and symmetrically made, though not perfect; and it was soft and slightly warm. IT ENDED AT THE WRIST.' Another chronicler of Home's feats described how one of these weird limbs picked up a handbell, rang it, and brought it to him. He tried to grab the hand: 'I had no sooner grasped it momentarily than it melted away, leaving my hand void, with only the bell in it.'

Home gave many demonstrations of such phenomena in London but, lacking an income, had to depend on the hospitality of his friends until 1858, when he married his

Above: ***Daniel Dunglas Home, claimed by his supporters to be the greatest 'physical' medium of all time. His repertoire of effects encompassed virtually every kind of paranormal manifestation produced in seances before and since – and some have never been repeated.***

Above: ***Daniel Dunglas Home levitates himself above the heads of his astonished onlookers.***

first wife Alexandrina, one of the Czar of Russia's god-daughters. With this, material insecurity vanished, and his social standing instantly changed. Home was lionized by the most brilliant and fashionable, as well as many of the weightiest intellectual members, of London society. The witnesses to his extraordinary powers thus included some of the least impressionable men and women of his day.

BIZARRE ABILITY

Home's seances were often held in good light, and he never hid inside a cabinet. He produced all the usual phenomena of the seance room: tables tilted or levitated (one, an occasional table with a single leg and claw feet, even managed to 'walk' up onto another table, 'exactly like a child trying to climb up a height'); an accordion that played by itself even when others held it in bemusement, watching the keys worked by invisible fingers; pens that wrote without visible assistance; materializations of human faces as well as his famous disembodied hands; raps and bangs; currents of air; and apports – among many others.

The Russian novelist and poet Count Alexey Tolstoy reported on the plethora of phenomena at a typical Home sitting, in a letter to his wife written in 1859. Besides the ringing bells, the levitations of furniture, the mysterious floating (and dissolving) hands, Tolstoy told how: 'The piano played with no one near it; a bracelet unclasped itself from the arm of Mrs Milner-Gibson, and fell on the table, where it lay surrounded by a luminous appearance. Home was raised from the ground... a cold wind passed round the circle very distinctly, and perfumes were wafted to us.'

But perhaps most striking of all his phenomena was not what Home did with other things, but what he did with his own body.

The levitations of Home, rising above the sitters – 'as if,' as he put it himself, 'I were grasping the unseen power which slowly raises me from the floor' – were part of the standard Victorian medium's fare. One of Home's truly original effects was his quite bizarre ability both to elongate himself and to shrink. He normally stood about 5 ft 7 in tall. At one seance at the home of the art magazine editors Mr and Mrs S.C. Hall, a journalist – a hardbitten species of witness – reported that:

'Mr Home was seen by all of us to increase in height to the extent of some eight or ten inches, and then sank to some six or eight inches below his normal stature. Having returned to his usual height, he took Lord Adare and the Master of Lindsay, and placing one beside each post

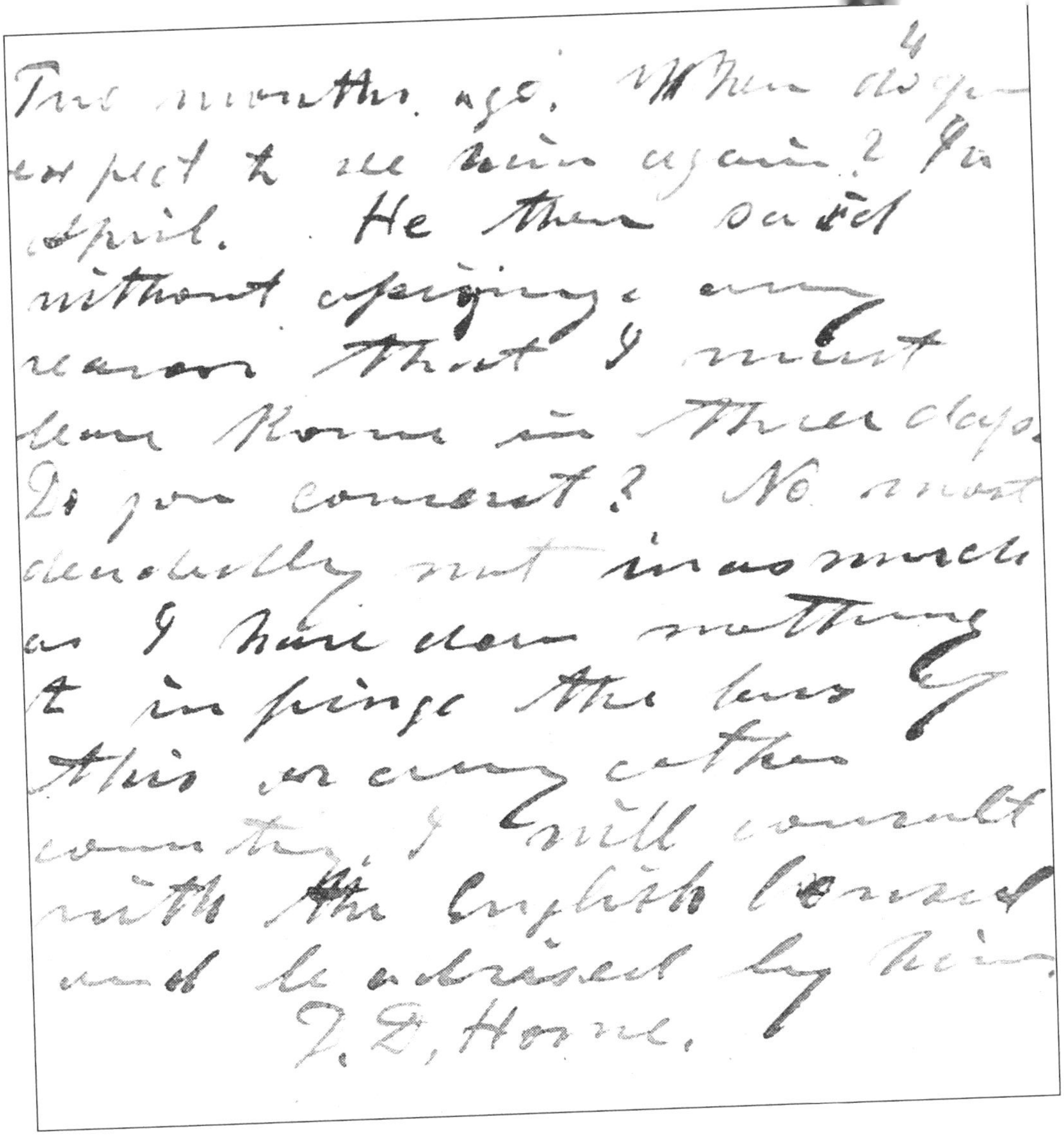
Two months ago. When do you expect to see him again? In April. He then said without assigning any reason that I must leave Rome in three days. Do you consent? No most decidedly not inasmuch as I have done nothing to infringe the laws of this or any other country. I will consult with the English Consul and be advised by him.
D. D. Home.

Left: ***Daniel Dunglas Home did not always impress. In this letter he protests about his eviction from Rome at short notice.***

of the folding door, lay down on the floor, touching the feet of one with his head and the feet of the other with his feet. He was then again elongated, and pushed both Lord Adare and the Master of Lindsay backward along the floor with his head and feet as he was stretched out…'

Hall, measuring the distance between the two startled noblemen, found that a space of more than 7 ft now separated them.

A GREAT WIND RUSHING

Still more extraordinary was Home's relationship with fire. On one particularly memorable occasion he created a kind of parody of the Pentecost. Tongues of flame darted from his head and he spoke in some unknown foreign language while, according to Lord Adare, 'we all distinctly heard…a bird flying round the room, whistling and chirping. There then came the sound of a great wind rushing through the room…'

This was not all. Numerous witnesses testified how Home was able to handle live coals for minutes at a time without feeling any pain. The supremely eminent physicist William Crookes reported one instance:

'Home removed from the grate a red-hot piece [of coal] nearly as big as an orange, and putting it on his right hand, covered it with his left…and blew…until the lump of charcoal was nearly white hot, and then drew my attention to the lambent flame which was flickering over the coal and licking round his fingers.'

Was any of this proof of life after death? Home certainly believed so. He had been a committed spiritualist since 1850, when he saw a vision of his mother dying in Scotland; the mail brought confirmation later that this happened on the day of her death. She continued to appear to Home throughout his life, giving him useful and moral advice. But he believed that his psychic powers were the work of several spirits – the chief among them was called 'Bryan' – over whom he had no control. His work was spirit work. And no one ever caught him cheating.

CONVERSATIONS WITH THE DEAD

Lord Archibald turned down an invitation to visit his tenant farmer that fateful evening. The blood-curdling events of the night were to make him regret that decision...

One snowy winter's afternoon some time before 1885, Lord Archibald Zealand had been out with his wife, visiting their acquaintances. As their carriage rolled up the drive to Zealand Manor, Lord Archibald saw one of the tenant farmers on his estate coming away from the front door, having found his landlord not at home. Lord Archibald stopped to talk to the farmer for a while and, before he went, the farmer invited him to drop in at his farmhouse later that evening. Lord Archibald had a busy evening ahead of him, and turned the offer down.

Later that night, at about 10 pm, Lord Archibald was in his breakfast room, working. He described what happened next to the editors of *Phantasms of the Living*, published by the Society for Psychical Research in London in 1886:

'I distinctly heard the front gate opened and shut again with a clap, and footsteps advancing at a run up the drive. When opposite the window, the steps changed from sharp and distinct on gravel to dull and less clear on the grass slip below the window, and at the same time I was conscious that someone or something stood close to me outside, only the thin shutter and a sheet of glass dividing us.

'I could hear the quick panting and laboured breathing of the messenger, or whatever it was, as if trying to recover breath before speaking. Had he been attracted by the light through the shutter?

'Suddenly, like a gunshot, inside, outside, and all around, there broke out the most appalling shriek – a prolonged wail... Of my [own] fright and horror I can say nothing – [but they] increased tenfold when I walked into the dining room and found my wife sitting quietly at her work close to the window, and in the same line and distant only ten or twelve feet from the corresponding window in the breakfast room. She had heard nothing.'

Too unnerved by this experience to go

Opposite: ***Doris Fisher Stokes, who for a decade personified spiritualist mediumship for millions around the world. Her unusual talent was to be able to hear the voices of the dead as they passed on their messages to those still 'this side' of the great divide between life and death.***

'I WAS CONSCIOUS THAT SOMEONE – OR SOMETHING – STOOD CLOSE TO ME OUTSIDE, ONLY THE THIN SHUTTER AND A SHEET OF GLASS DIVIDING US.'

Below: ***Surrounded by his family and a guard of honour, John F. Kennedy goes to his last long home. At least one Irish-American had the promising young president's untimely death announced to him by the unearthly howling of the banshee.***

THE BANSHEE LETS OUT A SPINE-CHILLING HOWL AS IT ANNOUNCES THE IMMINENT DEATH OF A MEMBER OF THE FAMILY.

outside immediately to look for whatever had made this blood-curdling sound, Lord Archibald waited till morning. No fresh snow fell in the night, but there were no signs of any footprints on the ground outside. Later that day, news came to the house that the tenant farmer Lord Archibald had spoken to the afternoon before had killed himself – apparently as the result of an unhappy love affair. He had ended his life by drinking prussic acid – and Lord Archibald's groom, who lived near the farm, had heard the man scream as he took the fatal dose and died.

The groom heard the dying man's cry at about 10 pm – 'as near as I can ascertain,' said Lord Archibald, 'at the exact time when I had been so alarmed at my own home'. The farm and the manor, however, were too distant from each other for him to have been able to hear the actual scream of the suicide. Lord Archibald's wife, after all, had heard nothing.

THE BANSHEE

Occurrences like this are known as cases of clairaudience – involving information that is passed on psychically through sound rather than through visual information. There are many cases of spontaneous, one-off clairaudience that, like the one above, occur only at moments of crisis and most often involve someone's death, but some people persistently and repeatedly hear information that they can only be receiving paranormally. And a few people claim to be able to hear the voices of the dead, speaking to them from the other side.

Among a number of old Irish families there is a tradition of clairaudience that is highly specialized, and not always welcome. This is otherwise known as the visitation of the banshee, which lets out a chilling howl as it announces the imminent death of a family member – though some say it comes to collect the departing soul.

The banshee is not only particular as to whose death it foretells; it is usually heard only by members of the family concerned. Irish tradition says that the banshee may also be seen – either in the form of an old hag or in the shape of a beautiful young woman – but reliable accounts of actually seeing the banshee are so rare as to be non-existent. The term itself comes from the Irish *bean sidhe* – 'woman of the fairies' – but the notion that the banshee is female seems to have arisen from the sound of its voice.

That, by all accounts, is unmistakably feminine, though the sound of its cries ranges from the most wistful, gentle and seductive entreaties to the most spine-chilling and vengeful shrieks. The difference in the nature of these sounds apparently depends on the attitude of the banshee toward the dying individual and his family. That in turn depends on whose spirit the banshee represents, and how the family treated them in earthly life, for it is reckoned always to be the spirit of a long-dead member of the family concerned.

DEMENTED WOMAN

Tales of the banshee's howl are not confined to the misty Irish past. The banshee howls in the late 20th century as loud and clear as it ever did – and its eerie voice is by no means confined to Ireland. One Irish-American businessman from Boston, Massachusetts, who preferred to hide behind the pseudonym 'James O'Barry', told journalist Frank Smyth of three occasions on which he had heard the unearthly voice. The first time, when he was but a small boy, he was unaware even of the existence of anything called the banshee.

'I was lying in bed one morning when I heard a weird noise, like a demented woman crying,' said O'Barry. 'It was spring...I thought for a moment that a wind had sprung up, but a glance at the barely stirring trees told me that this was not so. I went down to breakfast and there was my father sitting at the kitchen table with tears in his eyes. I had never seen him weep before. My mother told me that they had just heard, by telephone, that my grandfather had died in New York. Although he was an old man he was as fit as a fiddle, and his death was unexpected.'

In 1946, O'Barry heard the banshee the second time, when his father died; he himself was in the Far East, serving with the US Army Air Force. He was woken up at 6 am by 'a low howl': 'The noise got louder, rising and falling like an air raid siren.' On the third occasion, O'Barry was alone in Toronto, Canada, on a combined business trip and vacation. His account:

'I was in bed, reading the morning papers, when the dreadful noise was suddenly filling my ears. I thought of my wife, my young son, my two brothers and I thought: "Good God, don't let it be one of them." But for some reason I knew it wasn't.'

Indeed it was not. The time was just before noon, on 22 November 1963: the time that US President John F. Kennedy was assassinated in Houston, Texas. The president was a close friend of O'Barry's – and he was of Irish descent.

UNEARTHLY VOICES

As with other paranormal phenomena, there is nothing new about clairaudience. The ancient Greek philosopher Socrates was familiar with the promptings of what he called his 'daemon'. They were, he told his judges at his trial, 'constantly in the habit of opposing me even about trifles, if I were going to make some slip or error'. He had decided to stand trial for his life (albeit on somewhat frail charges) because his voices had not positively advised him to flee from Athens and, as he remarked to the court, he took this as a sign that 'those of us who think death is an evil are in error'.

Socrates, thus, seemed to think that his voices came from somewhere beyond this earthly life. In the Christian era Socrates would probably have been made a saint, and as such would have been in the company of two fascinating Christian women who too heard voices from unearthly realms.

One was Catherine of Siena (the Italian city where she was born in 1347). Catherine not only believed, like other mystics of her time, that among the voices she heard one came directly from God; she seems to have been actually clairvoyant, with the voices giving her information about ordinary human affairs. Some time after she had converted an aristocrat, Francesco Malevolti, to Christianity – and so taken him from a life of singular debauchery – the young man slid back into his former depraved existence. Catherine told him bluntly that she knew from her voices everything he did, and then recited to him a catalogue of his latest doings, sayings and sins.

Above: ***The ancient Greek philosopher Socrates, whose profound, still-relevant thought was prompted not by deep meditation, but by inner voices entirely outside of his control.***

'When I heard her tell me precisely all that I had done and said,' commented Malevolti, 'confused and shamed, and without an answer, at once and heedfully I fulfilled her command.'

DIVINELY INSPIRED

Possibly the most outstanding clairaudient in history was St Joan of Arc. Born in 1412 into a peasant family and illiterate all her life, Jean la Pucelle, 'the Maid of Orleans', first heard voices when she was only 13 years old. They told her that she could save her country from its enemies – France was then at war with England and the Duchy of Burgundy. Four years later, by sheer force

of character, she persuaded the Dauphin (crown prince) of France to let her join the French army that was attempting to relieve the siege of Orleans by the English. She effectively took command of the army, and 10 days later the English were defeated.

Other victories followed, and Joan persuaded the Dauphin to be crowned as Charles VII of France. He, however, did not follow up the moral and military advantage Joan had created, and when she attempted to break another siege more or less alone, she was captured by the Burgundians, who sold her to the English. They tried her for witchcraft, and – conviction being a foregone conclusion – she was burned at the stake in Rouen in

The brief but extraordinary life of Joan of Arc, the 'maid of Orleans' **(above)**, *was guided almost entirely by voices that dictated her actions and uttered astonishingly accurate predictions – to the extent that the civil authorities gave her unprecedented powers. Her greatest triumph came when she broke the siege of Orleans* **(opposite below)**. *The coronation of Charles VII of France* **(right)** *was another.*

1431, still not yet 20 years old.

Such a career would be astonishing enough, but it is all the more extraordinary that it was based on psychic ability. Joan's voices did not limit themselves to inspiring her to battle or to mystical utterances: they provided specific information. They directed her to the one man likely to introduce her to the Dauphin, for instance, and she impressed him less by her patriotic and religious fervour than by her ability to tell him, in a courtier's words, 'matters so secret and hidden that no mortal except himself could know them save by divine revelation'. These 'matters' had been revealed to her by her voices.

There are many other instances of the efficacy of Joan's voices, from her – or their – accurate prediction (recorded a fortnight before the event actually occurred) to the Dauphin that she would be wounded by an arrow at the siege of Orleans, to the information that there was a sword behind the altar in the church of St Catherine at Fierbois. She wrote to the clergy in Fierbois, telling them to look there; and they found a rusty sword.

Joan of Arc made no secret of her clairaudience, and it was this that condemned her in the eyes of the English court that tried her for witchcraft. As a later commentator put it, she died because of her 'resolute insistence on the truth of the very phenomena which were being used to destroy her'. Joan, naturally enough for anyone of her time, believed her voices were divinely inspired. To 20th-century eyes, she was a psychic, but there seems no doubt of her integrity or truthfulness concerning those voices and what they had to say, and little doubt either that they spoke with uncanny accuracy.

PHANTOM STEPS

Clairaudience, as these historical examples have shown, does not limit itself to precognition, telepathy – or to communication with the dead. Clairaudience is really the auditory awareness of *all* kinds of extra-sensory perception, and only a portion of recorded instances of the

Joan of Arc* (left), *still in her teens, was martyred as a witch by the English in 1431. To the end she insisted on the reality of the voices that had guided her all her life.

Above: ***Camille Flammarion, French astronomer and sometime president of the British Society for Psychical Research, among whose voluminous writings on psychic matters was an especially poignant case of clairaudience.***

LOUD FOOTSTEPS COULD BE HEARD PACING THE GALLERY, BUT THE DOORS WERE LOCKED AND THE SCIENTIST HAD THE KEY.

phenomenon can be said to offer any evidence at all of life after death.

Socrates seems to have taken his voices as implying that life continued in some form after death, although he did not assume that they came from the realm of the dead itself. St Catherine of Siena and Joan of Arc certainly attributed their voices to spirits, but they were very particular spirits indeed – the Archangel Michael, for instance, was among them. And it was perhaps inevitable that these two women, of such profound and visionary Christian belief, should have identified their clairaudience with the hosts of God. To the medieval Christian there was only one alternative – they were the work of the Devil.

The most commonly reported clairaudient communications with the dead have actually occurred at the point of death.

Karl von Linne (1707–78), the Swedish botanist who established the modern system of classifying living things by Latin names, was not so coldly scientific that he was immune to such events. His house in Uppsala contained a botanical museum, and one night in 1776 he and his wife were woken by loud footsteps pacing about the gallery. No one should have been there at all, since von Linne had locked the doors and, in fact, had the key with him. Then he recognized the footsteps as those of his closest friend, Karl Clerk, but he found neither Clerk nor anyone else in his museum. A few days later, he learned that his friend had died 'at precisely the same hour' as he had heard the phantom steps in his house.

A still surer indication that clairaudience acts as a channel between the living and the dead was recorded by Camille Flammarion in his 1922 book *Death and Its Mystery*.

In response to an appeal for such experiences, Flammarion had been told the story of a French girl named Clementine, who had suffered such a terrible life in the company of her alcoholic father that she decided to escape by entering a nunnery. Clementine's aunt gave her shelter when she first fled her father's house, but the older woman had a presentiment that Clementine did not have long to live. And she told the girl so.

Clementine seems to have had the same intuition, but made light of it. She knew she didn't have long to live, she said, but she would make sure her aunt knew when she died. 'I'll make an outrageous racket for you,' she promised.

Clementine in due course entered a convent, safe at last from the predations of her father. Some time after this, the aunt's entire household was disturbed one night around its usual bedtime by an 'outrageous racket' indeed. There were sounds from the roof as if it were caving in, and the very housebricks seemed to be slamming against one another. At the same time, there was no movement to be seen and no actual damage to the fabric of the house. Clementine's aunt guessed in a flash what had happened.

'Clementine is dead,' she said in a firm voice. At once, the uproar stopped as abruptly as it had begun. The next day, a telegram arrived at the house from the convent, breaking the news of Clementine's death – which had occurred at exactly the time that the clearly paranormal 'racket' had broken out.

UNCANNY VISIONS

By far the most renowned clairaudient of modern times was Doris Fisher Stokes, who for millions of people all over the world came to personify mediumship and contact with the next life. She was a natural star of television chat-shows and stage 'demonstrations' precisely because she was so natural – down to earth, unpretentious, unburdened by any New Age claptrap or desire to surround her talent with occult significance. Talking to the dead through Doris Stokes was an extraordinary experience just because she made it seem so everyday – and at the same time, she seemed hardly able to believe her own success.

In her early life she certainly had no reason to expect it. Doris Fisher Stokes was born the daughter of a blacksmith and a washerwoman, Tom and Jen Sutton, just after the end of World War 1, in Grantham, Lincolnshire.

In World War 2 Doris Stokes joined the Women's Royal Air Force and worked in operations rooms plotting the progress of Allied bombing raids on Europe. She found she had an uncanny and disconcerting foreknowledge of which aircraft would *not* return from their missions. It was only in 1944, after her husband John, a sergeant in the elite Parachute Regiment, failed to return (along with so many others) from the disastrous airborne assault on Arnhem in Holland, that Doris Stokes began to take either her own paranormal talent or evidence of survival after death very seriously.

At that time she had a vision of her father, who had died when Doris was only 13 years old. He told her two things: that John was alive, though a prisoner of war, and that their new-born son would shortly die. Both proved true. After that, she began attending her local spiritualist church. Her sensitivity developed, and she was soon practising as a medium herself.

TALKING TO THE DEAD

Doris Stokes said that she had two means of knowing when a soul from 'the other side' wanted to communicate. Either her spirit control – an entity claiming to be a deceased Tibetan Lama called 'Ramonov' (which is not the form of any known Tibetan name) would tell her 'in her ear', or she would see a small blue light appear over the head of a sitter, which indicated that someone close to them was trying to 'come through'.

Doris Stokes captivated huge audiences and many individual sitters too. She did so because time and again she produced information from the 'other side' that could have been known only to the individual she was talking to on 'our side' and to her unseen communicators. Yet some odd doubts remain about whether she was in fact able to converse in the easy way she had with the dead.

Doris Stokes has been accused of fraud since her death. She admitted to cheating once or twice during her lifetime. But to

The late Doris Stokes used to attract large audiences, such as that shown above – but she has been accused of fraud.

BUT WAS THE FAMOUS CLAIRVOYANT GUILTY OF SIMPLE, BASIC FRAUD?

offer some perspective on her mediumship, one has to give personal testimony.

The author of this book saw Doris Stokes in action three times: once at a private sitting in 1981, once at a press conference to launch one of her several books in 1982, and once (while on a flying visit to London) at a stage 'demonstration' in front of a packed house at the London Palladium late in 1985. The first two were highly impressive. The third was not, for reasons that will become clear.

The first occasion was as much a social one (in which I hoped to get some measure of Doris Stokes) as a formal 'sitting' as such. I was not the sitter (an old business colleague was) but over dinner before the sitting began, Doris Stokes made a number of casual observations about my life that were entirely accurate, although she had never met me before and as far as I know heard my name for the first time that evening. Two remarks in particular stand out: 'You've been a soldier, haven't you, love,' she said, 'and you don't know whether to be proud of what you've done or not, do you? But you don't talk about it.' All three of these statements were (and are) true.

Below: ***Doris Stokes takes a rest between sessions at a public demonstration in 1984. In the last few years before her death in May 1987 suspicions grew that her shows were not all that they seemed.***

Her second memorable remark concerned a ring I was wearing: 'That doesn't belong on that finger! You've moved that, haven't you, love?' The ring was on the little finger of my left hand. It was, in fact, my wedding ring. When my wife and I broke up, I moved it from the ring finger of my left hand to the pinkie, for a mass of tangled emotional reasons.

MIND READER?

The sitting itself was extraordinary for the wealth of detail that Doris Stokes produced about my colleague, some of which plainly embarrassed him because of my presence. But she told him nothing that he did not know already – nothing that he did not, then or later, confirm from his own knowledge. This is interesting because at about the same time the staff of the weekly magazine *The Unexplained* reported that they had invited Doris Stokes to a sitting that – reading between the lines – followed a curiously similar pattern. Settling on a young lady member of the staff whose grandmother had recently died, Doris Stokes found herself in communication with the old lady herself, but almost everything she had to communicate was already known to the girl.

No explicit conclusion was drawn from this significant fact in the magazine's report of the encounter, but in an assessment of the occasion written some years later, the editor of the magazine had this to say:

'When asked...whether she had considered the possibility that she was, in fact, reading the (unconscious) minds of her sitters, Doris Stokes replied that she would refuse to carry on her work if she felt she had been doing any such thing. "That would be an invasion of privacy," she said. "I don't think God would allow that." Nonetheless, the possibility remains that Doris Stokes is...highly telepathic, picking up memories from the mind of someone who knew the dead person [that is, of course, the sitter him- or herself]. These memories are then dramatized by Mrs Stokes's own subconscious, and come to her in the form of voices...

'Presumably the reasons for this are two-fold. In the first place, Doris Stokes has [a] very strong resistance to the notion that she is invading other people's most private space – the mind. And [in the second place]...she has been utterly convinced that we do survive death. She cannot prevent her talent manifesting itself, and so has rationalized it in a way that has brought her, and thousands of people who have sat with her, great comfort.'

SERIOUS QUESTION MARKS

This seems a very fair and logical deduction: Doris Stokes was not – as she undoubtedly, most sincerely, believed – in touch with the dead, but she was in touch with the minds of her sitters. But she was also, it seems, guilty of a quite different kind of touch – simple, basic fraud.

In *The After Death Experience*, published in 1987, author Ian Wilson described how he found out that Doris Stokes packed her public appearances with people (whom she placed in reserved seats at the front of the auditorium) whose personal details were, he and other researchers discovered, no secret to her. And the most impressive 'readings' at those appearances were, of course, for the people she had specially invited and with whose particular, intimate details she was already familiar.

Having attended such a demonstration – which followed exactly the pattern Wilson describes in his book – I can only agree with his conclusion: that at this stage in her career Doris Stokes was 'not all she seemed, and the most serious question marks hang over her'. In the same paragraph, Wilson generously suggests that Doris Stokes might 'really have been a genuine medium...rigging her shows through sheer fear of facing a huge audience' lest no 'other-worldly messages' came through. That is possible, but Wilson seems not to have taken one further factor into account.

When he saw Doris Stokes at the London Palladium – and discovered how she seemed so accurate in her readings – on 16 November 1986, Doris Stokes was dying of cancer, and she knew it. She actually 'passed over', as she would have put it, less than six months later, on 8 May 1987. The evidence that she rigged her last big public demonstrations is difficult to refute, but by then Doris Stokes had become part of show business – whose brave and tragic motto is 'The show must go on'. My own experience of Doris in less clouded and painful days suggests that she did have a genuine talent, and my experience of her later suggests that her last illness at least (there may have been other reasons) combined with a sad and mistaken sense of loyalty to her audience to override her own honesty and integrity.

The real question for students of the paranormal is whether, at the height of her power, Doris Stokes communicated with the dead, or simply made contact with the minds of her sitters. We know her own answer to that question. We do not know the real answer.

Doris Stokes* (above) *appearing before the public at one of her very popular demonstrations.

LIVING ART FROM A DEAD HAND

The teenager took up psychic art in the hope of ridding his family home of the destructive poltergeist, but as his pen and paintbrush re-created the masterpieces of the great artists, he found the demands made on him both baffling and exhausting.

There are two kinds of 'psychic artist'. There are those whose paintings, drawings, writings or musical compositions are guided by long-dead artists. And there is a handful of visual artists who draw or paint portraits of those they see 'in spirit'. What kind of evidence does the work of these two quite different groups of artists offer for life after death?

To some extent the answer to the question depends on the artist involved. In the early 1970s, the British healer Matthew Manning – then still a teenager – began what became a huge collection of paintings, drawings and sketches that were created 'through' him by artists as diverse as Leonardo da Vinci, Claude Monet, Aubrey Beardsley, Beatrix Potter, Paul Klee and Pablo Picasso. Manning did not go into trance to produce the pictures; he simply concentrated on the artist while sitting in front of a sketching block with pen, pencil or paintbrush at the ready.

In his book *The Link*, Manning admitted to being baffled by what was happening when he painted or drew these pictures. He commented: 'How do I ask Albrecht Dürer to draw through me…?…The fact that the person I wish to communicate with does not speak English is apparently no barrier.'

Strangely, what did prove a problem for many of these long-gone artists was how to use colour (Picasso was a notable exception). But this difficulty, paradoxically enough, may be a sign that the communication between Manning and the artists was genuine.

One is reminded of the frustration expressed by psychical researcher Frederic W.H. Myers (through a medium's automatic writing) five years after his death in 1901:

Opposite: ***Matthew Manning, now better known as a healer, was apparently guided by artists ranging from Leonardo da Vinci* (below left) *to Claude Monet* (below right) *when he produced his enormous number of artistic works in the 1970s.***

Right: ***Aubrey Beardsley, famous for his stylized black-and-white illustrations. One of his drawings for Oscar Wilde's*** **Salome** ***was reproduced by Matthew Manning.***

'I appear to be standing behind a sheet of frosted glass – which blurs sight and deadens sounds – dictating feebly to a reluctant and somewhat obtuse secretary.' At least the problem shows that Manning, if not in trance, was not in his normal state of consciousness. A reasonably talented painter in his own right, he had won prizes for art while at school, and should not have had any difficulty in using colour if he had been in full conscious control of his materials.

PSYCHIC COLLABORATION

Some of the pictures produced like this were very close to those created by the artists in their lifetimes. Manning – or the Renaissance artist himself – made a remarkably accurate reproduction of a sketch of a hanged man by Leonardo. Another such 'copy' was of Beardsley's famous drawing of Salome. In themselves, of course, these pictures prove nothing at all about survival. Manning speculated on this point: 'The only explanation I have is that the artist appears to be making a point of identifying himself beyond a shadow of doubt by reproducing something with which he is already known to be associated.'

Beardsley, however, was apparently also prone to make mistakes and to change his mind – as any living artist might – when working through Manning. 'More than any other...Beardsley made many mistakes while drawing,' said Manning, 'but instead of covering them over with paper, which obviously he could not do, he inked over them and changed them into something different.'

These works were often finished very fast – most in an hour or two, and without any preliminary sketching – far quicker and more spontaneously than a working artist would expect to complete a picture. This did not make the process easy, however. Picasso was a particularly demanding taskmaster: 'No other communicator tires me out as much as Picasso does,' wrote Manning. 'After only a few minutes, the time it takes him to do one drawing, I feel worn out and cannot continue for at least 24 hours.'

The Manning collection of psychic art seems authentic enough: but was it really produced by artists in the afterlife, using Manning as a medium? In *The Link* Manning states clearly of his psychic collaboration with Picasso: 'The first work from him came in July 1973, three months after he died. I specifically asked Picasso to produce a drawing for me.' But an equally valid interpretation is that Manning was unconsciously trying out – or trying on – a number of identities through his artistic efforts. He took up 'psychic art' and automatic writing, after all, in the hope of channelling his own inner conflict into less destructive paths than the particularly unruly poltergeist that had plagued him and his family for some years.

Manning in fact later distanced himself as far as he could from the idea that he was in touch with the spirits of the dead. In the early 1980s, he said, 'I have never [*sic*] claimed my drawings to have been communications from the spirits of deceased artists...I feel that I was merely attuning myself to the continuing inspirational force created in the first place by the artist. That is why many of my drawings are only copies, sometimes not very good, of drawings already made by the artist.'

PROLIFIC OUTPUT

Such a statement, complete with its economy with the truth, amounts to a recantation. Such qualms have never had to cross the mind of London medium Coral Polge, but she does not even pretend to be continuing the work of famous dead artists. Her specialty is drawing portraits of quite ordinary people who have died – and she draws them not from photographs, nor from any other kind of image, but from feeling their presence 'in spirit'.

'I know exactly what to draw,' she has said, 'without thinking about it. It's involuntary, like breathing or walking.'

Coral Polge did actually train as an artist, although ironically she was 'hopeless' at portraits as a student in the 1940s; in any case her real interest then was in textile designs. But she was interested in spiritualism, and became a medium herself in due course. When another medium suggested she had a future as a psychic artist, she responded first by producing portraits of the spirit guides – those in the afterlife who, according to spiritualists, act as individual 'guardian angels' for every one of us – of her sitters.

But many people (including Coral Polge) found these unsatisfactory, since they so frequently could not be identified easily from the historical records. They were often Red Indians, nuns, monks, Chinese sages or even Zulus, often from distant epochs. They were not the easiest people to track down in their earthly existences. Gradually she moved on to drawing portraits of the dead relatives, friends and loved ones of her sitters.

She cannot produce portraits of the dead on demand, however. 'It creates barriers when people come expecting or wanting me to draw someone in particular,' she has said. 'I draw whoever comes through.'

'I FEEL WORN OUT AND CANNOT CONTINUE.'

***Matthew Manning claimed to have had a special connection with Pablo Picasso* (shown above in his villa at Cannes).**

In doing that – without any visual stimulus at all – she has been both prolific and extraordinarily accurate. It has been estimated that between 1950 and 1970 she drew nearly 1800 portraits a year. Three out of the thousands of sittings that Coral Polge has taken over the years will show how precise her psychic vision can be.

AMAZING ACCURACY

One of her sitters was writing a book about the former UN Secretary-General Dag Hammarskjold, who had been killed in a mysterious aircraft crash in 1961. The visitor made no bones about her hope that Coral Polge would produce a portrait of the dead diplomat. Coral Polge did not feel able to oblige – as she says, such a demand 'creates barriers' – and her sitter was disappointed when Coral's pencil began to sketch the outline of what seemed to be a little girl with flowing blonde hair.

Coral's sitter in fact felt doubly disappointed, for she had been told by

Spiritualists often claim that each of us has an individual guardian angel. In this 19th-century painting,* Angel Slumber, *by Kaulbach* (above), *a sleeping child is tenderly rocked by an angel.

Right: ***Coral Polge with one of her portraits of a dead person, drawn through her awareness of their presence.***

Hammarskjold through another medium that she would have a portrait of him from a psychic artist. At first it seemed that it was not to be this psychic artist – until Coral Polge had all but finished, and her sitter realized that she had drawn not a portrait of Hammarskjold as an adult statesman, but as a child. In Coral Polge's drawing she recognized Hammarskjold as she had seen him in a photograph taken when he was aged only two – complete with long fair locks, not unusual in small children in 1907.

Another had a double confirmation of Coral Polge's abilities as an all-round medium as well as psychic artist at a public meeting at which Coral was producing drawings as they came to her, and then asking the audience if any of them recognized the resulting portraits. Mrs Phyllis Timms, from Salisbury, Wiltshire, was sure that one such picture, showing an elderly man with a drooping, bushy white moustache, was of her late maternal grandfather, Herbert Light. No one else in the auditorium made any move to claim it.

But Mrs Timms wanted some further sign that the picture was indeed intended for her. Coral Polge, picking up some further psychic impression about the man she had drawn, suggested the portrait might be for someone in a green dress. Mrs Timms was wearing blue. Coral Polge insisted that green was the key link between the man in her portrait and someone in the here and now. It was only at this point that Mrs Timms stopped thinking about colours and realized the significance of the word 'green'. Her maiden name, which she had not used for years, was Green. She claimed the picture.

These cases could be 'explained' by suggesting that Coral Polge had picked up her knowledge of her subjects' looks from the sitters – for it was the sitters she depended on to recognize whose likeness she had drawn. But in some cases the connection between sitter and portrait is not as direct or clear as that, and only later has the accuracy of Coral Polge's drawing come to light.

Singers Grace Brooks and Deirdre Dehn met when they were both working on the film of Lionel Bart's *Oliver!*. Deirdre, it turned out, had a talent for automatic writing. Through her scripts, another singer, who first identified herself as Maria Garcia, communicated with Grace. Later 'Maria' gave her surname as Malibran. Intrigued, Deirdre went to work to find out if this was indeed a historical person, and her research discovered that Maria Malibran had been born Maria Garcia in Paris in 1808. She made her debut as an opera singer in London in 1825, and died tragically at the age of 28 in Manchester, England, as the result of falling from a horse.

Maria Malibran was a real enough person, then. In due course, Deirdre Dehn went home to Australia, and that seemed to be the end of Grace Brooks's contact with Maria. Then she went to a sitting with Coral Polge. Coral drew a portrait of a young

Mediumistic art by Heinrich Nüsslein, showing the king of an unknown transgalactic civilization.

'IT CREATES BARRIERS WHEN PEOPLE COME EXPECTING OR WANTING ME TO DRAW SOMEONE IN PARTICULAR.'

Right: ***Maria Malibran, 19th-century opera singer who was in contact with Grace Brooks.***

woman with a hairstyle that was definitely not in any modern style. All Coral Polge could tell Grace Brooks was that 'This is a Spanish singer named Maria.'

Grace Brooks had no idea what Maria Garcia Malibran looked like, but she did know how to find out. Research in the British Museum turned up an engraving of a contemporary portrait of Maria Malibran. The likeness between this picture from the life, and Coral Polge's psychically received likeness is uncanny. It seems hardly likely that Coral Polge, producing more than 30 portraits a week, would have had time to research this one case in order to make an impression on Grace Brooks. And she certainly could not have been relying on telepathy to give her the image in Grace Brooks's mind.

THE PSYCHICALLY RECEIVED LIKENESS WAS UNCANNY – AND THERE WAS NO QUESTION OF TELEPATHY BEING INVOLVED.

THE STORY OF DOC TESTER

While Coral Polge gave up drawing portraits of spirit guides, there is a fascinating story concerning one portrait of a spirit guide that deserves to be retold. The picture involved so many different people in its long wait for its rightful home that it speaks for a real and mysterious consistency between psychics, and strongly suggests that there is a truth of some kind in the spiritualist belief in spirit guides – and in the survival of the individual identity after death.

In medium Tom Fox's consulting room in his house in Copthorne, West Sussex, hangs the portrait in oils of a rough-and-ready character who might have ridden the frontier in the days of Wild Bill Hickock and Doc Holliday. The tale of how this picture came to be on Tom Fox's wall is told here in his own words, taken from his autobiography *Medium Rare*:

'In the late Sixties I went for a private reading with a very well-known and respected medium, Billy Elton, the founder of the Spiritualist church in Aylesbury, Buckinghamshire. Among other things he told me that one of my spirit guides was an Australian doctor, whose name, he said, was Dr Tester. Now I'd never heard, seen, or sensed such a person at all, let alone known that I had such a character as a spirit guide. But I made a note of the name in my diary, as I always do put down details of a reading, imagining as I did so that this was some kind of fresh-faced modern colonial type – white coat, blond hair, maybe with glasses, and a cheerful and cheering manner for his rounds of the hospital wards.

'About a year or two later (during which there was no sign of Dr Tester in any shape or form) I was doing trance work in a development circle run by my old and dear friend Hilda Kirby. Among the members was another great friend, Jack Toyer. Just before we started one meeting – I remember he was sitting opposite me in the circle – Jack said, in a somewhat disapproving voice: "Tom...There's a spirit form, of a dirty old Mexican, standing behind you, you know."

'"Oh, is there?" I said. "Well, he's welcome. I don't know who he is, but he's welcome."

'I didn't give this "visitor" any more thought after that, because I soon went into trance. Blue Star, my Zulu guide, came through, and for some time was speaking through me about spiritual development and the world of Spirit. When he had finished Blue Star said, rather sternly, to Jack: "The man in the big black hat would like to talk to you."

'With that, he gave everyone a blessing and left, and I then started to come out of trance. I was nearly "round" when I suddenly went under again, under a very strong influence indeed. The person who'd taken control of me this time said – without any preamble, polite introductions, or anything:

'"Who the bloody hell d'ye think you're calling a dirty old Mexican? I'm no dirty old Mexican, mate. My name's Doc Tester."

'That caused a bit of stir in our polite gathering since nobody had any idea who that was, and I was in no position to tell them. Cutting right across the chatter, the blunt Doc just told them all to stop making so much noise and, in so many words, to shut up. Then he launched into quite a long talk about healing – and very lucid, very informative and, in fact, entertaining he was.

'Doc Tester is a very powerful character, but he's not intolerant: he gently and jovially mocks people, though, if he thinks they're not living up to the best in themselves. So that first appearance was also peppered with wisecracks at people who, he thought, were speaking without thinking, or asking him silly questions. And then, just as

'I'M NO DIRTY OLD MEXICAN, MATE. MY NAME'S DOC TESTER.'

Below: ***Tom Fox, through whom Doc Tester gave an informative talk about healing in the late sixties.***

Above: ***The painting of Doc Tester that hangs in Tom Fox's consulting room in Copthorne, West Sussex.***

'WE KNOW IT WASN'T SUICIDE. JUST A HIDEOUS ACCIDENT.'

Blue Star had done, he offered everyone a blessing and, with a promise to return another time, departed.

'After the meeting, as usual, we had a cup of tea all round. I needed it: I kept thinking that *that* couldn't be the Dr Tester that Billy Elton had mentioned.

'I said to Jack: "Are you really sure he had black hair?"

'"Absolutely," he said. "And the black hat. He was a scruffy old thing."

'I still couldn't believe it. This wasn't exactly the clean-cut young man that, for some reason, I persisted in thinking "my" Dr Tester had to be. And, as it happened, I personally heard no more from, or about, Doc Tester for a long time – about four or five years, in fact.

'In the early Seventies, I went to the Spiritualist church at Aylesbury one Sunday – just as an ordinary member of the congregation – and sat down at the back. During the service I became aware of a couple sitting in front of me – for, standing between them, with his arms around them – cuddling them, in fact – was the very strong visible presence of a teenage boy. He was about fifteen, I'd say, slimly built, and quite tall.

'The lady of the couple was, it turned out, an officer of the church, and after the service she made a point of speaking to the new faces, like me, who'd come to the church for the first time that day. I told her about the boy I'd seen with his arms around her and her husband.

'She called her husband over at once, and had me repeat the description. "That's our son," they agreed. "He died experimenting with a plastic bag – pulled it over his head and died of asphyxiation. We know it wasn't suicide. Just a hideous accident."

'We had quite a conversation after that. Their names, I discovered, were Vic and Pam Bradford. The next thing I knew I was being invited to tea with them for the following weekend.

'When I arrived at their house, the first thing I saw on their living-room wall was an oil painting of a man dressed in black, with black hair, and a big black hat. At once I asked the lady of the house who he was.

'"You tell me," she said.

'"His name's Doc Tester, he's Australian, and he worked in the outback," I heard myself saying without thinking. "And that's all I know."

'"Then he's yours," she said. "He's been waiting here three years for you."

'I was completely amazed. How could anyone else know about Doc Tester – especially when even I had doubted that he actually looked like *that*? How had anyone been able to paint this picture, or be sure that I would get to know about it?

'Then Pam told me the story.

'For her and Vic it began a couple of years after Doc – unknown to them, of course – had surprised our development circle. In Northampton there was a medium called Jack Burrell. He was also a psychic artist, who specialized in pictures of the family, friends, and spirit guides of people who came to him for readings. There were two unusual things about his art. He would paint only people who were dead, whom he had never seen in the flesh or in photographs, and he always painted with his eyes closed, because he worked in a state of trance.

'Among the pictures of spirit guides he painted was a portrait in oils of a black-haired man, who was wearing a black hat. Looking rather like a character from a Western, actually, except that in the background of the picture there are sheep, not long-horn steers.

'When Burrell had completed this picture, he gave it to his friends Pam and Vic Bradford.

'"It's not yours," he explained, "and it's not for you. But I want you to keep it. Hang it on your living-room wall. This is an Australian doctor, and he's somebody's healer in Spirit. Someone will be along eventually to collect it. But that's all I can tell you."

'And there I was, looking at that painting, and knowing that this really was Doc Tester. The painting hangs on the wall of my consulting room now, a reminder and an inspiration to me always. I think Doc would be one of my favourite people, with his blunt speech, rambunctious style, and dry style of humour, and I treasure his picture.

'I've found out a bit more about him since – from himself and from others in Spirit. He was an ordinary, country doctor, working out in the Australian outback in the Twenties. He'd spend weeks at a time riding from station to station and settlement to settlement on horseback – which is why his clothes are always so scruffy: they're old, travelling clothes, and they're covered in dust from his journeys in the bush.

'To tell the truth, Doc has done more talking to people in development circles and the like than he has made himself felt by doing healing through me. On the few occasions that I have done healing I've known he's there, but he tends to stay in the background.'

INCREDIBLY HE ALWAYS PAINTED WITH HIS EYES CLOSED.

PROOF AT LAST?

The authors of the Reader's Digest volume *Unsolved Mysteries of the Past* comment aptly on this singular example of psychic art: 'The most remarkable part of this story is that three mediums besides Fox himself independently either saw or were aware of Doc Tester, two of them before Fox had [learned] anything about his spirit guide; and the man who painted Tester's picture was someone whom Fox had never met.'

Whether or not they amount to proof of life after death, cases like this, and others – like Coral Polge's portrait of Maria Malibran – certainly confront us with a more than ordinary mystery.

Below: ***Narciso Bressanello, a mediumistic artist who used to be a ship repairer, in his studio on a boat in Venice.***

VISIONS OF AN AFTERLIFE

After a routine operation, something went frighteningly wrong. The doctors brought Iris Lemov back to life within minutes – but she was no longer the same woman.

When Mrs Iris Lemov went into hospital for a routine operation neither she nor her doctors expected anything unusual to occur. What actually happened was to change her outlook on life – and death – altogether.

'I was brought back to my room after surgery,' she recalled in a journal article in November 1979, 'and was speaking to my nurse, when a strange separated feeling between my body and my brain occurred. High above my body I floated wondering why so many doctors were around my bed...'

Mrs Lemov had slipped suddenly and unexpectedly into a coma. But the abrupt dislocation of her consciousness and her body was not to be any ordinary out-of-the-body experience. For while she watched from above, she went deeper into coma and her heart stopped beating. To Mrs Lemov, looking down on the scene, it appeared only that her face had gone terribly pale. And then everything went suddenly dark.

She found herself sucked into a long black tunnel. Light glowed at the end of it. 'I felt frightened and excited as I neared the end of the tunnel,' she said. 'I felt peace, without pain, and free. The light at the end of the tunnel was bright but easy on my eyes.'

When she came out into the light, Iris Lemov found herself in a verdant, peaceful valley, which was 'a sight to behold. There was velvety green grass and calmness. Music coming from nowhere made me feel comfortable and I began to feel as if I belonged. I saw figures of people dressed

Opposite: ***This tranquil valley is typical of the visions of peace and calm – interpreted as visions of Heaven – that people have reported seeing when on the point of death, just as they report being greeted by seemingly divine messengers as they slip out of contact with this life, as shown in the engraving below.***

AND THEN EVERYTHING WENT SUDDENLY DARK AS SHE WAS SUCKED INTO A LONG BLACK TUNNEL.

Above: ***Kenneth Ring, who has made a study of the experiences reported by people who have, for all practical purposes, died and then returned to life.***

in shrouds coming toward me and [they] called me by name. This man with a white beard told me to go back – your family still needs you – enjoy your life. This beautiful man was my grandfather who died two years before I was born…

'If we could all have the opportunity of seeing my valley during the course of our lifetime, how much more purposeful our lives would be.'

THROUGH THE MISTS

Iris Lemov's experience is typical of many who have clinically died, have been resuscitated and, in the brief period that they have been technically dead, have briefly visited the hereafter. Such people have, it seems, been vouchsafed a glimpse of the life after death. It is not surprising that the experience radically changes the attitude of most of these survivors toward death. For them, it no longer holds any fear, and, like Mrs Lemov's, their present lives are enriched as a result.

It is only with recent advances in medical technology – both drugs and equipment – that these 'near-death' experiences have been reported with any frequency – for the simple reason that they have allowed so many more people than ever before to be rescued from the very brink of death. But the truly striking thing about the reports of these brief sorties to the next world is their consistency. They may vary in detail, but the pattern of them is astonishingly uniform. Examples of other first-person accounts of such experiences will make this plain:

'I got up and walked into the hall to go get a drink, and it was at that point, as they found out later, that my appendix ruptured. I became very weak, and I fell down.

'I began to feel a sort of drifting, a movement of my real being in and out of my body, and to hear beautiful music. I floated on down the hall and out the door onto the screened-in porch. There, it almost seemed that clouds, a pink mist really, began to gather around me, and then I floated right straight on through the screen, just as though it weren't there, and up into this pure crystal clear light, an illuminating white light…

'It's not any kind of light you can describe on earth. I didn't actually see a person in this light, and yet it has a special identity…It is a light of perfect understanding and perfect love.

'The thought came to my mind, "Thou lovest me?" This was not exactly in the form of a question, but I guess the connotation of what the light said was, "If you do love me, go back and complete what you began in your life." And all the time, I felt as though I were surrounded by an overwhelming love and compassion.'

A woman who collapsed from a heart attack reported:

'I found myself in a black void, and I knew I had left my physical body behind. I knew I was dying, and I thought, "God, I did the best I knew how at the time I did it. Please help me."

'Immediately, I was moved out of that blackness, through a pale grey, and I just went on, gliding and moving swiftly, and in front of me, in the distance, I could see a grey mist, and I was rushing toward it. It seemed that I just couldn't get to it fast enough...Beyond the mist, I could see people...and I could also see something which one could take to be buildings. The whole thing was permeated with the most gorgeous light – a living, golden yellow glow...

'As I approached more closely, I felt certain I was going through that mist. It was such a wonderful, joyous feeling... Yet, it wasn't my time to go through the mist, because instantly from the other side appeared my uncle Carl, who had died many years earlier.

'He blocked my path, saying, "Go back. Your work on earth has not been completed. Go back now."

'I didn't want to go back, but I had no choice, and immediately I was back in my body. I felt that horrible pain in my chest, and I heard my little boy crying, "God, bring my mummy back to me."'

THERE AND BACK AGAIN

Those who have spent years collecting reports like these – the chief researchers include Drs Raymond Moody, Kenneth Ring, Margot Grey, Michael Rawlings and Michael Sabom – have compiled, from their analyses of hundreds of examples, a typical pattern of events that occur to people who are briefly clinically dead. They call this the 'core experience', on which almost every individual near-death experience is a variation.

This essential sequence of the journey from life to death and back is as follows:

- as people begin to die, they feel a blissful sensation
- as clinical death occurs, they have an out-of-the-body experience, floating above the scene in which their body is lying
- they go into a misty, or more often a dark area, and most see this transformed into a long tunnel with light at the end
- they hurtle with increasing speed down the tunnel
- as they emerge into the light, they are greeted by a relative or by a recognized religious leader such as Jesus of Nazareth
- the scenery at the end of the tunnel is often pastoral – a pleasant rural scene, or a beautiful garden
- soothing or 'heavenly' music is

'I DIDN'T WANT TO GO BACK BUT I HAD NO CHOICE...I HEARD MY LITTLE BOY CRYING.'

Left: *Jesus of Nazareth, depicted as* **The Light of the World** *in the famous painting by William Holman Hunt: Jesus is one of the divine figures who, survivors say, greet the dying as they enter the afterlife.*

Below: *The elect enter Heaven, as imagined by Luca Signorelli in a fresco in Orvieto cathedral. Those who believe they have had a glimpse of the afterlife report hearing strains of sweet music, as featured in Signorelli's painting.*

THE NEAR-DEATH EXPERIENCE IS THE BRAIN'S LAST FLING.

Below: ***The archangel Gabriel, one of the figures who reputedly greet the dead as they enter the afterlife.***

playing, though often its source is invisible

- sometimes, scenes from their earthly life pass before them, as if in a movie. These may also occur earlier in the sequence, before or during the passage through the tunnel
- a disembodied voice from 'the light', or the relative or other figure who greeted them, tells them to 'go back'
- the return from this celestial scene is usually instantaneous. At once, the body feels normal sensations – usually the pain from their injury or from the efforts of those trying to revive them
- as a result of the experience, people no longer fear death. They also tend to express a reduced interest in material things, and a heightened interest in spiritual matters, although conventional religions often lose much of any former attraction they may have had.

A PSYCHOLOGICAL TRICK?

The very consistency of the near-death experience argues for its truth: that there is a place we go when we die, and our loved ones are there to greet us and ease us past the shock of the transition from this life to the next. But that very same consistency can be interpreted in a quite different way.

For example, the highly regarded parapsychologist Dr Susan Blackmore has suggested that one near-death experience is so like another not because we all experience the same actual, objective reality at the point of death, but because our brains are essentially built in the same way – just as we all have noses above our mouths, and eyes to watch over both, and ears one each side of our heads. As our physical system collapses, the shards of consciousness interpret these symptoms of death in the best possible light, calling on the failing memory to create a marvellously benign and reassuring, but essentially fantastic, mental environment. Dr Blackmore concludes that 'what is generally now called the near-death experience is a psychological trick, played by the dying brain on the consciousness in order to lessen the trauma of dying. Essentially, this type of experience is the brain's last fling.'

Indeed it may be. But there are several aspects of near-death experiences as reported that don't fit with this analysis and that suggest there may be an objective reality to these accounts of what happens when we die. The very first problem with the sceptical view of near-death experiences is of its own making. What possible biological reason can there be for the mind (or brain) to have evolved a 'trick' to make dying easier to bear? How did the mind discover that it needed to learn this trick? How could anyone – other than through reincarnation, in which one suspects Dr Blackmore does not believe – inherit it?

Even if there is a materialist explanation for the near-death experience, this strange formula is hardly the best way to express it.

'GREETING FIGURES'

There are further facets of reported near-death experiences that indicate that something real lies behind them.

First, there is the figure who greets the migrating soul, or consciousness, on its arrival in the 'other' world. It would be interesting to know more about what distinguishes those who have been greeted on the 'other side' by standard religious figures such as Jesus, St Peter or the archangel Gabriel, from those who have been met only with a seemingly sentient, all-embracing, 'clear white light', and from those who have had close relations and loved ones there to meet them. While prior

Above: ***The City of God – that is, paradise – as conceived by St Augustine. According to those who have apparently been there, the afterlife does not conform to such complex ideas, although it may broadly reflect the religious beliefs of the witness.***

Above: ***Gustav Doré's illustration of Dante's vision of Heaven – winged, heavenly choirs floating on clouds to entertain the pious. Actual experiences of the pleasanter side of the afterlife suggest a more prosaic existence, if undoubtedly a pleasant one.***

expectations may create what (or whom) one perceives at this point, the figure (or lack of it) that people see may depend on their earthly circumstances.

It would be peculiar indeed if someone who had had a lifetime of almighty conflicts with relatives were suddenly to be greeted with boundless love and cosmic wisdom by the very same wicked grandad who had beaten them as children. It would be equally startling if an agnostic, who had never been averse to the existence of a Great Creator but had long suspected the prophet of Nazareth to be a con-man, were to find that the figure welcoming him to the paradisaical garden was none other than a smiling Jesus Christ himself – who would then add injury to insult by telling him to go back and finish his business on Earth.

Besides, there is a long and hardy tradition – within close-knit families, at least – of dead relatives coming to 'collect' a dying person and usher them into the next world. And from time to time these bailiffs of the grim reaper have been seen by people quite separate from the person who is dying.

D. Scott Rogo, in *The Return from Silence*, cites a fine instance of such an event from the memoirs of the New York nurse Margaret Moser:

'In the winter of 1948–9 I nursed a very sick old lady, Mrs Rosa B.…She was residing at that time at the Savoy Plaza Hotel on Fifth Avenue, and up to the last she was mentally competent.

'Early one afternoon…Mrs B. had been asleep, but suddenly I saw her sit up and wave happily, her face all smiles. I turned my head toward the door, thinking one of her daughters had come in; but much to my surprise it was an elderly lady I had never seen before. She had a striking resemblance to my patient – the same light blue eyes, but a longer nose and a heavier chin. I could see her very clearly for it was bright daylight; the window shades were only slightly lowered. The visitor walked toward my patient, bent down, and…they kissed each other. But then, as I got up and walked toward the bed, she was gone.

'Mrs B. looked very pleased. She took my hand and said, "It is my sister!" Then she slept peacefully again. I saw the same apparition twice later on, but never as clearly and always from another room. But every time she came the patient was obviously elated.'

Ms Moser later had corroborative evidence from her patient's sister's son that the apparition she and Mrs B. had both seen at the same time indeed resembled Mrs B.'s sister in all respects. Scott Rogo commented that 'this story…points to the objective existence of the "greeting figures" commonly seen by people having [near-death experiences]…We obviously need to collect more stories of this calibre…'

D. Scott Rogo, sadly, is himself now dead, but here is a small contribution to this needed literature, which was reported to the author of this book by a member of the family involved. (In the interest of privacy, certain personal details have been changed.)

In 1979 an exiled Iranian princess lay terminally ill from cancer in her house in London, England. Her husband was a doctor with a busy practice, and care of the dying woman fell largely to her elder daughter, Imrana, who was then aged about 14. She was with her mother in her final hours. At some point during that time, when it was obvious that no recovery was possible, the dying princess announced that her own father and an uncle, both long since dead, had arrived in her room.

She actually went so far as to introduce her daughter to the pair, although to Imrana they remained steadfastly invisible. Despite her feebleness, the fading woman then told them to go away, since she wasn't 'ready for them' yet. Apparently they did, for she soon ceased to be troubled by their presence. She next gave her daughter a long lecture on her future duties to the family. This responsibility discharged, she settled herself to wait for her 'guides' to come back to collect her. Her daughter saw her greet them before she finally gave up the ghost.

SWEET MELODIES

There is, then, some evidence that the 'greeting figures' reported by those who have had near-death experiences do have some objective existence. There is also evidence that the celestial music that dying people hear from, or in, the next world is not entirely of their own desperate imagining.

A close friend of a certain Mrs L. recorded the simultaneous experiences of several friends of the lady who, with her son, had gathered at her bedside shortly before she died in 1881. The report was given to Edmund Gurney, a senior member of the Society for Psychical Research in London, on 28 July that year, and it stated:

'Just after dear Mrs L.'s death between 2 and 3 am, I heard a most sweet and singular strain of singing outside the windows; it died away after passing the house. All [but one] in the room heard it, and the medical attendant, who was still with us, went to the window, as I did, and looked out, but there was nobody [outside]. It was a bright and beautiful night.

'It was as if several voices were singing in perfect unison a most sweet melody which died away in the distance. Two persons had gone from the room to fetch something and were coming upstairs at the back of the house and heard the singing... They could not, naturally, have heard any sound from outside the windows in the front of the house from where they were in the back.'

The only person who did not hear this sweet music was Mrs L.'s son, although the family doctor (the 'medical attendant') independently corroborated all the details of the first report, adding that the music consisted of 'a few bars...not unlike that from an aeolian harp – and it filled the air for a few seconds'. In his book quoted earlier, D. Scott Rogo remarked: 'The fact that the patient's son didn't hear the music implies that the sounds weren't from the street, but represented some form of psychic process.' He himself collected a number of reports of similar codas to

HAVING SETTLED HER AFFAIRS, THE DYING PRINCESS WAITED FOR HER 'GUIDES' TO COME BACK AND COLLECT HER.

Pictorial representation of celestial music (below) *by Fermoni, inside the cupola at Saronna.*

Impression of the Prince of Darkness **(above)** *from a 15th-century manuscript. An earlier manuscript* **(right)** *shows Christ at the door of Hell. Interestingly, those who have had near-death experiences tend to see Heaven rather than Hell.*

people's lives, although they seemed to be rare in 20th-century experience.

Finally, the view that the near-death experience is imaginary, a 'trick' dictated by biology and designed to obscure the fact of death, falls down over a crucial phase in the core experience. In fact the sceptics do not even address this question. And that is: if the experience is essentially imaginary, how does the imagination manage to put the procedure so neatly into reverse, as it were, when resuscitation is successful, and produce a suitable figure to pronounce the words 'Go back – your business on Earth is not yet finished' (or phrases to that effect), time after time, in so many different people? This is a surprising and unexpected sub-routine to find in a biological programme supposedly designed to ease one into oblivion.

THE FINAL CURTAIN

It might be argued that near-death experiences must be imaginary because they are simply too good to be true: no doubt most people would like to find themselves in green pastures and pleasant company on the other side of death. But not everyone who has glimpsed beyond that final curtain has had such a comforting vision. Some have seen Hell.

'I found myself in a place surrounded by mist...There was a big pit with vapour coming out and there were arms and hands coming out trying to grab mine...I was terrified that these hands were going to claw hold of me and pull me into the pit,' one such unfortunate told researcher Dr Margot Grey.

Another told Dr Raymond Moody that, as he travelled toward the realm of light during his near-death experience, he passed a place of terrible desolation, full of 'washed out', only partly human forms with an 'absolute, crushed, hopeless demeanour', who 'seemed to be forever

shuffling, moving around, not knowing where they were going, not knowing who to follow, or what to look for'.

Both these kinds of Hell have been reported by more than one witness. As Dr Michael Rawlings puts it, with black humour: 'It may not be safe to die.' Furthermore, the existence of the place of dreadful desolation has had some degree of objective verification.

APPALLING SORROW

In 1961, when serving with the British Army in Germany, medium Tom Fox spent a night at the site of the former Nazi concentration camp, Bergen-Belsen. He dozed off, and then:

'I woke up, and something very like Hell itself flooded my mind.

'No more than five yards away, clearly visible, there was a man standing. He was pale and thin, and a sense of appalling sorrow was welling from him.

'It very soon became obvious that he was by no means alone. His was the only form I could see, but I rapidly became aware of the presence of a whole crowd of souls. Occasionally, at the edge of things, I would see their blurred or fleeting images, as if they were on the brink of becoming visible...But there was no doubting that they were there. For I could hear them clearly enough. I was being overwhelmed with the turmoil of their suffering and heartbreak.

'At first I tried to close myself off from the agonized clamour of those tormented spirits. They were speaking in their own

Above: ***In a more peaceful representation in a French 12th-century manuscript, Christ is shown as supreme judge.***

Left: ***The light above the clouds. Some people who have had near-death experiences have felt they have risen above earthly things.***

Above: ***A traditional Christian view of the way to the ultimate end of mankind is shown in this representation of the Last Judgement.***

***In 1961 Tom Fox was overwhelmed with the anguish of tormented people when staying at the former Nazi concentration camp of Bergen-Belsen* (far right, the incinerator at Belsen).**

'SOME WERE CONSUMED WITH A DESIRE FOR VENGEANCE; OTHERS ASKED ONLY TO BE RELEASED FROM THE NIGHTMARE.'

languages, incomprehensible to me, but their anguish was unmistakable...Then, as I calmed down, I was able to distinguish personal voices and individual emotions.

'Some were consumed with the desire for vengeance; others asked only to be released from the nightmare of their experience, or to be freed from Belsen itself, the place to which they had become bound by their suffering. So many people had endured so many dreadful things in that camp, and in so short a time, that to those who had been there, it seemed that only those souls who had shared that terrible experience could possibly comprehend its enormity. Their time in Belsen had become their only reality. And so they had remained, tied to the place, to comfort one another.'

Fox prayed for them, and eventually the tormented host faded away. But, said Fox, 'I had learned more about human pain in those few hours at Belsen than many people do in a lifetime.'

The near-death experience seems to offer the best evidence so far that there is a life beyond death – and that, as might be expected, it is as challenging in its own way as life on Earth.

POLTERGEISTS AND THE PARANORMAL

HEARTS ON FIRE

When John Heymer, a former detective with the Gwent police, entered the council house, he was sickened by the grisly scene that met his eyes. After conducting his investigations he was forced to a conclusion that risked making him a laughing stock...

By the blast of God they perish, and by the breath of his nostrils are they consumed
Job, 4:9

In 1986, John Heymer, who had spent 25 years in the Gwent, Wales, police documenting minute details at the scenes of crimes, described the grisly scene that greeted him on 6 January 1980, when he investigated a mysterious death by fire in an Ebbw Vale council house:

'I opened the door [to the living room] and stepped into...a steamy, sauna-like heat...orange light emanated from a bare light bulb which was coated in a sticky, orange substance, as was the window...Heat had cracked one of the window panes.

'...On the floor, about one metre from the hearth, was a pile of ashes. On the perimeter of the ashes, furthest from the hearth, was a partially burnt armchair. Emerging from the ashes were a pair of human feet clothed in socks. The feet were attached to short lengths of lower leg, encased in trouser leg bottoms. The feet and socks were undamaged. Protruding from what was left of the trousers were calcined leg bones which merged into the ashes. The ashes were the incinerated remains of a man.

'Of the torso and arms nothing remained but ash. Opposite the feet was a blackened skull. Though the rug and carpet below the ashes were burned, the damage did not extend more than a few centimetres beyond the perimeter of the ashes. Less than a metre away, a settee, fitted with loose covers, was not even scorched. Plastic tiles which covered the floor beneath the carpet were undamaged.'

Heymer called in forensic scientists to confirm his suspicion that the victim had combusted spontaneously. They dismissed his proposal 'with knowing smiles', and suggested instead that the dead man had fallen into the coal fire in the room and ignited himself there. Heymer commented:

'Amazingly, the scientists saw nothing wrong in a man falling headfirst into a fire grate, igniting like a wax candle, then somehow picking himself out of the grate and sitting in his armchair to burn himself and most of his armchair to ash...the grate was tidy. It certainly did not indicate that anyone had fallen into the fire.'

A few weeks after this account appeared in the *New Scientist*, the journal published a letter from Dr Sidney Alford, who

Opposite: ***Officials search for clues to what started the fire in which Mrs Mary Reeser burned to death at her home in St Petersburg, Florida, on 2 July 1951. Despite the high temperature, flammable materials near her survived intact.***

PROTRUDING FROM WHAT WAS LEFT OF THE TROUSERS WERE CALCINED LEG BONES WHICH MERGED INTO ASHES: THE INCINERATED REMAINS OF A MAN.

Below: ***Mrs Mary Reeser, possible victim of spontaneous combustion. Similar cases have been recorded through the centuries, but the phenomenon still baffles modern medical science.***

Right: ***Hermann Melville and*** **(below)** ***Emile Zola. Both writers had fictional characters die from spontaneous combustion – a reflection of the 19th century's fascination with the idea that the human body can burst into flames of its own accord.***

probably knows more about explosives than anyone else in the UK, and who offered a possible explanation of such cases of spontaneous human combustion:

'Anaerobic fermentation within the gut...produces sometimes prodigious quantities of inflammable gas; consumption of eggs, for example, which are especially rich in phospholipids, might well add to the normal methane and hydrogen significant amounts of phosphine, and, worse, phosphorus dihydride, thereby imparting to the gas the property of spontaneous inflammability – the dreaded phosphinic fart. (How many of your readers have attributed singed underpants and burning thighs to mere frustration or, while strolling on a warm summer night after a second *soufflé*, have observed their breath glowing?)'

Alford's conclusion was clear enough: the right combination of circumstances and body chemistry 'might explain the precocious burning away which John Heymer describes'.

SPONTANEOUS HUMAN COMBUSTION IS MUCH MORE COMMON THAN THE OFFICIAL RECORD WOULD LEAD US TO BELIEVE.

BURNT TO CINDERS

The terrifying recurrence of spontaneous human combustion (SHC) – the hair-raising phenomenon in which a living person bursts into flames without warning or any sign of external ignition and is reduced to little more than a heap of ashes – has been the subject of fierce scientific debate for at least 300 years. Most scientists have regarded the very idea of SHC as ridiculous, and most medical textbooks omit any mention of it.

Yet hundreds of cases of mysteriously burned bodies have convinced the professionals on the spot – the firefighters and police – that nothing but spontaneous combustion could have caused the effects they have seen. Coroners are less easily persuaded, and many instances of SHC have been veiled by open verdicts. SHC is much more common than the official record would lead us to believe. Pathologist Dr David Price stated recently that he encountered a case roughly every four years.

Matters were not always so hedged about by fear of ridicule, as the literary record shows. There are nine famous allusions to SHC in pre-1900 fiction by distinguished authors, and there may well be more hidden in less celebrated works. The subject is mentioned in Washington Irving's *Knickerbocker History of New York* (1809); in Thomas de Quincey's 1856 revised edition of *Confessions of an Opium Eater*; and in Mark Twain's *Life on the Mississippi* (1883). Characters in Charles Brockden Brown's *Wieland* (1798) and Hermann Melville's *Redburn* (1849) succumb to a 'burning fiery death' without SHC being mentioned explicitly. SHC also features in Honoré de Balzac's *Le Cousin Pons* (1847)

Frederick Marryat **(above left)** ***and Charles Dickens*** **(above)** ***– two 19th-century novelists whose descriptions of spontaneous human combustion were based on real-life cases.***

and Emile Zola's *Le Docteur Pascal* (1893).

But the most detailed and revealing literary descriptions are based on real-life cases. Frederick Marryat used a London *Times* report of 1832 as the basis for his description of the death of the hero's mother, who is reduced to 'a sort of unctuous pitchy cinder', in *Jacob Faithful* (1833). The medical profession – when it deigned to notice SHC – regarded Marryat's description as a classic one, thanks to five 'typical' features: the victim was an elderly female; the victim was a chronic alcoholic; there was a lamp which might have started the fire; combustible materials in contact with the body were hardly burnt; and there was a residue of greasy ashes.

In *Bleak House* (1853), Charles Dickens killed off the sinister, alcoholic 'chancellor of the rag-and-bone department', Krook, by SHC. This fictional death echoes details of an inquest that Dickens attended 20 years earlier when he was a young reporter for the *Morning Chronicle*. Dickens was convinced of the reality of the phenomenon: in his preface, he bolsters his case for the plausibility of Krook's death by citing 30 press reports of death from SHC.

ACCUSED OF MURDER

The first medical writer to consider SHC was Thomas Bartholin, in *Acta*, published in Copenhagen in 1673. Then, in 1725, Nicole Millet was found burned to death in Rheims, in an armchair that remained unscathed by flames. Her husband was accused and convicted of her murder, but on appeal the court was persuaded that the death was a case of SHC. This inspired the scholar Jonas Dupont to gather together all the available evidence for SHC. His *De Incendiis Corporis Humani Spontaneis* was published in Leyden in 1763.

By the 19th century, Victorian moralists had concluded that SHC victims were invariably drunkards who had saturated their bodies with spirits – which were the

Above: ***William Guppy and Tony Weevle discover that the evil Krook has been mysteriously burned to a cinder, in an illustration from Charles Dickens'*** **Bleak House** ***(1853). 'Call the death by any name … attribute it to whom you will … it is the same death eternally – inborn, inbred, engendered in the corrupt humours of the vicious body itself, and that only – Spontaneous Combustion, and none other of all the deaths that can be died.'***

source of the retributive flagration. Unfortunately, this theory is nonsense: such an unrestrained drinker would die of alcohol poisoning long before becoming flammable. As the sceptical investigator Joe Nickell puts it, 'alcohol may have indeed been a contributory factor [in deaths apparently due to SHC], although not in the way some nineteenth century theorists imagined. A drunken person would be more likely to be careless with fire and less able to properly respond to an accident.'

But, as it happens, one of the first cases of apparent SHC, reported in the *Gentleman's Magazine* in 1746 and rehashed many times since, was of a woman not known for any close acquaintance with the bottle. She was the 62-year-old Countess Bandi, who burned to death near Verona in 1731. The sober noblewoman was reduced to a heap of ashes, though her legs and arms were untouched by fire. Despite the wealth of cases to choose from, the Bandi case, along with a handful of others (such as Grace Pett in 1744, Wilhelmina Dewar in 1908, Phyllis Newcombe in 1938 and Dr J. Irving Bentley in 1966), are repeated in nearly all the books and articles on SHC.

SELECTIVE DESTRUCTION

A strange feature of SHC deaths is the extraordinary speed with which the corpse – or what little may be left of it – decomposes once the flames have done their work. Another curiosity of such cases is the way that normally highly combustible furniture, linen and even clothing remains untouched by fire even though the victim's body – and the human body is one of the least flammable objects, consisting of about 75 per cent water – has been for the most part utterly destroyed.

This selective destruction is all the more mysterious given the intensity of heat needed to burn a human body. A crem-

atorium furnace, for example, maintains temperatures of at least 1700° F in a forced draught. A temperature of around 3000° F has to be maintained for several hours if there is no forced draught. But even a body burned in a crematorium fire at 2000° F for over eight hours will still leave recognizable bones, whereas the bones of many SHC victims are reduced entirely to ashes. Furthermore, crematorium fires are fed by copious external supplies of fuel. What can fuel the burning of a human body in a case of SHC?

Sceptical investigators say that the progressive release of body fat, soaking clothing or bedding, acts like the wick of an oil-lamp to provide the fuel for the fire. Pathologist Dr David Gee of Leeds University showed in the mid-1980s how this process might occur. He coated a test-tube with human fat, wrapped in human skin, to form a 'candle' 8 in long. He then wrapped cloth around it to simulate clothing. It took about a minute for a bunsen burner to ignite the 'candle', which then took about one hour to burn, the flame moving along the 'candle' against the direction of a draught from an extractor fan. But this demonstration proves nothing about cases in which people have apparently been burned to death when there is no external source of ignition, nor does it explain why they do not simply wake up early on in this grim process.

Researchers Vincent H. Gaddis (author of *Mysterious Fires and Lights*, 1967) and Ivan T. Sanderson (in *Investigating the Unexplained*, 1972) outline a possible sequence of events that might lead to SHC. This begins with loneliness, illness, or some similar emotional affliction that leads to a negative state of mind. This in turn affects the victim's metabolism in such a way that phosphagens, especially the vitamin B10, build up in his or her muscle tissue. (Phosphagen is a compound like nitroglycerine, and is extremely combustible in certain circumstances.) Electricity generated by intense sunspots, magnetic storms – or, later researchers have suggested, electrical energies produced by geological activity – then triggers the combustion.

Research by Livingston Gearhart,

Above: *The remains of a 65-year-old pensioner who died in a hayloft in Aberdeen, Scotland, possibly from spontaneous combustion. The body was considerably damaged; the floor around it had burned through, as had the roofing slats above, causing slates to fall onto the corpse, but the bales of hay surrounding the man did not catch fire. An account of the case featured in the* **British Medical Journal** *of 21 April 1888; this engraving was based directly on a photograph of the scene of death.*

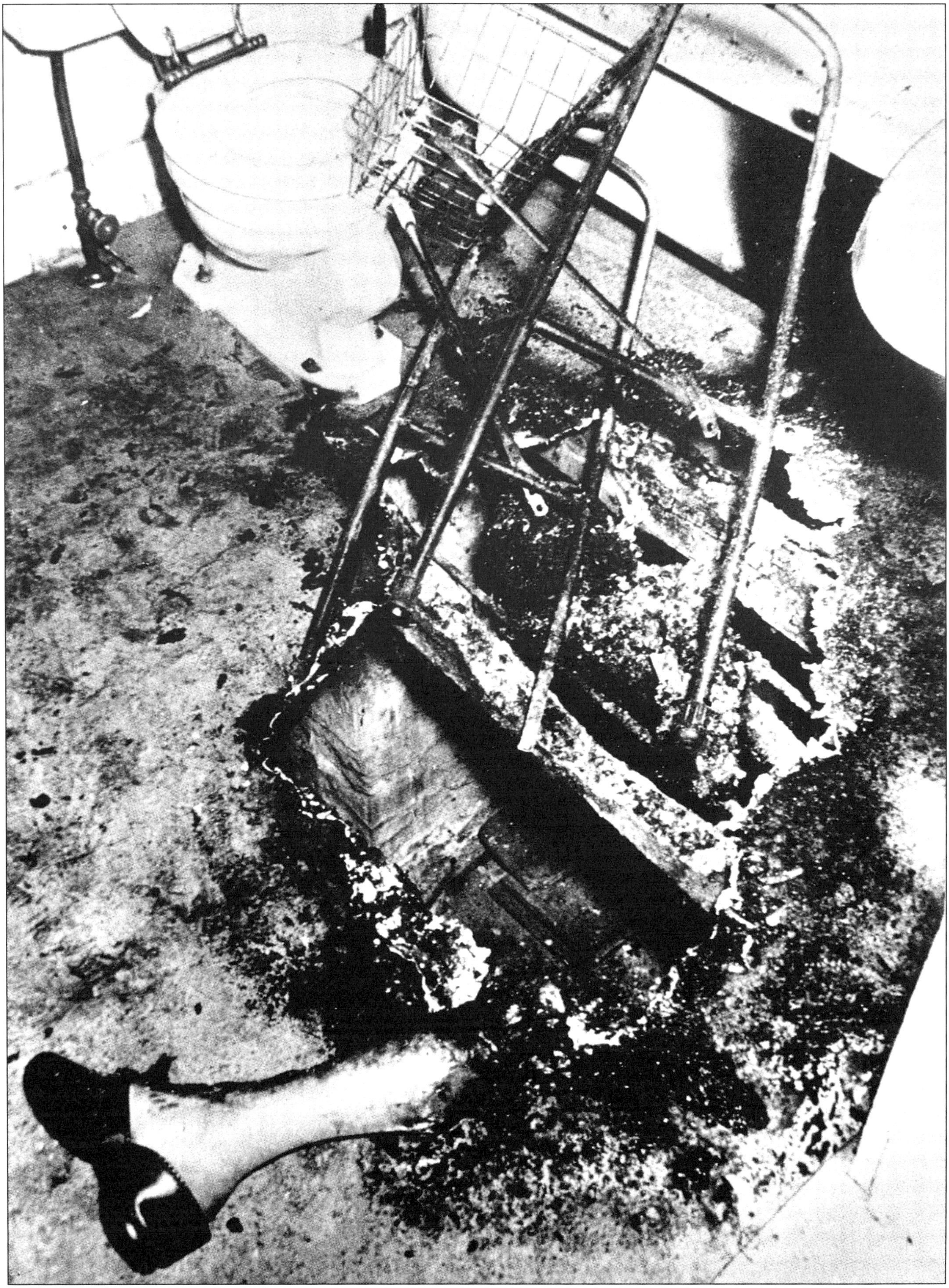

published in the journal *Pursuit* in 1975, showed that a significant number of SHC events coincided with local peaks in the Earth's magnetism. It is possible that high geomagnetism contributes to the formation of ball lightning, which in turn can generate short radio waves similar to those used in microwave ovens and radar equipment. (The reason warning notices and high fences surround radar aerials sited in places accessible to the public is simply that if you get in the way of a powerful radar array while it is scanning, it will cook your liver while you wait. External burns take some time to appear.) Some SHC victims appear to have burnt from the inside outwards, as if they had been subjected to this kind of microwave radiation.

A less materialistic theory is that SHC is caused by the Manipura chakra (the body's 'fire centre', which oriental medicine and acupuncture locate in the solar plexus) somehow running out of control. An advanced yoga adept can stimulate this chakra so that he literally glows in the dark. In the Tibetan practice of *tumo*, adepts have been known to generate so much internal heat while in a state of trance that snow melts around them. And it has often been noted that SHC victims seldom cry out or struggle, as if they were in a trance.

ORDEAL BY FIRE

Sceptics have striven mightily – and sometimes with success – to provide rational explanations for cases of *death* by SHC, but such reasoning after an event that itself lacked witnesses is easier than accounting for the occasions when people have burst into flames and survived.

On 15 November 1974, travelling clothes-salesman Jack Angel stopped for the night in his mobile home at the Ramada Inn in Savannah, Georgia. He awoke the next day to find his right hand burned and blistered, and further burns on his chest, leg, groin, ankles and back. Despite this damage he had felt no pain, and his sheets and clothes were unmarked. He staggered into the motel building and collapsed. When he woke again, he was in extreme pain, and in hospital. Doctors said the burns had begun inside his body, but did not explain how. As a result of his injury, Angel's burned hand and lower forearm had to be amputated. A Georgia law firm renowned for its success in product liability suits sued the makers of Angel's mobile home for $3 million damages – but after more than two years' investigation the cause of the fire remained elusive, even though the mobile home was dismantled down to its wheelbase in the search.

On 9 October 1980, Jeanna Winchester, then serving as an airwoman in the US Navy, was driving with a friend, Leslie Scott, along Seaboard Avenue in Jacksonville, Florida. Suddenly, yellow flames burst from Ms Winchester. Ms Scott tried to beat out the flames with her hands, and in the confusion the car crashed into a telegraph pole. The flames did die out, but not before scorching more than 20 per cent of Ms Winchester's body: burns disfigured

SOME PEOPLE HAVE BURST INTO FLAMES AND SURVIVED TO TELL THE TALE.

Opposite: ***The remains of Dr John Irving Bentley, retired physician, who died on 5 December 1966 in northern Pennsylvania, USA.***

Below: ***Ivan T. Sanderson, who suggested that SHC might result from an accumulation of certain extremely combustible compounds within the body, triggered by sunspots or magnetic storms.***

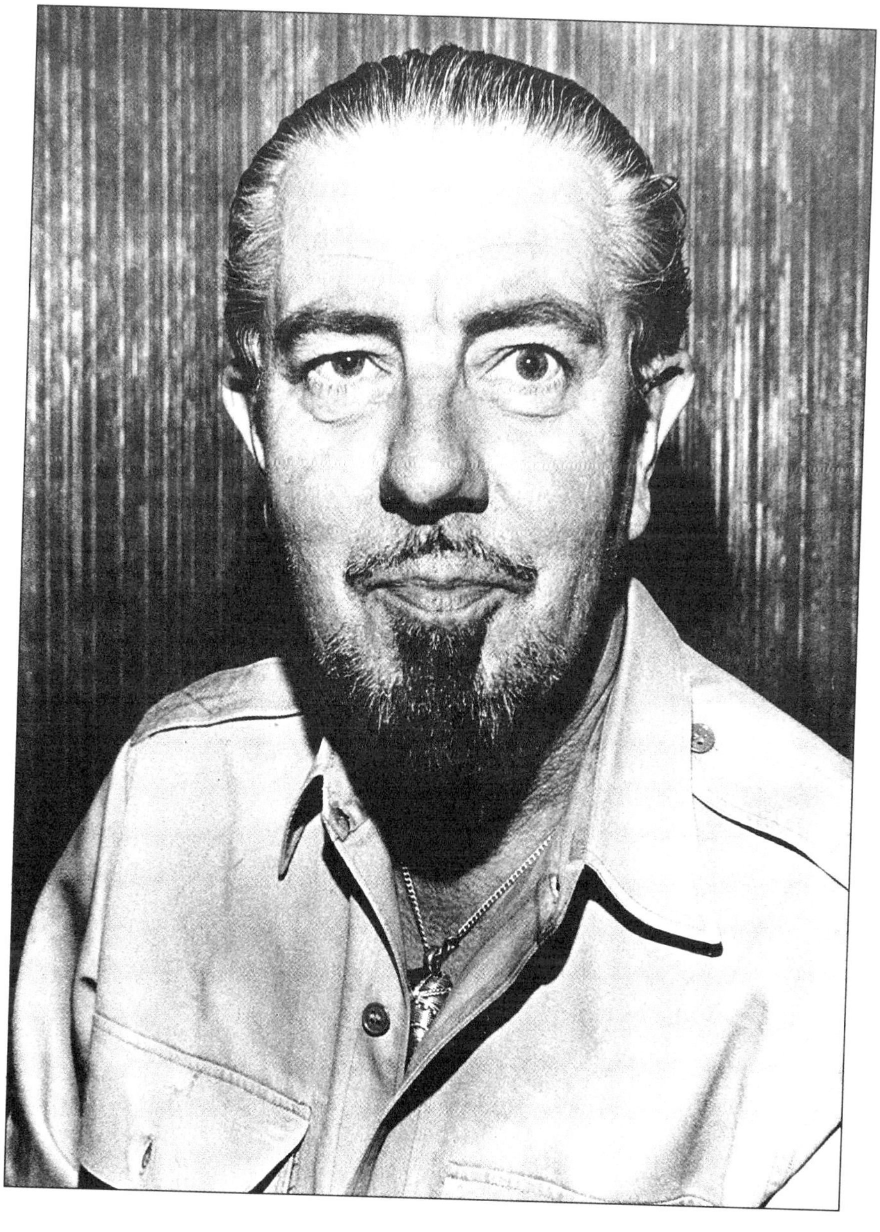

I THOUGHT I COULD HEAR MY BRAINS BUBBLING.

her right shoulder and arm, neck, side and back, and her stomach and breast. She said later: 'At first I thought there had to be a logical explanation, but I couldn't find any. I wasn't smoking anything. The window was up, so somebody couldn't have thrown anything in. The car didn't burn.' Nor had gasoline been spilled inside the car, police had confirmed. 'I finally thought about spontaneous human combustion when I couldn't find anything else.'

In the spring of 1978, the all-too-aptly-named investigative journalist Harry Ashbrook had just visited the Royal Free Hospital in London's Hampstead to have a leg injury treated. He then went to the local Haverstock Arms to meet fellow-journalist Peter Kinsley for a drink. While they were sitting in the pub, Ashbrook suddenly let out a scream of pain and almost passed out. Smoke was pouring from his bandaged leg. Kinsley helped him to return to the Royal Free, this time to the emergency room, where baffled doctors found that although the bandage was untouched, something had burned a hole in Ashbrook's leg down to the bone. But for the victim's account, they said, they would have assumed that only a red-hot iron or a point-blank gunflash could have caused such damage.

Below: ***Lightning. Sceptics implausibly claim this to be the cause of some SHC cases.***

Nineteen-year-old computer operator Paul Hayes, also a non-smoker, ignited without warning in the street in Stepney Green, east London, late at night on 25 May 1985. 'It was,' he said, 'like being plunged into the heart of a furnace. My arms felt as though they were being prodded by red-hot pokers from my shoulders to my wrists. My cheeks were red-hot, my ears were numb. My chest felt like boiling water had been poured over it. I thought I could hear my brains bubbling. I tried to run, stupidly thinking I could race ahead of the flames.'

In the end, he lay on the ground and curled up in a ball. Half a minute later, the flames subsided as quickly as they had burst out. Hayes stumbled to the London Hospital, a few streets away, where he was treated for burns.

BLAZING ROWS

Spontaneous fires do not have solely human victims, although they may be associated with individual people. These cases are apparently a fiery form of poltergeist. In these, the focus of the outbreaks (often, but not always, a child) live through a phase – often mercifully brief – during which they have the power to set nearby objects on fire.

Some such cases lead one to think that there really is a cosmic punster at work behind the world's multifarious scenes. 'Blazing rows' seem to have marked a series of outbreaks associated with a Mrs Barbara Booley – who seems to have had a fiery temper – between 1971 and 1975.

The first fire flared in August 1971 at the Berkeley Vale Hotel in Stone, Gloucestershire, after Mrs Booley had been sacked from her job as cook. The next broke out the following November, in a dormitory of St Hilda's School in Bridgwater, Somerset, where Mrs Booley was working, and had had a row 'with management' the day before. The third fire happened over Easter 1973 at Bath High School for Girls, Somerset. Mrs Booley said: 'Because I'd had a few words with a housemistress the previous day, police tried to pin the fire on me.' Fires numbers four, five and six erupted at the Swan Hotel, Tewkesbury, Gloucestershire, in August 1973. A parked car burst into flames in the hotel yard, and two days later flames broke out in a furniture store room. Mrs Booley left the hotel, and another fire broke out. The last reported incident was at the Torbay Hotel in Sidmouth, Devon. In early October 1975 Mrs Booley got the sack; the next day some bedding mysteriously caught light on a stair. Mrs Booley helped douse the flames, but was questioned once more by the police. She admitted that each blaze was preceded by an argument, but swore she did not set the fires. 'I wish I had been charged,' she said. 'Then I would be able to clear my name.'

Not all poltergeist-like fires are necessarily centred on anger. The talent, or affliction, of Benedetto Supino in this respect suddenly came to light in 1982. The son of a carpenter in Formia near Rome, Benedetto, then aged nine, was reading a comic in a dentist's waiting room when, unexpectedly and without visible assistance, it caught fire. One morning soon after this, Benedetto awoke to find his bedclothes on fire, and he was painfully burned. A plastic object held by his uncle burst into flames as Benedetto stared at it. Everywhere he went, furniture, fittings and objects smouldered.

Along with the fires came odd electromagnetic effects. Electrical equipment near Benedetto would function erratically and the power supply in his house failed several times. Top physicians and academics examined the boy without coming to any conclusions, while Archbishop Vincenzo Fagiolo pronounced the phenomenon 'not malign', to the relief of Benedetto's parents.

Another 'fire boy' made headlines in the Russian newspaper *Izvestia* in May 1987. In the presence of 13-year-old Sascha K, from Yenakiyevo in the Donets Basin of the Ukraine, clothes, furniture, carpets and electrical equipment had a tendency to burst into flames. The outbreaks, which resulted in over 100 fires, began in November 1986. He was taken to hospital for observation, and the clothing of a boy who shared his room suddenly caught fire. When Sascha was about, objects also flew in the air, and light bulbs would explode.

Perhaps the most famous 'fire-prone' person of recent years is the Scottish nanny Carole Compton, tried in Italy in 1983 for arson. On 2 August 1982, Carole, then aged 20, from Aberdeen, was arrested and held in jail in Livorno accused of trying to murder Agnese Cecchini, the three-year-old Italian child for whom she was employed as nanny, by setting fire to her cot. There had been a similar fire the previous night in the girl's grandfather's bedroom. On both occasions Carole was dining with the family, well away from the source of the fires. The girl's superstitious grandmother accused Carole of starting fires by using the 'Evil Eye'.

The trial opened in Livorno on 12 December 1983. Mrs Ricci, who had

Above: ***A group of farmworkers meet an untimely death on being struck by lightning, in an illustration from Camille Flammarion's*** **L'Atmosphere** ***(1888).***

EVERYWHERE HE WENT, FURNITURE, FITTINGS AND OBJECTS SMOULDERED.

Above: ***Fire damaged this building in Brazil at the height of a spate of poltergeist activity there. Investigators failed to identify the cause of the fire – it appeared to have been completely spontaneous.***

previously employed Carole, spoke of the nanny's obvious unhappiness both in her work and in her love affair with an Italian conscript. There had been unexplained fires in the household, and she said that her maid Rosa had complained of Madonnas falling off walls, an electric meter spinning while Carole was near it, and vases smashing off tables. Mrs Ricci's two-year-old son used to cry out that Carole was burning him whenever she touched him. All these are classic symptoms of poltergeist activity.

Nonetheless, Carole was found guilty of arson and attempted murder, and was sentenced to two and a half years in jail. She was, however, released immediately as she had already spent 16 months inside awaiting trial. She was back in Aberdeen the next day. The verdict was perhaps inevitable; it avoided the embarrassment of locking up a woman for witchcraft or of admitting her paranormal ability to start fires.

REPRESSED SEXUAL TENSION

There are numerous cases in the records of houses becoming affected by apparently spontaneous fires. On 6 August 1979, the Lahore family saw smoke pouring from an abandoned farmhouse on their property in Seron, in the Haute-Pyrénées, France. The fire was put out but, within two hours, two more broke out, this time in the family's modern farmhouse, which stands opposite the old one. In the month that followed, there were about 90 mystery fires in the house. For a while, 20 gendarmes camped near the farm but, despite a round-the-clock vigil, they neither saw nor apprehended any arsonists. One day, 32 separate fires sprang up within the house, burning towels, sheets, clothes and furniture. First there would be the smell of smoke; then an object would be found with a circular charred spot, which would burst into flames before being rushed out to be doused with buckets of water.

The Lahore family comprised father Edouard, 59, and his wife Marie-Louise, their sons Roger, 29, and Jean-Marc, 24, and a foster daughter, Michelle, 19, who had come to live with the family six years previously. Repressed sexual tension figures in many poltergeist cases, as do spontaneous fiery outbreaks, but it is idle to speculate about this case without more information. The prefect of police, an investigating judge, and Gregoire Kaplan, head of the Laboratory for Physical Analysis in the town of Pau, failed to establish how the fires were started. Like Carole Compton, two young scapegoats were jailed, tried and convicted (in that order), with no evidence, no witnesses and no apparent motive. But this satisfied the authorities' honour, and the pair were soon pardoned and freed.

But in some cases, no poltergeist focus or any other apparent natural or paranormal cause can be found for the visitation of the flames.

On a cold January morning in 1932, Charles Williamson of Bladenboro, North Carolina, heard his wife scream for help. He and his daughter rushed upstairs to find Mrs Williamson on fire. They quickly ripped off her burning cotton dress. The woman had not been standing near a flame, nor had her dress been in contact with a flammable substance. Two days later, a bed caught fire in the same bedroom, as did the curtains in an unoccupied room. Soon after that, a pair of Mr Williamson's trousers hanging in the wardrobe burst into flames. The bizarre series of 'spot' fires broke out over a five-day period. Arson experts investigated, but the results were inconclusive.

In 1990, a spate of unexplained fires hit the entire village of San Gottardo in the Berici Hills of northern Italy. Electrical equipment went haywire and objects of all sorts caught fire. Inhabitants complained of sickness, stomach pains and skin inflammations, all of which resisted medication. Animals were restless and off their food. People blamed UFOs, Martians and the 'excess of electricity produced by high-power generators at a nearby US communications base'. An army of investigators descended, but found no answers.

In that, they were hardly alone among those who have tried to discover the mechanism behind spontaneous fires of all kinds.

Below: ***More evidence of a fiery spirit at work in Brazil. In some poltergeist cases, the focus of the outbreak – often a child – develops the paranormal ability to set nearby objects on fire.***

POLTERGEISTS WITH A DIFFERENCE

Blood was everywhere. It spurted from the walls, drenching pots and pans, clothing and the doors. When the horrified occupants fled from room to room, their feet made bloody footprints on the floor.

On 12 March 1985, the occupants of a house in Aboro, a district of the city of Abidjan (which was once the capital of the Ivory Coast in West Africa), had the horrific experience of seeing blood spurt from their walls. It drenched articles of clothing, pots and pans in the kitchen, the shower, and some of the doors. Even more grotesque, when the occupants moved around inside the house, they made bloody footprints. Not a single person in the place, however, was wounded or injured.

In September 1987, a middle-aged couple, Mr William Winston and his wife, were subjected to extremely disconcerting flows of blood, apparently from nowhere, in their home in Atlanta, Georgia. The blood somehow splashed itself on the floors and walls of several rooms in the house; on one particularly grim occasion, Mrs Winston climbed out of her bath to find the bathroom floor covered in blood. 'I'm not bleeding, my wife's not bleeding. Nobody else was here,' said Mr Winston. Backing the truth of the story is the fact that the mysterious blood was analysed, and found to be human, type O. Mr Winston and his wife have type A blood, although they are undoubtedly human. So where did these grisly emanations come from?

Opposite and below: ***The work of a poltergeist at a house in Dodleston, Chester, in the spring of 1985. During the time it was active, a computer in the house received messages from a man who claimed to be living in the 16th century.***

Above and opposite: ***The Dodleston poltergeist displays its disturbing handiwork in the sitting room and the kitchen.***

UNDER TREMENDOUS PRESSURES AT WORK, IMPOTENT AND UNABLE TO SLEEP, THE FATHER WAS AT BREAKDOWN POINT WHEN THE POLTERGEIST OUTBREAK BEGAN.

SEXUAL DISTURBANCE

These poltergeist attacks contradict the stereotyped image of what a poltergeist does and what, so to speak, causes it.

The typical poltergeist throws things about, makes disembodied 'bumps in the night', hides everyday objects, and (these days) plays tricks with the telephone, TV and video. Sometimes it plays with fire. But, as we shall see, the range of mischief of which poltergeists are capable is far wider than this: so wide, in fact, that it has been truly said that no case is quite like another. Among other weird effects in the poltergeist's startling repertoire are apports – objects appearing out of thin air; teleports – things moving by unknown means from place to place, sometimes seemingly through solid walls or locked doors; sudden inexplicable chills; disembodied voices; levitation of people and things; and disgusting smells with no apparent source.

As for where poltergeists 'come from', the true answer to that question remains a mystery. The word 'poltergeist' is German in origin, and simply means 'noisy spirit' – from its traditional manifestation as bumps, raps and bangs. Whether or not a spirit or some so-far undefined reaction between someone's state of mind or emotions and the recognized 'scientific' forms of energy is involved, the blunt truth is that no one knows how poltergeists work or why one person sets them off while another, with perhaps identical stresses or problems, does not. Nor does anyone know whether their effects come directly from an individual, or if the affected person conjures up (or 'calls in') a separate entity that does the mischief on his or her behalf. Recognizing their own ignorance on this question, psychic researchers now use the neutral if somewhat tooth-jarring term 'repetitive spontaneous psychokinesis' (RSPK) to describe poltergeist cases. Itself translated, it means, essentially, that physical effects occur with a psychic cause, more than once, and without deliberate intention on anyone's part.

But it is true that poltergeist activity has often centred on adolescent children, especially around puberty. Few people do not experience turmoil at that time, and in some cases the inner disturbance spills over into the external world – with sometimes distressing results for those in the immediate vicinity. But by no means *all* poltergeists can be explained (as far as they can be explained at all) by the presence of pubescent children, especially when there is none around to point the finger at.

There are plenty of cases on record, however, that suggest that sexual disturbance of some kind is at the root of many poltergeist infestations. Some occur around women who are going through the menopause – which may, given the obvious symbolism of the blood involved, have had something to do with the Winston case in Atlanta, Georgia.

Grown men may also generate poltergeists. In the 1980s, researcher Andrew Green reported a case of 'psychic disturbances of all kinds' acting upon an outwardly happy and normal family of four in Somerset, England. The two children were in their teens and at first glance it seemed most likely that they were the focus of the disturbances. In the event, it turned out that it was the 49-year-old father of the family who was at the centre of the disruption. Under huge pressure at work, he had developed insomnia and then become impotent; he was near breakdown when the poltergeist outbreak began. Once he had proper medical attention and support, the disturbances stopped.

In many cases, it is not people but the place they live that is at the heart of the matter, and the commonest class of place that encourages poltergeists is council or public housing projects. One British analysis put the figure involving people in council houses as high as 86 per cent of all poltergeist incidents. This isn't necessarily to say that the families involved were faking the phenomena to improve their standard of living. Not all public housing is irresistibly attractive. A combination of the stress of moving, individual emotional conflicts within a family, and disappointment or even repugnance at the new home or its surroundings – and a house is, after all, the answer to a fundamental human need – may result in paranormal outbreaks.

LEWD PRESENCE

Some of the more bizarre poltergeist cases involve the apparent presence of discarnate spirits, and some of these are capable of extremely unexpected behaviour.

In early 1979, for instance, a poltergeist began shifting bottles and ornaments at the Whitchurch Inn, near Tavistock, Devon, but then stepped up the oddity of its attacks. While the landlady's family was out one night, a vase of flowers was upset, but the water in the vase 'simply

SHE TURNED ROUND TO RESPOND TO THE HAND CARESSING HER BOTTOM – ONLY TO FIND THE DOOR WAS CLOSED AND SHE WAS ALONE IN THE ROOM.

disappeared'. The climax came when landlady Sheila Jones received a warm hug, apparently from someone behind her: she thought it was a customer getting forward, and turned around to retaliate – only to find herself looking into thin air.

Another lascivious poltergeist, also associated with a pub, has plagued the Albion Hotel in Bolton, Lancashire – drying up the beer in the pumps or making beer flow incessantly from a bar-tap, as the whim takes it, and turning off gas-taps to the beer kegs in the cellar. One night in July 1979, landlady Barbara Barnes was getting into her bath when she felt a hand caressing her bottom. Thinking it was her husband, she didn't object: only when she turned around to see the bathroom door closed and no one there besides herself did her hair begin to rise. Just to make certain he wasn't playing tricks, she went to look for her husband – who was still in the bar, and had been all the time.

While some poltergeists appear to enjoy sex, others apparently disapprove. What they do in either case may well reflect the unconscious or repressed – unadmitted – fascinations and longings, or fears, or even feelings of revulsion on the part of those involved.

Wedding nights can reveal all of these and, especially for the inexperienced, can in any case be times of extreme tension. Add a very young bride – 17-year-old Debbie Mikloz, in this case – and a flat that was new to her, and it's just possible something strange will happen to spoil the initial joys of married life.

In November 1978 Debbie and her new husband, Steve Mikloz, went to spend their very first night together in their new flat in Raunds, Northamptonshire, and took

Below: ***John Glynn examines his wrecked bedroom during a poltergeist outbreak at his home in Runcorn, Cheshire, in 1952.***

themselves to bed. Debbie suddenly had the alarming feeling that they were not alone – and then Steve felt something grab him by the throat and haul him out of bed, struggling for breath. But there was no one else in the room besides the nuptial couple. With all amorous thoughts banished, the couple hurriedly got dressed and left. Since the assailant was invisible, the immediate assumption would be that this was the work of some kind of (jealous? puritanical? anyway, violent) ghost, but the landlords insisted that the flat had no history of haunting. Given the particular circumstances, a poltergeist remains the only plausible candidate. Whether the Miklozes were forcibly separated on any other occasion is, unfortunately for psychical research at least, not known.

With some libidinous phantasms it is difficult to sort out whether a species of poltergeist or a straightforward haunting is at work. When a council house is the setting, one might be forgiven for suspecting poltergeists, real or imagined; and there are other factors in the following case that make certain tensions at least possible. But the 'symptoms' of the case could just as easily apply to a haunting. But to say that is only to replace one unknown with another.

In 1978 the Hardie family – mother Bessie, then 57, her son Bob, 24, and her daughters Valerie, 20, and Margaret, 19 – had been living in a council house in Stockton, Teesside, for some time. They had been disturbed by odd noises coming from the loft, but these were as nothing compared to the events that occurred after the council had made some repairs to the house. One night shortly after this work was finished, Margaret was lying in bed when she heard a huge thumping coming from the landing outside her bedroom. Next, the bedroom door opened of its own accord. Margaret's bed began to shake. To her terror, her bedclothes were then slowly lifted up and what felt like a human hand slid from her shoulders down the front of her nightie and came to rest on her legs. Margaret was now paralysed with fright, unable to move.

It seems it was only at this stage that she was actually able to see her assailant, who appeared as a bald-headed man, wearing a Victorian cape; he kept his head down, so she could not see his face. But she did hear the apparition say 'Come to the bathroom, Margaret' – and he repeated this strikingly unromantic invitation three or four times. At this point, Margaret managed to let loose a loud shriek. Her mother rushed in to find Margaret drenched with sweat but no one else in the room. The teenager took to sleeping downstairs, but the apparition pursued her there as well. Others in the family began to catch sight of the entity, but it did not molest them. The family decided to have the house exorcized to rid themselves of the lewd presence.

Below: ***An illustration of the poltergeist that has come to be known as the demon drummer of Tidworth, from* Saducismus Triumphatus *(1681) by Joseph Glanvill, chaplain to Charles II and Fellow of the Royal Society. Glanvill's work at Tidworth was the first serious attempt to investigate a poltergeist haunting a private house.***

ELEMENTAL SYMBOLS

Without knowing a great deal more about the relationships between the individuals in the Hardie family, or the emotional history of the main victim, Margaret, it is impossible even to speculate on what might have lain behind these attacks – if, indeed, a revenant spirit was not at work, as seems quite possible. Psychic researcher Joe Cooper made the same point about the importance of seeking out the nature of a psychic victim's relationships, in his report of a particularly idiosyncratic poltergeist

THE TERRIFIED GIRL FELT THE BEDCLOTHES BEING SLOWLY LIFTED AND A HUMAN HAND SLIDING DOWN HER DEFENCELESS BODY.

Above: ***Drawings, found inside a sealed camera after the film had vanished, a sign of poltergeist activity in a house at Mulhouse, France, in the early 1980s. In a more bizarre manifestation, the ground level of the cellar rose 8 in*** **(below).**

that persecuted an elderly gentleman living on his own in a hotel in Yorkshire in the late 1980s.

He was afflicted by phenomena as varied as his clothes spontaneously igniting while hanging in a wardrobe, objects whizzing about under their own steam in the hotel lounge, and a pair of scissors that (also by itself) scratched crosses on the lid of a piano. But the most distressing, yet weirdly slapstick, aspect of the infestation was a deluge of water that repeatedly poured from thin air to drench the old man as he lay in bed reading.

Various attempts to get to the bottom of the mystery came to dead ends. Exorcism had no effect. A medium pronounced that at a certain spot in the hotel hallway a young soldier had slit the throat of a servant during World War 1, but neither the local newspaper archives nor older residents confirmed the story. Besides, even if they *had* existed, why would either of these characters soak an innocent old man in another part of the building with water, or set fire to his clothes? On a simple symbolic level it makes no sense unless, say, there had been some curious punning connection between their names. One could imagine such a link between a Private Waters, a waiter called Match and an old man called Box but, as the soldier and the servant were both figments of the medium's imagination, which did not stretch to the matter of anyone's names, even that devious path is a dead end.

Cooper suggested a change of room for

the old man, which seemed to stop the mysterious fires but did not entirely prevent the inconvenient floods of water. And the scissors persisted in vandalizing the hotel piano.

About a month after this change of accommodation, news came that the elderly gentleman's wife had died. She had been in a coma in hospital all the while – a fact that, it appears, neither the old man nor anyone else had imparted to the investigators, exorcists, mediums and so on who had become interested in the case. The poltergeist had started its mischievous work not long after the wife had been taken unconscious to hospital, however, and came to an abrupt and permanent halt when she died.

One can only wonder what kind of relationship the couple had had. He seems to have said nothing about her to anyone, let alone visited her. She visited elemental symbols of fire and water upon him (and, perhaps, symbols of death – graveyard crosses – that may also have been symbols of faith). That may be too grandiose an interpretation. Perhaps she was still burning with love for him: hence the fires. Perhaps he was not only indifferent (as he plainly was), but didn't wash often enough for her liking – hence the trials by water. Who can say? If the old man had only mentioned his wife and her coma, however, the investigators might have been able to learn a little about the relationship – and we might all be a little the wiser about the ways of poltergeists.

A CRY FOR ATTENTION

The renowned psychic researcher Harry Price characterized poltergeists in terms that were hardly complimentary, if accurate: 'mischievous, destructive, noisy, cruel, erratic, thievish, demonstrative, purposeless, cunning, unhelpful, malicious, audacious, teasing, ill-disposed, spiteful, ruthless, resourceful and vampiric'. The list reads like something from a thesaurus conceived in Bedlam. And for the vast majority of poltergeists, it remains an accurate description.

The literature of poltergeist infestations reads like a grotesque roll-call of the most mean-minded, petty and spiteful acts that human malice can devise. Looked at another way, such behaviour in human beings almost always erupts as a result of anger and rage – at oneself, at injustice, at emotional blackmail, at the impossible position (the double-bind) one has been shoved into mercilessly by others. It is irrelevant whether such an assessment is accurate, honest, truthful, or objective: indeed such a depth of emotion is rarely touched by people capable of a disinterested and impartial outlook. But scratch anyone, and – however rational they are – if there is one place in their lives about which they will reveal (and in some cases admit) such depths of feeling, that place will be their own family. There is nothing quite like the human family for creating massive, uncontrollable feelings of rage. And it seems to be on rage – the kind of crazed, lacerating destructiveness exhibited by a cornered animal – that poltergeists thrive.

And yet they can sometimes be kindly.

For more than a year, Derek Newman's family put up with a classic low-life poltergeist. It threw ornaments about, made a mess in the kitchen, and advertised itself importantly with bumps and thumps and bangs in their flat in Sheffield, Yorkshire. One night in January 1982, the usual

Below: ***Equipment installed at Mulhouse recorded inexplicable, sudden drops in temperature – a characteristic of poltergeist haunting.***

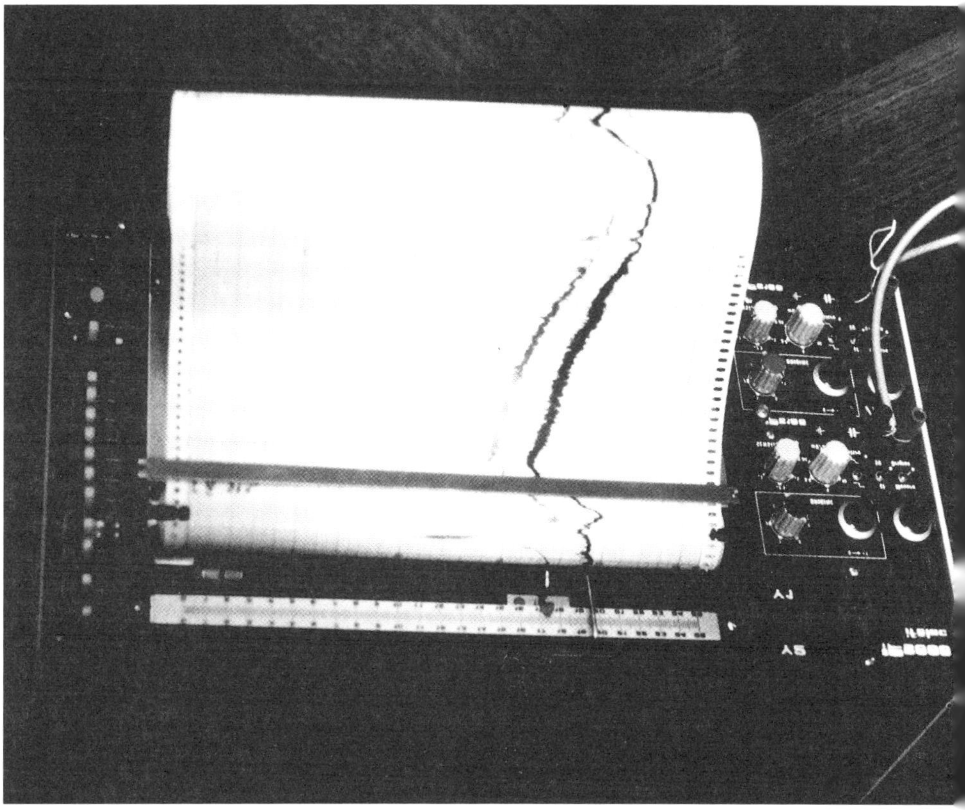

POLTERGEIST INFESTATIONS ARE A GROTESQUE ROLL-CALL OF THE MOST MEAN-MINDED, PETTY AND SPITEFUL ACTS THAT HUMAN MALICE CAN DEVISE.

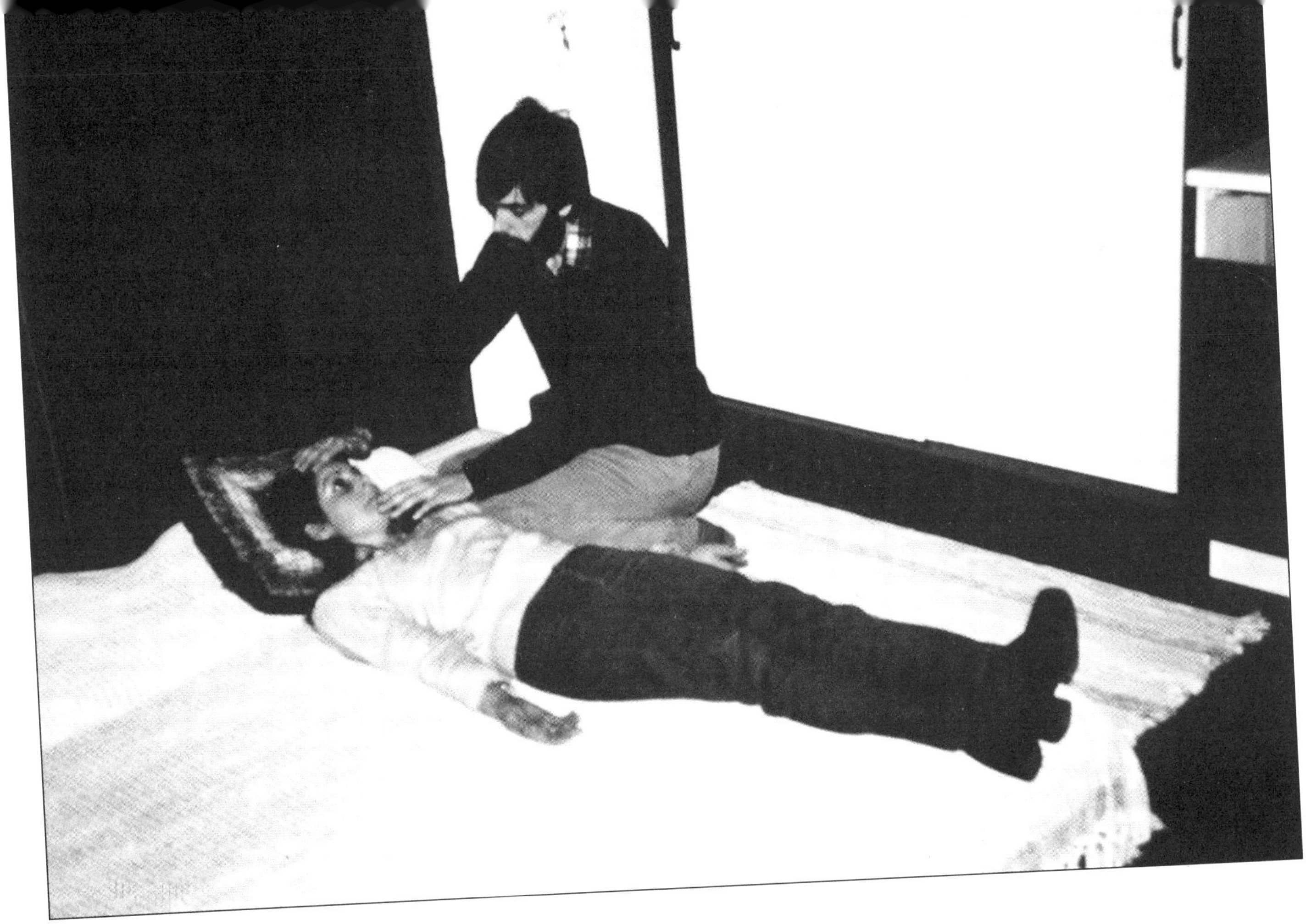

Above: ***Carla, the focus of the poltergeist activity at Mulhouse, undergoing hypnosis in an attempt to elicit poltergeist activity by means of post-hypnotic suggestion.***

commotion began, waking the family. Derek Newman said that the racket was 'like someone running round the lounge with a hammer'. He, however, had had enough, and decided to answer the poltergeist in kind. He picked up a hammer and opened his bedroom door. Dense, choking smoke poured in. Derek realized that his flat was on fire and dialled 999. As their flat went up in flames, firemen rescued the Newman family from their balcony.

Derek Newman has said that, were it not for the poltergeist, he and his family would have died in the blaze. But what started the fire in the first place? Was it the poltergeist – whatever that may be, or whatever it was expressing – or was it an accidental blaze that awoke the poltergeist because it *threatened* it with the worst fate any egotistical spirit could fear – namely, loss of attention?

This way of looking at poltergeists may not help explain the mechanics of the phenomenon, but it may illuminate one of its aspects. Put baldly, poltergeists seem sometimes, and perhaps more often than not, to be a way of crying out for attention. Harry Price's description of a poltergeist could as well be the characterization of a juvenile delinquent. Whether we can forgive such behaviour or not, it is not very difficult to understand. Few of us are not confused adolescents under our thin veneer of adult maturity – anxious for acceptance to the point of unconditional love, while demanding the room and a licence to be entirely, independently, and with splendid selfishness, ourselves.

There is a kindlier way of looking at the poltergeist, and that is to see it as the manifestation of the human spirit driven to extremes when its identity is under threat. While many children may regard the physical and emotional changes of puberty as an adventure and a source of pride, others may surely see them as a threat, fearing the loss of childhood simplicity (the besieged identity) and the sometimes alarming, often messy, onset of the unknown and the responsibilities it brings. If a child senses a risk of dubious sexual interest from a parent or sibling at this time, the whole turbulent process will be still less welcome.

Children are not alone in suffering crises of identity. Adults may feel trapped in a relationship, or stifled by their jobs or colleagues at work; a man suffering a bout of impotence, for whatever cause, may feel literally emasculated. Desperation is not the exclusive property of adolescents (although it often suits them to think so), and neither are poltergeists. In many cases, investigators are hampered in finding the roots of a poltergeist attack because they cannot bring themselves to enquire about intimate details of personal or family life, or because (not surprisingly) those involved are ashamed or afraid to reveal them to anyone, let alone comparative strangers.

At about this point, the usual objection rings out from the sceptics. But, they cry, if all that is true, why don't we *all* generate poltergeists when we're under stress?

This is really as pointless a question as 'Why do some people hate Beethoven?', or 'Why doesn't everyone breed racing pigeons?' Temperament, disposition, talent, environment, heredity – all or any of these may be involved. Some people have short tempers, others the patience of a saint. Some people work off their tensions, confusions, or rage by playing squash, listening to old Gong albums, drinking whisky, or even robbing banks. Some become comedians. Some produce poltergeists.

ROYAL OMENS

The link between a threat to the identity and poltergeist outbreaks is particularly plain in some cases.

In *The Paranormal*, scholar and historian of the paranormal Dr Brian Inglis relates how, on 28 January 1936, the funeral procession of the late King George V of England wound its way through the streets of London from St James's Palace. Among the regalia borne with the relicts of the King was the Imperial State Crown. At one point, the Maltese Cross that tops the crown fell

off. At this unexpected and somewhat undignified event the new king, Edward VIII, reportedly exclaimed: 'Christ! What's going to happen next?' He was overheard by the then Minister of Agriculture, Walter Elliott, who commented wryly to his companion Lord Boothby: 'That will be the motto of the new reign.'

Given the care with which the priceless British Crown Jewels are tended, such an occurrence would be unusual in any circumstances. But Edward VIII's identity was in question from several directions: apart from assuming the identity of the

Above and left: ***The funeral of King George V, which took place on 28 January 1936. During the procession, the Maltese Cross fell off the Imperial State Crown – an event that was so unexpected, so unlikely, and so shocking that some people suspected unseen forces were at work.***

Above: ***The Duke and Duchess of Windsor after their wedding in 1937. As Edward VIII, the Duke had been forced to choose between remaining king and marrying the divorcée Wallis Simpson. At his father's funeral the year before, the knowledge that he would have to make that decision and the tension he was undoubtedly feeling as a result could have produced the poltergeist-like activity that damaged the Imperial State Crown.***

monarchy (and having to give up his notorious social life for duties of state), he knew he would shortly have to choose between remaining king and marrying the divorcée Mrs Wallis Simpson – and their liaison indeed threatened the institution of the monarchy itself. Edward VIII's personal status and that of his royal office were thus in jeopardy. In the fraught emotional conditions of that particular royal funeral, then, it would not be surprising if a brief spasm from a poltergeist, centred on the new king, was responsible for distressing the major, most visible and most gorgeous of the symbols of monarchy on view that day. In the event, Edward VIII abdicated after just 325 days on the throne.

Dr Inglis cites another curious incident involving the British crown. When the former King James II entered Dublin in 1689 with the intention of raising the Catholic Irish against the new Protestant King William III, who had ousted him, his mace-bearer stumbled and fell. The cross on the crown of the mace lodged between two paving stones. James, who was to fail entirely in his attempts to regain the throne, was deeply troubled by the omen. We can only speculate on whether it was caused by psychokinesis from James's own subconscious recognition that his cause was lost, or whether it was no more than an ominous coincidence.

SAINTLY PRICE

Religion, for those who enjoy its certainties, is a powerful force in a believer's sense of his or her identity, and it's likewise unsurprising to find that the more ardent adherents of many religions have been surrounded by poltergeists when their beliefs were threatened. When they set about medieval Christian zealots, the poltergeists were invariably labelled 'demons' that were taken to be testing the victim's strength of faith – or simply setting about them with special vigour just because they were especially saintly and, therefore, a thorn in the side of the forces of darkness.

This may well have been the case, but it is worth remembering the psychologists' truism that people who profess an absolute, unbending belief in anything (from the joys of capital punishment to the flatness of the Earth) that is not amenable to direct proof must spend a great deal of energy repressing their awareness that they might possibly be wrong. It is a platitude that converts are particularly prone to intolerance of their former sins when they find them in others, and it takes no great psychologist to see that they are really resisting the temptation to backslide – in other words, they are projecting what is in fact an internal battle. So we may speculate with some justification that the poltergeists that beset the holy men and women of the Middle Ages were not precisely demons, but the projections of inner struggles. Scratches, pinching, showers of filth, and the usual harassment with loud noises were all part of the price the saintly paid for their faith.

Such outbreaks are not, however, confined to Christians. Dr Inglis cites the case of a Bishop Weston, who was

determined to show some native tribespeople in Zanzibar that the local demons could not faze a good Christian. He went into a reputedly haunted hut, only to stagger out covered in clods of earth that the 'demons' had plucked from the walls of the hut and liberally showered about when he stepped in. In this case, one might presume that behind the attack lay the faith of the local people, who might justifiably be incensed that their demons should not be accorded a proper respect.

Yet even the most assiduous psychological analysis of such idiosyncratic poltergeists can explain no more than the *conditions* that call them forth. It does not explain the mechanism of the poltergeist – how it picks things up and throws them about, or sets fire to someone's skirts, or speaks in gruff but disembodied voices. We are left somewhat in the position of someone who knows that buying an airplane ticket and boarding the aircraft will get them to the land of their choice – but from whom all knowledge of jet engines, aerodynamics or even the existence of the pilot has been kept hidden. The temptation to think that the ticket is the cause, and not the condition, of the journey is plain enough.

Above: ***A 16th-century illustration of the rite of exorcism. In medieval times, people troubled by poltergeists were believed to be possessed by evil spirits – and exorcism was the only known form of treatment.***

HUMAN ENIGMAS

At 4, Zheng Xiangling could see glowing auras surrounding people; at 6, she could accurately predict the sex of unborn babies; by the time she was 24 she had developed an X-ray vision which the leaders of the People's Republic of China found extremely useful.

When the Beatles chanted 'I'm looking throu-ou-ough yooou' on their 1965 album *Rubber Soul* they were giving a new twist to a common enough figure of speech. The unfortunate creature addressed by the foursome was so empty of interest that she was transparent. The following year, Pete Townshend of The Who used the metaphor in more traditional vein in *I Can See for Miles*, as he described how he could see into a certain lady's mind, heart and questionable motives with ease.

Being able to 'see through' other people's motives is a talent some are blessed with more than others, but a few rare individuals can apparently go further than that: they can see through human flesh.

Adepts of the ancient Chinese discipline of *qigong* have from time to time claimed to have developed X-ray vision, which they say is two-dimensional and limited to black and white imagery, by using a regime of breathing exercises to control their *qi*, or 'life-energy', as it flows through their bodies. But one modern adept has surpassed even that ability.

Reports of the wild talent of Miss Zheng Xiangling first surfaced in the West in 1988, when she was 24. A doctor who then worked at the General Staff headquarters

Opposite and below: ***Two of the photographs obtained by Margaret Fleming – not by using film and camera, but by holding a piece of photographic paper and concentrating on the image she wanted to appear.***

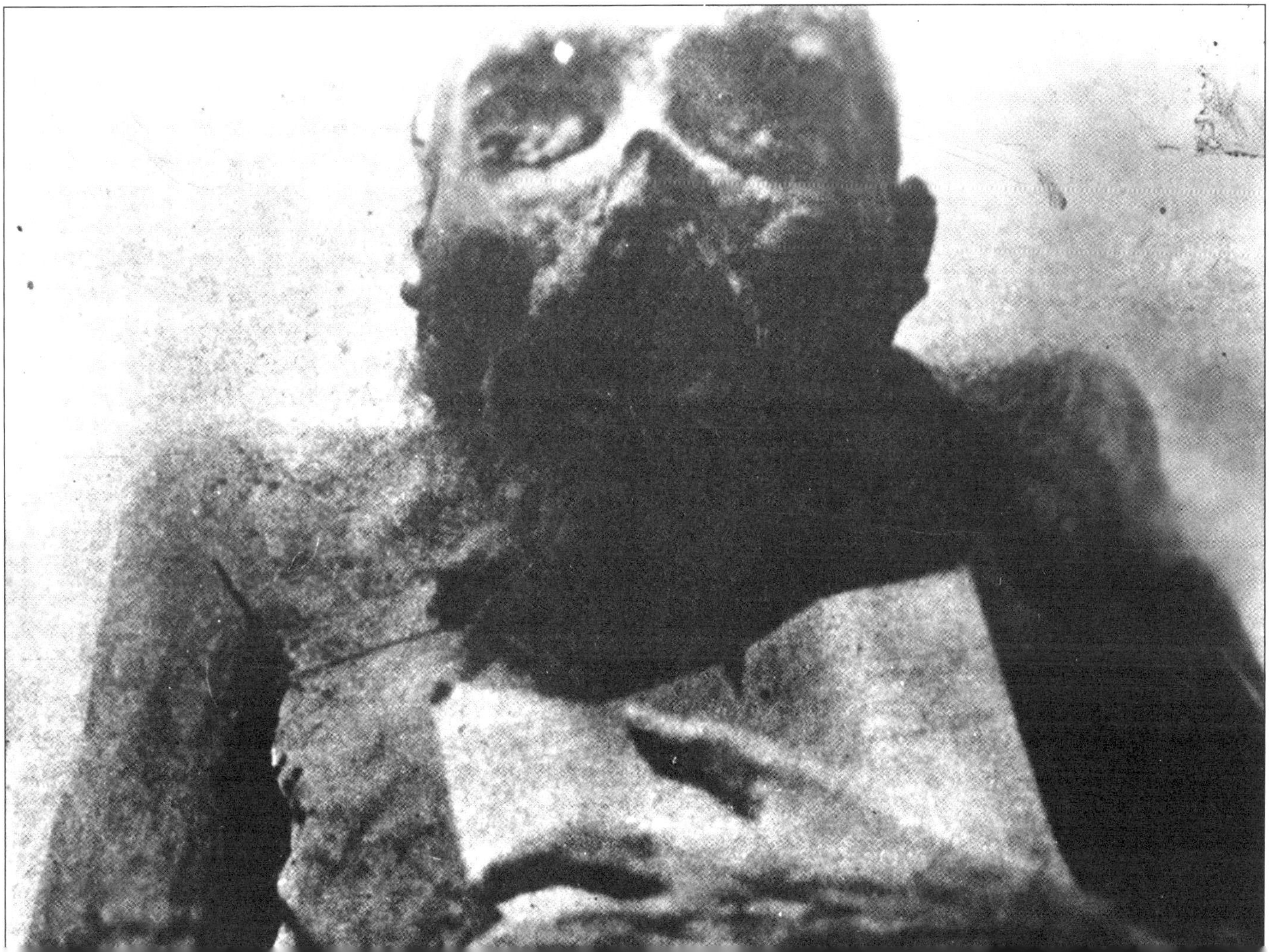

Above and opposite: ***Two more examples of Margaret Fleming's 'thoughtographs'. The ability to project images onto film or paper by mental energy alone is one of the most remarkable of paranormal talents.***

of the People's Liberation Army in Beijing, Miss Zheng can see her patients' bones, veins and internal organs in three dimensions and full colour – and can presumably see anyone else's as well, when and if she chooses. Her ability is not limited to human flesh: she can read words written – out of her sight – on paper that has then been tightly folded, for instance, and is reported to be able to will goldfish to die.

In her lifesaving role, Miss Zheng usually diagnoses her patients, who remain fully clothed, in the dark. She is particularly good at detecting cancers, heart disease, arthritis and respiratory problems, and with greater accuracy than standard hospital equipment. The process however is exhausting, and she sees patients only twice a week – and they, according to her friends, are a veritable 'Who's Who of the Chinese leadership'.

Miss Zheng believes she has inherited her extraordinary ability from her grandfather, whose reputation as a diagnostician in his native Shaanxi province was unsurpassed. The first sign of unusual powers came when she was aged four, when she discerned glowing auras around people. Within two years she was accurately predicting the sex of children carried by her pregnant relatives. Her brother, too, has similar powers, and is said to be employed by the police occasionally to spy on suspected criminals – by looking through the walls of their houses.

While Zheng Xiangling developed her ability through rigorous discipline, it can emerge spontaneously. In March 1978, 37-year-old crane driver Mrs Yuliya Vorobyeva was working in a mine near Donetsk in the Ukraine when she ran into an electricity line and received a massive 380-volt jolt. She was pronounced dead, and lay in the local mortuary for two days before a post-mortem was held. But no sooner had scalpel sliced skin than the 'corpse' began to bleed – and to shake uncontrollably. After that uncomfortable awakening, Mrs Vorobyeva did not sleep for six months. Finally, she succumbed to a long, deep sleep – which refreshed her in an extraordinary way.

'One morning,' she told the newspaper *Izvestia* in June 1987, 'I went out to buy bread. I got to the bus stop and a woman was standing there. I went up to her and suddenly I was paralysed with horror. I could see her intestines and straight through her as if she were a picture on a television set.'

Investigated by a Dr Yeizhertin at Donetsk hospital, she told him – correctly – within seconds of their meeting that his hearing was better in one ear than the other, and that his left eye was stronger than his right. In similar forthright fashion she correctly told the reporter from *Izvestia* that he had a red liquid in his stomach – which had once been a jelly. Mrs Vorobyeva now specializes in diagnosing rare diseases and, according to doctors at Donetsk, 'has never made a single mistake'.

THOUGHTOGRAPHY

Among the more exotic human talents, being able to see through solid matter has its unlikely parallel in the ability to produce images, as it were from nowhere, on film – without actually pointing the camera at the object it photographs.

The great exponent of thoughtography in modern times was former merchant sailor and Chicago bellhop Ted Serios. He was last reported, in the mid-1980s, to be living in obscurity in a slightly ramshackle house at the end of a dirt road near Mendon, Illinois, on the border with Missouri, and working as little as possible. 'If you gotta work and be poor,' he told visitors, 'you might as well not work and be good'n'poor.' But for a time in the 1960s and 1970s, Serios was famous.

He worked with a Polaroid camera, which at least proved that his effects were not the result of chicanery in the darkroom. And very strange effects they were, on occasion. Equally extraordinary was the lather into which Serios threw himself to get those effects. Much of his work was documented by psychologist Dr Jule Eisenbud, in Denver, Colorado – some distance from Chicago, to which city Serios would sometimes capriciously return without warning in the midst of a session. The sessions themselves were chaotic, as Eisenbud often had to pursue Serios around town and, even when settled, Serios himself would psyche himself up (he was never able to produce 'thoughtographs' to order) with copious amounts of beer, becoming ever more dictatorial and temperamental as he went on drinking.

Newscaster Bob Palmer described Serios's style: 'Ted would bolt out of his chair and charge the...camera. There, he would grunt, purr, curse, and squint, and with an incantation that would do a dice-roller proud, he'd wind up and let go. On

IT IS RUMOURED THAT HER BROTHER IS EMPLOYED BY THE CHINESE POLICE TO SPY ON SUSPECTED CRIMINALS – THROUGH THE WALLS OF THEIR HOUSES.

USING HER AMAZING POWERS MS FLEMING PSYCHICALLY PROJECTED THE IMAGE OF A LUSCIOUS NUDE ONTO THE FILM LOCKED INTO THE CAMERA.

the downhill side of these incidents he'd whirl round and demand, "Did you see anything? Did you see anything?"'

Nonetheless Serios did on many occasions produce photographs. Sometimes staring into the camera lens, sometimes in another room from the camera, sometimes with the camera pointing into empty space as he raged around it, Serios somehow managed to get images of distant locations onto the film. Sometimes they were pictures of specific targets that Eisenbud had asked him to 'thoughtograph', but they were often quite random images – and often strange in themselves.

In May 1965 Serios produced a string of pictures of a storefront rather strangely named the Wld Gold Store. This turned out to be the former Old Gold Store in Central City, Colorado. The curiosity was that when Serios 'took' his pictures, the store's name had been changed to the Old Wells Fargo Store. The 'W' in Serios's pictures, and on the storefront, was placed exactly where the letter 'O' had once been. Eisenbud was also unable to find any source that Serios might have used to fake the photograph. Another location in Central City that Serios 'thoughtographed' was Williams's Livery Stable. The oddity here was that his picture showed the building's windows bricked up, and the material of the façade was different from that of the actual building.

Central City is some 40 miles west of Denver, set in the mountains a little north of US Highway 40. It is conceivable that Serios went there on his unannounced departures from sessions with Eisenbud, or that he went there before the sessions, and he may have taken photographs of the place. What is clear enough is that he had no way of physically getting into the Polaroid cameras used in the experiments – they were in any case sealed and marked against interference – to plant these curious pictures. Still less likely is it that Serios – not, by all accounts, the most solvent or careful character on Earth – would have

Below: ***A 'thoughtograph' created by Mr Kohichi Mita on 11 October 1916. As the Japanese psychic focused his thoughts on Ohgaki Castle, the dim form of the building appeared on a photographic plate.***

Left: ***This pictogram appeared on a photographic plate after 31 seconds' concentration by psychic Mrs Ikuko Nagao.***

bothered to make a journey to Canada to fake up a picture of a building on an airstrip belonging to the Royal Canadian Mounted Police. And that photograph too has its internal anomaly. The word 'Canadian' is strangely misspelt, which it certainly is not on the actual building.

Serios is not alone in projecting thoughts onto film, nor are his necessarily the strangest results in the field. *Fate* magazine of June 1976 published two astonishing photographs obtained in a psychic experiment by Margaret Fleming. The first showed a leaping nude, which Ms Fleming had psychically projected onto film negative. A few days later she took another print from the same negative – but the image had subtly altered, as if it had continued to move. Nor was Serios the first to produce mental pictures on physical film. Japanese psychic Tenshin Takeuchi, working with investigator Dr Fukurai, produced numerous 'thoughtographs' in 1915. On one occasion he projected three pictograms, precisely those requested by Fukurai, onto a photographic plate; on another, he reproduced a whole sentence from a book.

MAGNETIC PERSONALITIES

Factory worker Leonid Tenkaev, of Saratov, Russia, is a very attractive man when he wants to be. His wife, his daughter, and his grandson are equally attractive. All four have the uncanny ability to make metal objects stick to their bodies at will.

According to Dr Valeri Lepilov, professor of physics at Saratov State University, the four have only to 'concentrate and think about generating heat inside their bodies' to turn on their magnetic ability. 'In a few moments objects can be attached to them.' The force these members of the Tenkaev family exert is considerable. Leonid, who was born in 1928, has made as much as 52 lb of ferrous metal stick to his person. Removing the objects, says Dr Lepilov, can be hard work – 'like dragging a metal object off a real magnet'.

The Tenkaevs say they have become aware of their strange talent only since

Below: ***One of many 'thoughtographs' produced during Dr T. Fukurai's experiments with psychic Tenshin Takeuchi in Tokyo in 1915.***

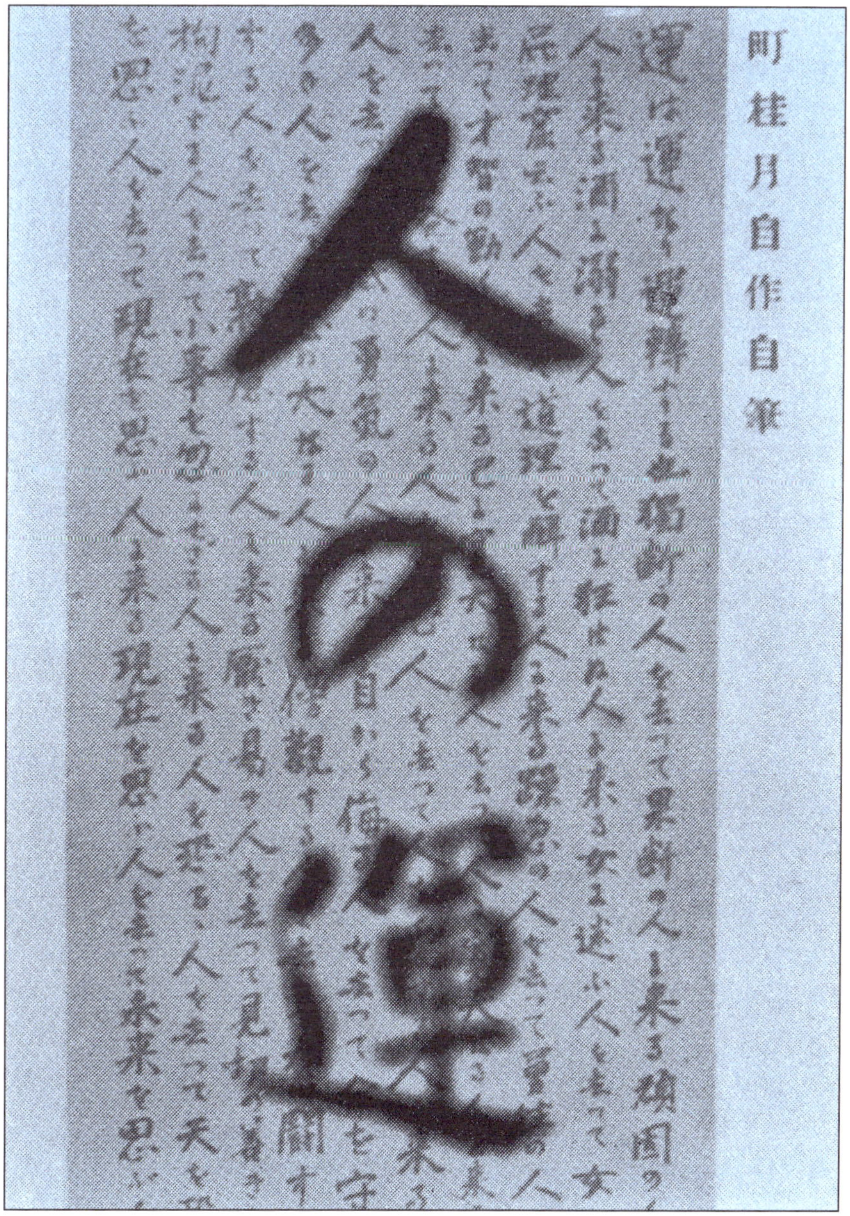

JUST A YEAR AFTER THE CHERNOBYL NUCLEAR DISASTER, THE TENKAEV FAMILY BECAME AWARE OF THEIR STRANGE NEW ABILITIES.

Below: ***Russian psychic Nina Kulagina looking into a camera and attempting to imprint an image onto the film: she usually made geometric shapes.***

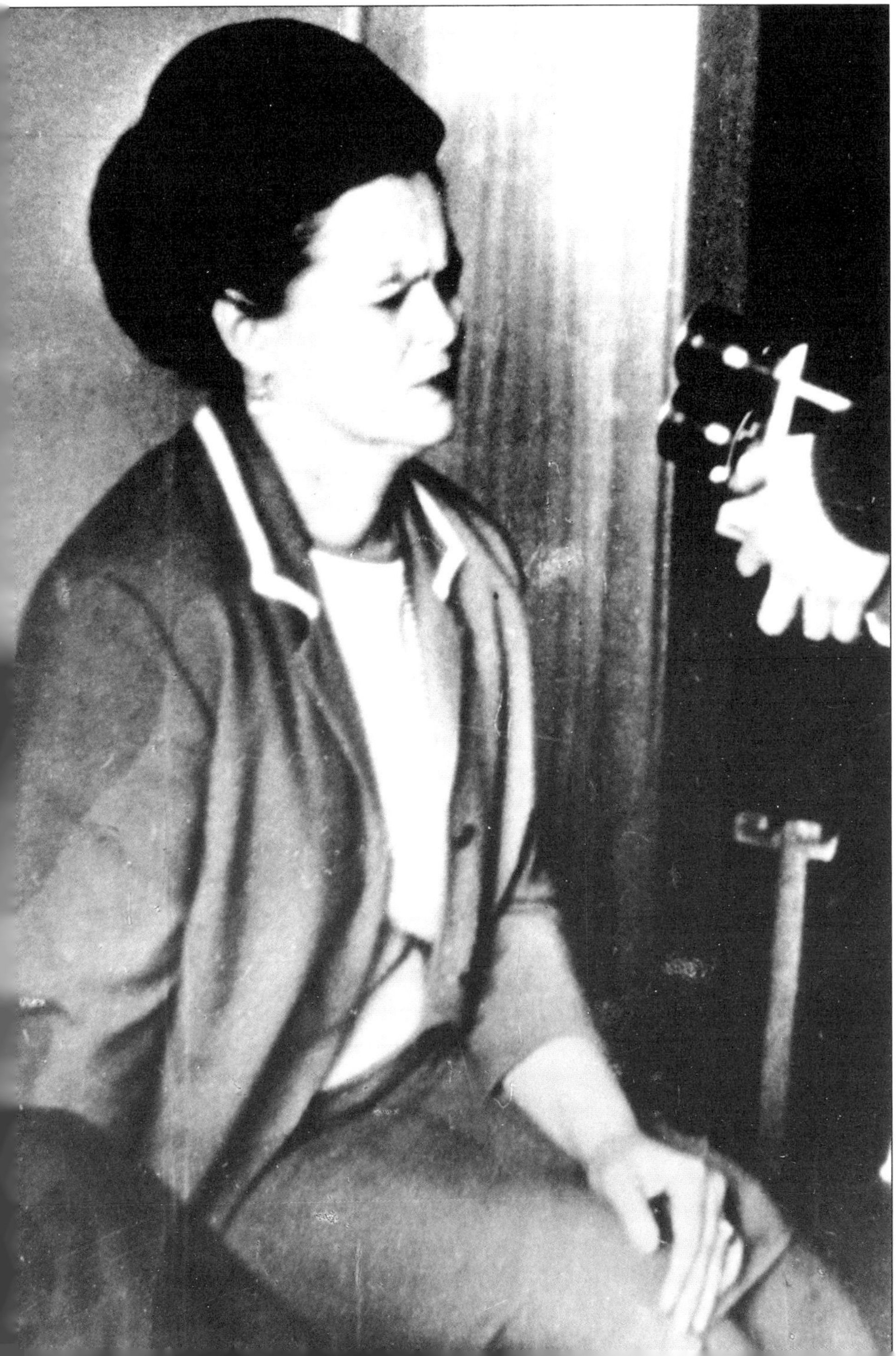

1987 – a year after the Chernobyl disaster. Certainly they are not the only Russians, or even Eastern Europeans, whose odd magnetic gifts have been in the news since then – but it is a moot point whether the cause of their fame has anything to do with the after-effects of a nuclear accident, or more to do with the greater freedom of the press in formerly communist countries.

Fifty-five-year-old militia patrolman Nikolai Suvorov, for example, was reported by Russia's *Soviet Weekly* in June 1990 as also being able to generate a magnetic force at will, so that things made of metal stick to his skin; while Bulgaria's Sofia Press agency reported in 1991 that no fewer than 300 'magnetic' people turned up at a contest to see who could keep metal objects on their bodies the longest.

But what creates this ability is a mystery, as is the ability such people have to turn it on and off whenever they want. Even stranger, it is not always strictly a magnetic effect. Unlike an ordinary iron magnet, the human magnet's powers are not limited to ferrous metals. Militiaman Suvorov, for instance, can attract plastic and glass as well as metal to his body. Inga Gaidochenko, from Grodno, Byelorussia, has been known to make a 9 lb sledgehammer stick to her, despite her youth (she was born in 1979), and can also attract plastic, wood and paper – but not glass. Something rather more like gravity than electricity or magnetism seems to be at work here – but why should glass be immune to it?

There are many such cases on record. In 1889, Frank McKinstry of Joplin, Missouri, was reported to feel himself becoming 'charged' early each morning, and then he had to keep walking – otherwise, his feet would stick to the ground, immobilizing him. If another person lifted his feet – as sometimes they had to – the effect would dissipate with a small, faint flash. McKinstry, interestingly, also had the reputation of being a good dowser.

In 1890 the Massachusetts College of Pharmacy studied the case of 16-year-old student Louis Hamburger, who made mincemeat of scientific preconception by lifting a glass jar full of iron filings, weighing about 5 lb, with the tips of three fingers. To do this, his fingertips had to be dry – a peculiarity because water is an excellent conductor of electricity, and children are constantly warned not to switch lights on and off with wet fingers. Hamburger's favourite demonstration was to draw his fingers up the *outside* of a glass beaker full of iron filings, so that they could be seen rising to follow the movement of his hands. In a more recent case, in 1938, Mrs Antoine Timmer demonstrated to a meeting of the Universal Council for Psychic Research in New York how her personal magnetism caused cutlery to stick to her hands; they could be removed only with a sharp tug.

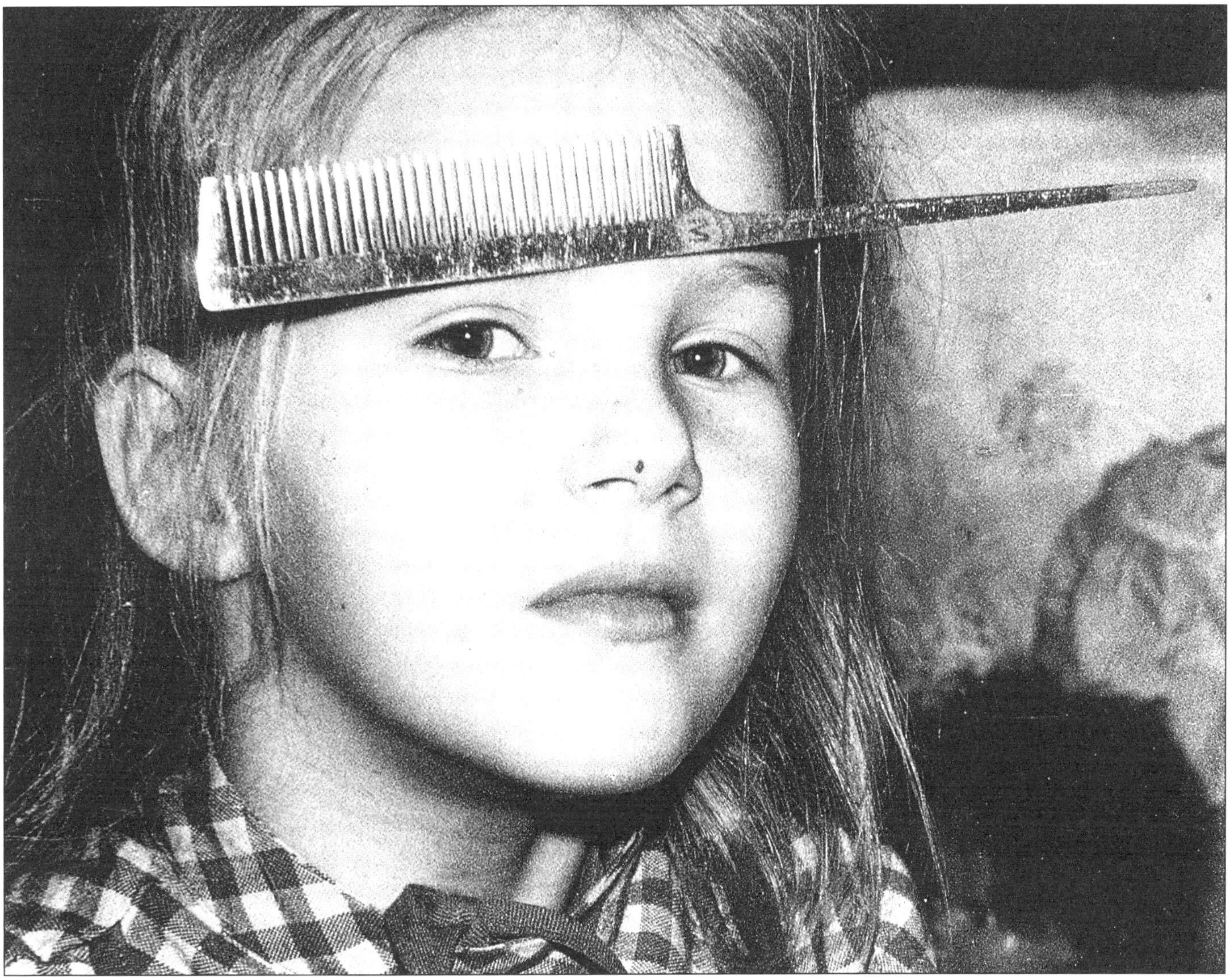

A SHOCKING STATE OF AFFAIRS

For some, their weird electrical abilities are more of a curse than a blessing. Oxford don Dr Michael Shallis discovered that Mrs Jacqueline Priestman, of Sale, Manchester, had more than 10 times the usual amount of static electricity in her body, which may explain her disruptive influence on household equipment, which began – for no discernible reason – when she was 22 years old. No fewer than 30 vacuum cleaners, five electric irons and two washing machines have succumbed to Mrs Priestman's electric personality, while her electric cooker cuts out when she tries to use it and her TV set changes channels at her approach.

Dr Shallis says: 'It's not certain what causes this severe build-up of static. Such people seem to be able to transmit miniature bolts of lightning that break down the insulation of some electrical appliances.'

He cannot explain why this build-up of electricity started when Mrs Priestman was 22, or why the effects are limited to her own home. However, by an irony, her husband Paul is an electrical technician. Is this perhaps some kind of real-life pun on the part of a poltergeist? More information about the Priestmans' domestic life might clarify matters, but in the circumstances they would probably prefer simply to be rid of their electrical plague than help develop the esoteric theories of psychic investigators.

The sudden onset of personal electrical power is not unusual, it seems, in cases of the kind – if anything about them can be called 'not unusual' in any sense. Xue Dibo, a 36-year-old boilermaker from Urumqi, in China's Xinjiang province, felt 'strange sensations' at the beginning of 1988, and then found that whenever he touched people he was giving them an electric shock that was strong enough to knock them over.

Above: ***Eight-year-old Svetlana Glyko displays her extraordinary powers of attraction. Svetlana, from the Commonwealth of Independent States, can hold combs, teaspoons and other small objects on her forehead.***

Right: ***Some paranormal electrical abilities can seriously disrupt domestic life. One woman found that all manner of household equipment – washing machines, vacuum cleaners, cookers, irons, televisions – refused to work in her presence.***

THE NUBILE 15-YEAR-OLD MADE A MOCKERY OF THE ACCEPTED LAWS OF PHYSICS.

REPELLENT

Not everyone who has such bizarre abilities is disturbed by them. Teenager Lulu Hurst was known as the 'Georgia Wonder' and at her parents' instigation appeared on stage between 1883 (when she was 15) and 1885 to demonstrate her capacity to defeat the usual laws of physics. She could draw all kinds of objects to her, metallic or not – even a straw hat – at will. With equal facility she could repel ordinary physical force: a favourite device was to line up a group of burly men at the end of a billiard cue, and invite them to push her over. Lulu Hurst could resist their combined force, just as she could resist any attempt to lift her against her will.

Still more famous was the similarly dubbed 'Little Georgia Magnet', Annie May Abbott, who toured the world in the late 1880s and 1890s. She weighed only 98 lb, but even Sumo wrestlers could not shift her from where she sat in a chair – which gave her no opportunity to exert a sideways deflecting force. She could also make objects immovable, simply by resting her fingers on them.

More recently, Welshman Brian Williams of Cardiff made the news in 1952, when he was photographed holding an electric lightbulb between finger and thumb – with the bulb glowing brightly from the electricity in his body.

Another human torch appeared at the Asian Games in Beijing in September 1990 to entertain visitors to the Olympic Hotel. Chun Tianzhao plugged himself into the mains and put a screwdriver to his temple until the tool glowed. Then he held hands with various members of the audience, apparently controlling the flow of electricity through his body so that they felt sensations ranging from mild tingling to a jolt that made them scream.

Like Miss Zheng mentioned above, Li Qinghong is a *qigong* master, and works in medicine – in his case, at the Railways Ministry Hospital in Beijing. The first unusual result of his training in *qigong* was his discovery that he could adjust the volume of his radio as he wanted it, without having to touch the dials. Li progressed to the point of soaking himself in water, standing in a puddle, and wiring himself into the 220-volt mains electricity supply. Having survived that experiment, he now acts as a human transformer in his healing work. He seems not only to be immune to electricity but to be able to augment current and voltage from the mains supply. He has been seen to put frozen fish on a pair of electric spits – which failed to cook the fish until Li took hold of them, whereupon the fish began to 'smoke, hiss and crackle'. Li's hands remained not merely unaffected, but quite cool throughout the operation.

INNER POWER

There is nothing strange about electricity in the human body: without minute electrical charges making connections between the synapses in the brain, we would not be able even to think, let alone wonder how strange are the ways of the world. And some animals can store and discharge electricity – electric eels can deliver a jolt of up to 500 volts, enough to kill the average would-be predator, and certainly enough to stun a human being. The existence of the electric eel suggests that electric people, if relatively few and far between, are not necessarily breaking the laws of nature, even if what brings about their unusual ability is little understood.

There may be another kind of explanation – or at any rate clue – to this kind of phenomenon in the notion of *qi* (often transliterated *ch'i*) energy cited and seemingly brought under control by Dr Zheng and other adepts. The concept of *qi* is not an easy one: writing in *Fortean Times* No 27, researcher Steve Moore noted that it is 'difficult of definition in any sort of everyday or scientific terms: it is at once "breath", spirit, non muscular energy, or "inner power". It is that energy which flows along the acupuncture meridians. It is also the energy developed by practitioners of the "Internal schools" of the martial arts, the most well-known of which is T'ai Chi Chuan.'

The electrical and magnetic powers that some Westerners exhibit or acquire by chance or accident are frequently reported among *qi* masters. Moore quotes a number of accounts of such talents that had been deliberately fostered through mental and spiritual discipline.

When, for instance, a female student of a martial arts master tried to attack him on one occasion, 'she found a force propelling her backwards, and then she started bouncing up and down until her feet began to hurt'. Another master, walking in the street with a friend, was hit in the back by a pedicab, which rebounded 10 ft and tipped over. The master, without a break in the conversation, walked on as if nothing had happened.' One particular instance is highly reminiscent of the 19th-century 'wonder girls' and their talents. The master Yang Ch'eng-fu 'could magnetize or attract his opponent's arm so that it stuck to his own as he moved'.

Western sages have yet to explain acupuncture in their own scientific terms. How they might come to grips with the whole concept of *qi* is a challenge few seem willing to take up. The broader lesson is that we all could probably learn much about other paranormal phenomena if scientists would but accept that the bizarre and inexplicable is not therefore impossible. Indeed because such things as electric people or poltergeists *are* inexplicable, they are all the more worthy of investigation. But to most scientists, probably for no better reason than their own preference for the quiet safety of conformity, such promising, tantalizing fields of research remain out of bounds.

HUMAN TRANSFORMERS OF ELECTRICITY – WHILE RELATIVELY FEW AND FAR BETWEEN – ARE NOT NECESSARILY BREAKING THE LAWS OF NATURE.

Below: ***Practitioners of acupuncture use needles to stimulate* qi*, the universal life force that flows through the body. Some researchers have suggested that a deeper understanding of* qi *and, for Western science, acceptance of its existence, could help to explain many paranormal phenomena.***

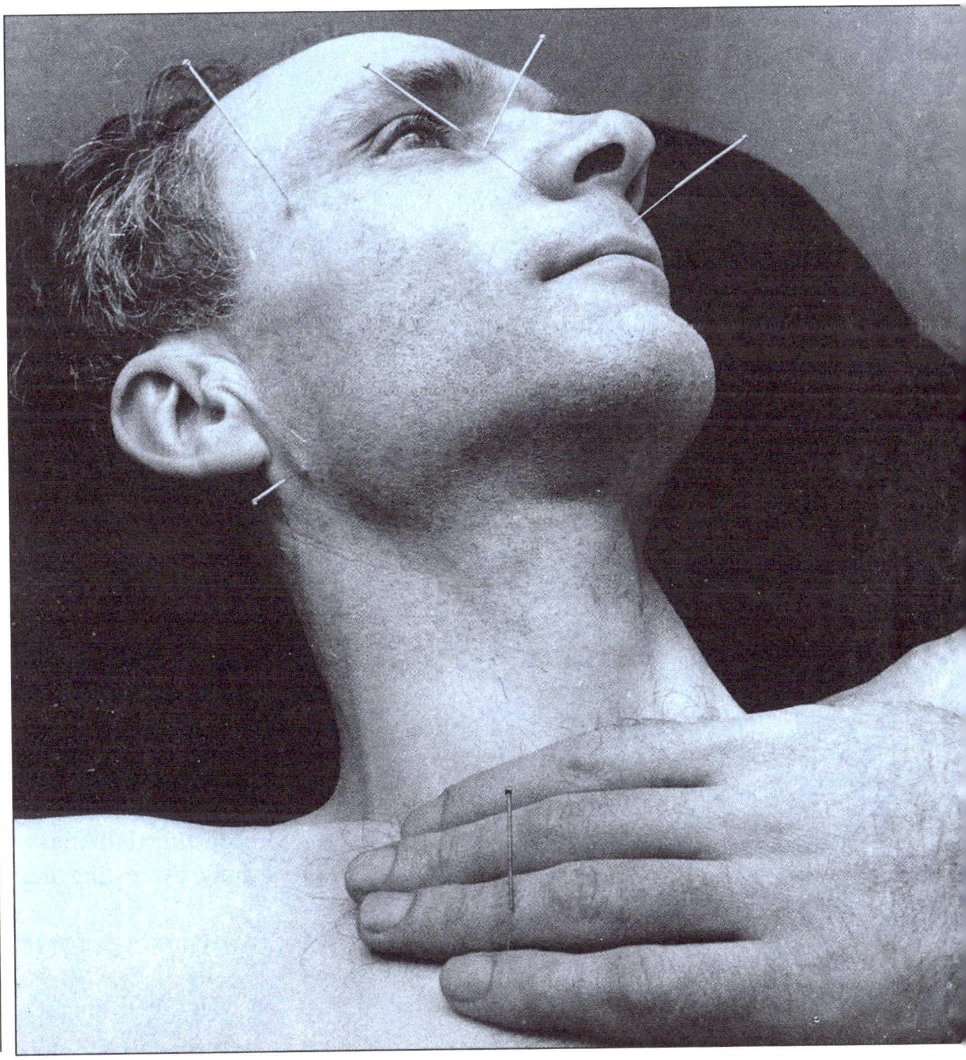

UNEXPLAINED ARRIVALS

The amputated human finger materialized out of thin air. The police combed the city's hospitals but no one claimed the missing digit. A clue to a grisly murder – or something far more horrific?

In March 1986, a respectable citizen of what was then West Berlin, Germany, was climbing into his car in the Tegel district of the city when he heard something land with a thud on the vehicle's roof. He looked out to see what had made the noise, and saw a human finger roll off the top of his car and into the gutter. He prudently left the grisly object where it was, drove off, and reported what he had seen to the police. On checking, the police found there was no mistake: there was an unmistakably human finger lying by the roadside. A search of the city's hospitals was ordered for its owner, but no one was found with a missing digit.

The finger seems to have had no Earthly owner in the immediate neighbourhood: so did it come from further afield, or did it come from some *un*Earthly realm?

The same question applies with even greater force to a small white bull that appeared apparently from thin air in a locked cowshed belonging to farmer Derek Steedman, on the Isle of Wight. One morning in January 1984, Steedman found that his herd of 12 Hereford calves had been joined by a two-week-old white Charolais crossbred. It had no identification, and 10 months after its arrival no one had claimed it, despite wide local publicity.

THROUGH LOCKED DOORS

The term 'apport' originally meant anything, either inanimate or alive, which materialized in the presence of a medium. The phenomenon was first reported by a Dr Billot in 1839. He described a seance he witnessed in 1819, during which a packet containing three small pieces of bone apparently appeared from nowhere on the floor in his presence. There are innumerable accounts of such things happening in the seance rooms

Opposite: ***Charles Hoy Fort, renowned researcher into anomalous phenomena. Fort was particularly interested in the many accounts of inexplicable showers of fish* (below), *frogs, snakes and eels and even of inanimate objects of many kinds.***

Right: ***A spider crab that fell from the sky at Brighton, Sussex, on 5 June 1983, and*** **(below)** ***a fall of rodents in Norway in 1680. Charles Fort put forward the idea that the natural world was originally equipped for us by using supplies of life 'airlifted' from elsewhere, and that this process continues today, with intermittent falls of fish and other living creatures.***

of the 19th century, and parapsychologists have made a definite distinction between *materializations* that psychic mediums produce apparently out of thin air, and *apports* as such, which seem to have been transported from one place to another, sometimes through solid walls with locked doors and windows, by some paranormal means.

In practice, it is extremely difficult to tell which is which, unless the mysteriously appearing objects are already known to the people they appear before. This has happened: the pioneering 19th-century scientist and psychical investigator Sir William Crookes had one such experience. In a locked seance room, he thought he heard a handbell ringing, as if someone were carrying it around the room. Then it fell beside him. It was indeed a bell – which, he later discovered, one of his sons had been playing with *while the seance was taking place*. There was no way the bell could have been brought into the locked room by any normal means.

On 3 December 1908 the citizens of Sydney, Australia, were no doubt amused to read in that day's *Morning Herald* newspaper that the Melbourne millionaire Thomas Welton Stanford, brother of the American railroad magnate and former US Senator Leland Stanford, had been visited by a customs official who suspected that the gentleman owed import duty on several certain small items.

But the reason Stanford had not paid

taxes on the curious assortment of dead singing birds, Babylonian clay tablets, ancient coins and other bric-à-brac was simple enough: they had been 'imported' through the agency of a Dr Whitcomb, a former general practitioner of Melbourne, but who had died in England, aged 47, in 1878. Dr Whitcomb was the spirit guide for the medium Charles Bailey, and Bailey had produced these and dozens of other objects as apports in seances.

No more was heard about the officious customs inspector, but many of the apports produced by Bailey are still in the keeping of Stanford University, California, founded by Senator Leland Stanford. His brother Thomas, an ardent spiritualist who employed Charles Bailey as his private medium between 1902 and 1914, also donated $500,000 to the university to establish a fellowship in psychical research.

Bailey's ability to produce apports was prodigious and spectacular. In March 1903, he was put to the test by Dr Charles McCarthy, an eminent Sydney physician, who sewed him into a stout, double-stitched canvas bag, which was sealed at the openings for his head and hands. In the course of six seances, Bailey apported Babylonian clay tablets inscribed with cuneiform writing, coins, semi-precious stones, an Arabic newspaper, a number of live birds, a crab, and foot-long shark.

In June 1903 Bailey underwent a second series of tests for McCarthy. Prior to the seances he was stripped and searched, made to wear boxing gloves and a fresh suit of clothes during the seance, and enclosed during it in a 'cage' made of mosquito netting. None of this appeared to daunt the medium or staunch the flow of exotic apports.

On other occasions, conducting seances for Thomas Welton Stanford, Bailey produced among other things many more live songbirds, nests with fresh eggs in, quantities of sand 'replete with aquatic fauna', a live turtle, live fish, a fishing net, ivory, beads, a human skull and leopard skin.

Researcher Ivan Sanderson once remarked of apports: 'We've got sound through matter, and sight through matter, why not matter through matter? Matter is 99 per cent holes anyway, and anyone can squirt a jet of water through a chicken wire fence.' Solving the problem may be a little more complex than that, and on a number of occasions medium Charles Bailey was caught out in circumstances that strongly suggested he had hidden his 'apports' about his person before entering the seance room. But he convinced many – and the things he brought into this world can still be seen in the library of Stanford University, California.

Above: ***A rain of crosses in 1503, reported by C. Lycosthenes in 1557. Inexplicable falls of objects have been reported through the centuries: their form and nature has tended to change with the development of modern technology.***

ON SEVERAL OCCASIONS THE MEDIUM WAS CAUGHT OUT IN INCRIMINATING CIRCUMSTANCES.

OUT OF THIN AIR

Such events at seances have become less and less common since the end of World War 1. This may be because mediums have concentrated on different kinds of spiritual manifestation – and is certainly partly explained by ever more rigorous tests designed to discourage frauds. What remains inexplicable are the hundreds of reports on record of objects that appear as

Above: ***Charles Fort at his 'supercheckers' table, devised to make the popular board game more challenging. Fort rejected the conventional scientific view that a phenomenon would be accepted as genuine only if it could be explained. To Fort, the fact that a phenomenon had occurred and been recorded was enough for him to accept its reality.***

if from nowhere in front of witnesses who are neither mediums nor even remotely interested in psychic matters of any kind. And in these cases it is impossible to say whether the objects involved have come from some other recognizable geographical location, or have materialized 'out of thin air'.

By far the most common apport met today is what Ivan T. Sanderson has called 'Fafrotskies': these are things that are alleged to FAll FROm The SKIES.

FAFROTSKIES

Fafrotskies have been recorded since the earliest written records began in Sumeria about 5500 years ago. Then, anything that fell from the sky was thought to have a divine origin. Falls of rain, ice, meteorites – let alone small creatures or artefacts – were seen as equally baffling and were believed to be the gift of the gods. The very idea of water suspended in the air, which was deemed to be empty space, must have seemed as unnatural as the idea that fish or fingers could be waiting in the sky to fall to Earth.

This kind of logic remains potent even in scientific circles in modern times, long after we have ceased to think that a thunderstorm is a sign of the wrath of God. In essence, this sceptical attitude says: 'If science can't explain something, that something can't exist.' Science, as the famed researcher into anomalous phenomena Charles Hoy Fort pointed out, is as much a faith in its own way as the most extreme religion; to reinforce the point, he called anything rejected or ignored by science 'the damned', and wrote a large book detailing how many and how various such 'damned' phenomena really are.

This prejudice of science was nowhere better demonstrated than in 1772, when a committee of the Académie Française, which included the famous chemist Lavoisier, investigated a stone that had dropped with a loud explosion on Luce in Maine, France, on 13 September 1768. The committee concluded that, as there are no stones in the sky, no stones can fall from the sky. (Unlike the ancient Sumerians, however, they were too inhibited to call the stone a gift of God.) Reports of meteorites – which was what the stone actually was – were due to either peasant superstition or faulty reasoning. Astronomers quietly abandoned this position in the 19th century, but more exotic fafrotskies remained, and still remain, among the 'damned' in orthodox scientific eyes.

TORRENTS OF STONES

In 1860, R.P. Greg published a report on meteorites in the *Report* of the British Association. It listed almost 2000 items, complete with dates, reaching back to AD 2. Besides the large amount of most unmeteoric behaviour that Greg documented – 'meteorites' that bounced along, hovered or made angular turns – there were many items said to have 'come down' with meteorites, such as delicately undefined 'gelatinous substances' and even, less delicately, blood.

Stones, whether meteorites or not, have

dropped out of nowhere in the most curious circumstances. Two fishermen at a lake in Skaneatles, New York, had their sport interrupted on the evening of 27 October 1973 when three stones, of ever larger size, fell into the lake in front of them. They looked around to find who had thrown them but, finding no one, went back to their rods – only to be battered by a rain of pebbles, which seemed to follow them as they abandoned their fishing and ran for their car. When they stopped to change their clothes, more pebbles fell on them, and on emerging from a bar to which they had repaired to recover, they were yet again showered with stones. When, at last, they parted outside the home of one of the pair, they were assaulted by 'torrents' of still more stones.

Yet more bizarre was the case, reported in 1957, of the young Aborigine farm-worker of Pumphrey, Western Australia, around whom stones fell even when he was indoors. Two witnesses swore that on one occasion stones fell at their feet when they were with the young man inside a closed tent (whose material also lacked holes). Scientists claimed, somewhat implausibly, that 'freak winds' were responsible, but did not explain how they collected the stones or why they should deposit their cargo exclusively around one individual.

SHREDS OF MEAT

Fortunately for those unconvinced by the claim that science has all the answers to everything all the time, Charles Hoy Fort produced a treasury of fafrotski reports in his books. In *The Book of the Damned* (1919) in particular, he bombarded the open-minded reader with data of falling ice, ashes, mud, sulphur, hot water, bricks, cinders, stone axes, nails, iron chains, snakes, eels, ants, worms, periwinkles (on the city of Worcester, England, on 28 May 1881), 'butter' (actually a foul-smelling dark-yellow substance that fell over large areas of southern Ireland in 1696), seeds, nuts, jelly, and more – including those most frequently reported mysterious apports, showers of fish and frogs – as well as rather more horrid apports of blood and meat.

On 20 July 1851, in the middle of a routine parade at the Benicia army base in San Francisco, California, troops were showered with blood and pieces of what seemed to be beef. Eighteen years later, on 1 August 1869, two acres of the farm owned by a Mr J. Hudson, of Los Nietos, California, were covered with a fall of blood, hair and shreds and strips of meat, some of them 6 in long. The day was clear and windless. This weird phenomenon was still going strong in 1968, when on 27 August blood and flesh fell for about five minutes on an area roughly 1000 yds square between the towns of Cacapava and São Jose dos Campos in Brazil, and it has been reported many times since.

SNOWED UNDER

When falls of lumps of ice occur, at least rationalists and sceptics can pull a more or

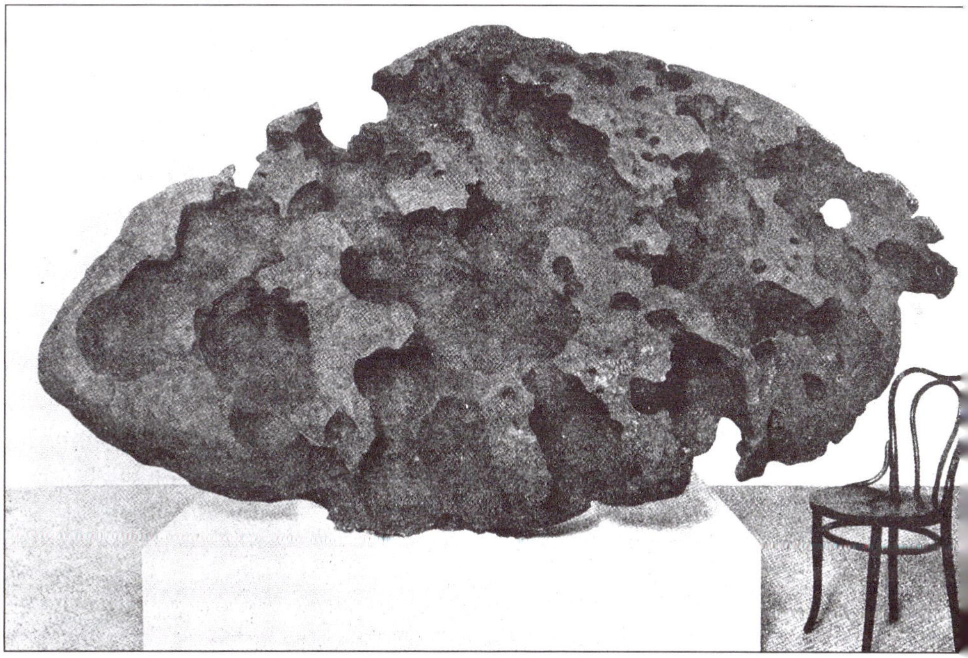

Top: ***The gigantic meteor crater near the Grand Canyon, Arizona, and*** **(above)** ***the Williamette meteorite, found in Oregon. Reports of meteorites falling from the skies were long dismissed as absurd by the scientific establishment – until the 19th century, when the evidence for their existence became irrefutable. Such a lesson should be heeded by those who dismiss paranormal phenomena out of hand.***

Above: ***A 15th-century illustration of a hazardous rain of steel ingots.***

NO MATTER WHERE THE FISHERMEN FLED, THE RAIN OF BATTERING PEBBLES PURSUED THEM.

less plausible explanation out of the hat: falls of ice are usually blamed on faulty aircraft de-icing equipment and leaking airborne lavatories. But in one study by atmospheric physicist James McDonald, the scientist found that only two out of 30 selected ice falls in the 1950s could be blamed on aircraft.

Inexplicable ice falls have been recorded throughout history. Even if planes had existed at the time to drop these ice bombs, many were so huge that they would have stopped the planes taking off in the first place. For example, a lump with a volume of 18 cubic feet fell on Hungary in 1802, and one measuring about 20 ft around, 'of proportionate thickness', and weighing about half a ton fell on Ord, in the Isle of Skye, Scotland, in 1849. And mysterious lumps of ice continue to fall from the sky.

A 'volleyball-sized' chunk crashed through a roof in Portland, Oregon, on 25 April 1989. It was milky-white in colour and smelled slightly of sulphur. (Other apports have been reported as smelling of sulphur, and some are positively hot when they first appear.)

A 70 kilo block of blue-green ice fell from a cloudless sky on a field near Belgrade in August 1989.

A chunk of ice the size of a football fell from a cloudless sky into a garden near Lake Vattern in Sweden in April 1990. It was 'milky' with shades of grey, brown and lilac. A Swedish TV report mentioned several pieces falling over a limited area, and showed several impact craters.

A 20 lb block of ice smashed through the roof of a house in Batley, West Yorkshire, on 11 October 1991. It fell into the kitchen, shortly after the occupant, Mrs Mavis Anderson, had left the room with a cup of tea.

When Mrs Pauline Reidy of Burbank, Illinois, went out to check her car one September evening in 1982, she was astonished to find a small 3 ft by 3 ft snowdrift lying on her front steps. Although it was a cool evening, snow was not expected; and indeed this was the only snow in sight. There was no indication that it had been dumped by a prankster.

BEANFEAST

But what can science make of showers of fruit and nuts, or even beans? In early March 1983, Rita Gibson of Topsham, near Exeter, found a scattering of strange pink beans in her back garden. They were larger than rice grains and smaller than orange pips. 'They could not have been thrown,' she said, 'because our house is surrounded by three walls around a courtyard.' Though they were out of season, they were quite fresh. This was not an isolated example of a bean fall – in September 1945, a lady from St Louis, Missouri, querulously telephoned the local weather bureau to ask if the world was about to end after a shower of beans had fallen around her house.

During the night of 8–9 November 1984, East Crescent, Accrington, in Lancashire, was bombarded with apples – best quality Bramleys and Coxes. Derek and Adrienne Haythornwhite found at least 300 on their back lawn, on the path and in the hedges, and more were found in nearby gardens. The couple were woken up in the night by a thunderous noise on the roof. According to Adrienne Haythornwhite, 'They kept on falling for an hour or longer.'

There was nothing new about this bizarre event, in a way. In 1687, the seeds of ivy berries were found inside hailstones that fell on Wiltshire, England, while on 9 May

1867, Dublin policemen were bombarded with 'nuts or berries' (some may have been hazelnuts) that rained down on them 'in great quantities and with great force'.

RAINING SPRATS AND FROGS

On the night of 27–28 May 1984, there was a fall of fishes in the borough of Newham, east London. Four had been found at the house of Ron Langton and his wife in Central Park Road, East Ham; three in the yard and one on the roof. Mrs Langton said that she had seen another fish on the same day, in a house gutter about half a mile away. The Natural History Museum in London identified the fish as flounders and smelts.

That day, too, a man in neighbouring Canning Town found 30 fish in his garden; his house is about one and a half miles east of the Langtons' house. Another Canning Town resident had found four fish. No one saw any fish fall; all were found in conditions suggesting they fell from above. It had rained heavily and thunderously during the night. All locations were within two miles of the River Thames, and the Natural History Museum suggested that the fish had been transported by a waterspout; but there had been no reports of waterspouts in the Thames that night, though flounders are found in the Thames Estuary.

Small freshwater fish, identified as thread fin shad, fell around Mr and Mrs Ellmers, and their neighbour Walter Davies, in Bonita, California, on the evening of 20 August 1984. They came down with 'harsh wet splats' from a cloudless sky. There was a population of these fish in the Sweetwater Reservoir about two miles away, but no funnel cloud capable of lifting the fish had been seen. Nor had anyone seen the flight of pelicans that, one wag suggested, had caught and then (for reasons that remained unexplained) had dropped the fish.

On the evening of 21 April 1985, there was a heavy rainstorm in the area of St Cloud, Minnesota. One couple noticed 'a white thing with five legs' in their

Above: ***An early cover of Lo!, one of Charles Fort's pioneering works.***

THE TOUGH GIs COWERED UNDER THE SHOWER OF BLOOD AND SHREDS OF FLESH.

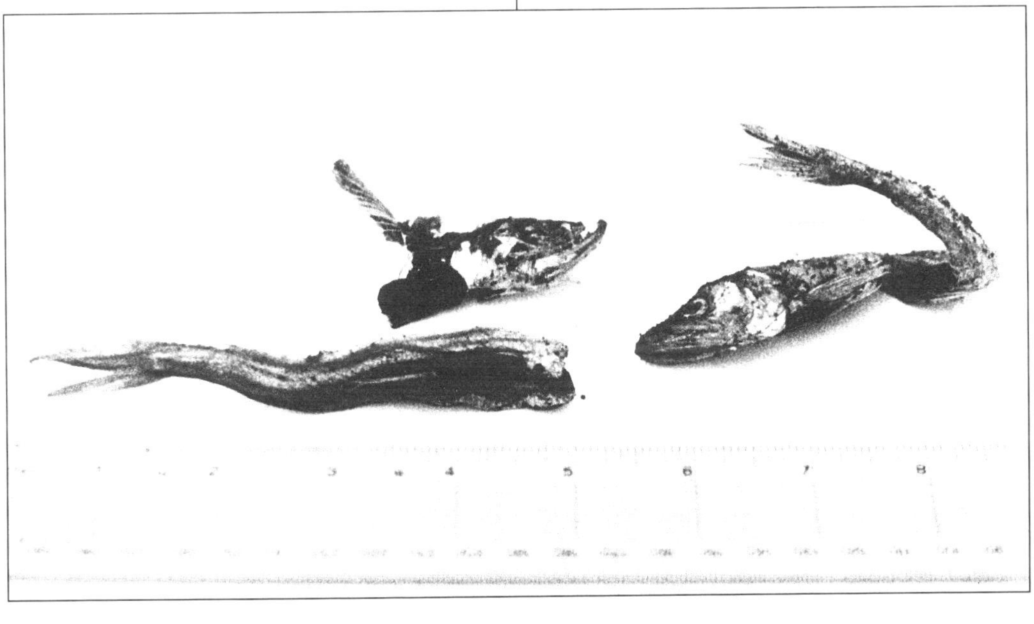

Left: ***Evidence of a fish fall in East Ham, London, in 1984. There was no doubt that the fish were real, but where they came from – and how – remains a mystery.***

Reports of bizarre rains of objects from the sky have been recorded for centuries (**above right:** *a woodcut from the 1555* **Historia de Gentibus Septentrionalibus** *by Olaus Magnus), and show no sign of abating as the 20th century draws to a close* (**above left:** *a classic cover from a 1958 edition of* **Fate** *magazine).*

Facing page: *An illustration of waterspouts from Camille Flammarion's* **L'Atmosphere,** *published in Paris in 1888. Some people suggest that inexplicable apports from the sky may have been sucked from the sea by a waterspout and deposited on land by the wind.*

THOUSANDS OF DEAD SARDINES FELL LIKE SHEETS OF SILVER RAIN.

backyard, which on closer inspection turned out to be a starfish. Turning on their outside lights, the couple saw more starfish on their lawn. There was one on the roof of a neighbouring garage roof and more in another garden. The starfish were ocean dwellers that were found only off the coast of Florida. The implausible explanation offered was that the creatures had been flung from a tall building at St Cloud State University a mile away as a joke by students, and then blown by strong winds before falling to the ground.

Many thousands of dead sardines fell 'like a sheet of silver rain' around the house of Harold and Debra Degen of Rosewood, near Ipswich, Queensland, Australia, on 6 February 1989. The Degens gathered a bowlful, some for their cat to appreciate and some to keep as souvenirs. The rest were 'gobbled by kookaburras'. According to the local police, the fall was confined to an area of only 2 acres.

After fish that fall from the sky, showers of frogs are the classic example of the inexplicable apport from the sky. Tiny – frogs that fall are always tiny, it seems – rose-coloured albino frogs fell in the neighbourhood of Stroud in the west of England during torrential rain some time in October 1987. Two similar falls had been observed in nearby Cirencester two weeks earlier, about the time Britain was dusted with 'Sahara' sand. There was a fourth incident in the Charlton Kings area of Cheltenham, Gloucestershire. According to one witness, the frogs bounced off umbrellas and pavements and hopped off in their hundreds to nearby streams and gardens. The Gloucester Trust for Nature Conservancy investigated the possibility that the frogs had arrived with the sand, possibly 'carried in atmospheric globules of water across land and sea'. The pink frogs seem to have settled in; they were observed in the area as late as the following June.

These recent reports form part of a tradition that reaches back at least as far as the second century AD, when the ancient Greek historian Athenaeus recorded a fall of fish that lasted for three days.

PENNIES FROM HEAVEN

If some of the things that fall from the sky are fairly revolting – like the tissue from the lungs of 'a human infant or horse' that fell from a cloudless sky on Bath County, Kentucky, on 3 March 1876 – some have been altogether sweeter in nature. Parts of Lake County, California, were showered with candy during the nights of 2 and 11 September 1857, and some of the local ladies made syrup from the crystals.

Still sweeter, to some, are falls of money. Several thousand silver coins fell near the city of Gorky in Russia on 17 June 1940; pennies fell in droves – along with lumps of coal, just to confuse the issue – in 1927 and 1928 in Battersea, London; a single, mint-fresh 2-franc French piece fell into a garden

in North Carolina in October 1958; 18 months earlier, however, 'thousands' of 1000-franc notes rained down on Bourges, France, although no one ever reported losing the huge sum involved. In December 1975, precisely $588 was handed to police by honest citizens of La Salle Street, Chicago, after a shower of dollar bills – though how much was kept by less upright folk is anyone's guess.

He admitted he'd been showered with coins on and off for six years.

Some falls of coins seem to cluster in particular places (and occasionally around a particular individual). Visitors to the graveyard of St Mary's Church, Kenardington, England, have more than once been showered with hot coins. In 1989, David and Sophie Gough witnessed just such a fall; the coins were dated between 1902 and 1953 – 'old' money in Britain, which changed its currency in 1971, and therefore no longer legal tender. Where had it been in the intervening years? The Goughs' comment that 'no aircraft were flying overhead' at the time seems hardly relevant: no one expects aircraft to scatter coins wherever they go, let alone money that has been useless for many years.

AN ILL WIND?

The standard explanation for mysterious apports like these is the innocent tornado. Since Jerome Cardan first put the argument forward in the 16th century, sceptics have fallen back on the claim that a whirlwind or waterspout has lifted up the fish, frogs, nuts or whatever else is involved, and deposited them at a distance.

As wind speeds of 280 mph have been measured in tornadoes, there is nothing surprising in the idea that they can lift heavy objects and dump them far away from their original location. A 'moderately devastating' tornado – called T6 on the conventional scale – is characterized thus: 'heavy motor vehicle levitated; strong houses lose entire roofs and perhaps also a wall;...less strong buildings collapse'.

Tornado damage is well-known for being highly localized and weirdly capricious. One tornado in Iowa destroyed one half of a house and left the other half intact, even leaving a clock ticking on the chimney piece. A baby was plucked from its mother's arms at Louisville in 1890 and set down unharmed six blocks away. In

Right: *The result of a tornado at Arreton, Isle of Wight, on 19 June 1985: dagger-sharp pieces of glass, 9–12 in long, lie deeply embedded in aluminium pipes. That strong winds can cause such freak happenings should by no means be taken as an explanation of all such events.*

Oklahoma in 1905, a tornado removed all the shoes from the people it struck and killed in its path. In 1911, a schoolgirl in Bradford, England, was lifted 20 ft into the air by a gust of wind and was dashed to the ground and killed. In 1943, in Lansing, Michigan, a tornado stripped a row of 30 chickens bare of their feathers.

Tornadoes (and waterspouts and freak winds) no doubt do account for some unexplained arrivals, and falling fish are the most obvious candidates; it's most likely that the waterspout responsible won't be seen, especially at sea or at night. The trouble with the tornado hypothesis when applied to other objects is that one never seems to hear of the corresponding loss of a harvest of apples, or nuts, or dollar bills – these showers of money, after all, can't all be ill-gotten gains, snatched by the winds of poetic justice from the hands of thieves, who might suffer further by admitting the loss. And tornadoes do not deposit calves in cowsheds with such care that they remember to lock the doors behind them afterwards.

Still less likely is it that tornadoes, or any other unusual weather conditions, would not only select coins to drop on the unsuspecting, but select one person upon whom to drop nothing but coins. A man who happened to come in the way of falls of frogs one month, fish the next, and coins a year later is not to be expected according to the laws of chance, probability and averages. Someone, like Albert Williamson of Ramsgate, Kent, who in 1989 admitted he had been showered with coins (and nothing else except God's own rain) on and off for six years, is not likely to believe, any more than anyone else, that anything as unpredictable as the weather was responsible.

Besides, these things keep falling from clear blue skies; in Chesterfield County, South Carolina, even *rain* fell for about 12 days out of a sunny cloudless sky in October 1886. Fish, frogs and toads in such falls are more often than not alive – a likely story if they have been suspended in the chill upper atmosphere for days on end. And how tornadoes find blood, meat and other grim organic matter to drop in highly selective areas is not easily explained, either.

Charles Hoy Fort suggested that such things came from a 'Super-Sargasso' sea in the sky. The notion is, to say the least, fanciful – but perhaps no more ridiculous, in the final analysis, than the all-embracing application of the explanation that tornadoes, waterspouts and 'freak winds' account for every one of such events. To anyone with an open mind – that is, to anyone with a genuinely sceptical outlook – where falls, or apports, of these things ultimately come from, remains as much a mystery as it ever was.

Below: ***A whirlwind at Roodegsvort, near Johannesburg, South Africa. The violent updraughts present in tornadoes and whirlwinds have proved strong enough to lift people and animals from the ground and carry them considerable distances. But in the case of apports, it is rare for the source of the object to be found.***

VANISHINGS

The stage magician discovered his astonishing ability by accident, but he was unable to control it. Then one evening, in front of a startled audience, his body started to become translucent...

Stage magicians can create extraordinary illusions when it comes to making people and things – even a pair of live leopards – seem to disappear, but none has matched the trick performed at least three times by Dr William Neff in the 1960s. On those occasions he became invisible, literally disappearing into thin air in front of witnesses.

The first time this happened was during his stage act while he was performing in Chicago. The second time, he was at home, when he vanished without warning – 'casually', as he put it – (and reappeared) in front of his wife, who was apparently not amused.

The third occasion was again during his stage show, at New York's Paramount Theatre. This time, radio broadcaster 'Long John' Knebel was in the audience – as reliable a witness as anyone could wish for, as Knebel was well-known for his hostility to claims of the paranormal. In his book *The Way Out World* Knebel says he saw Neff's form 'becoming minutely translucent' until 'you could see the traveler curtain clearly behind his translucent figure'. Yet more bizarre was that Neff's voice was unaffected by his invisibility, although it's unlikely, in the circumstances, that any of those present paid much attention to what he was saying. Knebel described Neff's reappearance like this: 'Gradually a rather faint outline, like a very faint pencil sketch...appeared again.'

The irony was that Neff himself was unaware of his own ability. He did not know when he had become invisible and had no way to control the phenomenon.

Opposite: ***In earlier times, a person's sudden disappearance would be explained as the work of the fairies, who lived in a parallel world that could rarely be perceived by mere mortals. If a human were to glimpse the delights of fairy life, it would prove impossible to resist*** **(below).**

Above: ***The German explorer Ludwig Leichardt, who was last heard of in the spring of 1848 while attempting to cross Australia from east to west. Over 100 years later, an expedition led by Zacharias Mathias set out to investigate rumoured evidence of Leichardt's fate, but Mathias too vanished without trace.***

DISAPPEARING TRICKS

The case of Dr Neff throws a huge spanner in the works of anyone trying to explain (or explain away) what happens when people 'mysteriously disappear'. We are not here considering cases in which the victims have simply dropped out of sight for their own reasons or almost certainly been the victims of crime. These are cases in which people vanish within minutes or seconds, and of whom no trace has been found despite immediate and intense searches, and who neither had any apparent wish or need to disappear, nor were snatched away by any natural agency.

If no natural cause can be found, the presumption is usually that such people have been translated into some 'other dimension'; once, people would have said they had been stolen away by the fairies. (In some cases, they may be taken through some other dimension to land up in another place on this Earth; these are known as 'teleportations'.) Perhaps that does happen; but in Neff's case since his voice could still be heard by his astonished audience the process was, at best, only partly begun – let alone completed – and reversed itself shortly thereafter. On the other hand, maybe disappearing people do what Neff did, but more thoroughly if no more willingly, and without the privilege of being allowed to be heard or to reappear. Perhaps we are surrounded by invisible people.

Whatever the mechanism of such events, the following cases leave one boggling at the speed and arbitrariness with which people (and occasionally things) are seemingly snatched from this existence – and, unlike many such stories in the literature of the paranormal, they are genuinely mysterious.

INTRIGUING CAVE PAINTINGS

In 1847, the German explorer Ludwig Leichardt set out to cross the Great Australian Desert from east to west, having already crossed the continent from Moreton Bay, Queensland, to Port Essington, Northern Territory, between 1844 and 1845. Nobel Prizewinner Patrick White based his novel *Voss* on Leichardt's next expedition, which took 50 bullocks, 20 mules and seven horses with them when they set out for Perth from the Darling Downs, west of Brisbane. Somewhere along the Cogoon River, the entire party vanished. Repeated searches found absolutely no trace of man, beast or equipment. A disappearance in the Australian outback is perhaps not inexplicable, but the story has a curious sequel.

In January 1975, Zacharias Mathias, a 40-year-old wildlife ranger, arrived in Darwin with photographs of a series of intriguing Aboriginal cave paintings. They depicted a pipe-smoking white man riding a horse, with a second white man on foot but carrying a saddle. A group of Aborigines was shown carrying a third white man. The

Right: ***A typical Mississippi riverboat. That a ship of this size could vanish into thin air is beyond belief, but that is exactly what happened to the*** **Iron Mountain** ***in June 1872: ship, cargo, passengers and crew all simply disappeared.***

President of the Northern Territory Historical Society immediately made plans to send an expedition, guided by Mathias, to investigate the paintings, which 'would give us the first positive clue to the disappearance…of Ludwig Leichardt'. But then Mathias himself vanished, and was never seen or heard from again.

DEEP TROUBLE

In June 1872, the Mississippi riverboat *Iron Mountain* (not *Iron Maiden* as some accounts have it) left Vicksburg, Mississippi, with 52 passengers plus a deck cargo of cotton bales and towing a string of barges laden with cotton and molasses. Some hours later, another riverboat, the *Iroquois Chief*, rounded a bend just outside Vicksburg and nearly ran into a haphazard, leaderless fleet of barges. They turned out to be from the *Iron Mountain*, and their tow-rope had been cut – a sure sign that the riverboat had been in deep trouble.

The only difficulty was that there was no sign of the *Iron Mountain*, nor had there been any since she had rounded the bend in the river and gone out of sight of Vicksburg. This is truly bizarre for, if the ship had sunk, her deck cargo at least would have been seen floating by someone on the busy river, and it is hardly likely that all 52 passengers (let alone the crew) would have drowned, let alone in such a way that not one of their bodies would float. No one heard an explosion – which would have scattered debris very obviously and very wide, for the *Iron Mountain* was one of the queens of the Mississippi – over 180 ft long, with a beam of 35 ft, and with five boilers to power her massive paddles. But searchers found nothing: no passengers, no crew – alive or dead – and no cargo or wreckage. The *Iron Mountain* had simply vanished.

THE LADY VANISHES

On 12 December 1910, socialite Dorothy Arnold, the 25-year-old niece of the US Supreme Court judge Rufus L. Peckham, left her family's fashionable home at 108 East 79th Street at about 11 am and went shopping for an evening dress. At about 2 pm, she met a friend, Gladys King, on Fifth Avenue. They chatted for a while, and parted, Miss Arnold giving her friend a cheery goodbye wave. Dorothy Arnold was never seen again. If she was kidnapped, no ransom was demanded. She had no cause to commit suicide or flee her comfortable and carefree existence as one of New York's elite. She just…disappeared.

In February 1975, Mr Jackson Wright was driving his wife Martha from New Jersey to mid-town Manhattan. It was snowing heavily and once they had entered the Lincoln Tunnel at Weehawken and were free of the weather, Wright drew up to clear the snow from his car and improve visibility. Martha, aged 36, began to clear the rear window, while Wright dealt with the windshield. When he had finished, Jackson Wright looked up to speak to his wife. She was nowhere to be seen.

On Saturday, 14 July 1990, an outing organized by the Orkney Heritage Society and the Royal Society for the Protection of Birds landed 88 ferry passengers on Eynhallow, a small uninhabited island off Rousay, for a short visit. Only 86 intrepid birdwatchers returned. Police and coastguards searched the island and the mainland coastline for the missing visitors, and a rescue helicopter with heat-seeking equipment scanned the area for signs of life. Nothing was found.

According to local tradition, Eynhallow is a sinister place. It is said that no mice, rats or cats can survive there, and that blood will flow from any corn cut after sunset. One legend has it that Eynhallow is a 'vanishing isle', appearing and reappearing as it will. To complicate matters concerning the missing

THE ENTIRE PARTY VANISHED...AND SHORTLY AFTER THE WILDLIFE RANGER STUMBLED ACROSS A CLUE TO THE MYSTERY, HE DISAPPEARED AS WELL.

THE SEARCHERS FOUND NOTHING – NO PASSENGERS, NO CREW AND NO CARGO OR WRECKAGE.

Below: ***When two birdwatchers went missing from the tiny island of Eynhallow in Scotland's Orkneys in the summer of 1990, local people offered two extraordinary explanations: either the missing pair had been abducted by mermaids, or they were themselves merfolk and had returned to their ancestral home.***

THE LOCALS SPOKE OF EYNHALLOW AS A SINISTER PLACE, WHERE BLOOD FLOWED FROM CORN CUT AFTER SUNSET.

pair, some believers in Orcadian folklore suggested that the two missing 'tourists' might actually be mermen or mermaids, returning to their ancestral home. The Fin Folk, as they are known in Orkney, are supposed to look much like humans. Their scales appear simply as clothing, the female tail as a shining skirt – although none of the other visitors to the island seem to have noticed anything so distinctive about their companions. Nor is it clear why merfolk should book their passage on a boat rather than make the journey in their natural element.

Another related (but no less farfetched) solution to the mystery was put forward: that the two humans had been kidnapped by mermaids. The reason: mermaids, although beautiful when young, grow repulsively ugly as they age, unless they can secure a human husband.

Sometime after midnight on 26 February 1985, Richard Brownell, aged 27, and his 25-year-old fiancée Sandra O'Grady left a bar in Newport Beach, California, with another man after they had told friends that they had paid him to fly them to Las Vegas for a spot of gambling. An hour later, a single-engine Cessna 152 light aircraft crashed into the Pacific Ocean off Newport Beach. The bodies of Brownell and O'Grady were found strapped to their seats inside. No engine faults were found, and three searches of the surrounding ocean failed to find another body.

Neither of the dead couple could fly a plane, so a third party, the pilot, had to have been on board. A car belonging to the plane's owner was found near the plane's tie-down spot at John Wayne Airport, but his whereabouts were unknown. The dead pair had had about $3000 on them when they set out, but only small change was found on their bodies. Did the pilot who offered them a lift rob them, then bail out, leaving them to die? Or did something more bizarre occur?

At 5 am on 17 January 1989, Graham Marsden, 45, a businessman from Poole, Dorset, filled up his red Volkswagen Polo at the Rownhams service area on the M27 motorway near Southampton, Hampshire. After paying his bill, he asked the way to the men's room. He was last seen walking towards it. His car stood unattended for an hour, and finally the worried cashier went to look for him. There was no sign of the man, and the police were called. They searched the surrounding woods with tracker dogs, but found nothing.

Marsden appeared to have no personal or financial worries – no reason, in fact, to want to disappear. 'If he planned to disappear,' a police spokesman commented, 'why did he fill his car with petrol first and leave it at the pumps? And why choose a service station miles from anywhere? We are mystified.'

A Venezuelan DC-9 jet took off from Maracaibo International Airport, 350 miles from Caracas, at 3.55 pm on 5 March 1991. It was on a routine flight, and was due to land at Santa Barbara el Zulia, another oil city in western Venezuela 135 miles away, 35 minutes later. Radio contact with the ground ceased after 25 minutes, although air traffic controllers on the ground received no distress signals. The official Venezuelan news agency, Venpres, released a list of the 38 people on board, including one child and five crew. A plane and a helicopter flew in daylight over the normal route the jet would have taken – a plains area on the rim of Maracaibo Lake – but found no sign of wreckage.

Below: ***The fate of Dorset businessman Graham Marsden remains a complete mystery. In the early hours of 17 January 1989, Marsden stopped at a service area near Southampton. After filling his Volkswagen car with petrol, he paid his bill, then walked off in the direction of the men's toilet. He never came back.***

TOP-SECRET EXPERIMENTS

These disappearances have every sign of being random and inexplicable. There is no reason why the people involved should have vanished, unless, by some extraordinary coincidence, every one of them (all 52 passengers of a Mississippi riverboat – and

Left: ***Scientist Morris K. Jessup first learned of the US Navy's alleged experiments with invisibility in 1956. Self-professed witness Carlos Allende claimed that an application of the theory of relativity by Albert Einstein*** **(below)** ***enabled a ship to be teleported from one dock to another.***

all 38 people on board a Venezuelan airliner?) had for instance a mole on their right arm that made them of irresistible if, to us, unfathomable interest to whatever powers took them away. And there may be perfectly prosaic explanations for all of them, although there seems not to be, according to our current knowledge. But unlike these random cases of mysterious disappearance, others attract the suspicion that some kind of determined intelligence lies behind the vanishings.

In one notorious instance, the agency responsible has been unequivocally identified: and there is nothing mysterious or paranormal about it. It is the US Navy.

The story goes that a top-secret experiment by the US Navy in 1943 first made a warship invisible and then, later, teleported it from one dock to another. The only evidence for this is the testimony of Carlos Miguel Allende (who also called himself Carl M. Allende), who first gave his version of what happened in two rambling letters to scientist and UFO writer Morris K. Jessup in 1956.

According to Allende, a US government scientist, Dr Franklin Reno, had developed an application of Einstein's relativity theory that enabled the US Navy to render the destroyer USS *Eldridge* and her crew invisible. This experiment was conducted at sea in October 1943 and was witnessed by Allende from aboard the steamer SS *Andrew Furuseth*. (The records show that Allende was indeed on this boat at this time.) Allende alleged that the *Eldridge* was bathed in a strange force field, which extended 'one hundred yards out from each beam of the ship'. The experiment was a success, except for side effects on the crew: some died, some went insane, and some continued to lapse into invisibility. Allende said the incident was reported in a Philadelphia paper sometime between 1944 and 1946.

This report has never been traced. Charles Berlitz and William Moore, who wrote a bestseller called *The Philadelphia Experiment*, reproduce an alleged news report about a brawl in a tavern near the Navy docks in Philadelphia, which says that during the mayhem two sailors vanished into thin air. This report came from an anonymous source and was a photocopy, not the original clipping, and shows neither the newspaper's name nor its date. It has not been proved authentic. It does not even look like an item from the Philadelphia newspapers of the time, all of which printed their news in narrower columns than the clipping that Berlitz and Moore reproduce.

Allende also said that, in a further experiment, the USS *Eldridge* was teleported from its Philadelphia dock to a dock in the Newport News area of Virginia, and back again. He was not a witness, but saw a report in a Philadelphia paper, which 'may have been in 1956'. This report has never been found either.

The US Navy has always denied the story, and said that the technology required does not exist. Dr Franklin Reno is untraceable, although Berlitz and Moore claimed that Franklin Reno is a pseudonym, and that they had talked to him. All he told them was that he had provided figures for a discussion on a project using electromagnetic fields to deflect torpedoes and mines. This hardly constitutes corroboration of Allende's story.

None of the crew of the *Furuseth* has ever made any statement about the alleged experiment. Even Berlitz and Moore admit that the Navy is unlikely to have conducted a top-secret experiment in open seas and in full view of merchant ships like the *Furuseth*. In any case, records of the two ships' movements rule out October as the month for the experiment; the only possible date is 16 August, and there is no direct evidence that either ship was near the other on this date.

If there is any doubt that the entire 'Philadelphia Experiment' story existed from start to finish purely in the mind of Carlos Miguel Allende (give or take a few writers), an extract from his original letter to Morris Jessup should allay it. Social workers and psychologists will instantly recognize the style:

'"Results" of My friend Dr Franklin Reno, *Were used*...The Result was & stands today as Proof that The Unified Field Theory (*) to a certain extent is correct... The "result" was complete invisibility of a ship, Destroyer type, *and all* of its crew. While at Sea. (Oct. 1943) The Field Was effective in an oblate spheroidal shape, extending one Hundred yards (More or Less, due to Lunar position & latitude) *out* from each beam of the ship. Any Person Within that sphere became vague in form BUT He too observed those Persons aboard *that* ship as though they too were of the same state, yet, were walking upon nothing. Any person without that sphere could see Nothing save the clearly *Defined shape of the Ships Hull in the Water*...

'There are only a very few of the original Expierimental D-E's Crew Left by Now, Sir. Most went insane, one just walked "throo" His quarters Wall in sight of His Wife & Child & 2 other crew Members (WAS NEVER SEEN AGAIN), two "Went into

Right: ***British troops in Gallipoli in 1915. According to three witnesses, a whole regiment of men was abducted, apparently in a mysterious cloud, during the ill-fated Gallipoli campaign.***

'The Flame'", i.e. They "Froze" & caught fire, while carrying common Small-Boat Compasses...THEY BURNED FOR 18 DAYS...The expieriment Was a Complete Success. The Men Were Complete Failures.'

INEXPLICABLE LOSSES

Another highly dubious disappearing act, which was first made public in 1965, is the one involving an entire regiment of British troops, the First-Fourth Norfolks, who allegedly vanished into a cloud (which may have been a UFO) in the midst of the battle for Hill 60 in Suvla Bay, Gallipoli, Turkey, on 21 August 1915. According to three eyewitnesses, who were serving with the New Zealand Army, manning an observation post in a neighbouring sector, that day was cloudless and bright but for a group of clouds that, oddly, did not move despite a breeze blowing at about 4–5 mph. One cloud – an 'absolutely dense, solid-looking structure' – seemed to be resting on the ground across a creek near Hill 60. The New Zealanders, whose post overlooked Hill 60 by some 300 ft, then observed:

'A British regiment, the First-Fourth Norfolk...marching up this sunken road or creek towards Hill 60. However, when they arrived at this cloud, they marched straight into it, with no hesitation, but no one ever

Left: ***William Moore who, with Charles Berlitz, wrote the best-selling book*** **The Philadelphia Experiment,** ***published in 1979. Their claim that a US destroyer had been made to vanish was based on flawed and flimsy evidence, and the US Navy has always denied the charge.***

Above: ***General Sir Ian Hamilton*** **(left)*****, who commanded the allied operation at Gallipoli. He described the disappearance of the Norfolks as 'very mysterious'. But given the appalling and chaotic conditions at the battlefront, it is hardly surprising that men should vanish seemingly without trace. Indeed, of the 34,000 British and allied troops who died at Gallipoli, only 7000 have a known grave.***

came out to deploy and fight at Hill 60. About an hour later, after the last of the file had disappeared into it, this cloud very unobtrusively lifted off the ground and, like any cloud or fog would, rose slowly until it joined the other similar clouds which were mentioned at the beginning of this account. On viewing them again, they all looked alike "as peas in a pod"... as soon as the singular cloud had risen to their level, they all moved away northwards...In a matter of about three quarters of an hour they had all disappeared from view.

'The regiment mentioned is posted as missing or "wiped out" and on Turkey surrendering in 1918, the first thing Britain demanded of Turkey was the return of this regiment. Turkey replied that she had neither captured this regiment, nor made contact with it, and did not know it existed...Those who observed this incident can vouch for the fact that Turkey never captured that regiment, nor made contact with it.'

This story has been repeated time and again in books and broadcasts about 'unexplained mysteries', but there are plenty of proven errors in this account, as researcher Paul Begg divulged in 1979, in his meticulously researched book *Into Thin Air*. The first mistake should have been obvious to anyone with any acquaintance with British Army organization, let alone to those who fought alongside the British in Gallipoli: the First-Fourth Norfolks is the first *battalion* of the Fourth Norfolk Regiment, not a regiment in its own right. Second, that particular battalion did not disappear that day or any other, but went on to fight with distinction in Gallipoli until the end of 1915, when it was relieved and posted elsewhere. However, on 12 (not 21) August, the First Battalion of the *Fifth* Norfolk Regiment's Colonel, 16 officers and 250 men did vanish. On that day, they were in hot pursuit of the enemy when night fell; the next day, there was no trace of them. But they were operating 4 1/2 miles from the position of the New Zealanders, and nowhere near Hill 60.

Sir Ian Hamilton, the general commanding the operation, described the disappearance of the First-Fifth Norfolks in despatches as 'a very mysterious thing', but it has to be remembered that the Gallipoli campaign was one of the most disastrously mismanaged of World War 1: conditions both in and out of combat were appalling, confused and lethal, and of the 34,000 British and allied troops who died there, no less than 27,000 have no known grave. That less than 1 per cent of this number vanished without explanation in the heat of battle – and at night – in one small incident is not so surprising.

Why should three New Zealand veterans make up such an outlandish tale? Perhaps the answer is that they did not. Begg suggests that they simply fused together their 50-year-old memories of August 1915 and two separate accounts in an official account of the Gallipoli expedition, *The Final Report Of The Dardanelles Commission*. The two accounts are on facing pages in the report.

The first describes the disappearance of the First-Fifth Norfolks on 12 August. The second describes the peculiar weather conditions of 21 August, when a combined Australian and New Zealand force attacked Hill 60: 'By some freak of nature Suvla Bay and Plain were wrapped in a strange mist on the afternoon of 21 August.' On that day, too, the Sherwood Rangers attacked Hill 60 and were wiped out; it is possible that the old soldiers confused the disappearance of the Norfolks with the carnage, and unusual weather, that they witnessed around Hill 60.

Significantly, the report was published in full only in 1965 – the year the three New Zealanders published their curiously conflated account of these two incidents (and dates), and which was the 50th anniversary of the battle – making it all the more likely that the 'witnesses' would have read it. Simple human error would account for the creation of the 'kidnapping' of the Norfolks by a cloud. Wishful thinking, and a shortage of the kind of research that distinguishes Paul Begg's work, accounts for the story's repetition and acceptance at face value. The fate of 267 men from the First-Fifth Norfolks *is* still a mystery – but it is not a mystery that has any connection with the paranormal.

However, some very weird clouds do certainly exist, as a report in the Philadelphia *Inquirer* on 1 August 1904 testifies. The British SS *Mohican* had just berthed at Philadelphia, having arrived, the paper said, from Ibraila, Rumania (in fact, later research has established, it was on its way there). According to Captain Urquhart, the *Mohican*'s master, the ship had been on a heading for the Delaware breakwater when a weird 'magnetic' cloud had descended around it at latitude 37° 16' North, longitude 72° 48' West. For half an hour it enveloped the ship and 'made everything glow'. The compass spun wildly, while iron chains on deck were magnetized, clinging together so powerfully that no one could move them. The cloud was grey, with glowing spots in it, and so dense that nothing could be seen beyond the decks. 'It appeared as if the whole world was a mass of glowing fire,' said Urquhart. 'The hair on our heads and in our beards stuck out like bristles on a pig...all the joints of the body seemed to stiffen...there was a great silence over everything that only added to the terror.' Then the cloud lifted and moved off over the sea.

The *Mohican* did not disappear, however, and neither did any of her crew. But there is no lack of ships that, if they themselves have remained untouched, have indeed suffered the inexplicable loss of their crews.

A CARGO OF GOLD

The most celebrated of these cases is undoubtedly that of the *Mary Celeste*, which was found in the Atlantic Ocean on 5 December 1872 at latitude 38° 20' North, longitude 17° 50' West – about 400 miles west of Lisbon, Portugal – with her jib, fore topmast staysail and fore lower topsail set, her cargo intact, and in sound condition. The only things missing were the ship's boat,

WHEN THE 'CLOUD' MOVED AWAY, THE REGIMENT HAD VANISHED.

THERE WAS A GREAT SILENCE OVER EVERYTHING THAT ONLY ADDED TO THE TERROR.

The sudden disappearance of the entire crew of the* Mary Celeste (right) *is one of the greatest of sea mysteries. The ship was found adrift in the Atlantic in December 1872. When sailors from the* Dei Gratia *boarded her* (opposite), *they found that she was in sound condition – but there was not a soul on board.

and her entire crew of seven. Stories that sailors from the *Dei Gratia*, the ship that found her, went aboard to find the captain's breakfast laid and the food still warm upon the plates are fiction, but there is no doubt that the *Mary Celeste* was in almost perfect order and that no satisfactory explanation has ever been found for the peculiar disappearance of her crew. There is equally no doubt that the *Mary Celeste* was a jinxed ship; what forces were really at work, whether normal or paranormal, about this boat, is anyone's guess.

But the *Mary Celeste* is by no means the only ship to have lost its crew for reasons that remain unexplained. Paul Begg cites the following in his invaluable book *Into Thin Air*.

On 28 February 1855, the barquentine *James B. Chester* was sighted about 600 miles south-west of the Azores, in the Atlantic Ocean, 'yawing back and forth and [apparently] sailing with no one at the wheel'. That, indeed, proved to be the case, nor was anyone else on board. The boarding party, from the *Marathon*, found signs that the ship had been abandoned in a hurry, but the evidence could as well point to the crew being kidnapped, for drawers had been rifled, and none of the ship's lifeboats had been launched. On the other hand, the ship's compass and papers were missing, indicating a deliberate and calculated departure by officers and men. To confuse the issue further, the ship was completely sound, and the cargo intact.

One of the most tantalizing tales of lost ships is that of the wool clipper *Marlborough*, which sailed for England from New Zealand in 1890. She was carrying a cargo of gold bullion, even then worth perhaps as much as £2 million; a temptation, perhaps, for someone in the know, for she was never seen again. But, nearly a quarter of a century later, the Wellington (New Zealand) *Evening Post* of 13 November 1913 reported that the crew of the British ship *Johnson* had made a curious discovery off the coast of Chile that year. (The standard New Zealand–England voyage in those days was first to Iquique, Chile, then round Cape Horn and across the Atlantic to Cape Town, South Africa, with a final leg up the Atlantic, often calling at Hamburg before finally dropping anchor in the Pool of London.) The *Johnson*'s crew had come across a derelict ship, its sails mouldy and in tatters, its timbers rotten, and with a score of skeletons as its only crew. The ruined hulk's prow bore, in faded letters, the name *Marlborough*. The report does not say whether or not the ship's fabled cargo of gold was still aboard, or even if anyone looked for it – perhaps for the simple reason that by then the *Marlborough* and her gold had been forgotten.

In October 1917, the *Zebrina* set sail in fair weather from Falmouth, Cornwall, for Brieux, France. Two days later she was found with no crew but in perfectly good condition. There was no clue as to why she had been abandoned – or her crew abducted, if that is what happened.

In July 1941, the French cutter *Belle Isle* was found drifting with her sails set near the Gulf of Lyon. She was perfectly seaworthy but for the lack of her crew. There were no signs of violence on board.

NORMAL OCCURRENCES?

Mysterious disappearances do occur, but only when someone like the dematerializing Dr William Neff returns from such a vanishing to describe the experience will we be sure that something paranormal is afoot. Which does not mean that something paranormal is *not* afoot in these cases – it only means that we have no evidence for it. But then we have no evidence that anything 'normal' occurred, either.

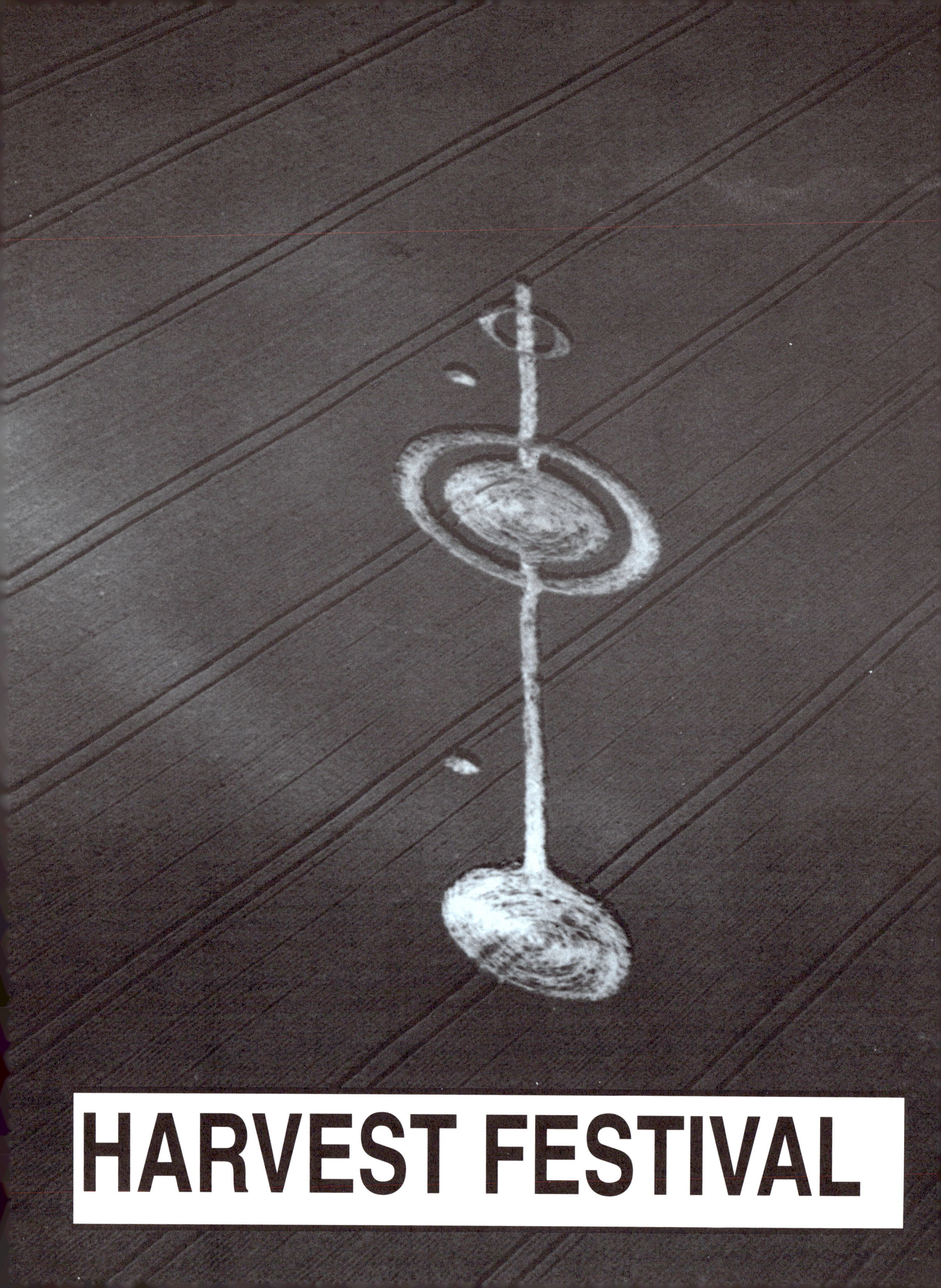

HARVEST FESTIVAL

Crop circles became big news in the 1980s; as the sightings multiplied, so did the complexity of the markings. But are these weird phenomena the work of hoaxers, UFOs, or some freak of nature? The cautious British army major preferred to reserve judgement, despite what he had witnessed with his own eyes...

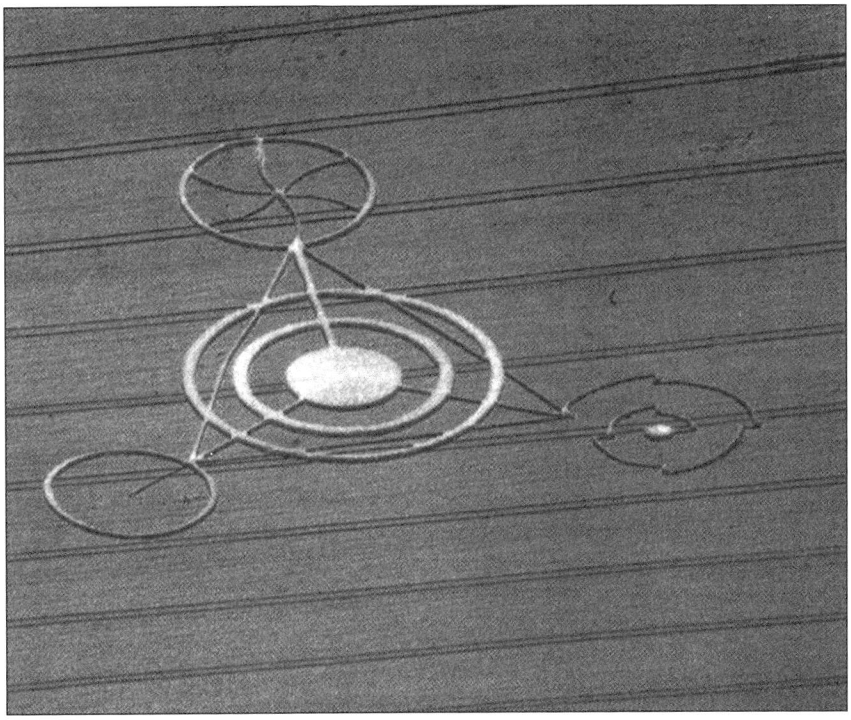

Just after 4.30 am on 10 August 1965, a truck driver, heading south on the Warminster–Westbury Road in Wiltshire, came around the bend at a point called Colloway Clump and drove straight into a UFO. The object was a huge crimson ball of light. To the driver's amazement the thing seemed to fasten itself to the windscreen, generating 'enormous vibrations'. The driver swerved, and the truck ended up by the fence on the verge, and on the wrong side of the road. At this point, the object spun away with a whistling sound.

'It was so huge,' the driver said, 'much larger than my truck. I would say it measured a good 30 to 40 ft across at the base.'

Almost a month later, at about 7.30 pm on 7 September, a British army officer,

This page and opposite: ***Three examples of the many crop circles that have mysteriously formed in the Wiltshire countryside in recent years. In 1990, more than 1000 circle formations were reported in England alone.***

Right and below: ***Crop circles in Canada that formed in 1990 and 1991. The photograph of the 1990 formation*** **(below)** ***shows the typical characteristics of a corn circle: the crop is flattened but not broken and there is a sharp cut-off between the disturbed area and the rest of the field.***

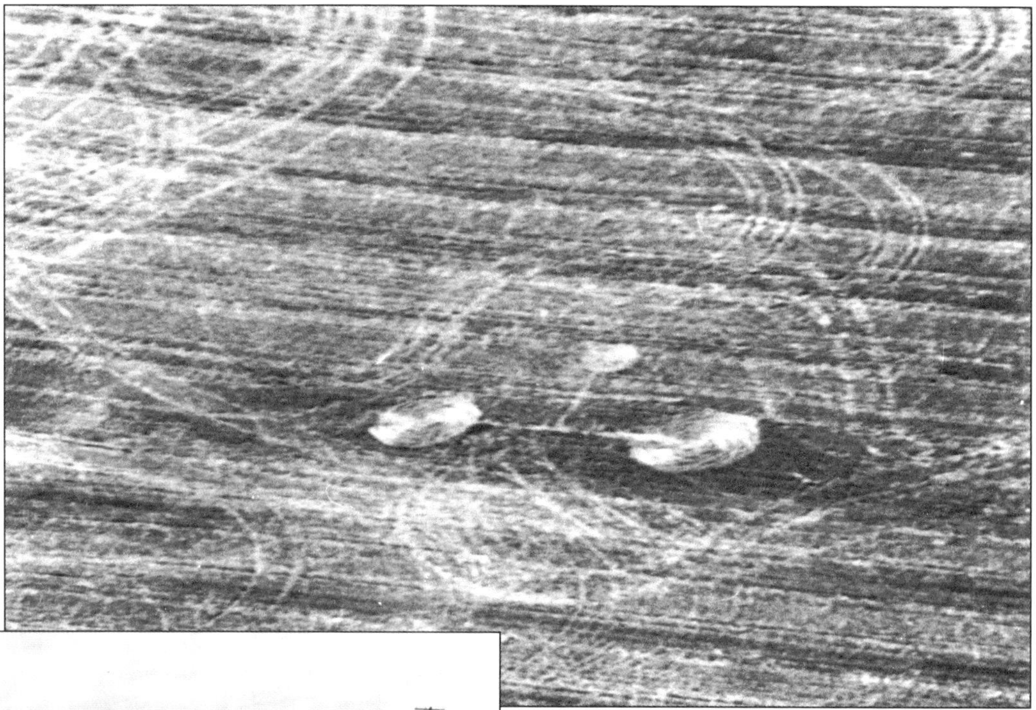

Major Hill, was driving past the same spot at about 45 mph when his car engine suddenly cut out. As the car came to a stop it was seized by huge vibrations. The body swayed, and Major Hill jumped out. Around him the air was pulsating, and there was a noise 'on a par with the sounds of high-powered refrigeration units or deep-freeze equipment, but...magnified many times'.

Less than three minutes later, he said, 'everything was back to normal. I pressed the starter button, and the car purred away perfectly, just as if nothing had happened at all.'

These reports bear all the hallmarks of classic kinds of UFO encounter. And, in the field just by that bend in the road, precisely circular depressions have been found and photographed in the crops – what, in 1965, many ufologists would immediately have dubbed 'UFO nests'. The question is: what connection is there between UFO reports like the two cited above, and what are now known as 'crop circles'? Are they made by UFOs, or by some freak of nature – or are the UFOs concerned themselves some kind of natural phenomenon?

COMPLEX PICTOGRAMS

Crop circles became big news in the 1980s. From the early years of the decade, more and more of them seemed to be appearing each year, especially in southern England, while reports came in too from Australia, New Zealand, Argentina, Brazil, South Africa, Mexico, the USA, Canada, France, Spain, Switzerland, Austria, Germany, Sweden, the former Soviet Union and, by no means least as to numbers, Japan.

As, year by year, the number of sightings multiplied so, it seemed, did the complexity of the markings. At the beginning of the decade people found only plain circles. Their sizes ranged from the diameter of a cartwheel to that of a circus arena. Sometimes the circles were laid out in tantalizingly neat patterns, but as the years passed – and especially from 1990 onward – the marks became noticeably weirder and consequently posed more difficult questions for researchers to answer.

From simple circular depressions, the phenomenon developed into circles with rings around them, or consisting entirely of rings. There were symmetrically placed circles, or single large ones with minor, precisely aligned 'satellites'. Towards the end of the decade, astonishing pictograms appeared: some resembled the more elaborate and mysterious ground markings at ancient sites like Nazca, Peru. Perhaps the most astonishing of these later patterns was the 'Mandelbrot set' found in August 1991 at Ickleton, about 10 miles south of Cambridge – which consisted of a closely connected pattern of circles that exactly reproduced one of the visual depictions of the currently fashionable chaos theory in mathematics. The forgivable presumption that it was a fake was confused by the fact that the wheat stalks were reported to be 'laid in multiple swirled layers to create the characteristic plaited effect which no human imitators of crop circles have been able to reproduce'.

And as the mysteries grew so did the number and kind of speculations about the circles' origins. Believers in paranormal explanations became increasingly bold in their assertions, while most scientists became progressively more sceptical. But all wanted to know – whatever suspicions they harboured – how the increasing complexity of the circles could be reconciled with the rising number of reliable eyewitnesses – who, perplexingly, persisted in seeing only simple circles being made?

Some complex formations can be likened to the enormous designs in the ground at ancient sites such as those in Peru* (above: *the Andes Candelabra, a 70 m carving south of Lima;* below: *markings in the desert at Nazca, fully appreciable only from the air).

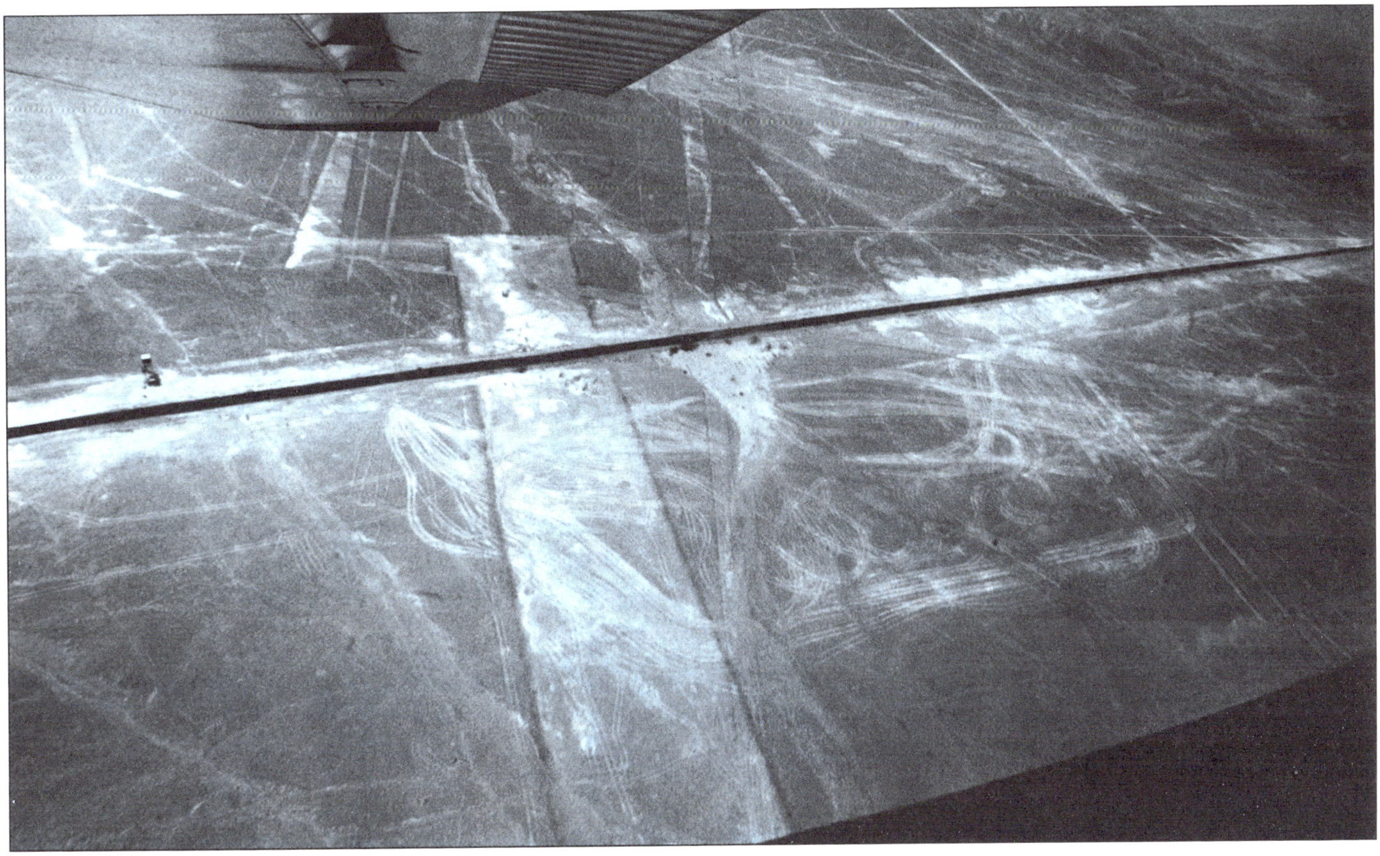

HORDES OF RUTTING HEDGEHOGS!

Some researchers suspected hoaxers were hard at work, while the more imaginative sceptics produced some of the most surreal 'rational explanations' ever to adorn an anomalous phenomenon. The least of these blamed deer, who had supposedly trampled the crops with geometrical exactitude in order to give birth and raise their young in orderly surroundings. Deer – and vixens, too – have been known to use the circles as 'nurseries', but they are rather more likely to have taken advantage of the shelter they had found, than to have trampled circles of such precision. The most baroque 'solution' to the mystery put the circles down to hordes of stampeding hedgehogs – or to rutting hedgehogs, still more amazingly.

Others developed extraordinary mystical 'New-Age'-style theories that, in essence, saw the circles as 'signs of the times' – as if something (perhaps the Earth itself) was writing urgent coded messages to us on the ground. From this point of view it was possible to see esoteric cosmic symbols in the circles, from 'the Divine Hermaphrodite' to signs of the zodiac.

Other researchers, notably Colin Andrews and Pat Delgado, concluded in their book *Circular Evidence* that 'the circles are created by an unknown force field manipulated by an unknown intelligence', and that 'Nothing in the current state of conventional science can account for all that has been described in this book.' What that hypothetical intelligence was could perhaps be guessed from Delgado's publishing his research summaries in *Flying Saucer Review*. At the end of 1986 he wrote there: 'Maybe these circles are created by alien beings using forcefields unknown to us. They may be manipulating existing Earth energy...'

THE CHARACTERISTIC PLAITED EFFECT WAS ONE WHICH NO HUMAN IMITATORS OF CROP CIRCLES HAVE BEEN ABLE TO REPRODUCE.

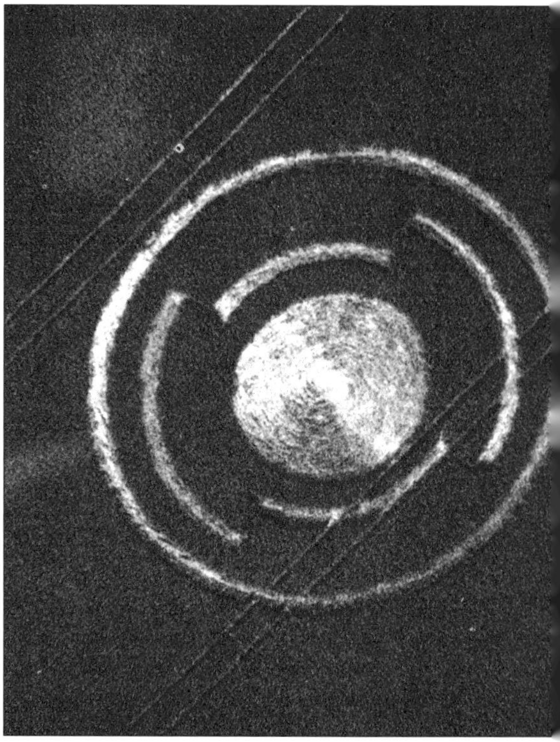

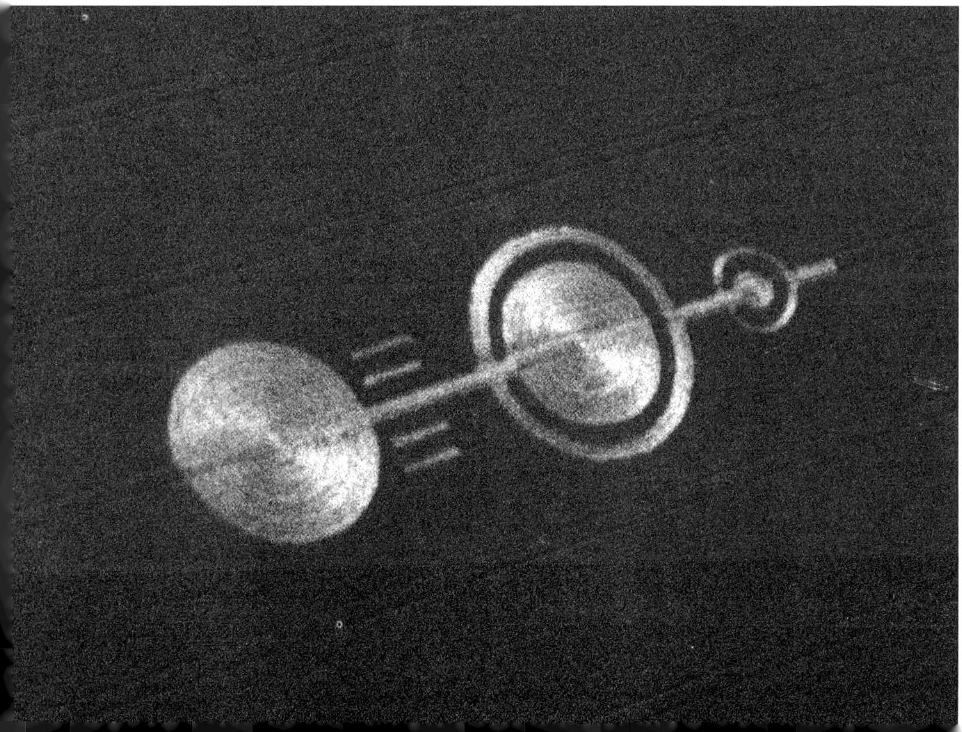

Right and below: ***Crop circle formations near Winchester, Hampshire, in the summer of 1990. Over the years the patterns of crop circles have become ever more intricate, leading many to believe that they are nothing more than the work of hoaxers. But the truth is not so simple.***

THE RESEARCH CONCLUDED THAT THE CIRCLES WERE CREATED BY ALIEN BEINGS USING FORCEFIELDS UNKNOWN TO HUMANITY.

That there are UFOs, and that UFOs have been seen at around the same time that crop circles have been created, is not in doubt. But the idea that such UFOs are necessarily under 'intelligent' control has yet to be proved.

ANCIENT SITES

Other 'rationalist' attempts to explain the circles have blamed the downdraft from helicopters – but the effect from chopper rotors does not create a precise 'edge' typical of the circles – and spreads of fungus, which do create exact circles as they reproduce (as in fairy rings of toadstools and mushrooms); but field investigators found no evidence of fungoid growth or disease among the crops in the circles. Some archaeologists have suggested that the circles were forming over ancient prehistoric sites, which were often circular in form. There may well be a connection with these sites, but the proponents of this form of the theory failed to explain why an ancient site should make an area of crops fall down.

Other scientists entered the fray with the hypothesis that the biochemistry of the soil had been disturbed (perhaps by over-indulgence in pesticides), so that the crop had weakened. But that did not explain the random appearance of the circles, their exact construction, the complex patterns, or the fact that circles would sometimes appear in the same field at widely spaced intervals.

Still other researchers took a strictly scientific but less prejudiced line and made steps toward explaining the phenomenon in terms of unusual, but perfectly natural and explicable, meteorological conditions – Delgado's and Andrews's claims that this was impossible notwithstanding. This last group also suspected that hoaxers were muddying the waters by producing the most complicated of the patterns found in the fields.

'EVERYONE HAS BEEN FOOLED'

Then, in September 1991, Douglas Bower and David Chorley hit the headlines. The pair, both artists in their sixties, claimed that since 1978 they had been faking crop circles in England. 'Everyone has been fooled,' they crowed. The two hoaxers showed a delighted press contingent how they had done it: using nothing but wooden boards and lengths of twine, they repeated a complex insect-like pattern that researcher Pat Delgado (promoter of the 'unknown force/unknown intelligence' hypothesis) had declared indubitably genuine at a private showing three days earlier.

Most circle researchers were underwhelmed by the claim that everyone had been fooled. Delgado and other officers of the Centre for Crop Circle Studies and other organizations whose leaders had embraced paranormal explanations for the phenomenon rejected the idea that hoaxers – including Bower and Chorley – could be responsible for creating crop circles.

But even before Bower and Chorley had dropped their bombshell, members of the scientific organization CERES (Circles Effect Research Group) already knew, in founder Dr Terence Meaden's words, that 'pranksters were rampant', and that some had nearly been caught. CERES had spent the entire 1991 season seeking out and exposing hoaxed circles – and netted some 150 fraudulent patterns in the process.

THE MOWING DEVIL

It was also apparent that Bower and Chorley were not merely pretending to be hoaxers, as the paranormalists preferred to believe. Since 1978, the pair had created hundreds of circles, but they had worked in only a small part of southern England. And they never claimed they had fabricated any of the pre-1978 circles already known to researchers.

In his book *The Circles Effect And Its*

'EVERYONE HAS BEEN FOOLED,' CROWED THE HOAXERS.

Below: ***Meteorologist Dr Terence Meaden has been studying crop circles since 1980 and founded the scientific body CERES (Circles Effect Research Group) to help further his research. His theory, widely held among scientists, is that the circles are formed by an atmospheric phenomenon.***

Right: ***A fascinating account of a crop circle, the case of the 'mowing devil', appeared in a four-page pamphlet published in 1678. The circle appeared in a field of oats on the night after a dispute between a mower and a farmer: angered by the price the mower had quoted, the farmer declared that he would rather the Devil himself should mow his oats than that the poor mower should have anything to do with them. A strange light was seen in the field that night – and a circle was found there the next morning.***

Mysteries Dr G. Terence Meaden cites cases that occurred in Britain as early as 1918 – this actually appeared in a Kentish field of beans, rather than corn – but the earliest detailed instance on record from Britain is the so-called 'mowing devil' report of 1678.

In August that year, according to a contemporary four-page pamphlet, a Hertfordshire farmer had three half-acres of oats standing ripe and in need of harvesting. He approached 'a poor mower' to do the job, but the mower's price was too high for the farmer, and they exchanged a few sharp words. Infuriated, the farmer snapped that 'the Devil himself should mow his oats before he should have anything to do with them'. The pamphlet continues:

'...that same night this poor mower and farmer parted, his field of oats was publickly beheld by several passengers to be all on a flame, and so continued for some space, to the great consternation of those that beheld it, which strange news being by several carried to the farmer next morning...the inquisitive farmer no sooner arrived at the place where his oats grew, but to his admiration he found the crop was cut down ready to his hands, and as if the Devil had a mind to show his dexterity...he cut them in round circles, and plac't every straw with that exactness that it would have taken up above an age for any man to perform what he did in one night – and the man that ow[n]s them is as yet afraid to remove them.'

Here, once again, we have the peculiar, luminous, UFO-like phenomena that are associated with later circles. What is odd is the report that the oats were cut, as in genuine crop circles the stalks are bent over just above the ground. But one might also surmise that no one was prepared to approach 'the Devil's work' that closely, and certainly the bent stalks can look as if they have been cut. The neat arrangement too suggests the characteristic outward swirling of the crops from the centre noted by modern investigators.

If the hoaxers could not have produced these circles from times past, nor could they possibly have created the many hundreds of circles reported elsewhere in the world.

A crop circle found in 1967 in the north-eastern USA was featured in the infamous Condon Report on UFOs. The circle was 30 ft in diameter and had affected a small swamp: 'cattails had been squashed down and found to lie in a clockwise spiral pattern,' said the report. A lady eyewitness had seen a large glowing light at that spot the night before. Another instance is the 45 ft wide ringed circle that appeared at Orebro in Sweden in April 1972. Witnesses in this case saw a red light descend prior to the discovery of the circle. Within the mark, the crops were swirled clockwise. Its overall shape was oval, but within it was a 10 ft wide anti-clockwise ring.

In 1975, geologist Dr Alan Wells photographed a series of overlapping swirled circles at the snow-covered foot of a mountain in a remote part of the Munzur range in Turkey. Each circle was about 35 ft in diameter. In 1968, Dr Wells had also found similar swirled, circular markings in snow in the Elburz Mountains near Tehran, Iran.

Crop circles appear in huge numbers in Japan. Recent incidents include the 10 ft rayed and blasted circle that formed in reeds on 9 August 1986, in Yamagata prefecture, and interfered with TV signals. Another formed within the double-fenced grass compound of a Nippon Radio station in the early hours of 1 September 1991. It seems to have been responsible for the massive amount of radio interference that occurred at the same time. There are, too, many Japanese reports from long before the 1980s, some dating back centuries.

It seems a reasonable conclusion that the more complex and elaborate 'circles' and their attendant patterns are hoaxes, while the simpler ones are not. In these simpler formations, a typical pattern can be seen in the bent crops: an outward swirling of the stalks (noted above), interwoven layers of stalks, twisted straws and, occasionally, a centre with crops still standing.

But that still leaves the fundamental question unanswered: what causes the circles to form in the first place?

A RUSTLING VORTEX

Some people have actually witnessed crop circles coming into existence, and the best clues to the solution of the mystery have come from examining what they have seen. And it is worth noting that not one of these eyewitnesses, nor any other known witnesses of the making of a crop circle, reported supernatural experiences.

In July 1982, at Westbury, Wiltshire, Ray Barnes saw a huge circle take shape close by him, within a mere three or four seconds, to the accompaniment of a weird humming noise. Late one evening in 1983 Melvyn Bell saw a circle appear in wheat as dust spun in a typical whirlwind. Near Dundee, Scotland, in 1989, Sandy Reid was out at dawn one morning when he heard a tremendous noise in the air; then he saw a crop circle take rapid shape.

At about 9 pm, as the sun was setting on 17 May 1990, Gary and Vivienne Tomlinson were walking along the edge of a wheatfield in Surrey, when a vortex formed next to where they were standing. From a soft rustling, the sound of the wind changed to something like a high-pitched flute. Pressure of the air from above and beside them forced them into the corn,

IN SECONDS IT WAS ALL OVER.

Below: *Mysteriously flattened reeds at Nishikawa-cho, in Yamagata prefecture, Japan. This event occurred overnight on 8–9 August 1986: it was accompanied by interference with TV signals and the appearance of a bright orange light of ball lightning.*

Above: ***Vivienne and Gary Tomlinson witnessed a crop circle forming near their home. They found it increasingly difficult to stand, and only with a great deal of effort were able to get free.***

Below: ***Balls of light are often associated with the formation of crop circles, leading many to believe that the marks are left by alien landing craft.***

where they found themselves right in the centre of a corn circle as it formed. Gary Tomlinson's hair was standing on end from static electricity; both were almost knocked to the ground by the force of the wind roaring around them. But in seconds, it was all over. As the mass of swirling air drifted away it cut out a second circle and then a third, further off.

In Gloucestershire, at dusk one day in July 1988, Tom Gwinnett saw a large orange-yellow ball of light spinning just above a field of wheat. A crop circle was found next day at the spot where he judged the light to have been.

SPECTACULAR LIGHTS

It seems, then, that comparatively simple circles are formed from a combination of wind and electrical effects, and that at night an associated spinning ball of light may develop – or at any rate, be more obvious: it is this that forms the 'UFO' component in crop circles.

For such a vortex to form, the air has to be virtually calm, which happens more often in the evening, at night, or early in the morning than by day. When a wind butts against a hill, the downward airflow can produce vortices that, within a small area, can be quite violent. And when the air is also humid, they become visible as the whirling columns or hollow spheres that witnesses have also on occasion reported.

According to Professors John Snow and Tokio Kikuchi, when eddies of wind 'break down', they move towards the ground and sweep out the circles in the crops. Professor G. Terence Meaden suggests that, as this happens, friction in the moving air separates and concentrates existing electrical charges in the atmosphere. This accounts for the humming noises reminiscent of high-tension power lines (a sound not unlike a deep-freeze unit at work, incidentally) and for the sometimes spectacular lights that have been seen accompanying the high-powered winds. Alarmed witnesses have taken the lights to be UFOs – which in the strict sense they were, until this explanation for their presence was put forward.

SACRED BURIAL GROUNDS

Whatever the origin of real crop circles, they have always been with us. There is evidence that prehistoric peoples too noticed circle-making vortices, and the seemingly magical nature of the phenomenon may well have made them sacred in those peoples' eyes. The crop-circle effect may even account for the circular shape of so many prehistoric sacred sites.

The peoples of Neolithic and Early Bronze Age Britain built some 40,000 round burial mounds, around 1000 stone circles and many thousands of ring ditches, timber circles and the like. Many were not exactly circular. Like crop circles, some

Perhaps prehistoric rings of stones and burial grounds were sited in places made sacred by the visitation of whirling winds and inexplicable lights.

were oval, others elliptical in shape. It may be that the rings of stone, burial mounds and so on were laid on top of sites made sacred by the visitation of whirling winds and inexplicable lights, and that burials took place at the crop-circle centre. It is possible that Stonehenge was built on just such a site.

And here, too, may be an explanation of the association so often noted between ancient sites and UFOs, for certain features of the landscape seem to favour the formation of crop-circle vortices – similar features to those so frequently chosen by the ancient builders for their sacred places.

In the opinion of one of the world's most eminent scientists, Professor Stephen Hawking, crop circles are entirely explicable by natural atmospheric vortices on the one hand and hoaxing on the other. Circle researcher Paul Fuller remarked, no less pertinently, after Bower and Chorley went public: 'When the media stop promoting the phenomenon as a supernatural mystery, the hoaxers will go away and leave us with the real circles.' Those two comments make a fair conclusion. And they do not make the existence of crop circles any less a matter for wonder.

Left and below: *These three crop circles in Cornwall were all formed between 11 July and 10 August 1991. In each case, a bluish white light was reported over or inside the circle.*

CURSES

The pregnant serving maid, cruelly abandoned by her aristocratic seducer, put a curse on the noble family. Even when his brother committed suicide at the age of 26, the young 8th Earl of Craven refused to believe in the curse. He was proved fatally wrong.

At 2 am on 30 August 1990, 28-year-old Simon Craven was driving to his home, Peelings Manor, near Pevensey, Sussex; he was cruising along the seafront in Eastbourne, Sussex, when his car collided with parked vehicles. Craven died in the ambulance that rushed him to hospital. This was no ordinary traffic accident, however: the dead man had been the 8th Earl of Craven, and his death appeared to fulfil a 350-year-old curse on his family. The late Lord Craven's grandfather, the 5th Earl, died aged 35 during a wild party aboard a yacht. The 6th Earl died of leukaemia at 47. Simon Craven succeeded to the title in 1983 when his elder brother Thomas, the 7th Earl, shot himself in a fit of depression at the age of 26. Apart from the original Earl Craven – who was granted the title by King Charles II in 1664, and died aged 91 in 1697 – it is said that no one who has held the earldom has lived beyond the age of 57.

The curse is in fact supposed to hang over the Cravens' ancestral home, Morewood House in Hamstead Marshall, Berkshire – the first peerage to be granted the family was the Barony of Hamstead Marshall – and, according to tradition, was laid on the family by a servant girl, whom one of the dynasty's sons had made pregnant and abandoned. The house was sold after the 7th Earl's suicide, but the sale seems neither to have saved the 8th Earl from an untimely end, nor to have left the house. Only a week before Simon Craven's death, a verdict of suicide was recorded on Morewood's latest owner, Dr Robert Reid. (The double tragedy is not necessarily a result of the curse being somehow confused: 'house' and 'family' are often used synonymously of great families, as in 'the House of Windsor' for the present British Royal Family, so the curse would presumably affect both.) Despite this grim history, the Cravens' lawyer maintained that

Opposite: ***William, 1st Earl of Craven, on whose family a curse was laid by a serving girl. According to the 350-year-old curse, all the Earls of Craven are doomed to die young – a fate that befell both William Craven, the 2nd Earl*** **(above)** ***and his successor to the title, George*** **(below).**

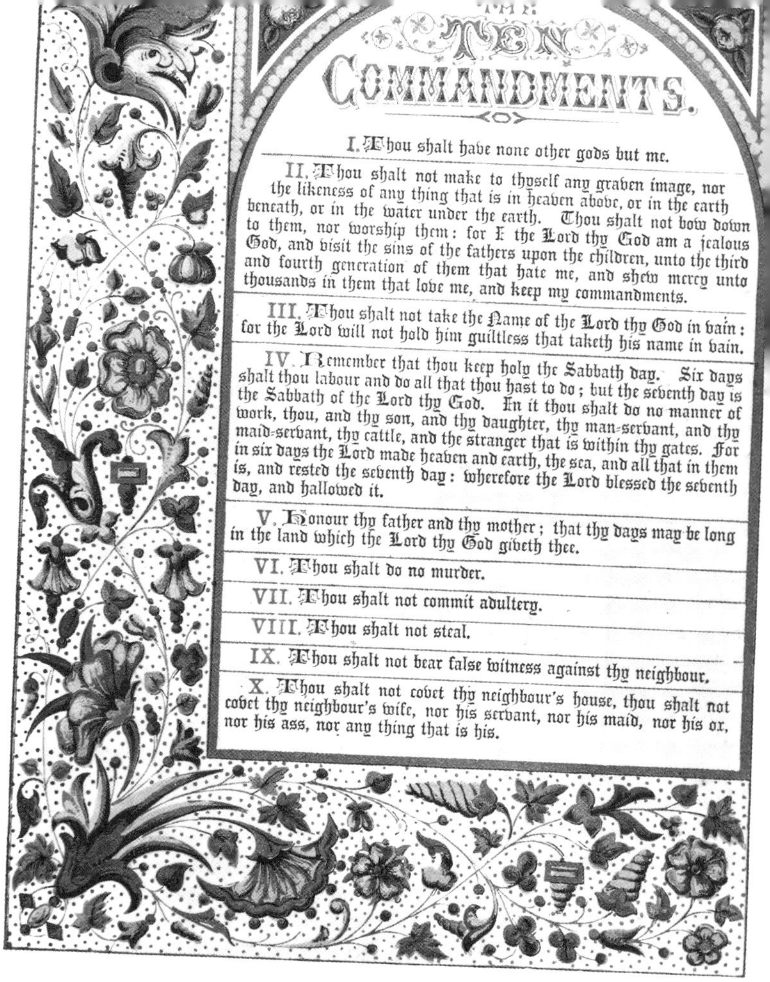

THE TEN COMMANDMENTS.

I. Thou shalt have none other gods but me.

II. Thou shalt not make to thyself any graven image, nor the likeness of any thing that is in heaven above, or in the earth beneath, or in the water under the earth. Thou shalt not bow down to them, nor worship them: for I the Lord thy God am a jealous God, and visit the sins of the fathers upon the children, unto the third and fourth generation of them that hate me, and shew mercy unto thousands in them that love me, and keep my commandments.

III. Thou shalt not take the Name of the Lord thy God in vain: for the Lord will not hold him guiltless that taketh his name in vain.

IV. Remember that thou keep holy the Sabbath day. Six days shalt thou labour and do all that thou hast to do; but the seventh day is the Sabbath of the Lord thy God. In it thou shalt do no manner of work, thou, and thy son, and thy daughter, thy man-servant, and thy maid-servant, thy cattle, and the stranger that is within thy gates. For in six days the Lord made heaven and earth, the sea, and all that in them is, and rested the seventh day: wherefore the Lord blessed the seventh day, and hallowed it.

V. Honour thy father and thy mother; that thy days may be long in the land which the Lord thy God giveth thee.

VI. Thou shalt do no murder.

VII. Thou shalt not commit adultery.

VIII. Thou shalt not steal.

IX. Thou shalt not bear false witness against thy neighbour.

X. Thou shalt not covet thy neighbour's house, thou shalt not covet thy neighbour's wife, nor his servant, nor his maid, nor his ox, nor his ass, nor any thing that is his.

For many people a coincidental connection with the great and the good provides a little pleasure. Not so for the unfortunate Chapple family of Devon. For three generations, a boy was born into the family on 29 September – the birthday of Horatio, Lord Nelson **(above)*****. And, like the celebrated naval hero, each man lost his right eye in an accident.***

none of the family believes in the curse.

If not quite a curse, something very similar afflicted the family of Doreen Squires of Riverdale, Devon, for several generations. She felt she had reason to worry when her son Martin, aged 25, had a piece of steel fly into his right eye while working in a saw mill in nearby Totnes. Her father, grandfather and greatgrandfather had all lost their right eyes in accidents. Jim Chapple, a stone cracker, lost his eye to a stone chipping. His son Jim, a blacksmith, lost his to a piece of steel while making a horseshoe, and his son Adrian, Doreen's father, lost his in a quarry blast. All had been born on 29 September, which is the birthday of the British naval hero Horatio, Lord Nelson. He lost his right eye during the blockage of Corsica in 1794: he was in the way of a bit of gravel that was sent flying when an enemy cannonball landed near him. Martin Squires, however, recovered from his accident with no lasting damage to his sight. But he was not born on 29 September.

THE HIDEOUS CHILD WAS HIDDEN IN A BASKET.

The second of the Ten Commandments (**above right*****) given to Moses (*****right,*** ***in a Dutch painting by M. de Vos) warns the Hebrews against worshipping idols, threatening divine retribution on three generations of children.***

A GRISLY MONSTER

Curses on families and their succeeding generations are by no means new. The second of the ten commandments given to Moses on Sinai contains the threat of just such a retribution should the Hebrews fall into idolatry; Exodus 20, verse 5, says plainly: 'for I the LORD thy God am a jealous God, visiting the iniquity of the fathers upon the children unto the third and fourth generation of them that hate me'.

The ancient Greeks took curses seriously. Not even animals were exempt. The reason, according to Greek myth, that crows are black is entirely due to the wrath of the goddess Athene; once, they were pure white, and were her favourite birds besides. The tale goes that the god Hephaistos was besotted with Athene, and tried to rape her, but he bungled the dreadful business, so that his sperm fell on Mother Earth and made her pregnant instead. The result was a grisly monster, part boy, part serpent. Athene felt a curious obligation to look after this strange creature, but (in the way of goddesses) delegated the task to the daughters of King Kekrops of her patron city, Athens.

Athene secreted the hideous child in a basket, and insisted the princesses never look inside it. Naturally, they peeped, and were so disgusted at what they saw that they promptly threw themselves off the Acropolis. This is where a crow, whose identity has never been established, made a fundamental error of judgement. Thinking he was doing Athene a good turn, he told the goddess what had happened. Athene was outraged, and rewarded the crow, and all his kind, by turning his feathers black. The truth of this story is plain to anyone who has seen the hooded crows of Greece: a sad reminder of their former brilliant whiteness is preserved in the dull grey-pink plumage on their bodies – while all the rest is deep black.

THE MUMMY'S CURSE

A good curse, like a diamond, it seems, is forever. The most famous ancient curse is probably the one allegedly uttered by those who buried the Egyptian boy king, Tutankhamun, who died at the age of 18 in approximately 1340 BC.

Above: ***Lord and Lady Carnarvon at Ascot in 1921. Carnarvon funded the excavations of archaeologist Howard Carter, who discovered the treasure-filled tomb of the boy-king Tutankhamun in Egypt's Valley of the Kings. Only weeks after the official opening of the tomb, the Earl fell ill and died in Cairo, the apparent victim of an ancient curse that promised death to anyone who disturbed the sleep of the pharaohs.***

Rumours that tampering with Tutankhamun's grave were fraught with psychic danger began with the death of the 5th Earl of Carnarvon in 1923. This happened just a few months after the discovery of the boy Pharaoh's tomb, and Carnarvon had sponsored the dig that uncovered it. Carnarvon had first employed the English archaeologist Howard Carter, who found Tutankhamun's last resting place, to search for antiquities in Egypt in 1907. By 1922, Carter had unearthed a number of tombs and made some interesting finds, but in Carnarvon's eyes the expense involved, by now some £40,000, was beginning to seem onerous in view of his meagre returns – archaeology then being largely a matter of digging up what treasures one could, and selling them to the highest bidder: essentially, it was grave-robbing made respectable by the interest of aristocratic European gentlemen and a dash of accompanying scholarship.

In October 1922, Carter persuaded Carnarvon to keep financing his searches for one more season and, perhaps to celebrate his continued employment,

This page: ***Howard Carter, on the brink of discovering the dazzling splendours of Tutankhamun's tomb, in the Valley of the Kings at Luxor. Carter himself did not believe in the curse that was rumoured to be linked with the Pharaoh. However, by 1929, six years after Carter's historic opening of the tomb, 22 people who had been associated with the excavation had died prematurely.***

bought himself a yellow canary. His Egyptian workers said it would bring him luck. On 26 November 1922, Carter, literally, struck gold: he broke into the grave of Tutankhamun, along with Carnarvon, his daughter Lady Evelyn, and Carter's assistant, Arthur Callender. Four days later, Carnarvon received a prophecy of his death in Egypt which the noted mystic, Count Hamon, had received by automatic writing.

THE ILL OMENS CONVINCED THE EGYPTIAN WORKERS THAT A HUMAN DEATH WOULD FOLLOW SHORTLY.

The front of the decorated head-dress on the mummy's golden mask bore the image of Wadjet, the cobra goddess who protected Egyptian royalty; when Carter's canary was gobbled up by a cobra, the Egyptian workers on the site were convinced a human death would shortly, and surely, follow. It did.

By the end of February Carnarvon was ill; his teeth were falling out, and he was racked by fever. He went into a coma – the cause was diagnosed as blood poisoning – and he died, aged only 57, on 4 April 1923. At the same time, it is said, his pet fox terrier Susan howled, and died with her master.

At this point the notion began that the Pharaoh's tomb was cursed. The first to fuel the flames of the 'Curse of the Pharaohs' were, of course, the hacks of Fleet Street, who with red-rimmed eyes reported that carved above the entrance to Tutankhamun's tomb were the words 'Death shall come to him who touches the tomb' – or perhaps they were 'Death will slay with wings whoever disturbs the peace of the pharaohs', depending on the reporter.

Such protective threats certainly were written on some royal tombs in Egypt. One states bluntly that anyone disturbing the sanctity of the last royal resting place 'shall hunger, thirst, faint, and sicken', but Howard Carter resolutely maintained that no such curse was attached to Tutankhamun's grave. In the early 1980s, Richard Adamson, a former military policeman who had worked as a guard on the dig, stated that the rumour of a curse had been started by Carnarvon himself – simply to keep thieves away from what he knew was a fabulous treasure.

Nevertheless, there have been other sudden and not altogether explicable deaths among those who have visited the tomb or come in contact with its riches. A Professor La Fleur died the very evening of the day he visited the tomb; the American millionaire George Jay-Gould died after developing a fever on the day he went; A.C. Mace, one of Carter's assistants, resigned in 1924 after persistent bouts of fever and died in 1928; Richard Bethell, another assistant, died at the age of 45. Arthur Weighall, a third, died of an unknown fever. Of those who were associated with the find, he was claimed as the 21st victim, after Carnarvon's half-brother, who killed himself.

Howard Carter, however, not only led the team who broke into the grave but removed a number of treasures from the tomb for his personal collection; he was surely the prime candidate for supernatural vengeance, but he lived another 17 years without mishap and died unspectacularly, aged 65, in 1939.

The latest theory to explain the apparent curse is that some mummies are radioactive. In January 1992, a Cairo University professor was reported in *New Scientist* as suggesting that Carnarvon and others may have died from radiation sickness. But Howard Carter, it seems, was immune even to that.

A WEREWOLF

In February 1972, brothers Colin and Leslie Robson were clearing weeds in the garden of their council house at Hexham, about 20 miles from Newcastle upon Tyne, Northumberland, when they found two carved stone heads, each about the size of a tennis ball. One, which the Robsons called 'the boy', was greenish-grey, glinting with quartz crystals, and very heavy; the other was of rougher material, and its witchlike appearance made the Robsons dub it 'the girl'. The brothers took the heads inside, but then odd things began to happen: the heads turned around spontaneously, a mirror frame was found shattered in a frying pan, mysterious whiplash sounds were heard and one of the Robson daughters had her mattress showered with glass.

Above: ***Rough copies of the allegedly Celtic heads that were found in a garden in Hexham, Northumberland, and identified as ritual sculptures dating from the 2nd century AD. The objects appeared to have some malign influence, not only on the household in whose garden they had been found, but also on the family of the Celtic scholar, Dr Anne Ross, who identified the heads and subsequently took possession of them. A man who had formerly lived in the house at Hexham claimed he had made them from concrete, as toys for his small daughter, in the 1950s. Since the whereabouts of the heads themselves is now unknown, the truth about their origin may never be established.***

The effects were not limited to the Robsons' household while the heads were in their house. One night the next-door neighbour's 10-year-old son thought something was touching him in the dark as he was trying to sleep. His mother told him not to be silly, and was promptly horrified to see a 'half-human, half-sheep' shape come towards her, touch her, and slink out of the room on all fours. The Robson boys said too that a luminous flower had grown one Christmas at the place where the heads were found, and a mysterious light was seen hovering above the spot one night while the heads were in the house.

When, later in 1972, the heads were borrowed for study by Celtic scholar Dr Anne Ross, an archaeologist at Southampton University, the Robsons' house was troubled no more by unpleasant and

DID THE SEVERED HUMAN HEADS STILL HOLD THE MAGICAL POWERS INVESTED IN THEM NEARLY 2000 YEARS BEFORE?

unearthly events. Initially, Dr Ross identified the heads as typical Celtic sculptures, about 1800 years old. She kept them in a box in her study. A few nights later, she woke up cold and frightened, and saw a tall figure, in her bedroom doorway:

'It was about six feet high, slightly stooping, and it was black against the white door...The upper part I would have said was wolf and the lower part was human. It was covered with a kind of black, very dark fur. It went out and I just saw it clearly and then it disappeared and something made me run after it – a thing I wouldn't normally have done, but I felt compelled to run after it...I could hear it going down the stairs. Then it disappeared toward the back of the house. When I got to the bottom of the stairs I was terrified.'

Above: ***A man is attacked by a werewolf, in a 16th-century woodcut from* Die Emeis *by Johann Geiler von Kaiserberg. Both Dr Anne Ross and her daughter were threatened by what appeared to be a werewolf during the period while the Hexham heads were in Dr Ross's keeping.***

Dr Ross then returned to wake her husband. A search revealed nothing.

A few days after this, Dr Ross's teenage daughter Berenice came home from school and saw a large entity – which she described as 'as near a werewolf as anything' – rush down the stairs towards her. It vaulted over the banisters and landed on the floor with a 'kind of plop'. Like her mother, Berenice felt compelled to follow the thing as it padded away, and it vanished by the door of the Rosses' music room. Subsequently, Dr Ross occasionally felt a cold presence in the house, and heard the thing's footsteps. Her study door would fly open on its own.

The entity, although described as a 'werewolf', bore some resemblance to the wulver – half-man, half-sheep, of Northern European myths, which has been sighted several times this century in the Shetlands. The wulver is reputedly well-disposed towards people unless it is provoked, although visitors to the Rosses' house said the air of evil was palpable as long as the heads were there.

Even after she had removed the heads from her house, Dr Ross was still periodically aware of the entity in her house. She said it was as if it had been 'locked in' to the other Celtic heads in her possession. Eventually, she disposed of the whole collection and had the house exorcized.

Dr Ross assumed that the ancient heads – which were cult objects among the Celts, who would also place severed human heads over their doors to ward off evil – still held the magic powers invested in them nearly 2000 years before. But then, later in 1972, the previous occupant of the Robsons' house, truck-driver Desmond Craigie, revealed that he had made the heads with cement in about 1956 for his daughter, and that they had been thrown in the garden where they were later found.

Dr Ross countered that the heads were indisputably Celtic in appearance, at least, and noted that spectrographic analysis had shown no sign of calcium silicate, the major component of cement. But she also remarked that:

'no matter when and by whom these heads were fashioned, the phenomena they engendered...seem at least irrefutable, if inexplicable...I do *not* maintain that the heads are Celtic in origin; but that they have in some way drawn to themselves powers such as were attributed to real [i.e. severed human] or manufactured heads in the pre-Christian world.'

There is, of course, another interpretation. It is worth remembering that in the three households apparently affected by the heads, there were adolescent children – who are frequently the focus of weird psychic manifestations if there is a poltergeist about. (They may indeed 'manufacture' the poltergeist at some strange interface between mind, emotion, energy and matter.) Did adolescent turmoil and ancient magic meet to produce the singularly disturbing entities that disrupted the Robsons, their neighbours, and the Rosses?

LASH OF FIRE

The Celtic heads of Hexham may have been the bearers of an ancient Druidic curse. Perhaps surprisingly curses are still cast by the priests of the world's major religions, even today. The story of the jackdaw of Rheims, against whom the bishop pronounced an anathema 'with bell, book and candle' is well known.

Even the traditionally rather mild Church of England has its Service of Commination, which first appeared in the 1662 *Book of Common Prayer*. The service contains 12 curses – some of them for what today seem rather minor offences: 'Cursed is he', for example, 'that removeth his neighbour's landmark', while others are obscure to the modern ear: 'Cursed is he that smiteth his neighbour secretly.' Slander and drunkenness too lay one open to being 'cast into utter darkness'. The service leaves room for other sinners and their wickedness to be cursed, and was used against church thieves as recently as 1981 – by the Rev. Robert Nesham of Down Ampney.

Judaism has its *pulsa de nura* (Aramaic for 'lash of fire'), also known as the Rod of Light ceremony. This is held in a room lit by black candles where a *minyan* (at least ten righteous men) have gathered to recite cabbalistic incantations and burn a paper inscribed with the names of the one to be accursed and his or her mother; during the service the *shofar* (ram's horn) is blown to dispel *shedim* (evil spirits).

In September 1981, Rabbi Moshe Hirsch threatened to invoke the Rod of Light against archaeologist Yigal Shilo, whose excavations of a part of ancient Jerusalem apparently threatened to disturb a medieval Jewish cemetery. 'This ceremony is an absolute last resort,' said the Rabbi, adding: 'It has been invoked only twice in the last 30 years, both times with horrible consequences. There are many ways of dying, some less pleasant than others.' Shilo denied that the 'threatened' cemetery existed, and in the end escaped unscathed, as Rabbi Hirsch was unable to discover the name of the archaeologist's mother.

In January 1991, during the Second Gulf War (Operation Desert Storm), the ultra-orthodox Eda Haredit group in Israel did indeed perform the ceremony, and pronounced a death curse on President Saddam Hussein of Iraq. At the time of writing, he was still alive.

The entire state of California was once placed under a ritual curse of sorts, and by a judge – for even the secular law, it seems, can pronounce anathemas. In the case of US District Judge Samuel King, his order of the court had perhaps a more profound effect than he expected. Annoyed because jurors could not attend his San Francisco court because of heavy rains, Judge King declared in 1986: 'I hereby order that it cease raining by Tuesday.' Five years of severe drought promptly afflicted

Above: ***The Druids were the priestly class of the Celts, and were responsible for passing on philosophical and scientific wisdom, as well as knowledge of sacrificial rites and herbal medicine. They were also known to have a firm belief in magical charms. Could the Hexham heads have somehow become imbued with ancient magical powers – powers that worked only for evil?***

THERE ARE MANY WAYS OF DYING, SOME LESS PLEASANT THAN OTHERS.

California. Once he was reminded of his motion, Judge King proclaimed: 'I hereby rescind my order of February 18, 1986, and order that rain shall fall in California beginning February 27, 1991.' Later that day – well within the deadline set by the judge – a fierce Pacific storm drenched California with more than 4 in of rain, the state's heaviest rainfall in ten years. The judge, apparently unimpressed by the coincidence, said this was 'proof positive that we are a nation governed by laws'.

AN ANTI-CURSE

Chiang Mai, Thailand's second largest city, suffered a far more complex fate in 1991. That summer, a story began to circulate that the town was cursed.

The origins of the trouble went back to 1986. Then, a construction firm proposed building a cable railway to the holy mountain, behind the city, which was the seat of an ancient temple. The monks at the temple were enraged by the plan; students gathered a 20,000-signature petition against the project. Feelings among both people and monks were obviously rising, for Royal Thai Air Force pilots who flew over the city reported seeing monks sitting on clouds in the lotus position. But, attracted by the prospect of the railways, construction companies began to build modern apartment blocks and hotels around it. This, said popular opinion, was upsetting the geomantic harmony of the city.

When building started for a 24-storey apartment block next to an old temple on the banks of the River Ping, and the citizens of the Old City realized there was nothing they could do to stop it, they decided to invoke evil spirits against the developers.

There was a large demonstration in August 1989. To arouse the spirits, people carried various symbols of disharmony, such as broken plates, and women mocked the holy sutras. At the climax of the ceremony, the sky darkened and there were three dramatic lightning flashes. Three days later, the city was shaken by an almighty earthquake. The people had no doubt that evil spirits had been aroused.

In April 1991, a strong wind uprooted the oldest holy Bodhi tree at the Suan Dork Temple. At the beginning of May, when the rainy season normally starts, the paddy fields continued to be parched. The property market collapsed. New projects

Below: ***US troops in Operation Desert Storm, the successful operation to free Kuwait from occupation by Iraqi forces in 1991. In response to Iraq's missile attacks on Israel during the war, an extremist Jewish group performed the rare Rod of Light ceremony, in which a death curse was pronounced on Iraqi president Saddam Hussein. By early 1993, the curse had yet to be fulfilled.***

were cancelled. The governor promised a stop to high-rise building. At the end of May, a Lauda Air Boeing crashed killing 13 VIPs, including the governor and his wife. Four days later, the abbot of one of Chiang Mai's most important Buddhist monasteries died.

People started to desert the ill-starred city in droves. The only thing to do was to bring the evil spirits abroad back under control. 'The evil spirits are so powerful that only an extra-strong anti-curse can drive them away,' explained Mani Pajomjong, Professor of Pedagogy at Chiang Mai University, and a former monk. The city council appointed him Master of Ceremonies for the spirit cleansing.

At sunrise on 8 June 1991, women arrived at the main gate of the city with trays of offerings, which were then laid out in seven different corners of Chiang Mai. The offerings had been paid for by banks and construction companies and consisted of fish, raw meat, bamboo shoots, fruit, sugar cane and cheroots laid out on banana leaves. The largest offering was reverently placed at a crossroads where the founder of the city, King Meng Rai, had been struck down by lightning in AD 1311. 'We invite the spirits to a feast and ask them to leave the city,' announced Professor Mani enticingly. At 5 pm, 108 monks began chanting a sutra to break the spirits' power.

'This has nothing to do with superstition; it's about our relationship with Nature,' said a professor at the university. 'With all this modernization we are losing our roots. The curse has forced us to think about the environment.'

The monks had just finished their chant when a light rain fell. As the offerings were taken to the river to be thrown in, the sky opened and the sun shone on the city. 'If people are angry with the new high-rise buildings,' said Professor Mani afterwards, 'they can always invite the evil spirits back.'

A SHIP OF ILL FORTUNE

The *Mary Celeste* is one of the most famous ships in maritime history; her discovery some 400 miles east of the Azores on 5 December 1872, her sails set, and all in order aboard – but for the minor detail that not one of her crew was present, and not one has been seen, dead or alive, since – has made her the supreme example of the mystery ship.

But the mysterious disappearance of the *Mary Celeste*'s crew is only the high point in the story of a ship that seems to have been doomed from the start – and whose ill luck did not cease on that eerie winter day in the north-east Atlantic.

Sailors have long held that to change a ship's name will bring her bad luck. The *Mary Celeste* was launched in 1861 as the *Amazon*, from the shipyard of Joshua Dewis on Spencer's Island, Nova Scotia. She was a brigantine, a two-masted vessel square-rigged and with three jibs on the foremast, with a gaff-rigged mainsail, a staysail and four foresails on the mainmast. She measured 99 ft 4 in from stem to stern, with

Below: ***A woman selling amulets at a witch-doctors' market in La Paz, Bolivia. The ancient practice of using amulets to ward off evil spirits or protect against black magic still flourishes in many cultures.***

Above: ***Benjamin Spooner Briggs, captain of the*** **Mary Celeste.** ***The ship seems to have been jinxed from the start of her career; after the disaster in which Briggs and his crew vanished without trace in 1872, things went from bad to worse. The vessel changed hands no fewer than 17 times in a dozen or so years – but she brought nothing but ill fortune to each of her owners.***

a beam of 25 ft 6 in, and her gross weight was 198.42 tons. Her maiden voyage had not even begun when her first designated skipper, Robert McLellan, fell ill and died. A new master, John Nutting Parker, took the *Amazon* out on her maiden voyage but, somewhere off the coast of Maine, she ran into a fishing weir – a set of stakes driven into the seabed to trap fish – and gashed her side. While she was being repaired ashore, a fire broke out. Captain Parker lost his job.

The *Amazon* acquired a third skipper, who took her across the Atlantic. In the Straits of Dover she collided with a brig, which sank. While the *Amazon* was being repaired, her master resigned his command to find another berth.

Matters now become a little vague, but it seems that the *Amazon* went back across the Atlantic after her repairs in England – only to run aground off Cape Breton Island, Nova Scotia. She was probably then sold to an Alexander McBean, who may actually have salvaged her; he spent $16,000 repairing and enlarging the vessel, and in the process he may have changed her name to *Mary Celeste*. True to her nature, the ship bankrupted McBean, and she then went through a succession of owners until finally being bought by a New York consortium, J.H. Winchester & Co. On 7 November 1872, under her new name, she set out on the voyage that was to make her name a byword. She was carrying 1701 barrels of commercial alcohol, insured for $36,943, to Genoa, Italy.

Twenty-eight days later she was discovered by the British brigantine *Dei Gratia* in perfect order but with no one on board. After a lengthy legal wrangle as to salvage rights in the ship, ownership of the *Mary Celeste* was restored to the Winchester company in New York, and in March 1873 she finally delivered her cargo to Genoa. Winchester then promptly sold her – and she changed hands 17 times in the next dozen years.

No one, it seems, had any luck with the *Mary Celeste*. She had an incorrigible and depressing tendency to lose her cargo, her sails, and on some occasions her sailors, to run aground, and to catch fire. In the end a notorious old salt named Gilman C. Parker bought her late in 1884. Parker has been called 'undoubtedly guilty of every maritime crime short of piracy', and he clearly had no intention of trying to make an honest penny out of the *Mary Celeste*. He loaded her with a cargo insured for $30,000 but worth at most $500, and sailed her from Boston to Haiti, where he deliberately ran her aground in the Gulf of Gonave on 3 January 1885. He unloaded the cargo, and then set the ship alight.

The insurance companies involved smelled a rat as well as a sinking ship, and soon discovered the truth. Parker and his associates were arrested, and would have been tried for barratry – maritime insurance fraud – which then carried the death penalty. They walked free thanks to a legal technicality, but were not yet free of the jinx of the *Mary Celeste*. Parker himself soon went bankrupt, and died in penniless obscurity. One of his associates went mad; another committed suicide. The *Mary Celeste*, it seems, brought ill fortune to all who sailed in her.